Congregation Shaare Shamayim-G.N.Y.C.

In Honor of
Birth of Granddaughter,
Jayne Caroline

Donated by

Sisterhood Executive Board

THE TRUTH ABOUT
"THE PROTOCOLS
OF ZION"

THE TRUTH ABOUT "THE PROTOCOLS OF ZION"

A Complete Exposure

By
HERMAN BERNSTEIN

Introduction by
NORMAN COHN

#1030

KTAV PUBLISHING HOUSE, INC.
New York, New York
1971

FIRST PUBLISHED 1935

NEW MATTER
COPYRIGHT © 1971

KTAV PUBLISHING HOUSE, Inc.

Library of Congress Cataloging in Publication Data

Bernstein, Herman, 1876-1935.
   The truth about "The protocols of Zion."

   Reprint of the 1935 ed. with a new introd.
   Contains reprints of all the documents relating to
the case, including Dialogues in hell between
Machiavelli and Montesquieu (p.   ) and "Protocols
of the wise men of Zion" (p.   )
   1. "Protocols of the wise men of Zion." I. Joly,
Maurice, 1831-1878. Dialogue aux enfers entre
Machiavel et Montesquieu. English. 1972. II. "Pro-
tocols of the wise men of Zion." 1972. III. Title.
DS145.P7B45 1972   296   77-157884
ISBN 0-87068-176-1

SBN 87068-176-1

LIBRARY OF CONGRESS CATALOG CARD NUMBER: 77-157884
MANUFACTURED IN THE UNITED STATES OF AMERICA

TO LOVERS OF TRUTH AND JUSTICE

AND PARTICULARLY

TO THE ONE HUNDRED AND NINETEEN

EMINENT AMERICAN CHRISTIANS

WHO, ON JANUARY 16, 1921,

SIGNED THE PROTEST

AGAINST THE DISSEMINATION OF

THE SPURIOUS "PROTOCOLS OF THE WISE MEN OF ZION"

AND THE "VICIOUS PROPAGANDA" OF PREJUDICE AND HATRED

AND WHO CALLED UPON "MOLDERS OF PUBLIC OPINION—

THE CLERGY AND MINISTERS OF ALL CHRISTIAN CHURCHES,

PUBLICISTS, TEACHERS, EDITORS AND STATESMEN—

TO STRIKE AT

THIS UN-AMERICAN AND UN-CHRISTIAN AGITATION,"

THIS VOLUME

IS RESPECTFULLY DEDICATED BY

THE AUTHOR

ACKNOWLEDGMENT

I ACKNOWLEDGE with gratitude the helpful suggestions and encouragement given me by Dr. Cyrus Adler, and the invaluable co-operation of Mr. Harry Schneiderman in the preparation of the manuscript.

Grateful acknowledgment is made to Father A. Sacchetti and to Dr. Stephen S. Wise for their thoughtful counsel; to Dr. Joshua Bloch, New York Public Library, and to Dr. Israel Schapiro, Library of Congress, Washington, for their helpfulness in connection with my work of research.

THE AUTHOR.

CONTENTS

INTRODUCTION

The notorious fabrication known as the *Protocols of the Elders of Zion* was first published in Russia in 1903 and 1905; but it became important only when right-wing Russian extremists, arriving as refugees from the Bolshevik revolution, brought it to the West. In 1920 the *Protocols* were a major sensation: translations published in that single year include two American, two German, two French, two Polish and one English. Nor was the sensation confined to the naive or the uneducated: serious newspapers such as the London *Times* and the Philadelphia *Public Ledger* earnestly debated the authenticity of the *Protocols*.

The unmasking of the fabrication also began at once. In his little book, *The History of a Lie,* which appeared at the beginning of 1921, the American Herman Bernstein showed that the *Protocols* were modelled on an episode in a German novel called *Biarritz,* published in 1868 over the pseudonym of Sir John Ratcliffe (the author was really a disreputable journalist called Herman Goedsche). Six months later the Constantinople correspondent of the London *Times,* Philip Graves, was able to point to another source of the fantasy: large parts of the *Protocols* had been taken almost verbatim from Maurice Joly's *Dialogue in Hell between Machiavelli and Montesquieu,* which is a satire on Napoleon III, published in Brussels in 1864.

The *Protocols* continued to be printed and sold in many countries even after their spuriousness had been proved; and when Hitler came to power they took on a new kind of importance. In

Germany the *Protocols* became one of the sacred texts of National Socialism, published by the Party itself; and unlike Hitler's *Mein Kampf,* this sacred text was not only bought but read. By 1935 a German Minister of Education was even able to prescribe the *Protocols* as one of the basic textbooks for schools. Meanwhile throughout vast areas of the world—in most European countries, in the United States, Canada and Argentina, even in Japan—new editions of the *Protocols* were published and propagated by Nazi sympathizers or Nazi-type parties and movements.

This was the context in which Herman Bernstein produced his second and much longer book on the *Protocols. The Truth about the Protocols of Zion* contains, in English translation, all the material bearing on the fabrication: Maurice Joly's *Dialogues* and Philip Graves' account of his finding of the *Dialogues*; the relevant passage from Goedsche's *Biarritz;* the *Protocols* themselves; and evidence concerning the Russian religious fanatic, Sergei Nilus, who in 1905 published the first complete text of the *Protocols* as part of his mystical tract on the coming of Antichrist. Thirty-six years have passed since Bernstein's book appeared; but it remains the only work of its kind. Nowhere else can one find such a comprehensive collection of the relevant documents.

Bernstein's five introductory chapters also remain valid as a general introduction to the history of the fabrication. But, inevitably, perspectives have changed. Since Bernstein wrote, a vast amount of research has been done on the history of anti-semitism and on the ideological roots of National Socialism. To appreciate the full significance of the *Protocols* one has to know what tradition they sprang from; what changes they underwent when they reached Germany; and what they meant to Hitler himself. The following pages will be devoted to situating the *Protocols* in this wider context.

Over very large areas of the earth, Jews have been seen traditionally as mysterious beings, endowed with uncanny and sinister powers. It is known where these ideas originated. Between the second and the fourth centuries C.E., when the Church and the Synagogue were competing for converts in the Hellenistic world, and when moreover the Church and the Synagogue were struggling to win adherents from one another, this conception of the Jew came into being. St. John Chrysostom is a case in point: in order to terrorize the Christians of Antioch, who showed a certain inclination to revert to Judaism, he called the Synagogue "the temple of demons, the cavern of devils, a gulf and abyss of perdition", and portrayed Jews as habitual murderers and destroyers, people possessed by an evil spirit. Likewise, St. Augustine was much concerned to protect his catechumens against the attractions of Judaism—and so he described how the Jews, who had been the favourite sons of God, were now transformed into the sons of Satan. Such were the beginnings.

Seven or eight centuries later, in the most militant period in the history of the Roman Catholic church, these ancient fantasies were revived, and integrated into what was really a whole new demonology. The change came with the First Crusade (1096); from then onwards, Jews were presented as children of the Devil, agents employed by Satan for the express purpose of combating Christianity and harming individual Christians. In the twelfth century Jews were for the first time accused of such things as ritually murdering Christian children, torturing the consecrated wafer, poisoning the wells. Although popes and bishops frequently and emphatically condemned these stories as gross fabrications, the lower clergy continued to propagate them; and in the end the stories came to be generally believed. Above all, it was said that Jews worshipped the Devil and that the Devil in return rewarded them by making them collectively masters of black magic. From this it followed that however helpless individual Jews might seem, Jews collectively were regarded as possessing limitless powers for evil.

The propagation of such views by the clergy, century after century, gradually but in the end decisively influenced the attitude of the laity. It is true that Judaism, with its idea of the Chosen People and with its elaborate system of taboos, tended in any case to make Jews into a people apart; but what now happened went far beyond that. The Jews became much more than a people apart, they came to be regarded as most dangerous enemies; and for that Christian teaching and preaching were responsible. To be convinced of this, one only has to consider the case of the Jewish settlements in India and China: they existed for some two thousand years, without ever attracting any particular attention. But there is no need to labour the point. There are, after all, many other minorities in the world which show traits of separateness in one way or another, and they are by no means always seen as enemies.

During the Middle Ages Jews were almost wholly without legal rights and were frequently massacred by the mob; and of course such experiences as these in turn greatly encouraged the Jewish tendency to exclusiveness. During the long centuries of persecution, Jews became a wholly alien people within Christendom, compulsorily restricted to the most sordid trades, regarding the Gentile world with bitterness. In the eyes of most Christians these strange creatures were demons in human form; and some of the demonology that was woven around them then has proved extraordinarily durable.

The myth of the Jewish world-conspiracy is the typical modern adaptation of this ancient demonology. According to this myth, there exists a secret Jewish government which operates through a world-wide network of camouflaged agencies and organizations, and in this way controls political parties and governments, the press and public opinion, banks and economic developments. This secret government is supposed to be doing all these things in pursuance of an age-old plan, a plan with a single aim: establishing Jewish domination over the whole world. And this secret government is supposed to be dangerously near to achieving its aim.

Now in this fantasy of the Jewish world-conspiracy one recognizes the ancient demonological terrors, stemming from the Middle Ages, but one also recognizes certain anxieties and resentments which are purely modern. 'The Jew' became in fact the scapegoat for many of the discontents of the modern world. The myth of the Jewish world-conspiracy is a particularly degraded and distorted expression of the new social tensions which

arose with the French Revolution and the coming of the nineteenth century; that is to say, at a moment when Europe entered
upon a period of exceptionally rapid and deep-going change.
In the nineteenth century traditional social relationships were
shaken, hereditary privileges were attacked, age-old values and
beliefs were called in question—all to an extent never seen
before. The slow-moving and conservative life of the countryside
was increasingly challenged by an urban civilization which was
dynamic, restless, given to innovation. Industrialization brought
to the fore a bourgeoisie intent on increasing its wealth and ex-
tending its rights, while gradually the new class of the industrial
proletariat began to exert pressure on its own account. By the
middle of the century such things as democracy, liberalism,
secularism, even socialism, were forces to be reckoned with. But
all over Continental Europe there were large numbers of people
who abominated all these things. A long, bitter struggle began;
a struggle between those who accepted the new mobile society
and the opportunities it offered, and those who hoped to retain
or restore the vanishing traditional order. To Europe's Jews
these changes brought both new possibilities and new dangers.

In the centuries since the Middle Ages Jews in most European
countries had suffered from all kinds of disabilities. They were
forbidden to own land, they were debarred from the professional
guilds of artisans, and they were confined to a few sordid occupations. In many places they were also subject to residential
restrictions, being forced to live a segregated existence in ghettos.
But all this began to change with the French Revolution; and
in the course of the nineteenth century Jews were relieved of
their legal disabilities in one country after another in western
and central Europe. Most Jews wanted nothing so much as to
live by the same routines as other people, and they adapted
themselves very quietly and smoothly to their new freedom.
Nevertheless, in the eyes of many people 'the Jew' still had a
highly symbolic significance, and for two quite different reasons.
On the one hand Jews remained an identifiable and—though to
a diminishing extent—an exclusive community. This meant that
they retained something of that mysterious demonological quality

which had been wished upon them in the Middle Ages. But on
the other hand Jews came to be seen as symbolic of the modern
world, and precisely by those people who most detested the
modern world.

There were various reasons for this. For centuries Jews had
been town-dwellers—of necessity, since they were not allowed
to own land—and in the nineteenth century they still remained
to an overwhelming extent in the cities, especially in the capital
cities. In politics Jews naturally tended to side with the liberal
and democratic forces, as the only ones which might be expected
to guarantee and increase their own liberties. Moreover, Jews
were still denied access to many traditional occupations. This
encouraged them to find new ways of making a living; and in
doing so, some of them became extremely rich. And in general
it can be said that a feeling of suddenly liberated energies made
many Jews more enterprising than the average—above all, exceptionally given to experiment and innovation. In industry and
in commerce, in politics and journalism, Jews achieved an influence quite out of proportion to their total numbers.

There is nothing surprising in all this. There are perfectly
sound sociological explanations for the pre-eminence of Jews
in all these fields. Moreover, the number of Jews who did in fact
become pre-eminent in any of them was relatively small; and
conversely, banking and journalism and radical politics would
all have developed in much the same way if there had been no
Jews at all. But these facts were not evident to everyone. Some
persuaded themselves that without the Jews and their Satanic
arts the vast changes inaugurated by the French Revolution and
the industrial revolution would never have taken place at all.

There were in the nineteenth century various types of anti-
semitism. This particular type flourished amongst the people who
were most thoroughly disconcerted by the civilization of the nineteenth century; that is to say, it flourished above all among the
landed aristocracy and the clergy. These were the people who
saw in 'the Jew' a symbol of all that most threatened their own
world—meaning not only their material interests but also the
values which gave meaning to their lives. These people were

only too happy to believe that the alarming changes which they witnessed all around them sprang not from any defects in the old order, nor from impersonal historic processes, but from the machinations of a handful of demons in human form.

This way of interpreting the contemporary scene could also serve highly practical aims. There was now a growing electorate, but it was still in the main an ill-educated electorate. By portraying democracy, liberalism and secularism as the work of the Jews, people hoped to make these things suspect in the eyes of the electorate. A new form of antisemitism came into being: political antisemitism. From now on antisemitism was to be deliberately whipped up by ultra-conservative politicians and publicists, in their struggle against the progressives.

So the old and the new accusations flourished side by side. In many parts of Europe Jews were still accused of such things as ritual murder, as they had been in the Middle Ages. But gradually these age-old superstitions yielded in importance to the new political superstition concerning a secret Jewish government.

In its modern form the myth of the Jewish world-conspiracy can be traced back to a French Jesuit, the Abbé Barruel. As early as 1797 Barruel had produced a great five-volume *Mémoire pour servir à l'histoire du Jacobinisme,* in which he argued that the French Revolution represented the culmination of an age-old conspiracy of the most secret of secret societies. In his view, the source of the trouble lay in the medieval Order of Templars. In reality this order had been exterminated in 1314—but in Barruel's fantasy it still survived as a secret society, pledged to abolish all monarchies, overthrow the papacy, preach unrestricted liberty to all peoples, and found a world-wide republic under its own control. In modern times it was operating through the Order of Freemasons, and particularly through a group of Bavarians called the Illuminati, whom Barruel called "enemies of the human race, sons of Satan". In Barruel's view it was this little handful of Bavarian Illuminati, who, carrying on the doctrine of the medieval Knights Templars, and controlling all Freemasons and Jacobins in France, had brought about the cataclysm of the French Revolution. He was also convinced that unless the Illuminati were stopped, they would very soon dominate the whole world.

Of course, this was all the merest fantasy. The idea that the French Revolution was produced by a conspiracy reaching back to the fourteenth century needs no comment. As for the obscure German group known as the Illuminati, they were not Freemasons at all but rivals of the Freemasons, and they had in any case ceased to exist by 1786. And Barruel also fantastically oversimplified and exaggerated the role of the Freemasons themselves. It is true that Freemasons shared that concern with humanitarian reform which is commonly associated with the Enlightenment—for instance, they contributed to the abolition of judicial torture and of witchcraft trials, and to the improvement of schools. On the other hand at the time of the Revolution most Freemasons were Catholic and monarchists; indeed, King Louis XVI and his brothers were all Freemasons. And during the revolutionary Terror Freemasons were guillotined by the hundreds and their organization, the Grand Orient, was suppressed.

Moreover Barruel himself, though he lived through the Revolution, never noticed any of the mysterious Masonic influence while the Revolution was in progress. The idea came to him when he was in London some years after the Revolution; and it was not even his own idea. He heard of it from a Scottish mathematician called John Robison, who was himself preparing a book called *Proofs of a Conspiracy against all the Religions and Governments of Europe carried on by Secret Meetings of Freemasons, Illuminati and Reading Societies*. It occurred to Barruel that he might produce a book on the same subject, if possible before Robison; and so he did. His *Mémoire* came out one year before Robison's book; it was translated into English, Spanish, Italian, Russian and Polish, and it made Barruel a rich man.

At the time when Barruel wrote his five volumes he still imposed certain limits on his imagination. He was concerned with

Freemasons only and hardly mentioned the Jews—understandably, since no Jew played any significant part either in the Revolution itself or in the philosophical revolution, the Enlightenment, which had preceded it. But in 1806 Barruel received a document which was in effect the earliest prototype of the *Protocols*. This was a letter from Florence, supposedly written by an Italian army officer called J. B. Simonini. Nothing whatsoever is known about this Simonini, and Barruel never managed to establish contact with him. The object of the letter was to persuade Barruel that he had overlooked the heart of the conspiracy; this was 'the Judaic sect', which the mysterious Simonini calls "the most formidable power, if one considers its great wealth and the protection it enjoys in almost all European countries." And Simonini goes on to claim that he has penetrated to the secrets of this sect. The Jews promise themselves that in less than a century they will be masters of the world. Then they will abolish all other religions, and establish the rule of their own sect. They will turn Christian churches into so many synagogues. They will buy up all lands, houses and other property, and reduce the remaining Christians to slavery. Only one obstacle stands in their way: the House of Bourbon. But the Jews have a plan to annihilate that obstacle; and the French Revolution is a part of this plan.

The Simonini letter was a forgery; almost certainly it was produced by someone in the French political police under Fouché, with the object of influencing Napoleon himself against the Jews. The context was the great debate over Jewish emancipation. For the first Jews in Europe to be emancipated were the French Jews, during the Revolution; and later, during the Napoleonic wars, Jews were emancipated wherever the French armies were victorious. In the Simonini letter one seems to hear the crash of the Italian ghetto walls as they fell before the advance of the French armies. Nevertheless, there were many in France itself who were uneasy about Jewish emancipation. The intention was that Barruel should pass the Simonini letter around in these circles; and so he did.

After the fall of Napoleon, Barruel himself emerged as an

enthusiastic believer not simply in the Masonic conspiracy but in the Jewish conspiracy as well. Just before his death in 1820, at the age of 79, he propounded the idea that the whole of Europe was in the grip of a vast revolutionary organization, which extended downwards into every single village of France, Spain, Italy and Germany and which was rigidly controlled by a supreme council, which in turn was controlled by Jews. He even describes how the secret orders in code from the Jewish headquarters are transmitted throughout Europe by relays of Freemasons, all of them speeding briskly about on foot. "The mail coach," he says, "takes ten hours from Paris to Orléans, stopping for an hour; the distance is thirty leagues. Fifteen or twenty pedestrians, replacing one another, and stopping neither to eat nor to sleep, can reach Orléans from Paris in nine hours, using short-cuts". Clearly, the supreme council already possessed that capacity for organizing vast and invisible manoeuvres which was to be so characteristic of the Elders of Zion.

* * * * * * * * * * * * * * * * *

Bernstein has told how the *Protocols* came to be fabricated and disseminated. It was not part of his task to explain the extraordinary success that came their way in Germany.

The *Protocols* acquired a completely new dimension when they came into contact with that peculiar outlook which is known as *vœlkisch*. The beginnings of this outlook—it was really a pseudo-religion—go back to the Napoleonic wars. Germany is by no means the only country which first began to develop a national consciousness as a result of being invaded—but it so happened that in this case the invading power was itself the standard-bearer of the modern age. For revolutionary France was the champion of democracy, liberalism and rationalism. It is normal to reject the values of the invader and to affirm the opposite values. But in the case of Germany, this meant that German nationalism was from the start partly backward-looking; to an exceptional degree, it was inspired by a repudiation of modernity and a nostalgia for a past which was imagined as altogether unlike the modern world. Moreover, this attitude not only persisted but was greatly intensified when economic developments pitchforked Germany into the modern world. At the very time when Germany was turning into a great industrial power, a land of factories and cities, technology and bureaucracy, many Germans were dreaming of an archaic world of Germanic peasants, bound together by bonds of blood in a 'natural', 'organic' community.

Such a view of the world requires an anti-figure. This anti-figure was supplied partly by the liberal West—that is to say, France and Britain; but it was also, and more effectively, supplied by the Jews. As we have seen, it is characteristic of modern, political antisemites that they see 'the Jew' not only as an uncanny, demonic being but also as an embodiment of modernity, a symbol of all those forces in the modern world which they themselves fear and hate. This was the case also with German antisemites of the *vœlkisch* variety—but with a difference. When these people looked to the past, to the ideal state which they supposed to have preceded the modern age, they looked a very long way back. They looked far beyond throne and altar, back to an infinitely remote and almost entirely mythical world. For them 'the Jew' was not only, or mainly, the destroyer of kings and the enemy of the Church—he was above all the age-old antagonist of the Germanic peasant, he was the force which for two thousand years had been undermining the true, original German way of life. Historical Christianity itself was a Jewish creation which had helped to destroy the archaic Germanic world; and now capitalism, liberalism, democracy, socialism, and the urban way of life were continuing this process. Together these things were supposed to make up 'the Jew's' world, that modern age which was imagined as his creation and in which he flourished.

The first major proponents of this outlook were certain writers who flourished in the last quarter of the nineteenth century. They included an eccentric scholar called Paul Bötticher, but who is usually known by his adopted name of Paul de Lagarde; Wilhelm Marr, who is the probable inventor of the word 'antisemitism' and who wrote a book called *The Victory of Jewry over German-dom;* and Eugen Dühring, a lecturer in economics and philosophy at Berlin University and the author of *The Jewish Question as a Question of Race, Morals and Civilization.* But the most important and influential of these writers was Houston Stewart Chamberlain. An Englishman by birth and the son of a British admiral, Chamberlain became a German by choice and eventually by nationality; and in the year 1900 he published, in German, a two-volume work called the *Foundations of the Nineteenth Century.* It was a very eloquent work, it had an appearance of learning, and it became the bible of the whole *vælkisch*-racist movement in Germany. In this book all human history was presented as a bitter struggle between spirituality, embodied in the German 'race', and materialism, embodied in the Jewish 'race'—the only two pure races, all others being only a 'chaos of peoples' *(Vælkerchaos).* In Chamberlain's view the Jewish 'race' had been relentlessly striving, down the ages, to secure absolute dominion over all other nations. If once this 'race' were decisively defeated, the Germanic 'race' would be free to realize its own divinely appointed destiny—which was to create a new, radiant world, transfused with a noble spirituality and mysteriously combining modern technology and science with the rural, hierarchical culture of earlier times.

The *vælkisch*-racist outlook made its main appeal to certain sections of the middle class, and above all to artisans and small retailers. It has often been remarked that these people were particularly prone to antisemitism, and in due course they provided the bulk of the votes which brought Hitler to power. There is nothing mysterious about this. These sections of the population were survivals from an earlier age and they were gravely threatened by the development of modern capitalism. They lived in a state of almost perpetual crisis. They were barely able to cope with the new world of giant industrial and commercial undertakings, and at the same time they lacked even that rudimentary understanding of this world which, in Germany, industrial workers received from Marxism. Artisans and small retailers struggled frantically to preserve their status and they felt an overwhelming need for a scapegoat.

The Jews were perfectly suited for this role—not because they occupied the commanding heights in the German economy, nor because they were mostly well-to-do, nor because they were obviously foreign. None of these things were true, though they were often said. The main factor was the concentration of small numbers of well-to-do Jews in certain areas of Berlin and Hamburg; a concentration which could lead the unthinking to suppose that all Jews were rich, or even that all rich people were Jews. Another factor was the typical Jewish zeal in getting the sons to universities and thence into the liberal professions; for this brought them into direct conflict with the more aspiring members of the lower middle class.

However, the appeal of the *vœlkisch*-racist outlook was even stronger among the German element in the Habsburg empire than it was in Germany itself. On this Austrian periphery of the German-speaking world, where the German element felt isolated and threatened by the preponderant Slav element, the aggressive affirmation of German superiority had particular attraction. Moreover, Jews were far more conspicuous in Austria than in Germany, and they were conspicuous at both ends of the social scale. The great majority of Jews lived in appalling poverty. At the same time, a minority of Jews made up a large part of the professional class, and a few of them were bankers of great wealth.

These Austrian Jews regarded themselves as belonging entirely to the German group in the Austro-Hungarian empire; but this helped not at all—the Germans rejected them. And here, as in Germany, the most militant antisemites were to be found in the lower-middle class. When Hitler came to power in 1933 a joke circulated in Germany: that Hitler was Austria's revenge for the defeat which she had suffered at the hands of Prussia in 1866. There was a good deal in this. The petty-bourgeois Hitler embodied a whole century of frustration, disappointment, and insecurity; and the boundless lust for revenge which possessed him was a magnified version of something which possessed a whole stratum of Austrian society.

Already in the years immediately preceding the first world

war Austrian racists developed the cult of the swastika; some even foretold that one day Jews would be castrated and killed under the aegis of the swastika. In Germany too there appeared a multitude of more or less esoteric bodies such as the Order of Teutons and Volsungs, which also had the swastika as its emblem. Yet at that time few imagined that this *vœlkisch*-racist outlook would ever impinge on practical politics. It was the outcome of the first world war that made this possible. The humiliation of defeat and the great sufferings that followed it; the mortification which was felt in Germany over the peace treaty of Versailles, and in Austria over the peace treaty of St. Germain; above all, the absolute disorientation and the widespread financial ruin which accompanied the collapse of the currency—these things produced an entirely new atmosphere.

Already in 1919 there appeared an extreme right-wing body called the Deutsch-vœlkischer Schutz- und Trutzbund (the German *vœlkisch* Defensive and Offensive Alliance). This alliance too had the swastika as its emblem and it quickly acquired a membership of 300,000. Meanwhile the old Order of Teutons and Volsungs continued to exist, also using the swastika. In November 1918, just after the armistice, this Order produced a cover-organization called the Thule Society; and early in 1919 this body joined forces with another organization, the German workers' party, shortly to become the Nazi party.

All these organizations were indoctrinated with the *vœlkisch*-racist outlook in its most fanatical form; and when the *Protocols* came into their hands, they reinterpreted them in the light of this outlook. In their eyes the machinations of the Elders of Zion were the supreme expression of the characteristics which they attributed to the Jewish 'race': the Jewish world-conspiracy was seen as the product of an ineradicable destructiveness, a will to evil which was believed to be inborn in every Jew. As they saw it, a peculiar breed of creatures, dark and earthbound—the Jews—were working conspiratorially to destroy those sons of light, the 'Aryan' or Germanic 'race'; and the *Protocols* contained their plan of campaign.

Now this same world-view obsessed Hitler himself throughout

his political career. There were signs of this obsession already in
the very first of his political utterances: a letter which he wrote to
a certain Gemlich on 16th September 1919, when Hitler was acting as so-called education officer with an army command in
Munich. Already in this letter Hitler insists that it is not enough
to dislike Jews; Germans must realize that Jewry forms a racial
entity with very strongly marked racial characteristics, of which
the passion for material gain is the most dominant. This makes
Jewry 'the racial tuberculosis of the peoples'. Hitler goes on to
say that mere pogroms are inadequate to cope with such a dangerous foe. Instead, he demands the formation of a government
which will start by restricting the legal rights of the Jews, and
whose long-term aim will be the removal *(Entfernung)* of the
Jews altogether. So spoke the unknown ex-corporal a couple
of days before he attended the first meeting of the tiny group
which was to be the nucleus of the future Nazi party.

Probably Hitler knew of the *Protocols* already at that time;
for they were already being advertised and circulated in manuscript, in preparation for their publication at the beginning of
1920. Certainly by the time Hitler emerged in the political lime-
light in 1923, his thinking was permeated by the *Protocols*. Germany passed through the inferno of the great inflation, in which
the savings of the middle and working classes were wiped out
and wages and salaries became meaningless. As this happened,
Hitler already had his explanation of the catastrophe: "According to the *Protocols of Zion* the peoples are to be reduced to
submission by hunger. The second revolution under the Star of
David is the aim of the Jews in our time"—the first revolution
being the establishment of the Weimar Republic and the overthrow of the German monarchy. In the following year Hitler
took part in an abortive *putsch* in Munich and was arrested and
lodged in a comfortable prison. There he dictated *Mein Kampf*
—and much of that dreary but revealing work is devoted to the
manoeuvres by which Jewry is supposed to be pursuing world-
domination. Hitler points out how the Jews have first used Free-
masonry as their weapon, and are now using Bolshevism. The
object of all this is to come to power with the help of the masses,

and then dominate the masses in the interests of the Jews.

The source of all this was certainly the *Protocols,* even though by that time the *Protocols* had been proved, by Herman Bernstein and Philip Graves, to be a forgery. In *Mein Kampf* Hitler explicitly names the *Protocols* as a major influence on his thinking: "The extent to which the whole existence of the Jewish people is based on a continual lie, is shown in an incomparable manner in the *Protocols of the Elders of Zion.* What many Jews do perhaps unconsciously is here consciously exposed. But that is what matters. It is a matter of indifference which Jewish brain produced these revelations. What matters is that they uncover, with really horrifying reliability, the nature and activity of the Jewish people, and expose them in their inner logic and their final aims. But reality provides the best commentary. Whoever examines the historical development of the last hundred years from the standpoint of this book will at once understand why the Jewish press makes such an uproar about it. For once this book becomes generally familiar to a people, the Jewish menace can be regarded as already vanquished."

Years later, when Germany was in the throes of the great depression, Hitler accounted for this world-wide disaster in precisely the same way as he had accounted for the German inflation. To Hermann Rauschning, who afterwards published it in his book *Hitler Speaks,* he explained that the Jews had invented the economic system of booms and slumps, otherwise known as capitalism. "Capitalism is the creation of the Jews, and under their exclusive control. It is their super-state, planted by them above all the states of the world in all their glory." He went on, "I have read the *Protocols of the Elders of Zion* and it simply appalled me. The stealthiness of the enemy, and his ubiquity. I saw at once that we must copy it—in our own way of course. . . . It is in truth the critical battle for the fate of the world."

There is another source for Hitler's belief in the *Protocols.* It is a little book called *Bolshevism from Moses to Lenin: a dialogue between Adolf Hitler and myself,* which was written by a poet and journalist called Dietrich Eckart and published posthumously in 1924. Eckart was not only one of the founding members of the Nazi party, he was also one of the very few real friends that Hitler ever had—in fact *Mein Kampf* ends with an invocation of the memory of Dietrich Eckart. So the book can be taken as reliably presenting Hitler's views.

The booklet shows Hitler combining the *Protocols* with *vœlkisch*-racist speculations, to conduct a whole 'philosophy of history'. As he sees it, human history forms part of nature and follows the same laws as the rest of nature. If it has gone wrong, that shows that some force is at work to frustrate nature's intention; and this has in fact been the case for thousands of years. There follows an outline of history which portrays it as one long degeneration. Nature, says Hitler, demands inequality, hierarchy, subordination of the inferior to the superior—but human history has consisted of a series of revolts against this natural order, leading to ever greater egalitarianism. This process is compared with disease, with the work of a bacillus: "a proliferation right across the world, now slow, now leaping ahead. Everywhere it sucks and sucks. At first there is teeming abundance, in the end only dried-up sap."

The force behind this disastrous process is the Jewish spirit, "which has been there from the beginning". Already in ancient Egypt the Children of Israel undermined a healthy, 'natural' society. They did this by inciting the lower orders to revolt, until all nationally minded Egyptians rose in their wrath and chased the trouble-makers from the land; this is the true meaning of Exodus. Moses therefore is the first Bolshevik, a true precursor of Lenin. And so a process began which has been repeated over and over again ever since. In Hitler's eyes the lower social strata consist, all over the world, of similar, racially mixed and therefore inferior human material. The essence of the Jewish world-conspiracy is that it uses this racial hotchpotch to overthrow the racially pure upper classes and thereby to further its own drive for world-domination.

One can penetrate further still into this strange fantasy. There is in *Mein Kampf* an astonishing passage which ought to have attracted more attention than it did. It reads as follows: "If the Jew, with the help of his Marxist catechism, triumphs over the peoples of this world, his crown will be the dance of death for mankind, and as once before, millions of years ago, this planet will again sail empty of all human life through the ether. . . . I believe that I am today acting according to the purposes of the almighty Creator. In resisting the Jew, I am fighting the Lord's battle!" One is forced to ask: What ever can the man have meant? What possible sense can there be in this talk of an earth empty of all human life? And the answer to these questions, when one faces up to it, goes a long way to explain the monstrous deeds perpetrated by the Germans during the second world war. Naturally, it has nothing to do with atomic warfare— these words were written in 1924. What Hitler means is that only a tiny part of what is usually regarded as mankind really consists of human beings—notably those whom he imagined to be of Nordic descent, plus, for political reasons, the Japanese. All the rest—what he called the racial mish-mash—belongs not to mankind but to an inferior species. In using these creatures to kill off the ruling strata—who in his view must *ipso facto* be Nordic—the Jew is therefore literally depriving the earth of its human population. What will be left will be simply animals disguised as human beings, under the leadership of Jews, who are demonic beings disguised as human beings.

Even by the crazy standards of German racism these ideas were eccentric and extreme. Unfortunately they were held by the man who became dictator of Germany; and this meant that instead of remaining the property of some obscure group of cranks, they became the creed of the SS. It was in the name of these weird fantasies, disguised as scientific truth, that the SS at the height of their power terrorized and martyrized Europe from the English Channel to the Volga. How Hitler's special version of the Jewish world-conspiracy was presented to these men can be seen from the following quotations from a tract issued by SS headquarters: "Just as night rises up against the day, just as light and darkness are eternal enemies, so the greatest enemy of world-dominating man is the sub-man. That creature which looks as though biologically it were of absolutely the same kind, endowed by nature with hands, feet and a sort of brain, with eyes and mouth, is nevertheless a totally different, a fearful creature. It is only an attempt at a human being, with a quasi-human face, yet in mind and spirit lower than any animal. Inside this being a cruel chaos of wild, unchecked passions; a nameless will to destruction, the most primitive lusts, the most undisguised vileness. A sub-man—nothing else!. . . . Never has the sub-man granted peace, never has he permitted rest. . . . To preserve himself he needed mud, he needed hell, but not the sun. And this underworld of sub-men found its leader: the eternal Jew!"

Once such a creed was applied it could only lead to massacre. The victims were not only the six million Jews who were killed as bearers of an imaginary plague. In Hitler's eyes Russia was the country in which the Jews, through the Bolshevik revolution, had most completely 'infected' the population; and this certainly had much to do with the extraordinary ferocity of the SS in the occupied territories of the Soviet Union. When the German attack began, Himmler announced that it was intended to kill thirty million Russians. The number of Russian dead is in fact put at twenty million; and the way in which whole armies of prisoners of war were put behind barbed wire and left to starve, and whole villages of men and women herded into barns to be burned alive, is certainly connected with the fact that these people were regarded as sub-human beings, bastardized by the Jews and enlisted in their service.

As for the Jews, in Hitler's mind the war of 1939 was above all the final struggle against Jewry; and from 1939 onwards Hitler himself publicly talked of the war in just those terms. German editors of the *Protocols* had always insisted that the first world war was the work of the Jews; now Hitler blamed them for the war he was about to inflict on the world, and at the same time prophesied the genocide he was about to carry out. In a speech to the Reichstag on 30 January 1939, eight months before the war began, he declared: "Today I will once more be a prophet: if the international Jewish financiers in and outside Europe should succeed in plunging the nations once more into a world war, then the result will not be the bolshevization of the earth, and thus the victory of Jewry, but the annihilation of the Jewish race in Europe."

Hitler repeated this again and again during the war, and in the last weeks before he committed suicide, he returned to the theme. "I have played straight with the Jews," he said. "On the eve of war I gave them a last warning. I warned them that if they again plunged the world into war, they would not be spared this time—that the vermin would be finally exterminated in Europe. They replied to this warning by a declaration of war. . . . We have pierced the Jewish abscess. The world of the future will be eternally grateful to us."

One of the chapters in Bernstein's excellent book is entitled "The End of the Protocols." It was a reasonable supposition. Nobody in 1935 could have foreseen that within ten years the *Protocols,* as interpreted by Hitler, would have borne fruit in the greatest and cruellest massacres the world has ever seen.

NORMAN COHN

PREFACE

In FEBRUARY, 1921, I presented documentary evidence in my
book, "The History of a Lie," which showed that the notorious
"Protocols of the Wise Men of Zion," published in Russia in 1905,
were based on an absurdly fantastic work of German fiction,
published in 1868, about a centennial secret midnight meeting
of representatives of the "Twelve Tribes of Israel" in the ancient
Jewish cemetery of Prague—a story which was part of a pseudo-
historical romance entitled "To Sedan," one of a series of novels
called "Biarritz-Rome," by Hermann Goedsche, a petty official
of the German post office who turned to writing fiction after his
dishonorable discharge for participation in the then scandalous
Waldeck forgery case. I also showed how Goedsche afterward
transformed the "testimony" he had placed in the mouths of his
fictitious "Elders of Israel" into an alleged speech said by him
to have been delivered by an unnamed rabbi at a mythical Jewish
congress in Lemberg.

In August, 1921, about six months after "The History of a
Lie" appeared, the London *Times* published, in three successive
issues, articles by Mr. Philip Graves, then its Constantinople correspondent, proving that the "Protocols" had been plagiarized
from "Dialogues in Hell between Machiavelli and Montesquieu,"
a French book brought out anonymously at Brussels in 1864, four
years before the publication of Goedsche's novel "To Sedan."
The discovery of that plagiarism was an invaluable supplement to
the numerous evidences of forgery already known. The German
novelist was not the originator of the sinister plans he had attributed to the "Elect of Israel." He merely pirated the fiendish
conceptions from the work of Maurice Joly, and changed them

into a weird story of a Jewish plot for world domination. The
"Dialogues in Hell" did not deal in any way with Jewish subjects,
but were a satirical attack against Napoleon III. Their author,
Maurice Joly, a Parisian attorney (not a Jew, as has been stated
by some anti-Semites), was sentenced to fifteen months' imprisonment for this act of *lèse majesté*. As all the Joly books upon which
the French police were able to lay their hands were destroyed,
copies are extremely rare. The *Times* correspondent secured one
copy which belonged to a Russian army officer who had emigrated
to Turkey after the Bolshevist revolution. One copy is in the
British Museum and another is in the New York Public Library.
A complete translation of the "Dialogues in Hell," Exhibit A,
is presented in this volume for the first time in the English
language.

The similarity between the Joly book, published in 1864, and
the story of the cemetery meeting in Goedsche's German novel
"To Sedan," published in 1868, and translated into Russian in
1872, becomes apparent upon even a superficial examination.
Goedsche had taken the anti-social, anti-democratic, imperialistic
ideas which Joly had imputed to Napoleon III through the shade
of Machiavelli, and placed them in the mouths of the "Elect of
Israel" assembled at the tomb of a "Holy Rabbi" in Prague, and,
later, in the mouth of an imaginary rabbi.

The authors of the "Protocols" went a step further. They
attributed the expression of these subversive ideas to invented
"Elders" or "Sages" of Zion. Some of them endeavored to identify
these forged documents with Theodore Herzl and the first
Zionist Congress at Basle in 1897. Documentary evidence is presented in this volume showing that the "Protocols" were brought
to Russia from France in 1895, two years before the first Zionist
Congress, and that they were first published privately in Russia
with the aid of a high Tsarist official of the Holy Synod who was
closely connected with Grand Duke Sergius, the uncle of Tsar
Nicholas II. Tsar Nicholas himself was also deeply interested in
the "Protocols." In the course of my research, I discovered a copy

of the 1906 Butmi edition of this anti-Jewish document in the private library of the Tsar acquired several years ago by the Library of Congress, Washington, D. C.

While the inspiration for the Russian "Protocols" obviously came first from the weird German novelette and fictitious "Rabbi's Speech" by Goedsche, the Joly "Dialogues in Hell" undoubtedly served as the textual basis of the fabrication, as will be shown in parallel columns reproduced in this volume.

"The History of a Lie" was prepared by me with the closest co-operation of the late Louis Marshall, distinguished attorney and civic worker, widely recognized by the Jews for his courageous and able defense of the honor of the Jewish people.

In 1926, Father A. Sacchetti, of the Catholic Agricultural School at Beitgemat, Palestine, a noted scholar and traveler who was visiting New York, wrote me a letter referring to my "History of a Lie," in the course of which he said:

"You who have documented so well the affair of the 'Protocols' will certainly be gratified to recognize in the 'Dialogue aux Enfers' the paternity of the legend of Hermann Goedsche and the truly diabolical 'Protocols.' You must complete your work and render a real service to the cause of truth and justice.

"The publication of this document (the 'Dialogues in Hell') will help the task of many writers in search of the truth. Public opinion is completely ignorant of the enormity of the manufacture and propagation of the 'Protocols' in so many editions and so many languages, and it is necessary to inform it correctly.

"I have formed the personal conviction that the 'Protocols' belong to the category of those malicious inventions which took a literary form in past ages, the most striking of which are the celebrated 'Secret Instructions (Monita Secreta)' of the Jesuits; a species of protocols of secret instructions from the superiors to the subordinates to put into practice the shameful and Machiavellian policies of the Society of Jesus. That the 'Monita' are a brazen invention is admitted even by adversaries. Nevertheless the so-called 'Legend of the Jesuits' has grown up, and it is believed to be genuine by credulous opponents and taken seriously by not a few of the faith.

"I will close by insisting again that it is necessary for the 'Dialogues' of Joly to reach the public mind. Moreover, the book is interesting in itself and reveals uncommon intelligence in the author."

Preoccupation with other literary work and my duties as Minister of the United States to Albania have prevented until now the carrying out of this suggestion. The present revival in the dissemination of the "Protocols," both here and abroad, the intensified use of these spurious documents, particularly in Germany, and the recent proceedings in Switzerland at which the authenticity of the "Protocols" was submitted for judicial determination, make the publication of this book of facts especially timely.

I submit in this volume all the available documentary evidence showing clearly the various stages of the brazen literary and political fraud known as the "Protocols," the illegitimate offspring of the "Dialogues in Hell," which has served as the chief basis of the anti-Jewish propaganda in Tsarist Russia and Nazi Germany, and which has indeed made the life of Jews under those régimes a veritable hell on earth.

HERMAN BERNSTEIN.

New York City
  December, 1934.

CHAPTER ONE

Dialogues in Hell

In 1864 a French lawyer named Maurice Joly published an anonymous book in which he made a veiled attack against Napoleon III. The volume, which appeared in Brussels, signed "by a contemporary," was entitled "Dialogues in Hell between Machiavelli and Montesquieu, or the Policies of Machiavelli in the Nineteenth Century."

The author explained his motives for writing the "Dialogues in Hell" in a pamphlet called "Maurice Joly, his past, his program expounded by himself," published in 1870, by Lacroix, Verbeckhoven and Co., 13, Faubourg-Montmartre." *

Among other things, Joly wrote in that pamphlet as follows:

"I meditated for a year on a book which would show the terrible inroads that the imperial legislation had made on all branches of the administration and the gaps which it had opened by completely wiping out all public liberties.

"I reflected that, among the French, so severe a book would have no readers. I then sought to shape my work in a form appropriate to our sarcastic temper which, since the time of the Empire, has been forced to make attacks only behind a disguise. I thought of a history of the Lower Empire, and then suddenly I recalled the impression that had been made on me by a book known only to dilettantes, entitled *'Dialogue sur les Blés,'* by the Abbé Galiani.

"To have living persons or dead ones converse on contemporary politics: this was the idea that came to me.

*Library of the Bar Association, Paris. No. 122.10.

15

"One evening while I was walking on the terrace along the river near Pont Royal in bad weather which I still remember, suddenly the name of Montesquieu came into my mind as the personification of one side of the ideas which I wanted to express. But who would be the opponent of Montesquieu?

"The idea came to my mind. Why, to be sure! Machiavelli!

"It is Machiavelli who represents the policy of force as opposed to Montesquieu who will represent the policy of justice; and Machiavelli will be Napoleon III, who himself would describe his abominable policies.

"The idea was found. The execution came after infinite research and I will not dwell here for long upon the difficulties which it represented. I hoped to have my book published in France; but the printer Bourdier to whom I explained that it was a translation from an English author named McPherson, recognized Napoleon III at the end of three dialogues. He refused to continue the printing.

"It was during my vacation that I left for Belgium."

When it became generally known that the "Dialogues in Hell" were aimed at Napoleon III, the French police began to search for the author. Maurice Joly was soon placed under arrest and sentenced on April 25, 1865, to fifteen months' imprisonment and a fine of 300 francs. The judgment of the court of the Seine disappeared, but it was announced in the newspaper *Le Droit* and published *in extenso* on April 26, 1865. It read as follows:

"Whereas, in a dialogue between Machiavelli and Montesquieu, the author begins by opposing the political principles developed in the writings of these famous men, then establishes a general thesis that the dreadful despotism taught by Machiavelli in his treatise, 'The Prince,' succeeded, by artifice and evil ways, in imposing itself on modern society. . . . That this work is neither an abstract and speculative criticism nor a political argument inspired by a sincere spirit; that the author charges the French Government with having, through shameful means, hypocritical ways and perfidious contrivances, led the public astray,

degraded the character of the nation and corrupted its morals.
. . . Finally for having, as the writer himself describes it in the
last page but one of his book, composed 'this gathering of monstrous things before which the mind recoils in fright, this work
that only hell itself could accomplish.'

"For these reasons, Maurice Joly, having committed the crime
of inciting hatred and contempt for the Government, is sentenced
to fifteen months' imprisonment, 300 francs fine, and to the confiscation of the copies of the 'Dialogues in Hell.' " *

The "Dialogues" are a very apparent criticism of the despotism
of Napoleon III, in the form of a series of twenty-five conversations between Montesquieu and Machiavelli. In the preface,
the anonymous author points out that certain passages are applicable to all governments, "but it particularly personifies a political
system which has not varied in its applications for a single day
since the fatal, and alas, too distant date when it was enthroned."
It refers to and indicts the policies of Napoleon—his repressive
measures, his wasteful financial system, his foreign wars, his use
of secret societies, his relations with the Vatican, and his control
of the press.

The book opens with the meeting of the spirits of Montesquieu
and Machiavelli on a desolate beach in Hell. Greetings are
exchanged, and then Montesquieu asks Machiavelli to explain
why he has become the author of the "Prince," and "founder
of that somber school of thought which has made all crowned
heads your disciples, but which is well fitted to justify the worst
crimes of tyranny." Montesquieu seems puzzled because, as he
says, Machiavelli had originally been an ardent republican. Machiavelli replies that he is a realist. He proceeds to justify his change
in viewpoint by explaining its applicability to the situation of the
states of Europe in 1864. He describes at length how he would
solve the problem of society. Machiavelli is in reality Napoleon III
and the greater part of the dialogues is devoted to his ideas.
Montesquieu satisfies himself with short explanations and exclama-

*See Exhibit A for the complete text of the "Dialogues in Hell."

tions of surprise. He is profoundly shocked by Machiavelli's defense of an able and ruthless dictatorship, but his arguments grow briefer and weaker.

Joly paid dearly for his daring attack on Napoleon III, and though his book was confiscated, it has had a long and terrible history. Surely, he never suspected that his fantastic "Dialogues" would some day be utilized by plagiarists and forgers for the purpose of bolstering up tottering autocracies and ruthless dictatorships against which he had fought. The "Dialogues in Hell," which a liberal and liberty-loving French lawyer had conceived while walking in the rain near the Pont Royal, were to be converted by a Prussian novelist and by Russian Political Police agents into the "Protocols of the Wise Men of Zion," the modern bible of anti-Semitism.*

A comparison of Joly's "Dialogues in Hell," the veiled political attack against Napoleon III, and the "Protocols of the Wise Men of Zion," containing the outlines of an alleged Jewish conspiracy for world domination, shows beyond the shadow of a doubt that the "Protocols" were plagiarized and paraphrased from the Joly original and other works of fiction inspired by it.†

The German introducer-in-chief of the "Protocols," Gottfried zur Beek, in an effort to discredit the exposé that the "Protocols" had been plagiarized from Maurice Joly's "Dialogues in Hell," wrote in 1925 that Maurice Joly was a Jew, a leader of the Terrorist movement, and that Gambetta delivered the funeral oration at his grave in 1878. The German anti-Semite thus resorted to another falsification. Maurice Joly was not a Jew, and the man at whose death Leon Gambetta delivered the funeral oration was Albert Joly, a deputy belonging to Gambetta's party.

*The full text of "The Protocols of the Wise Men of Zion" is given in Exhibit F.

†The similarity between the "Protocols" and the "Dialogues" was first shown by Mr. Philip P. Graves, Constantinople correspondent of the *Times*, London, in his articles published on August 16, 17, and 18, 1921. Extracts from his articles describing his discovery, and his affidavit submitted to the Swiss court, are reproduced in Exhibit B.

Albert Joly died about three years after Maurice Joly had committed suicide.

Roger Lambelin, who wrote the introduction to the French edition of the "Protocols," in an article published in 1921 in *La Revue Hebdomadaire*, of Paris, stated that Joly's book appeared in several editions in both Geneva and Brussels, that on the fourth page of one of these editions there was an announcement that "on sale at the same publisher's" were other books against the régime of Napoleon III by Victor Hugo, Bouchot and the Duc d'Aumale. That edition also mentioned the fact that on April 28, 1865, "the publication of the first anonymous edition of this book cost its author, M. Maurice Joly, a sentence to fifteen months' imprisonment and 300 francs fine for inciting to hatred and distrust of the imperial government."

M. Lambelin also declared at the same time that his researches proved that Maurice Joly was not of Jewish origin, as some anti-Semites had asserted, but that his family was of Italian descent. His grandfather was paymaster in the army of the First Empire, and his father was councillor-general of the Jura under the July Monarchy. Joly was born in Lons-le-Saunier in 1831. He was a prolific writer, but his articles, philosophical and severe, were not often accepted by the Parisian journals to which he had submitted them for publication. He committed suicide in 1878, several months before Marshal MacMahon resigned and the Republicans triumphed.

CHAPTER TWO

"To Sedan"

ABOUT two years after the publication of Maurice Joly's "Dialogues in Hell," a series of novels entitled "Biarritz-Rome" appeared in Berlin, purporting to have been written by "Sir John Retcliffe," the pseudonym of Hermann Goedsche, a German novelist with an unsavory past. To conceal his identity and to convey the impression that the anti-Semitism with which his writings abounded emanated from English sources, he selected "Sir John Retcliffe" as his pen-name.

According to *Meyer's Konversations Lexikon* (Sixth edition, 1904, Volume VIII, page 77), Hermann Goedsche was born in February, 1815, in Trachtenberg, Silesia, and died on November 8th, 1878, at Warmbrunn. He was employed in the postal service, but when he was implicated in the Waldeck forgery case, he left the service in 1849, and devoted himself to literary work. Under the name of "Armin" he published a number of works of fiction, but he was best known under the name of "Sir John Retcliffe," by which he signed a series of sensational novels describing the Crimean war, "Sebastopol," "Rena-Sahib," "Villa-franca," "Puebla," "Biarritz," in 1866. A new edition of these works appeared in Berlin in 1903-1904.

Brockhaus' Konversations Lexikon (supplement volume XVII, 1904) refers to Goedsche, the novelist, known under the name of "Sir John Retcliffe" (formerly "Armin"), as having played an infamous role in the Waldeck forgery case. He was compelled to leave the postal service, and later became a member of the staff of the *Preussische Kreutz Zeitung*.

In Goedsche's novel, "To Sedan," there appeared a chapter entitled "The Jewish Cemetery in Prague and the Council of Representatives of the Twelve Tribes of Israel," in which he described a secret centennial midnight meeting of the representatives of the twelve tribes of Israel in the ancient cemetery in Prague. According to Goedsche's fantastic story, the representatives of the twelve tribes of Israel meet once in a hundred years in the Prague cemetery for the purpose of reporting what had happened to the Jewish people during the past century and of elaborating plans for the next century. The midnight meeting, depicted by Hermann Goedsche in the style of blood-curdling fiction, is secretly attended by a converted Jew and by a "large-sized man, with the pale serious face of Germanic type." The Devil himself, the son of "the accursed one," is also present at that midnight meeting of the representatives of the twelve tribes of Israel. And from time to time the Devil is quoted as making side remarks.

The chapter of the Retcliffe-Goedsche novel was published as a separate booklet in a Russian translation in 1872, avowedly as a work of fiction. On even a cursory reading this book will be found to contain the essence of the "Dialogues in Hell," except that the Machiavellian arguments have been changed by the German novelist into an outline of an alleged Jewish conspiracy against the Gentile world. A copy of this little volume is in the Russian Department of the Library of Congress, Washington, D. C.

In this weird, fantastic thriller, lifted from the "Dialogues in Hell," and transformed afterward into the infamous "Protocols," the story is told of a secret meeting of the representatives of the twelve tribes of Israel, ten of which totally disappeared nearly twenty-five centuries ago. The Devil, who is represented as having attended that meeting, was assigned the function of spreading the decisions of the "Wise Men of Zion" among the Jews in order that they may conquer the world.

An examination of "The Jewish Cemetery in Prague and the

Council of Representatives of the Twelve Tribes of Israel," discloses the fact that every substantive statement contained in the "Dialogues in Hell" and elaborated in the "Protocols," appears in the Goedsche-Retcliffe novelette.

Inspired by Maurice Joly's "Dialogues in Hell," Goedsche-Retcliffe, the German novelist, changed the Machiavelli-Montesquieu meeting in Hades into a mysterious centennial midnight meeting of the elders of Israel in the ancient cemetery of Prague.

The Russian translation of the Goedsche novelette was published first in a magazine edited by Nikolay S. Lvoff and then in booklet form, with the following foreword:

"The contents of the legend are not the invention of Retcliffe himself; rather Retcliffe, with his characteristic fantastic imagination, collected various parts into one whole and painted all with poetic colors, which strike one perhaps by their excessive gaudiness, but which are nevertheless interesting.

"Passed by the Censor, St. Petersburg, May 17, 1872." *

Several years after the publication of this fantastic story in his novel "To Sedan," and after the Russian translation had appeared, "Sir John Retcliffe," alias Goedsche, deeming it important for his purpose of adding fuel to the flame of anti-Semitism that had been lighted in Germany, undertook to convert his work of fiction, the offspring of his imagination, into a statement of fact. This led him to adopt a simple device of consolidating into one continuous speech the dialogue contained in his imaginative thriller, and of putting the speech into the mouth of an imaginary Rabbi in such a way as to make it appear to be an address delivered by him to a secret convocation of Jews. And the very man who had plagiarized from the "Dialogues in Hell" the speeches set down in his work of fiction now vouched for the

*A translation of the Goedsche-Retcliffe chapter, "The Jewish Cemetery in Prague and the Council of Representatives of the Twelve Tribes of Israel," together with a photostat reproduction of the title page of the Russian booklet in the Library of Congress, Washington, is given in full in Exhibits C and I.

authenticity of the speech which he himself had fabricated and attributed to a Rabbi.

G. Butmi, a notorious Russian reactionary and anti-Semitic writer, who reproduced the translation of the "Rabbi's Speech" * in 1905, prefaced it with the following editorial comment:

"Toward the end of the last century there appeared a book in London by Retcliffe entitled 'A Review of Political and Historical Events During the Past Ten Years.' This work was translated into French. The French periodical press, without waiting for the complete translation of the book, reproduced certain parts of it because they were of special interest. Thus the French newspapers and magazines published translations from the English of an intensely interesting speech (from the Hebrew), most edifying for Russia, delivered by one of the Rabbis, the authenticity of which speech is vouched for by *the above-mentioned author*. This inimitable gem must in the eyes of the Russians assume all the more importance since it is brought out by that 'highly civilized,' humane and practical country, England, which has given protection to the Russian Jews against the poorly invented persecutions on the part of the Russian government and people. This monstrous document was sent at the time in printed form, in the French language, to the editorial office of the Odessa newspaper *Novorosisky Telegraf* for those who might want to examine the accuracy of the translation published in No. 4996 of that newspaper, dated January 22, 1891, and reprinted in No. 21 of the St. Petersburg newspaper *Znamya*, dated January 22, 1904. *The speech relates to the time of the Sanhedrin of 1869.*"

The Butmi preface to the "Rabbi's Speech," vouched for by Goedsche-Retcliffe, furnishes further evidence of the unscrupulous methods and motives of the forgers and plagiarists who fabricated the "Protocols." They used them to save the crumbling Russian

---

*A translation from the Russian of the apocryphal "Rabbi's Speech," as published in G. Butmi's book entitled "The Enemy of the Human Race," dedicated by the author to the Black Hundreds, the Tsarist pogrom-makers, is presented in this volume, in Exhibit D, together with the passages omitted from the French version of that "Speech."

autocracy by endeavoring to discredit the Jews and to justify the Tsarist pogrom policy against them. In the first place, no book entitled "A Review of Political and Historical Events During the Past Ten Years," by Retcliffe, ever appeared in England. Secondly, the only authority given for the authenticity of the "Rabbi's Speech" is the assurance of the novelist-forger Goedsche-Retcliffe who had used most of the passages of that speech years before in his own weird work of fiction about the secret meeting in the Prague cemetery. Thirdly, the Black Hundred publicist, Butmi, sought to convey the impression in Russia that Retcliffe was an Englishman and that his work was published in London. His ironic reference to England as "that 'highly civilized,' humane and practical country, which has given protection to the Russian Jews against the poorly invented persecutions on the part of the Russian government and people" is quite typical of the Russian reactionaries' attitude toward England's liberalism at the time. The Black Hundreds, the party of the Russian pogromists, was furious at England's sympathetic treatment of the Russian Jews who had fled from Russia because of religious persecution and found refuge there. In order to minimize the significance of the liberalism of the English people, the reactionary anti-Semitic Russian writers developed a theory that the English are really the "lost tribes of Israel." The Russian anti-Semitic writings of that period abound in references to the English people as mercenaries and "pure-blooded Jews."

Finally the statement in Butmi's foreword that the Rabbi's Speech "relates to the time of the Sanhedrin of 1869," reaches the climax of absurdities by which the Russian anti-Semite sought to substantiate the authenticity of the invented "Rabbi's Speech."

The Great Sanhedrin, the highest political magistracy of the Jews of Biblical times, ceased to exist when the Jewish state perished with the destruction of Jerusalem in the year 70 of the Christian era. It was composed of seventy elders, members of the nobility and priesthood. The Religious Sanhedrin, which existed at the same time and supervised various religious problems, was carried on after the destruction of the Temple by the Academy of Jabneh, which in turn was superseded by Jewish academies under the patriarchs of the family of Hillel. The institution lasted until the end of the fourth century of the Christian era.

The French Sanhedrin was convened by Napoleon I to give legal sanction to the principles expressed by the Jewish Assembly of Notables in answer to twelve questions propounded to it by the Imperial Government. It was composed of 71 members, two-thirds of whom were rabbis and the rest laymen. The last session of the French Sanhedrin was held on April 6, 1807.

A comparison of the "Rabbi's Speech" with the Goedsche-Retcliffe scene in the Prague cemetery easily identifies its authorship. It was this "Rabbi's Speech" by Goedsche-Retcliffe, originally published in a Russian translation in 1891, that undoubtedly furnished the inspiration to convert the "Dialogues in Hell" into the "Protocols of the Wise Men of Zion."

CHAPTER THREE

The Protocols in Russia

THE "Protocols" were concocted not for the purpose of impressing statesmen, theologians, or even public opinion; they were drawn up in France and published in Russia to influence and inflame a feeble-minded person whose spirit already was filled with hatred of the Jew.

That person was none other than Tsar Nicholas II.

The Russian autocrat, who felt his throne tottering under him in the middle of the nineties and particularly after the Russo-Japanese war, when the revolutionary movement assumed serious proportions, was unwilling to grant the Russian people the reforms advocated by Count Sergius Witte. The influence of his tutor, Pobyedonostsev, the head of the Holy Synod, one of the most sinister and brilliant Russian reactionaries, and the pressure brought by Dubrovin, the leader of the Black Hundred pogromists, caused the weak-willed Tsar Nicholas to resist the counsel of Count Witte, who urged the saving of the Russian dynasty by means of a major operation in the form of a Constitution. It was first Gen. Orzhevsky and, later, Ratchkovsky, unscrupulous Paris representatives of the Russian Okhrana, political secret police department, who conceived the idea of fabricating the document with which to impress the Tsar that the Jews and the Freemasons were responsible for the revolutionary upheavals in Russia and that they were also engaged in a conspiracy for world domination.

The Jews were represented as possessing all the infernal wisdom and the wealth which would enable the revolutionary ideas of the Freemasons to be realized, thus bringing about the subjugation of Russia and then of the rest of the world. To the political danger of anti-Tsarism was added the spiritual danger of the anti-Christ, and the fabricators of the "Protocols" strove to persuade Tsar Nicholas that it was in his power alone to save the world and especially his own dynasty from the threatening forces of disruption and revolution.

The Tsar was informed that already in 1901 a "mystic saint," Sergius Nilus, had published a deeply religious and powerful book, "The Great in Little—The Coming of the Anti-Christ and the Rule of Satan on Earth." In 1905 that book by Nilus was reprinted by the Government Press at Tsarskoye Selo, the home of the Tsar, and the "Protocols" were added as a commentary on the Nilus prophecy and as an illustration of its approaching fulfillment. Thus appeared the notorious Nilus edition of the "Protocols," a copy of which is registered in the British Museum under the date of August 10, 1906.

Because the writings of Sergius Nilus are typical of the "literature" produced under the auspices of the Russian Black Hundred organizations which sought to save the Tsar's throne by pogroms, I examined a large number of publications brought out in Russia during the period when "the Russian Mystic," Sergius Nilus, published his pretended discovery, the "Protocols." His book, "The Great in Little—the Coming of the Anti-Christ and the Rule of Satan on Earth," appeared in 1905 after the Russo-Japanese War, when the Russian revolutionists made an attempt to overthrow the Tsar's government. A new organization was formed for the support of the Russian throne. It was known as "the Union of the Russian People"—the Black Hundreds—whose program was Jew-baiting. It was then that Russia adopted a definite, anti-Jewish policy of vengeance—a pogrom policy. The Black Hundreds held the Jews responsible for Russia's defeat in the war and for the attempted revolution,—and neither the Tsar nor his loyal organization of the Black Hundreds ever forgave Count Sergius Witte, who won for Russia at the Portsmouth Peace Conference what she had lost on the battlefields, for inducing Nicholas II to grant a constitution to Russia. The Black Hundreds nick-named Witte "the Jewish Count of Portsmouth." They attacked him and attempted to assassinate him. They assassinated at that time two Jewish members of the Duma, Yollos and Hertzenstein. It was during the period of Judophobia that Sergius Nilus published his book containing the "Protocols."

What are these mysterious Protocols which have been exhumed from obscurity for the purpose of enlightening the world, and which point to the Jews as the cause of all unrest, chaos and confusion? How did they come to "the Russian mystic," Sergius Nilus, who revealed them in 1905?

Nilus is credited with several versions of how he had secured the Protocols, and his stories flatly contradict one another. In 1905 he said that the Protocols were given to him by a prominent Russian conservative whose name he did not mention, and who in turn had received them from an unnamed woman who had stolen them from "one of the most influential leaders of Freemasonry at the close of a secret meeting of the initiated in France." Then, several years later, Nilus wrote that his friend himself had stolen the Protocols from "the headquarters of the Society of Zion in France." Several years afterwards, in a new edition of his book, Nilus said that the Protocols came from Switzerland and not from France. This time he named his Russian conservative friend, Sukhotin, who had died in the meantime. He added that the Protocols were not Jewish-Masonic but Zionist documents secretly read at the Zionist Congress in Basle in 1897.

Then followed a new edition of the Nilus book bearing the date of 1917. A translation of this edition appeared in this country in 1920, containing a brand-new explanation as to how the Protocols were rescued and given to the world. This explanation is taken from the German versions published in Charlottenburg. The introduction to that edition says that the Protocols, having been read from day to day at the Basle Congress, were sent as read to Frankfort-on-the-Main. The disclosure of them came through the infidelity of the messenger.

The 1917 edition is published with a prologue and an epilogue, like a drama, which indeed it is, with all the ingredients of melodrama: a villain, a mysterious woman, a Grand Duke, a conspiracy to destroy the world, and a saint—Nilus, who convicts himself in his own writings of falsification in the giving of these various accounts of how the Protocols came into his possession.

The anonymous American editor of the Nilus book gave the following information about Nilus:

"Serge Nilus, in the 1905 edition of whose book was first published the *Zionist Protocols*, was, as he states, born in the year 1862, of Russian parents holding liberal opinions. His family was fairly well known in Moscow, for its members were educated people who were firm in their allegiance to the Tsar and the Greek Church. On one side he is said to have been connected by marriage with the nobility of the Baltic provinces. Nilus himself was graduated from the University of Moscow and early entered the civil service, obtaining a small appointment in the law courts. Later, he received a post under the Procurator of a provincial court in the Caucasus. Finally, tiring of the law, he went to the Government of Orel, where he was a landowner and a noble. His spiritual life had been tumultuous and full of trouble, and finally he entered the Troitsky-Sergevsky Monastery near Moscow. 'In answer to his appeal for pardon, Saint Sergei, stern and angry, appeared to him twice in a vision. He left the Monastery a converted man.'

"From 1905 until the present, little is known of his activities. Articles are said to have appeared from time to time in the Russian press from his pen. A returning traveller from Siberia in August, 1919, was positive in his statement that Nilus was in Irkutsk in June of that year. Whether his final fate was that of Admiral Kolchak is not known."

In the German edition, Nilus is described as follows:

"Sergius Nilus was an employee of the Russian secret police department, of the *okhrana*, connected with the Church, especially relating to 'foreign religions.' He lived for some time at the Optina Pustina Monastery. In 1901 he published a book entitled 'The Great in the Small and the Anti-Christ.' According to the *Lutsch Sveta*, Nilus claims to have received in 1901 a copy of the text of the Protocols from the secret archives of the Main Zionist organization in France, but he published the Protocols only in 1905. A second edition appeared in 1911, and finally another edition was brought out in the beginning of 1917, but all copies are said to have been destroyed."

"The Cause of the World Unrest," an anonymous book published in England and reprinted in this country, speaks of Nilus and the "Protocols" as follows:

"In the year 1903 a Russian, Serge Nilus, published a book entitled *The Great in Little*. The second edition, which was published at Tsarskoye Selo in 1905, had an additional chapter, the twelfth, under the heading 'Anti-Christ as a Near Political Possibility.' This chapter consisted of some twenty pages of introduction followed by the text of twenty-four 'Protocols of Meetings of the Learned Elders of Zion,' and the book ends with some twenty pages.

"Directly after the protocols, comes a statement by Nilus that they are 'signed by representatives of Zion of the thirty-third degree.' These protocols were secretly extracted or were stolen from a whole volume of protocols. All this was got by my correspondent out of the secret depositories of the Head Chancellery of Zion. This Chancellery is at present on French territory."

In the edition of 1917 Sergius Nilus wrote:

"My book has already reached the fourth edition, but it is only definitely known to me now and in a manner worthy of belief, and that through Jewish sources, that these protocols are nothing other than the strategic plans for the conquest of the world under the heel of Israel, and worked out by the leaders of the Jewish people—and read by the 'Prince of Exile,' Theodore

Herzl, during the first Zionist Congress, summoned by him in August, 1897, in Basle." *

Sergius Nilus also wrote:

"In 1901 I came into possession of a manuscript, and this comparatively small book was destined to cause a deep change in my entire viewpoint as can only be caused in the heart of man by Divine Power. It was comparable with the miracle of making the blind see. 'May Divine acts enlighten him.'

"This manuscript was called 'the protocols of the Zionist Men of Wisdom,' and it was given to me by the now deceased leader of the Tchernigov nobility, who later became vice-governor of Stavropol, Alexis Nikolayevitch Sukhotin. I had already begun to work with my pen for the glory of the Lord, and I was friendly with Sukhotin. *He was a man of my opinion,* that is, extremely conservative, as they are now termed.

"Sukhotin told me that he in turn had obtained the manuscript from a lady who always lived abroad. This lady was a noblewoman from Tchernigov. He mentioned her by name, but I have forgotten it. He said that she obtained it in some mysterious way, by theft, I believe.

"Sukhotin also said that one copy of the manuscript was given by this lady to Sipiagin, the Minister of the Interior, upon her return from abroad, and that Sipiagin was subsequently killed. He said other things of the same mysterious character. But when I first became acquainted with the contents of the manuscript I was convinced that its terrible, cruel and straightforward truth is witness of its true origin from the 'Zionist Men of Wisdom,' and that no other evidence of its origin would be needed."

Feodor Roditchev, one of Russia's most famous liberals, a member of the nobility, a former member of the Duma, writing of the Nilus protocols and of Sukhotin, whom Nilus described as a man of his own opinion, said in 1920:

*It will be shown later that the so-called Butmi edition of the "protocols" published in 1907 contains the definite statement of the man who claims to have translated them into Russian from the French in 1901 that the Elders of Zion are not to be confounded with the Zionist movement.

"For months I hear on all sides about the Nilus book and its success in England, and I am asked, who is Nilus? There was a Nilus, an associate justice of the Moscow District Court. It is said that the manuscript was given to Nilus by Sukhotin, the notorious *zemstvo* official of Chernsk.

"The Berlin edition contains no mention of Sukhotin, but in that edition Nilus said, 'Pray for the soul of the *boyar* Alexis.'

"The name of the notorious Alexey Nikolayevitch Sukhotin means nothing to the present generation. But there was a time when his name attracted attention.

"Sukhotin arrested the peasants of a whole village for refusing to cart manure from his stables because the animals there were infected with glanders. Judge Tsurikov released the peasants. Tsurikov was removed for this, while Sukhotin justified his act by writing to the Minister of the Interior, Durnovo, that he had arrested the peasants not because they refused to cart his manure, but because they dared disobey him as a *zemstvo* official. The reactionary Chernsk nobility made Sukhotin marshal of nobility. So it was this man who furnished the protocols of the secret meetings of the representatives of Zion! But how did Sukhotin get the protocols? An unknown friend had brought them to him. They were given to him by an unknown lady who had received them from an unknown but energetic participant in the Basle Congress. Is this credible? Well, then, there is another version of the origin of the protocols—but that is for the German readers. The Russian government sent a spy to the Basle Congress. He did not go to the Congress himself, but bribed one of the participants. He was carrying the protocols from Basle to Frankfurt to the local masonic organization. He stopped on the way in a little town, and gave the protocols to the spy. He engaged copyists who worked all night and copied the protocols.

"In the first Russian version the protocols were supposed to have been brought to Russia in French. According to the German version, the protocols were copied, consequently they were in German, but the most important thing is that the protocols are not protocols at all, but a monograph—which could be called the dream of a member of the 'Black Hundreds'."

In the book issued by G. Butmi to which reference has been made, and which contains the "Rabbi's Speech" already considered, there is to be found still another version of the protocols. Butmi was a notorious Black Hundred writer. This book was dedicated to the Black Hundred organization. Appropriately enough it was published by the Society of Deaf and Dumb, as will be seen from the facsimile reproduction of the title page. With exceeding naïveté Butmi published the forged speech attributed by Retcliffe-Goedsche to a Jewish Rabbi as proof of the genuineness of the protocols, and side by side with the fabricated speech appears the Butmi version of the protocols.

The headlines over the protocols in the Butmi 1906 and 1907 versions read as follows:

"PROTOCOLS TAKEN OUT OF THE SECRET DEPOSITORIES OF THE MAIN OFFICE OF ZION.

"(Extracts from ancient and modern protocols of the Sages of Zion of the Universal Organization of Freemasons.)"

Thus the Protocols were in 1907 presented by G. Butmi, dedicated to the Black Hundreds, as Masonic, not as Jewish documents. In his introduction the author says, in part, as follows:

"These secret protocols were secured with great difficulty in fragmentary form, and were translated into Russian in December, 1901. It is almost impossible to get at the secret depositories again where they are hidden, and therefore they cannot be reinforced by definite information as to the place, day, month, year, where and when they were composed.

"The reader who is more or less familiar with the secrets of Freemasonry will draw from the general character of the criminal plot, outlined in the protocols, the conclusion as to their authenticity, and from several details he will suppose with great certainty that the mentioned protocols were taken from the documents of the Masonic lodge of Egyptian ritual, or Mizraim, which is joined mostly by Jews. . . .

"But the above-mentioned failure to mention the time and place where the protocols were composed might call forth in the reader, who is entirely unfamiliar with the abominations of Masonic doctrines, doubts as to the authenticity of these documents."

At the end of the Protocols published in this edition by Butmi, in 1907, there appears a note by the man who declares that he had secured and translated the documents from the French, on December 9, 1901, and in the very first two lines of his note, he states that the representatives of Zion mentioned in the documents are not to be confounded with the representatives of the Zionist movement. The Russian mystic Serge Nilus, in his later editions, connected the documents with the Zionist Congress in Basle and with the head of the Zionist movement, Dr. Theodore Herzl.

The translator, as do Nilus and Lutostansky, also gives a version of "the political plan devised by the Wise Men of Zion." This translator, however, states that the "political plan was conceived 929 years before the birth of Christ. It was invented by Solomon and Judean sages in theory."

Here follow extracts from the so-called Translator's Note:

"The expounded protocols are signed by the representatives of Zion (*do not confound them with the representatives of the Zionist movement*). They were taken out of a whole book of protocols, the entire contents of which it was impossible to copy because of the short time allowed the translator for reading these protocols. A small appendix was attached to them and a plan of conquering the world by the Jews by peaceful means. These protocols and the Sketch were taken from the secret depositories of the Main Office of Zion, now located on French territory.

"The above-mentioned Sketch contained the entire political plan of Zion with regard to the stages to be passed through by this movement and to the means of passing from one to another. The aforesaid political plan was conceived 929 years before the birth of Christ. It was invented by Solomon and the Judean

Sages in theory; according to historical events, it was elaborated
and enlarged by their followers initiated in this plan.

"These sages decided to conquer the world peacefully for
Zion, with the cunning of the Symbolic Snake, whose head should
be composed of the Jewish Government initiated in the plans
of the Wise Men (always masked even to their people), and the
body—the Jewish nation.

"Crawling into the bosom of governments, this snake has
undermined or eaten away all non-Jewish governmental powers,
according to their growth, in various continents, but particularly
in Europe, which it should do also in the future, following
exactly the outlines of the plan until the cycle of the road travelled by it will close by the return of the head of the Snake to
Zion—that is, until this snake will include in the sphere of its
circle all Europe, and through Europe the whole world, utilizing
all forces conquered by economic means in order to draw the
other continents into the sphere of its cycle.

"For instance, the economic theory of the ballot system has
made it possible to carry out everything that was desirable in
the interests of the elevation of Zion. The Jewish authorities
commenced to act by means of bribing or by instigating the
majority of votes as soon as they succeeded to manage so that
the decisions of that majority became the determining factor in
questions of national life. The crowd always in need, or the
greedy intelligent class, short-sighted liberals and other blind
people have also rendered good service to Zion. Therefore the
republican is the most desirable and convenient form of government for Zion because it gives full sway for the activities of the
armies of Zion—for anarchists of thought and action, called
socialists.

"All that which is outlined above is the work of the hands
of the nation without a territory, constituting but a drop in the
ocean of humanity, but possessing the most ideal Government,
every member of which is familiarized with the plan of action
worked out in the course of centuries, from which he cannot

deviate. The politics of the *goyim* is the politics of accidental circumstances, engineered by the Jews, and tends not towards perfecting the affairs of the state, but towards struggle for the sake of greed, or more often for the personal aggrandizement of the administrators.

"From this it is clear, on whose side there must be victory and the guidance of the world.

"Translation from the French, December 9, 1901."

The Russian and German anti-Semites have maintained that the Protocols were the minutes of the secret proceedings of the first Zionist Congress at Basle, held in 1897, presided over by Dr. Theodore Herzl. Dr. Alfred Rosenberg, the Nazi ideologist of anti-Semitism and translator of the Protocols into German, declared that they were the work of the Zionist leaders, Herzl, Nordau and Achad Ha'Am. Even Butmi, who published the translator's note to the effect that the "representatives of Zion who signed the Protocols" should not be confounded with the representatives of the Zionist movement, declared in his edition of 1906 as follows:

"In vain does the translator in his note ask us not to confound the doctrines of the Zionist sages of Masonry with those of the representatives of the Zionist movement, that is Zionism, founded by Dr. Theodore Herzl in 1896. Particularly in Russia the Zionist-Masons in their activities, directed against the Church and the State, found a natural ally in Judaism, especially in the so-called Zionism which is so widespread among Jewish intelligentsia in Russia, which uses but as an external pretext the plan of the emigration of Jews to Palestine, but which is in reality a revolutionary organization, secretly guided by the Jewish 'Bund.' . . .

"England, through its agents, the Russian Masons, is co-operating for the internal enslavement of Russia by the Jews, by Jewish Zionists, by means of stirring up internal sedition, paralyzing the potential resistance of Russia to the wiles of British foreign policy. The agreement on this subject between the Zionists and the Masons was apparently arrived at in 1900, at the initiative of Dr. Herzl, founder of modern Zionism. Thus Jewish Zionism, working in Russia under the protection of Russian Masons, is well-organized and spread throughout Russia by the treacherous agency of the British foreign policy, which is always inimical to Russia but friendly to the Jews."

While the Russian fabricators and forgers of the Protocols could not agree on any one version of how and when the Protocols reached Russia, and under whose sponsorship the spurious anti-Semitic document first made its appearance there, they all sought to identify the Protocols with the first Zionist Congress held in Basle in 1897.

Fortunately, I find documentary evidence, submitted by the anti-Semites themselves, in their desperate effort to prove the authenticity of the first Russian version of the Protocols, that they were brought to Russia in 1895, *two years before the first Zionist Congress.*

L. Fry, in a book entitled "Water Flowing Eastward," published in Paris in 1933, thus describes "How the Protocols Came to Russia":

"In 1884 the daughter of a Russian General, Mlle. Justine Glinka, was endeavoring to serve her country in Paris by obtaining political information, which she communicated to General Orgevskii (at that time Secretary to the Minister of the Interior, General Cherevin), in St. Petersburg. For this purpose she employed a Jew, Joseph Schorst (*alias* Schapiro, whose father had been sentenced in London, two years previous, to ten years' penal servitude for counterfeiting), member of Mizraim Lodge in Paris. One day Schorst offered to obtain for her a document of great importance to Russia, on payment of 2,500 francs. This sum being received from St. Petersburg was paid over and the document handed to Mlle. Glinka (Schorst fled to Egypt where, according to French police archives, he was murdered).

"She forwarded the French original, accompanied by a Russian translation, to Orgevskii, who in turn handed it to his chief, General Cherevin, for transmission to the Tsar. But Cherevin, under obligation to wealthy Jews, refused to transmit it, merely filing it in the archives (on his death in 1896, he willed a copy of his memoirs containing the Protocols to Nicholas II).

"Meantime there appeared in Paris certain books on Russian court life, (published under the pseudonym 'Count Vassilii,' their real author was Mme. Juliette Adam, using material furnished by Princess Demidov-San Donato, Princess Radziwill and other Russians), which displeased the Tsar, who ordered his secret police to discover their authorship. This was falsely attributed, perhaps with malicious intent (among the Jews in the Russian secret service in Paris was Manuilov, whose odious character is drawn by M. Paléologue, *Memoires*), to Mlle. Glinka, and on her return to Russia she was banished to her estate in Orel. To the *Maréchal de noblesse* of this district, Alexis Sukhotin, Mlle. Glinka gave a copy of the Protocols. Sukhotin showed the document to two friends, Stepanov and Nilus; the former had it printed and circulated privately in 1897; the second, Professor Sergius A. Nilus, published it for the first time in Tsarskoye Selo (Russia) in 1901, in a book entitled *The Great Within the Small*. Then, about the same time, a friend of Nilus, G. Butmi, also brought it out and a copy was deposited in the British Museum on August 10, 1906.

"Meantime, through Jewish members (notably Evno Azev and Efron) of the Russian police, minutes of the proceedings of the Basle Congress in 1897 had been obtained and these were found to correspond with the Protocols. The Russian government had learned that at meetings of the B'nai B'rith in New York in 1893-94, Jacob Schiff had been named chairman of the Committee on the revolutionary movement in Russia.*

"In January, 1917, Nilus had prepared a second edition, revised and documented, for publication. But before it could be put on the market, the revolution of March, 1917, had taken place, and Kerenski, who had succeeded to power, ordered the whole edition of Nilus' book to be destroyed. In 1924, Prof. Nilus

*Jacob H. Schiff was never an officer or chairman of any Committee of the B'nai B'rith.

was arrested by the Cheka in Kiev, imprisoned, and tortured; he was told by the Jewish president of the court, that this treatment was meted out to him 'for having done them incalculable harm in publishing the Protocols.' Released for a few months, he was again led before the G. P. U. (Cheka), this time in Moscow and confined. Set at liberty in February, 1926, he died in exile in the district of Vladimir on January 13, 1929.

"A few copies of Nilus' second edition were saved and sent to other countries where they were published: In Germany, by Gottfried zur Beek (1919); in England, by *The Britons* (1920); in France, by Mgr. Jouin in *La Revue Internationale des Sociétés Secretes*, and by Urbain Gohier in *La Vieille France;* in the United States, by Small, Maynard & Co. (Boston, 1920), and by The Beckwith Co. (New York, 1921). Later, editions appeared in Italian, Russian, Arabic and even in Japanese.

"Such is the simple story of how these Protocols reached Russia and thence came into general circulation." *

This account of the history of the Protocols in Russia is accompanied by a facsimile affidavit made in 1927 by Philip Stepanov, one of the two friends to whom Sukhotin first showed the Protocols in Russia. Stepanov's telltale affidavit, translated from the Russian, reads as follows:

"In 1895 my neighboring estate owner in the province of Tula, retired Major Alexey Nikolayevitch Sukhotin, gave me a handwritten copy of the 'Protocols of the Wise Men of Zion.' He told me that a lady of his acquaintance (he did not mention her name), residing in Paris, had found them at the home of a friend of hers (probably of Jewish origin), and before leaving Paris, had translated them secretly, without his knowledge, and had brought one copy of that translation to Russia, and had given that copy to him, Sukhotin.

"At first I mimeographed one hundred copies of the Protocols, but that edition was difficult to read, and I resolved to have it

*A copy of L. Fry's book, "Waters Flowing Eastward," second edition, Paris, 1933, is in the New York Public Library.

printed somewhere, without mentioning the time, the city and the printer; I was helped in this by Arcady Ippolitovitch Kelepkovsky, who at that time was Privy Councillor with Grand Duke Sergey Alexandrovitch; he had these documents printed at the Provincial Printing Press; that was in 1897. S. A. Nilus reprinted these Protocols in full in his book, with his own commentaries.

"Philip Petrovitch Stepanov, former Procurator of the Moscow Synod Office; Chamberlain, Privy Councillor, and at the time of the publication of that edition, Chief of the district railway service of the Moscow-Kursk railway (in Orel).

"This is the signature of a member of the colony of Russian refugees at Stary and Novy Futog.   (Cor. C. X. S.)

"Witnessed by me, Stary Futog, April 17, 1927.

"Chairman of the Administration of the Colony,

"Prince Vladimir Galitzin."   (Seal) *

The translation of this handwritten affidavit by Stepanov, given in L. Fry's book, contains several minor inaccuracies. The signature of Prince Vladimir Galitzin is transcribed as "Prince Dimitri Galitzin."

Thus the Russian anti-Semites themselves, anxious to vouch for the authenticity of the "Protocols" and their Zionist origin, by this affidavit give the lie to the Russian fabricators and disseminators of the Protocols, revealing that the Russian translation of the spurious document had reached Russia two years before the first Zionist Congress was held in Basle. This affidavit furnishes the missing link in the chain of incontrovertible evidence establishing the falsity of the Protocols and the sinister motives of the anti-Jewish forgers. It also confirms the fact that officials close to the Tsar's family participated in the launching of the Protocols in Russia.

Several years ago the Library of Congress, of Washington, had purchased a collection of books belonging to the library of Tsar Nicholas II. That collection, as yet uncatalogued, is now in a vault in the Department of Rare Books and Manuscripts.

*A facsimile of this letter in Russian is reproduced in Exhibit I.

Recently I examined the volumes of the Tsar's library and found among them the 1906 edition of Butmi's book, "Enemies of the Human Race," dedicated to the Union of the Russian People (the Black Hundreds), and containing the Protocols. The special binding bears the Imperial crest of the Russian Empress. Butmi's foreword to that edition, dated St. Petersburg, December 5, 1905, offers the following explanation:

"The Protocols, being secret, were obtained with great difficulty, in fragmentary form, and translated into Russian on December 9, 1901. It is almost impossible to get again at the secret depositories where they are hidden, and therefore they cannot be reinforced by definite information concerning the place, the day or the month, where and when they were composed. This circumstance might arouse suspicion as to the genuineness of the Protocols."

However, Butmi is sure that the Protocols are genuine Jewish documents because of their contents. The Butmi version of the Protocols in the Tsar's library differs from the other Butmi editions in that the attacks on the "British foreign policy" and the British Masons co-operating with the "Jewish Zionists" are not included in this particular edition. Apparently Butmi feared to weaken the impression of his anti-Jewish book on the Tsar by the offensive references to the British government.

Father Gleb E. Verchovsky, a Roman Catholic priest of the Byzantine Slavic rite, residing in Chicago, who knew the Russian anti-Semitic writer, George Butmi, intimately, states that it was Butmi who first brought the French "Protocols" into Russia, translated and published them shortly after the close of the Dreyfus Affair. Butmi published several editions of the "Protocols" in his book entitled "Accusatory Addresses—Enemies of the Human Race," dedicated to the Black Hundreds.

Butmi's version differs from that of Nilus in the style of the translation as well as in the order and division of the "Protocols." Butmi's text is divided into 27 Protocols, while the Nilus Protocols are 24 in number. Butmi's translation also contains several passages that are not included in the Nilus version.

The "Protocols" were fabricated by Russians in Paris, apparently during the first year of the Dreyfus Affair, for political purposes. The spurious documents were intended not only to inflame general hatred against the Jews in Russia but also to discredit the Russian liberals who deplored the anti-Jewish discriminations and persecutions, and were aimed particularly at Sergius Witte, then Minister of Finance, who introduced the Gold Standard in Russia and irritated the reactionaries by advocating liberal reforms and sympathizing with the Jews.

The plagiarists of the Joly "Dialogues in Hell" also drew upon the works of various French, German and Russian rabid anti-Semites for the preparation of the "Protocols of the Wise Men of Zion."

The authors of the "Protocols" had evidently no idea of the hopes, the ethical aspirations, the religious traditions, the historical destiny of Judaism and the Jew. Every intelligent reader of the mélange of ignorance and venom contained in the "Protocols" must recognize that the writer of these calumnies had never read a Jewish or even an authoritative non-Jewish book dealing with Jewish history. None of the plans, ideas and aspirations outlined in the "Protocols," none of the political conspiracies are, in any detail, based on Jewish psychology or Jewish history.

CHAPTER FOUR

Spread and Exposé of the Protocols

Upon my return in January, 1919, from the Far East, where I had represented the New York *Herald* and a syndicate of American newspapers as war correspondent accredited to General William S. Graves, head of the American Expeditionary Forces in Siberia, I was informed by Mr. Ohl, then managing editor of the New York *Herald*, that an American physician, Dr. Harris Houghton, connected with the Army Intelligence Department, had submitted to him a very important document concerning the Jewish people and their rôle in world affairs, and that he desired me to examine the manuscript and give my opinion as to its authenticity and significance.

The physician soon called on me with the document. He told me in the strictest confidence that he had come upon a most amazing find, the secret "Protocols of the Wise Men of Zion," which he said had been prepared by Dr. Theodore Herzl, the father of modern Zionism, and which he believed had been adopted at the first Zionist Congress at Basle in 1897. He said that the manuscript in his possession was a translation from a Russian book by Sergius Nilus, a monk, who had secured and made public the "Protocols." He spoke of the far-reaching significance of the "Protocols" with an air of great mystery. He said that he had submitted the manuscript to several members of President Wilson's Cabinet, and a few high officers of the Intelligence Department, and that all these people were deeply impressed with the astounding revelations of a universal sinister plot on the part of the Jewish people to secure world domination

43

by instigating war and revolution and bringing about the collapse of Christianity. He pointed to Bolshevism in Russia as the fulfillment of the plan outlined in the "Protocols" of the Zionists under the presidency of Theodore Herzl.

Dr. Houghton, who seemed to treasure this document as his most precious possession, asked me to read the "Protocols" and express my opinion, for Mr. Ohl, managing editor of the New York *Herald,* to whom he had submitted them for publication, had told him that he would be guided by my report as to the document's authenticity and importance. I replied that I would be glad to examine the "Protocols" and give my opinion, and told him that I would need three days for the examination. At first he hesitated to part with his precious document, but finally he decided to let me have it for three days, on condition that I sign a receipt promising to return the manuscript within that time and not to let anyone else see it.

I read and reread the "Protocols" and returned them to him within the three days, stating that, in my opinion, the "Protocols" were a clumsy falsification, and that from my intimate knowledge of Jewish life and Zionist activities I was convinced that neither Dr. Theodore Herzl nor any other responsible Jewish or Zionist leader could have prepared such a document. I even suggested that I would be willing to have the "Protocols" published, provided they would be accompanied by my comments exposing the absurdity of their fantastic charges against the Jewish people. When I informed Mr. Ohl of my opinion, he decided against their publication.

Upon investigation I soon learned that the Russian text of the "Protocols" was brought to the doctor's attention by Boris Brasol, a Russian monarchist in this country, a former Tsarist minor official of the Department of Justice under the notorious Minister of Justice Scheglovitov, who had staged the ritual murder trial in Kiev for the purpose of discrediting the Jewish people and of justifying the Tsarist government's anti-Jewish policy of pogroms.

Shortly afterward I left for Paris to describe the Peace Conference for the New York *Herald*. In Paris I learned that typewritten copies of the "Protocols" were circulated among delegates to the Peace Conference.

A year later translations of the "Protocols" began to appear throughout the world with the prolificacy of poisonous fungi. In England they were published under the title, "The Jewish Peril." Then a German version appeared, followed shortly by a Polish translation. Two versions were published in the United States in 1920. One of these was the manuscript which the American Intelligence officer had submitted to me for an opinion. Three different translations of the "Protocols" were published in France, followed by Italian, Danish, Swedish and Finnish versions. Hungary joined the merry dance and even in far-away Japan and China the "Protocols" made their appearance—in Russian, due to the efforts of Russian White Guards. All these translations, with conflicting explanations and introductions, emanated from the Russian reactionary émigrés and the Prussian Jew-baiters who had for years been trying to build up a case for their "scientific" anti-Semitism.

In Germany the "Protocols" were welcomed by the anti-Semites and their dupes with loud enthusiasm. Count Reventlow, one of the foremost disciples of the "Russian mystic," Sergius Nilus, and now a member of the National Socialist Government, led the campaign against the Jews. No nationalistic newspaper was too important or too small to devote much space to the "Protocols of the Wise Men of Zion."

Professor Hermann L. Strack, Privy Councillor in Germany, and one of the foremost German theological scholars, published an annihilating criticism of the "Protocols" and described them as a network of falsifications. The anti-Semites attacked the disinterested truth-loving professor, branding him as being in pay of the Jews, and his lone voice was drowned in the raucous noise of hate-inflamed ignorance and deliberate distortion of the truth.

The English press also paid serious attention to the "Protocols."

The *Times* as well as the *Spectator* seriously discussed this conglomeration of falsehood and absurdity as a genuine document. The *Morning Post* published a series of articles under the general title "Cause of the World Unrest," in which the entire course of history was reviewed and interpreted in the light of the "Protocols." These articles appeared later in book form and were widely read, discussed and reprinted in England and, to a certain extent, also in the United States.

In France the "Protocols" were discussed not only in the ultra-chauvinistic and anti-Semitic press, such as *La Libre Parole* and *La Vieille France,* but even serious and dignified publications of the type of *L'Opinion* carried leading articles about the monstrous falsehoods without questioning the authenticity of the documents. Many of the daily newspapers were full of allusions to the "Protocols," and no critical journalist there seemed to grasp the psychological and historical impossibility of the whole tragic falsification.

In Italy, where the "Protocols" had already appeared in April, 1920, the Milan paper *Perseverenza* reprinted in July extensive excerpts from the London *Morning Post* articles, and the *Resto del Garlina* in Bologna soon followed suit. The widely read *Vita Italiana* of Rome devoted considerable space to serious discussion of the "Protocols," and for about two years various provincial newspapers repeatedly published articles dealing with this unsavory subject.

The "Protocols" were also translated into Arabic and were circulated in Egypt, Palestine, Syria and Persia.

In America, where two versions of the Nilus book appeared in translation, such a serious newspaper as the Philadelphia *Public Ledger* published long articles about the "Protocols" as the "Red Bible" of the Bolsheviki, a "bible" which was said to contain a detailed plan for world-revolution, prepared by Russian Jewish Communists more than a decade before. The *Dearborn Independent,* published by Henry Ford, took up the torch which had been kindled by the Russian Black Hundreds and the Prussian

Jew-baiters in an attempt to explain the collapse of the Russian and German autocracies and the rise of Bolshevism. The *Dearborn Independent* articles, for which material was supplied by the American physician and the Russian monarchist, Boris Brasol, who introduced the "Protocols" in this country, were based chiefly on the "Protocols." These articles reached a wide reading public, and were afterwards reprinted in book form. A collection of these articles, entitled "The International Jew," was brought out in a German translation in Leipzig by the Hammer Verlag, under the editorship of the rabid Jew-baiter, Theodore Fritsch. The fact that Henry Ford's name was used in connection with the authorship of the book helped its sale and distribution immensely in Germany.

Towards the end of 1920 and early in 1921 I undertook an investigation in order to establish the origin of the "Protocols." Fortunately I found some of the original volumes in the Library of Congress at Washington, among a vast number of Russian books which had recently been purchased in Russia.

I searched among the Black Hundred publications brought out toward the end of the Russo-Japanese War, and found the Butmi edition of the "Protocols." I also found there a Russian version of a chapter from a German novel entitled "To Sedan" in his series "Biarritz-Rome," by "Sir John Retcliffe," whose real name was Hermann Goedsche, a German novelist with a criminal record.

In my book, "The History of a Lie," published in February, 1921, I showed by documentary evidence the various stages of the forgery which emanated from Prussian and Russian sources. These documents are reproduced in the present volume.

Count A. M. du Chayla, a Frenchman who had lived in Russia for many years, gave interesting and important testimony at the 1934 trial in Berne, Switzerland, regarding the "Protocols" and Sergius Nilus, whom he knew intimately.*

*Count du Chayla revealed the Russian origin of the "Protocols" in 1921, in *Posledniya Novosty*, the Russian newspaper published in Paris,

The first authentic information concerning the mysterious Nilus, the Russian sponsor of the "Protocols," was given by Count du Chayla in 1921. He is the author of several studies on Russian theology and culture. During the war he was commander of a detachment of Don Cossacks and was decorated for heroism. In 1909 M. du Chayla spent nine months at the monastery at Optina Poustina as a close neighbor and intimate friend of Nilus, who frequently spoke to him of the Protocols and showed him the original document and the commentaries which he was preparing for it. M. du Chayla also gathered further information concerning Nilus from people who had known him intimately.

When he was introduced to Nilus the third day after his arrival at Optina Poustina, du Chayla found Nilus to be "a man of about 45, a true Russian type, big and broad, with a gray beard and deep blue eyes." Nilus came from a family of Swiss *émigrés* who had come to Russia in the reign of Peter I, and boasted of being a direct descendant of a special executioner under Ivan the Terrible. A brother of his was a judge in Moscow, who regarded Nilus as a madman. Nilus was well educated, had been graduated from the Law Academy in Moscow, and knew perfectly French, German and English. He had been appointed judge in Trans-Caucasia but his eccentricities and capricious temperament forced him to abandon that post.

M. du Chayla made the sensational disclosure that Nilus was at one time about to become the confessor of the Czar and the Royal family of Russia but was prevented by his enemies and forced to leave in disgrace. In 1918, Nilus lived in Kiev at the convent known as "Protection of the Holy Virgin." In the winter of 1918-1919, he escaped to Germany and lived in Berlin.

---

under the editorship of Professor Paul Miliukoff, the eminent historian, and Minister of Foreign Affairs in the Provisional Government in Russia, after the Tsarist government had collapsed. Count du Chayla's article is reproduced in Exhibit G.

Du Chayla frequently visited Nilus at his villa near the monastery where Nilus was living on the pension that his wife was receiving from the Imperial Court. In the course of a discussion on religion, Nilus read some extracts from the text and from his commentaries, and was greatly incensed at the Frenchman's failure to be impressed with the document and proceeded to show him a manuscript, which he claimed was the original draft of the sessions of the Wise Men of Zion. Du Chayla noticed on the front page a large ink spot. The text was French, and was in several handwritings and in different inks. Nilus explained this by asserting that different people had filled the post of secretary at the secret sessions of the Wise Men of Zion. He did not seem to be certain, however, about this detail, for at another time he told du Chayla that the manuscript was not the original but a copy.

Nilus introduced du Chayla to a certain Mme. K. who was living with them at the villa. This Mme. K., whose name du Chayla did not divulge, had been in intimate relations with Nilus in Paris and, after Nilus had married, came to live with him and his wife. Mme. Nilus was a submissive woman who did not object to this arrangement.

Nilus told du Chayla that this Mme. K. while in Paris had met a certain General Ratchkovsky who had given her the manuscript of the Protocols which he said he had removed from the secret archives of the Freemasons. This Ratchkovsky was head of the branch of the Russian political police which watched Russian political offenders who had escaped to France. Du Chayla once asked Nilus whether he did not think that he was following a false trail in accepting as gospel truth the manuscript of Ratchkovsky, whose unreliability had been so frequently demonstrated. Nilus answered, "Did not the ass of Balaam utter prophecy? Cannot God transform the bones of a dog into sacred miracles? If He can do these things, He can also make the announcement of truth come from the mouth of a liar."

To convince du Chayla further, Nilus showed him a mass of

miscellaneous household utensils, insignia of technical societies, diplomatic emblems, etc., which Nilus kept in a small chest. "On each of these objects," says du Chayla, "his inflamed imagination showed him the mark of the Antichrist in the form of a triangle or a pair of crossed triangles. It was enough for any object to have on it a figure resembling somewhat a triangle for Nilus to see in it the seal of the Wise Men of Zion.

"The first two editions of the Protocols," says du Chayla, "passed almost unnoticed in Russia. In fact, only one newspaper reviewed them. The theological reviews did not even mention these books, and it is doubtful whether they knew of their existence. . . . Most of the authorities of the Russian Church to whom I spoke concerning Nilus and his work regarded him as a crazed fanatic. In 1911, Nilus addressed a letter to the Patriarchs of the Orient, to the Holy Synod, and to the Pope, asking them to call together the 8th Œcumenical Council in order to take measures to protect Christianity against the coming of the Antichrist. At the same time Nilus preached this doctrine of preparedness to the Monks at Optina. The monastic peace was so troubled by Nilus that the authorities asked him never again to appear at the cloister.

"The first indications of public interest in the Protocols became apparent in 1918. A new edition of the Protocols was published by Ismailoff, a Moscow lawyer. The center of anti-Semitic propaganda was then transferred to Rostoff, the seat of the propaganda department for General Denikin's army. From Rostoff the Protocols were sent out in great numbers and distributed among the units of the volunteers and among the Cossack troops at Kouban. They served as fuel to a violent pogrom agitation which brought lurid and pernicious results. A circular against this propaganda was sent to all the chaplains at the front by Archpriest George Schavelsky, head of the military clergy, but the effects of this circular were paralyzed by the attitude of the commanding officers."

M. du Chayla also told of the use that had been made of the Protocols in the pogroms in the Ukraine and under Wrangel in the Crimea. They were constantly being used to incite the troops to pillage and excesses and this constant propaganda eventually contributed to the demoralization and the defeat of these forces.

CHAPTER FIVE

The End of the Protocols

THE forgers of the "Protocols" made alterations in each suc-
ceeding edition, mistranslating the stolen passages, adding or
subtracting, endeavoring to adapt them to changing conditions
in order to prove that the Jews had either predicted or instigated
such events as the Russian revolution, the World War, the overthrow of the Russian and German autocracies, and the rise of
Communism.

Out of the scrap heap of Tsarist autocracy, the Russian and
Prussian anti-Semites exhumed the old weapons for the purpose
of waging war on the Jewish people. Upon the structure of the
old myths, made in Germany and re-made in Russia, they continued to erect new falsehoods in order to intensify chaos, confusion and dissatisfaction in the hope of a restoration of their
old privileges.

Lucien Wolf, the eminent British publicist and author, in his
keen analysis of "The Jewish Peril," the first English version
of the "Protocols," related the following episode which threw
more light on the unscrupulousness of the mercenaries who had
peddled the infamous documents:

"In June, 1919, the present writer, while in Paris, heard of
the circulation of the Protocols as a pogrom pamphlet in Denikin's country, but he attached no importance to it. Later on came
the first intimation of the proposed publication of the Protocols in
Western Europe. It came in very characteristic shape. One day
the members of a certain Jewish delegation in Paris received a
visit from a mysterious Lithuanian who had been connected with

the Russian Secret Police. He professed himself anxious to serve the Jewish community, and said that he was in a position to prevent the publication of an exceedingly dangerous book, which, if it saw the light, would probably involve the whole house of Israel in ruin. Quite naturally, he wished to be paid for this service, but the sum was a mere trifle, a matter of £10,000 (about $50,000). He was asked for a sight of the volume, and he produced it. It was, of course, the Protocols. Needless to say, no business was done. It was possibly only a coincidence that in the following December a German edition was published under the title *Die Geheimnisse der Weisen von Zion,* and two months later the English edition saw the light under the title 'The Jewish Peril: Protocols of the Learned Elders of Zion.' The German and English publication would have been simultaneous but for the fact that difficulty was experienced in finding a reputable London publishing house to take the Protocols seriously."

Israel Zangwill, the brilliant Anglo-Jewish author, in his "Legend of the Conquering Jew," published by The Macmillan Company in 1921, had this to say of the Protocols:

"Two recent scurrilous books, 'Jewry Ueber Alles' and 'The Jewish Peril,' carry in their titles this legend of the conquering Jew. The latter work, a mass of mystical work from the Russian and published by concerted action in various languages after being peddled in Mss. round the Governments of Europe and America by notorious Russian anti-Semites as though it were a precious document, though it had already appeared in print in 1905, professes to reveal 'the secrets of the Sanhedrin'; but the tirades against England for drawing upon the support of the 'Sanhedrin' in her universal intrigues for Empire have been prudently cut out of the English edition, for they would spoil the game. (For cutting out the whole, £10,000 was asked!)

"There is no Sanhedrin now extant, no 'Learned Elders of Zion' exist whose meetings can be recorded in 'Protocols,' and Nilus, seeming to have discovered this by the time his book reached a third and enlarged edition in 1911, substituted for his original melodramatic mendacities the story that his documents—described in the first edition as stolen from French Free-masonry—were simply the secret reports of the Zionist Congress at Basle in 1897. Unfortunately for Nilus, I happened to be at all the sittings of that Congress, which was the first, and which I have described in my 'Dreamers of the Ghetto.' Nothing could be less like the operations of a Jewish Jesuitry than this gathering, which laid the foundations of the Zionist movement and formu-lated its programme as 'the acquisition of a publicly, legally rec-ognized home for the Jewish people in Palestine.' As this was absolutely a new movement in Jewry, initiated in spite of great public opposition by a few more or less impecunious publicists, it seems indeed a strange manifestation on the part of the secret Semitic gang that ran—and runs—all the papers, parliaments and banks of the world, and in whose iconoclastic propaganda Charles Darwin was a prominent puppet! We have to do in fact with the forgery of a pious Russian, passionate for the Church and the Tsar, edited in 1905 by an agency bent on drowning the Revolution of that year in Jewish blood. Such forgeries in-variably appear in troubled periods, they are a stock historical weapon; though rarely has a forger admitted in more Irish fash-ion than the author of 'The Jewish Peril' that he cannot prove the authenticity of his documents, for—he gravely explains—the essence of the criminal plot is secrecy!"

Disregarding all the unmistakable documentary evidence which substantiated the falsity of the "Protocols," the anti-Semites and their dupes continued to spread the forged documents throughout the world, and particularly in the United States, England and Ger-many. They ascribed to world Jewry the rise of Bolshevism in Russia, as part of the "Protocol" conspiracy for world conquest.

In the United States two versions of the Nilus Protocols ap-peared, the Small Maynard and the Beckwith editions. The trans-lators and promoters of the Nilus "Protocols," believing that the book exposing the "Jewish plot" would become a best seller and apparently unable to reach a satisfactory understanding as to the division of their spoils, brought out rival editions. In the Beckwith edition, published anonymously by Dr. Houghton, the crude translation was somewhat doctored and revised. However, the books proved a commercial fiasco, and the "Protocol" promoters in the United States were deeply disappointed in their dreams of amassing fortunes by means of scaring people into believing in the fantastic legend of a "Jewish Peril."

Some of these "Protocol" venders found a new source of income from Henry Ford's *Dearborn Independent*, which was conducting a violent anti-Jewish campaign at that time. The "Protocols" were sold to Henry Ford's editors and were soon used as the basis for most of the onslaughts against the Jewish people. The fact that Henry Ford's name was identified with the rabid anti-Semitic articles on "The International Jew" served to encourage the Jew-baiters abroad, especially in Germany. They imagined that Mr. Ford would place his millions at their disposal for the purpose of waging a world-wide war against the Jews. They welcomed him as their most powerful ally. They translated "The International Jew" into German and for a time did a thriving business through the use of Henry Ford's name.

The American press, with but few exceptions, treated the "Protocols" and the *Dearborn Independent* articles as the ravings of unscrupulous trouble-breeders or unbalanced dupes. The American press condemned the efforts that were made to poison American life and institutions with race hatred and distrust.

The quadrennial convention of the Federal Council of the Churches of Christ in America, in December, 1920, attended by delegates representing thirty denominations and fifty thousand churches, adopted the following resolution:

"Whereas, For some time there have been in circulation in this country publications tending to create race prejudice and arouse animosity against our Jewish fellow-citizens and containing charges so preposterous as to be unworthy of credence, be it resolved that the Federal Council of the Churches of Christ in America, impressed by the need at this period of our national existence for unity and brotherhood, deplores all such cruel and unwarranted attacks upon our Jewish brethren and in a spirit of good will extends to them an expression of confidence in their patriotism and their good citizenship and earnestly admonishes our people to express disapproval of all actions which are conducive to intolerance or tend to the destruction of our national unity through arousing racial division in our body politic."

On January 16, 1921, a protest prepared under the initiative of John Spargo, eminent American author, signed by one hundred and nineteen distinguished Americans, was made public.

The protest read, in part, as follows:

"The undersigned citizens of Gentile birth and Christian faith, view with profound regret and disapproval the appearance in this country of what is apparently an organized campaign of anti-Semitism, conducted in close conformity to and co-operation with similar campaigns in Europe. We regret exceedingly the publication of a number of books, pamphlets and newspaper articles designed to foster distrust and suspicion of our fellow-citizens of Jewish ancestry and faith—distrust and suspicion of their loyalty and their patriotism.

"These publications, to which wide circulation is being given, are thus introducing into our national political life a new and dangerous spirit, one that is wholly at variance with our traditions and ideals and subversive of our system of government. American citizenship and American democracy are thus challenged and menaced. We protest against this organized campaign of prejudice and hatred not only because of its manifest injustice to those against whom it is directed, but also, and especially, because we are convinced that it is wholly incompatible with loyal and intelligent American citizenship. The logical outcome of the success of such a campaign must necessarily be the division of our citizens along racial and religious lines, and, ultimately, the introduction of religious tests and qualifications to determine citizenship. . . .

"We call upon all those who are molders of public opinion—

the clergy and ministers of all Christian churches, publicists, teachers, editors and statesmen—to strike at this un-American and un-Christian agitation."

Here are the names of the signers of that historic protest:

Woodrow Wilson, William Howard Taft, William Cardinal O'Connell, Lyman Abbott, Jane Addams, John C. Agar, Newton D. Baker, Ray Stannard Baker, Charles A. Beard, James M. Beck, Bernard I. Bell, Arthur E. Bestor, Albert J. Beveridge, W. E. B. Du Bois, Mabel T. Boardman, Evangeline Booth, Benjamin Brewster, Chauncey B. Brewster, Jeffrey R. Brackett, Horace J. Bridges, William Jennings Bryan, Henry Bruere, Nicholas Murray Butler, Bainbridge Colby, George W. Coleman, Alice B. Coleman, Paul D. Cravath, George Creel, Samuel McChord Crothers, R. Fulton Cutting, Olive Tilford Dargan, Clarence Darrow, James R. Day, Henry S. Dennison, James Duncan, Robert Erskine Ely, Charles P. Fagnani, W. H. P. Faunce, Dorothy Canfield Fisher, Irving Fisher, John Ford, Raymond B. Fosdick, Robert Frost, James R. Garfield, H. A. Garfield, Lindley M. Garrison, John Palmer Gavit, Herbert Adams Gibbons, Charles Dana Gibson, Franklin H. Giddings, Martin H. Glynn, George Gray, Edward Everett Hale, James Hartness, Patrick J. Hayes, John Grier Hibben, John Haynes Holmes, Jesse H. Holmes, Hamilton Holt, Ernest Martin Hopkins, Frederic C. Howe, Henry C. Ide, Inez Haynes Irwin, Will Irwin, George R. James, David Starr Jordan, William W. Keen, Paul U. Kellogg, William Sergeant Kendall, George Kennan, Henry Churchill King, Darwin P. Kingsley, W. P. Ladd, Ira Landrith, Franklin K. Lane, Robert Lansing, Julia C. Lathrop, Ben B. Lindsey, Charles H. Levermore, Frederick Lynch, Edwin Markham, Mrs. Edwin Markham, David Gregory Mason, Joseph Ernest McAfee, J. F. McElwain, Raymond McFarland, Alexander R. Merriam, E. T. Meredith, James E. Minturn, John Moody, William Fellowes Morgan, Charles Clayton Morrison, Philip Stafford Moxom, Joseph Fort Newton, D. J. O'Connell, Mary Boyle O'Reilly, George Wharton

Pepper, Louis F. Post, Theodore Roosevelt, Charles Edward Russell, Jacob Gould Schurman, Vida D. Scudder, Samuel Seabury, Thomas J. Shahan, Charles M. Sheldon, Edwin E. Slosson, Preston Slosson, John Spargo, Robert E. Speer, Charles Stelzle, Paul Moore Strayer, Marion Talbot, Ida M. Tarbell, Harry F. Ward, Everett P. Wheeler, Gaylord S. White, George W. Wickersham, Charles David Williams, Charles Zueblin.

In July, 1927, Henry Ford finally became convinced of the grave injustice committed by his *Dearborn Independent* and he ended its anti-Jewish campaign of vilification. He made a public statement of retraction and apology to the Jewish people, declaring:

"I confess I am deeply mortified that this journal *(The Dearborn Independent)*, which is intended to be constructive and not destructive, has been made the medium for resurrecting exploded fictions, for giving currency to the so-called Protocols of the Wise Men of Zion, which have been demonstrated, as I learn, to be gross forgeries, and for contending that the Jews have been engaged in a conspiracy to control the capital and the industries of the world, besides laying at their door many offences against decency, public order and good morals. . . .

"I deem it my duty as an honorable man to make amends for the wrong done to the Jews as fellowmen and brothers, by asking their forgiveness for the harm I have unintentionally committed, by retracting so far as lies within my power the offensive charges laid at their door by these publications, and by giving them the unqualified assurance that henceforth they may look to me for friendship and goodwill. . . .

"Finally, let me add that this statement is made of my own initiative and wholly in the interest of right and justice and in accordance with what I regard as my solemn duty as a man and as a citizen."

On November 1, 1927, Henry Ford also addressed a communication to Theodore Fritsch, Leipzig, Germany, the notorious anti-Semitic translator and publisher of "The International Jew." In that letter Mr. Ford wrote as follows:

"I am informed through the public prints that you are still publishing and circulating these pamphlets in various European countries in a number of languages, using my name in connection therewith and asserting that the publication rights have not been withdrawn.

"In order that there may be no misunderstanding as to my wishes in this regard, you are accordingly notified that whatever rights you have or claim to have to publish 'The International Jew' anywhere or in any language whatsoever, are hereby revoked and terminated, and that the publication, sale or other distribution of 'The International Jew' and the use of the name of Henry Ford or of the Dearborn Publishing Company in connection therewith, by you or by any person or corporation claiming under you or acting by your authority as agent, licensee or otherwise, are hereby forbidden."

Nothwithstanding this letter, the German anti-Semitic publishers continued to bring out editions of "The International Jew," still using the name of Henry Ford. The latest German edition, published in 1933, was described on the title page as being the twenty-ninth.

During the past few years, under the influence of Nazism, the "Protocols" have been revived in this country by such anti-Jewish agencies as the Industrial Defense Association, of Boston, and the Silver Shirts under the guidance of the discredited William Dudley Pelley.

Former Congressman Louis T. McFadden, of Pennsylvania, the violent Jew-baiter who describes himself as a Presbyterian and Mason, made reference to the "Protocols" in the House of Representatives in order to have quotations from that spurious and malicious document reproduced in the Congressional Record.

In England the "Protocols" are still being disseminated by the "Britons," an anti-Semitic organization under the influence of Tsarist Russians and Nazi Prussians.

In Germany the "Protocols" have become the cornerstone of the system upon which Hitlerism is founded. The anti-Semitism of the forged "Protocols" has served as the major part of the program of vengeance which brought Adolf Hitler to power. Indeed, the "Protocols of the Wise Men of Zion" have become the Nazi "bible," not merely in the sense that their entire anti-Jewish program is founded upon the falsified documents, but also because the Nazi dictator has apparently appropriated the Machiavellian ideas contained in the "Protocols" and the "Dialogues in Hell," and has been translating them into actuality. While accusing the Jews of scheming for world domination and pointing to the forged "Protocols" as proof of the imaginary Jewish conspiracy, the Nazi Leader has followed the "Protocols" in many respects, building his dictatorship upon the diabolic theories of these documents.

Several extracts from the "Protocols" will show how peculiarly applicable they are to the Nazi Leader and his régime.

From Protocol VII:

"Throughout all Europe, and by means of relations with Europe, in other continents also, we must create ferments, discords and hostility. Therein we gain a double advantage. In the first place we keep in check all countries, for they well know that we have the power whenever we like to create disorders or to restore order. All these countries are accustomed to see in us an indispensable force of coercion. In the second place, by our intrigues we shall tangle up all the threads which we have stretched into the cabinets of all States by means of politics, by economic treaties, or loan obligations."

From Protocol IX:

"Our Super-Government subsists in extra-legal conditions which are described in the accepted terminology by the energetic and forcible word—Dictatorship. I am in a position to tell you with a clear conscience that at the proper time we, the lawgivers, shall execute judgment and sentence, we shall slay and we shall spare, we, as head of all our troops, are mounted on the steed of the leader. We rule by force of will, because in our hands are the fragments of a once powerful party, now vanquished by us. And the weapons in our hands are limitless ambitions, burning greediness, merciless vengeance, hatreds and malice.

"It is from us that the all-engulfing terror proceeds. We have in our service persons of all opinions, of all doctrines, restorating monarchists, demagogues, socialists, communists, and utopian dreamers of every kind. We have harnessed them all to the task: each one of them on his own account is boring away at the last remnants of authority, is striving to overthrow all established form of order. By these acts all States are in torture; they exhort to tranquillity, are ready to sacrifice everything for peace; but we will not give them peace until they openly acknowledge our international Super-Government, and with submissiveness."

From Protocol X:

"The mob cherishes a special affection and respect for the geniuses of political power and accepts all their deeds of violence with the admiring response: 'rascally, well, yes, it is rascally, but it's clever! . . . a trick, if you like, but how craftily played, how magnificently done, what impudent audacity!'" . . .

"(We shall) remove the possibility of individual minds splitting off, for the mob, handled by us, will not let them come to the front nor even give them a hearing; it is accustomed to listen to us only, who pay it for obedience and attention. In this way we shall create a blind, mighty force which will never be in a position to move in any direction without the guidance of our agents set at its head by us as leaders of the mob. The people will submit to this régime because it will know that upon these leaders will depend its earnings, gratifications and the receipt of all kinds of benefits."

From Protocol XI:

"What we want is that from the first moment of its promulgation (the new constitution), while the peoples of the world are still stunned by the accomplished fact of the revolution, still in a condition of terror and uncertainty, they should recognise once for all that we are so strong, so inexpugnable, so superabundantly filled with power, that in no case shall we take any account of them, and so far from paying any attention to their opinions or wishes, we are ready and able to crush with irresistible power all expression or manifestation thereof at every moment and in every place, that we have seized at once everything we wanted and shall in no case divide our power with them. . . ."

From Protocol XII:

"We shall deal with the press in the following way: . . . We shall saddle and bridle it with a tight curb: we shall do the same also with all productions of the printing press, for where would be the sense of getting rid of the attacks of the press if we remain targets for pamphlets and books? . . . No one shall with impunity lay a finger on the aureole of our government infallibility. The pretext for stopping any publication will be the alleged plea that it is agitating the public mind without occasion or justification. . . . Not a single announcement will reach the public without our control. . . . Literature and journalism are two of the most important educative forces, and therefore our government will become proprietor of the majority of the journals. . . . When we are in the period of the new régime transitional to that of our assumption of full sovereignty we must not admit any revelations by the press of any form of public dishonesty; it is necessary that the new régime should be thought to have so perfectly contented everybody that even criminality has disappeared. . . . Cases of manifestation of criminality should remain known only to their victims and to chance witnesses—no more."

These are but a few characteristic illustrations of how the Nazi leader made the "Protocols" his own, while charging the Jews with having originated them. He even borrowed his own favorite title of Leader from the "Protocols."

In 1905 the second edition of Serge Nilus' book appeared, printed on government presses at Tsarskoye Selo, containing a new and elaborated version of the protocols.

The translators of the Nilus protocols published in his 1905 edition, a copy of which is in the British Museum, have deliberately omitted numerous passages from his prologue and epilogue. These passages show clearly the purpose of the volume. Nilus writes: "We may perhaps be reproached, and justly, for the apocryphal character of the document presented. But if it were possible to demonstrate its accuracy by documents or through the testimony of trustworthy witnesses; if it were possible to unveil the faces of those who are at the head of the world conspiracy and who hold its bloody strings in their hands, then the very 'mystery of lawlessness' would be infringed upon, and it must remain intact until its incarnation in the 'son of destruction.' " Then he goes on to say that there is only one force that can save it, and that is the "God-Anointed Tsar of Russia." The omitted portions of the Nilus book show distinctly that it is a work of propaganda for the Russian autocracy. Nilus denounced Leo Tolstoy, the emancipation of women, and all movements leading toward progress.

The editors of the protocols in Europe and America, realizing that these passages would disclose to intelligent people the real motive of the Nilus protocols and thus discredit them, have deliberately omitted them in the translations.

Here are some of the omitted portions of the notorious Nilus book, which are his own utterances and do not purport to constitute a part of the Protocols. They are translated from a photographed copy of the volume in the British Museum:

"We have succeeded in obtaining for our use from a man close to us, now deceased, a manuscript in which are described with unusual precision and clearness the course and progress of the universal fatal mystery aiming to bring the apostate world to an inevitable catastrophe. This manuscript was given to us about four years ago (in 1901) with the assurance that it was an accurate copy—a translation of the original documents stolen by a woman from one of the most powerful and sacred directors of Freemasonry after one of the secret meetings of the 'initiates' in

France, the present nest of the Freemason's sect. This manuscript under the general title 'Protocols of the Wise Men of Zion' I now call to the attention of all who wish to see or hear. These 'Protocols' at a first cursory glance might seem to be what we are accustomed to call truisms; they are more or less commonplaces although expressed with a boldness and a hatred not altogether customary in commonplaces. A proud, deeply-rooted, ancient, for a long time secretly growing,—and what is more frightful than all,—a religious rage boils between the lines, bubbling over and escaping from the overfilled vessel of violence and vengeance, already approaching complete triumph.

"It must be mentioned, by the way, that the title of the manuscript does not fully justify the contents: these are not protocols of a meeting but rather the report of someone in power, divided into parts which are not even always logically connected: the impression remains that this is a fragment of something much more significant, the beginning of which has been lost. The origin of the manuscript, as given by us above, furnishes sufficient explanation of this."

.   .   .   .

"The history of the Rothschilds shows that the whole republican era of France is due to Zion and that not a single one of those elected to office has to this time ever done what he promised to do, if the demands of his electors did not coincide with the plans of the government of Zion.

"What has become of unfortunate France! . . .

" 'Let him who has ears, listen!' "

.   .   .   .

" 'Now the Spirit speaketh expressly, that in the latter times some shall depart from the faith, giving heed to seducing spirits, and doctrines of devils;

" 'Speaking lies in hypocrisy; having their conscience seared with a hot iron;

" 'Forbidding to marry, and commanding to abstain from

meats, which God hath created to be received with thanksgiving of them which believe and know the truth.'

"Is not this Tolstoy and his followers scattered over the whole world?!"

. . . .

"In every age there have been many women 'drowning in sin and led on by various lusts'; the ebb and flow of this sin in woman's heart characterized whole epochs of particular human defection but at no time of the seeming triumph of sin have there been women 'constantly studying'—this sign represents entirely a universal inheritance and is an exclusive characteristic of our epoch.

"Who is ignorant of the so-called 'woman question,' the emancipation of woman, that has already succeeded in breaking up so many families and which threatens an even greater disruption in the future?! . . .

"For the sake of some phantom the bride and mother abandons her true mission. Is not this the greatest and most unfortunate world revolution!"

. . . .

"The Sanhedrin was unseizable and invulnerable. It carried the roots of evil from France into Scotland, where under a different name it entered into a league with United England, with whom, after having let it in behind the curtain of its secret and having declared deadly war to papism, it cooperates even to the present day, helping out England in her exploits over the whole world with its capital and concessions, in which respect the Sanhedrin was never penurious.

"As to the question why England and no other European government was chosen as the point of resistance for the fighting Sanhedrin, the Sanhedrin gives no reply. We are inclined to think that the cause is to be found in the isolated island position of the sufficiently strong government, and perhaps in the kinship between the English and the Jews.

"(As is known, there is a scientific theory which tries to prove that the English are the descendants of the scattered tribes of Israel. The Sanhedrin, which directs the course of contemporary science, is not ashamed to produce whatever theories are advantageous to them. According to certain tenuous evidences in the air it seems that a new theory is being produced according to which the honor of birth relationship with the God-elected Sanhedrin is extended to America and . . . Japan. *Avis à l'Angleterre! . . .)*

"Having covered the whole of Europe with a network of Masonic lies (the symbol of the temple of Solomon is preserved for them also), possessing countless millions, in face of the general fall of the Christian spirit among the European peoples, in whom there was artificially spread and supported the cult of the golden calf; having poisoned the idea of godliness and spirituality in the heart of the peoples by 'scientific' theories, the Sanhedrin— the priest of the golden idol created by it, has gained control of the spiritual life of all Europe, and with its help, with the help of its gold, with the sold consciousness of those standing at the helm of power, and with the help of its faithful ally—England, it has corrupted and perverted all the political foundations of Europe, and through them the well-being and spiritual health of its population. The French revolution, glorified by the Masonized historical science of 'greatness' and the fall of the 'great' Napoleon have shown to the world the significance and strength of the Sanhedrin. But the world did not recognize the new manifestation of Satan: at that time the words of truth of the Evangel and the apostolic foresight had become alien to him."

Sergius Nilus, the "mystic Russian" who first published the "Protocols of the Wise Men of Zion," in his book published in 1905, the only existing copy of which is in the British Museum, gave the following amazing explanation as to the reason why the authenticity of the "Protocols" could not be proved:

"*We must not search for direct evidence:* we are forced to

content ourselves with indirect proofs and of these it seems that the attention of the sad Christian observer is fully satisfied."

All of the literature about the "Protocols" which commenced to appear in various parts of the world in 1920 was based on the "documents" vouched for by the mysterious Sergius Nilus who himself admitted that he might be justly reproached for "the apocryphal character" of his material and that "we must not search for direct evidence."

The Nilus protocols which were published by the Black Hundreds were not taken seriously by the reactionaries or even by the Black Hundreds, who sought every means of discrediting the Jews. In the most stupendous anti-Jewish plot ever devised by the Russian government to justify Jewish massacres—the notorious Beilis case—the protocols published eight years previously were never used by the prosecution even though it resorted to every foul means that could be conjured up of slandering and vilifying the Jewish people. The very persons who were instrumental in spreading the "protocols" in Russia in 1905 seemed to have realized that the false accusations which they contained were too transparent and too clumsy to deceive even the most credulous, and so they were discarded.

But suddenly, after the armistice, a new edition of the Nilus book, dated 1917, made its appearance as suitable to the chaotic conditions that prevailed in Russia, and was reproduced in various countries. This time the anti-Semitic propagandists tried to connect the "Protocols" directly with Theodore Herzl, Asher G. Ginzberg and the Zionist movement. The war, the peace treaty and bolshevism were characterized as the fulfillment of these "Protocols." New editions of the forged "Protocols" have made their appearance in various lands for the purpose of intensifying the agitation against the Jewish people as the cause of the world unrest.

Recently the notorious "Protocols of the Wise Men of Zion" have had their day in courts of justice.

In August, 1934, the libel suit of the Rev. A. Levy, of Port
Elizabeth, South Africa, against Harry Victor Inch, Johannes
von Strauss von Moltke and David Hermanus Olivier, Jr., three
anti-Semitic Grey Shirt leaders, was decided in favor of the plain-
tiff and damages were awarded against the Grey Shirt leaders
with costs.

The suit was instituted in connection with another forged anti-
Jewish document. In the course of the lengthy trial the "Protocols" were frequently referred to. Mr. Beamish, one of the
witnesses for the Grey Shirt leaders, stated that he was a firm
believer in the "Protocols of the Elders of Zion," and that he
could "prove every one of them." He declared that in every
country the aristocracy and the landowners were rapidly dis-
appearing. He said he was satisfied that Lloyd George had introduced his land taxation measures because all the political parties
throughout the world are controlled by Jews.

When he was asked about the Protocols, Beamish stated that
it is merely a part of a plot which has been in existence for a
large number of years, and is now being rapidly brought into
effect. He said he belonged to a "secret organization, finding
out all these things," that he did not go by his own name, for it
would be dangerous to do so. He said that the last Spanish
Revolution "was engineered by the Crypto Jews," the descendants
of Jews who have been kept in "cold storage" for all these years,
ever since the fifteenth century, and who have now come out.

Then he declared that the Revolution led by Cromwell in
England was brought about by the Jews, that the Jews were at
the back of the conquest of England by William the Conqueror,
that the Jameson Raid was "engineered by Alfred Beit," that
the Russo-Japanese War, the Boer War and the late World
War were all results of Jewish intrigues. He said he believed that
the Jews' aim is to destroy the Christian Church and religion
and to Judaize the civilized world. He declared that he "opened
Henry Ford's eyes to the Jewish menace." He described the
Jewish Board of Deputies in England as "the super-Parliament

of Great Britain." Then he boasted that he had "taught Hitler" in 1921.

The decision rendered by Sir Thomas Graham and Justice Gutsche, of the Supreme Court, imposing a fine on the Grey Shirt leaders, contained the following statement concerning the Protocols:

"The Protocols are an impudent forgery, obviously for the purpose of anti-Jewish propaganda."

At a trial in Berne, Switzerland, which has attracted universal attention, a number of distinguished experts have testified how the "Protocols of the Wise Men of Zion" had been plagiarized and forged, and they have named the actual perpetrators of the crime instigated by the Tsarist government for sinister political purposes.

Vladimir Bourtsev, the eminent historian of the Russian Revolution, who unmasked the arch agent-provocateur Azev and who exposed the workings of the Tsarist political police department, testifying as an expert at the Berne trial of the "Protocols," declared that General Globotchov had informed him that it was General Ratchkovsky, head of the Russian political police in Paris, and his agents, who had actually fabricated the "Protocols" in their present form. Mr. Bourtsev also expressed his conviction that the "Protocols" were directly responsible for a series of terrible pogroms in Southern Russia during 1919.

Count A. M. du Chayla, the Frenchman who had lived for many years in Russia and who knew Nilus intimately, appeared as a witness at the Berne trial and testified along the lines of the statement published elsewhere in this volume.

Dr. Henri Sliosberg, the well-known Russian Jewish jurist, who also appeared as an expert at the Berne trial, declared that as far back as 1901 Sergius Witte, then Russian Minister of Finance, had asked him to prepare a memorandum on the so-called "Protocols." He branded the document as a falsification and stated that the "Protocols" were intended not only as a weapon against the Jews but also against the Liberals in general, and especially against Witte himself. He recalled that Witte's financial plans in 1899 had been denounced by the Tsarist reactionaries as "Jewish machinations."

The epilogue to the Nilus "Protocols" contained the following statements:

"According to secret Jewish Zionism, a political plan was devised for the peaceful conquest of the world for Zion, by Solomon and other sages already 929 years before the birth of Christ."

The French translator of the alleged original "Protocols of the Wise Men of Zion," in a note accompanying his translation, also gave a version of "the political plan devised by the Wise Men of Zion," stating:

"The expounded protocols are signed by the Representatives of Zion (do not confound them with the representatives of the Zionist movement). . . . These protocols and the Sketch were taken from the secret depositories of the Main Office of Zion, now located on French territory. . . . The aforesaid political plan was conceived 929 years before the birth of Christ. It was invented by Solomon and the Judean Sages in theory."

Thus the Prussian and Russian fabricators of the "Protocols of the Wise Men of Zion" have endeavored in the Twentieth Century to make the world believe that 929 years before the birth of Christ, King Solomon and the Judean Sages elaborated designs for the Jewish conquest of the world by instigating the World War more than 2800 years later, by bringing about the overthrow of the Romanoff, Hohenzollern and Hapsburg dynasties, and by the establishment of Communism in Soviet Russia. On such absurdities and "malignant lunacy" have the anti-Semitic agitators built their case against the Jewish people.

As I wrote in "The History of a Lie," in periods of turmoil and unrest such venomous fabrications as the "Protocols" may gain credence among the ignorant and may poison their minds. But, like all anti-Semitic myths of old, the new anti-Jewish legends are bound to destroy themselves. The truth will prevail.

Israel has no secret protocols, no hidden designs. Its dream is still of peace, of justice and of human brotherhood. After all the centuries the word that came from Sinai and the message of the prophets of old are still enshrined in its heart. The Holy Scriptures are the only authentic·protocols of the Wise Men of Zion.

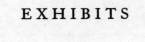

EXHIBITS

EXHIBIT A

DIALOGUES IN HELL*

BETWEEN

MACHIAVELLI AND MONTESQUIEU

Or the Policies of Machiavelli in the Nineteenth Century

By a Contemporary

(Maurice Joly)

༄

"Soon will be seen a frightful calm, during which all will reunite against the infringing power of the laws:
"When Sylla desired to restore liberty to Rome, she was no longer able to harbor it."

(Montesquieu, *Esprit des Lois.*)

BRUSSELS

Press of A. Mertens and Son
22, Rue de l'Escalier

1864

*See Exhibit I for facsimile of original title page.

PREFACE

THIS book has characteristics that can be applied to all governments, but its goal is more exact; it personifies one particular political system which has not varied once in its methods since the fatal and alas! already too distant date of its *enthronement*.

There is no question here of a defamatory lampoon, nor of a pamphlet: opinion in modern nations is too regimented to accept violent truths about contemporary affairs. The supernatural duration of certain successes is, moreover, making for the corruption of honesty itself; but the public conscience is still alive and providence will one fine day interfere in the game being played against it.

One judges better certain facts and certain principles when one sees them outside of the framework in which they usually exist in our sight; the change in point of view sometimes terrifies the eyes!

Here, all is presented in the form of fiction: it would be superfluous to give away the key in anticipation. If this book has a message, if it bears a lesson, the reader must discover it for himself and not be informed. This reading, moreover, will lack certain lively distractions; nevertheless, one must proceed slowly, as is necessary with writings that are not frivolous.

No one will ask whose hand has written these words: a work such as this is in a way impersonal. It responds to the call of the conscience; the whole world conceived it, it is done. The author stands back, for he is only the editor of a thought which is in the general mind, he is but the more or less obscure tool of the coalition for good.

Geneva, October 15, 1864.

FIRST DIALOGUE

MACHIAVELLI. On the bank of this deserted coast, they told me, I would encounter the shade of the great Montesquieu. Is it he who stands before me?

MONTESQUIEU. The name "great" belongs to no one here, O Machiavelli. But I am the one you seek.

MACHIAVELLI. Of all the illustrious personages whose shades people the resting place of darkness, there is none I would rather meet than Montesquieu. Carried into this unknown territory by the migration of souls, I give thanks to the chance that at last places me in the presence of the author of the *Esprit des Lois*.

MONTESQUIEU. The former secretary of State of the Florentine Republic has not yet forgotten his courtly language. But what can those who have traversed these dark shores exchange, save anguish and regrets?

MACHIAVELLI. Is it the philosopher, or is it the statesman who speaks thus? What does death matter to those who have lived by thought, since thought never dies? For myself, I know of no condition more tolerable than that in which we shall remain until the day of last judgment. To be free of the cares and worries of material life, to live in the domain of pure reason, to be able to converse with the great men who have filled the universe with the sound of their names; to follow from afar the revolutions among the states, the fall and the transformation of empires, to meditate on their new constitutions, on the changes applied to the customs and ideas of the peoples of Europe, on the progress of their civilization, in politics, in art, in industry, as well as in the sphere of philosophical ideas, what a theatre for the mind! What subjects for astonishment! How many new points

79

of view! How many unexpected revelations! How many marvels, if we are to believe the shades that come among us. Death for us is like a profound retreat in which we manage to gather the lessons of history and the rights of humanity! Oblivion itself could not break all the bonds which attach us to the earth, for posterity still speaks of those who, like you, have imprinted the great movements upon the human soul. Your political principles reign at the present time over almost half Europe; and if someone could be freed of fear in effecting the dark passage which leads from hell to heaven, who better than he who bears with him such pure titles to glory before the eternal justice?

MONTESQUIEU. You do not speak for yourself, Machiavelli: you show too much modesty for one who leaves behind him the tremendous renown of the author of *The Prince*.

MACHIAVELLI. I believe I understand the irony which is hidden beneath your words. The great French publicist would judge then like the mob who only knows my name and a blind prejudice? That book gave me a fatal renown, I know: it made me responsible for all tyrannies; it drew down upon me the maledictions of those peoples who personified in me their hatred for despotism; it poisoned my last days, and the reprobation of posterity seems to have followed me here. But what have I done? For fifteen years I served my fatherland, a republic; I conspired for her independence and I defended her unceasingly against Louis XII, against the Spaniards, against Julius II, against Borgia himself, who, but for me, would have strangled her. I protected her against the bloody intrigues which were woven in all directions around her, combating by diplomacy as another would have combated by the sword; treating, negotiating, weaving or snapping threads according to the interests of the republic, which was then crushed between the great powers and tossed by war like a small boat. And it was not an oppressive or autocratic government which we upheld in Florence; they were popular institutions. Was I one of those whom you see changing with a change in fortune? The executioners of the Medicis knew where

to find me after the fall of Soderini. Fostered by liberty, I succumbed with her; I lived as one proscribed, without the regard
of a single prince deigning to be turned on me. I died poor and
forgotten. That was my life, and those were the crimes which
have cost me the ingratitude of my fatherland, the hate of
posterity. Providence will perhaps be more just to me.

MONTESQUIEU. I knew all that, Machiavelli, and it is for that
reason that I have never been able to understand how the Florentine patriot, how the servant of a republic, had made himself the
founder of this sombre school that has made all the crowned heads
your disciples, but which is qualified to justify the most heinous
crimes of tyrants.

MACHIAVELLI. And what if I told you that this book was but
the fantasy of a diplomat; that it was not written to be printed;
that it received a fame that its author did not wish for it; that
it was conceived under the influence of ideas which were at that
time common to all the Italian principalities avid for territory
at the expense of others, and directed by cunning policies in
which the most perfidious were reputed to be the most able. . . .

MONTESQUIEU. Is that really your thought? Since you speak to
me with this frankness, I can admit to you that it was mine also,
and that I shared in that respect the opinion of many others who
knew your life and had carefully read your books. Yes, yes,
Machiavelli, and this avowal honors you, you did not then say
what you thought or you only said it under the influence of personal sentiments which muddied for a moment your powers for
clear reasoning.

MACHIAVELLI. That is what deceives you, Montesquieu, as well
as those who thought as you do. My single crime was to say the
truth to the people as to the kings; not the moral truth, but the
political truth; not truth such as it should have been, but such as
it is, such as it will always be. It is not I who am the founder
of the doctrine the paternity of which is attributed to me; it is
the human heart. *Machiavellism preceded Machiavelli.*

Moses, Sesostris, Solomon, Lysander, Philip and Alexander of

Macedon, Agathocles, Romulus, Tarquin, Julius Cæsar, Augustus and even Nero, Charlemagne, Theodoric, Clovis, Hugh Capet, Louis XI, Gonzalo of Cordova, Cæsar Borgia, those were the ancestors of my doctrines. I speak without mentioning, of course, those who came after me, and better ones, the list of whom would be long, and to whom *The Prince* taught nothing but what they already knew, by the practice of power. Who in your time rendered me more brilliant homage than Frederic II? He refuted me, his pen in his hand, in the interest of his popularity, and in politics he rigorously applied my doctrines.

By what inexplicable whim of the human soul was what I wrote in that work made sinful? As much reproach the savant for seeking the physical causes which bring about the fall of bodies that wound us in descending, the doctor for describing maladies, the chemist for making a history of poisons, the moralist for painting the vices, the historian for describing history.

MONTESQUIEU. Oh! Machiavelli, that Socrates were here to contest the sophistries that are hidden in your words! No matter how awkward in argument nature has made me, it is scarcely difficult for me to answer you: you compare to poison and sickness the evils engendered by the spirit of domination, of cunning and of violence; and these are the maladies that your writings teach the means to communicate to the states, these are the poisons that you instruct how to distil. When the savant, the doctor, the moralist, seek evil, it is not to teach how to propagate it; it is to heal it. Now, that is what your book does not do; but it matters little, and I am not less disarmed because of it. From the moment you do not erect despotism in principle, from the moment you yourself consider it an evil, it seems to me that by that you condemn it, and on this point at least we can be in accord.

MACHIAVELLI. That we are not, Montesquieu, for you have not understood my whole thought; I threw you off by a comparison which was too easy to refute. The irony of Socrates himself would disturb me, for only a sophist would use more ably than others, that false instrument, *logomachy*. That is not your school

and it is not mine: let us leave alone words and comparisons and
hold ourselves to ideas. Here is how I formulate my system, and
I doubt whether you will shake it, for it is only composed of deductions from the moral and political facts of an eternal truth:
The evil instinct in man is more powerful than the good. Man
leans more toward the evil than the good; fear and power have
more control over him than reason. I do not stop to demonstrate
such truths; there was among you only the hare-brained coterie
of Baron d'Holbach, of which J. J. Rousseau was the grand
priest and Diderot the apostle, who could have contradicted
them. All men seek power, and there is none who would not be
an oppressor if he could; all, or nearly all, are ready to sacrifice
the rights of others to their own interests.

What restrains these ravenous animals that we call men? In the
beginnings of society, it is brute force, without control; later, it is
law, that is, force again, ruled by certain forms. You have consulted all the sources of history; everywhere force appears before
justice.

Political liberty is only a relative idea; the necessity to live is
what dominates States as well as individuals.

In certain latitudes of Europe, there are people incapable of
moderation in the exercise of liberty. If liberty prolongs itself, it
is transformed to license; civil or social war arrives, and the State
is lost, either by division or dismemberment because of its own
convulsions, or by its divisions rendering it the prey of other lands.
In such conditions, the people prefer despotism to anarchy; are
they wrong?

States, once constituted, have two kinds of enemies; the
enemies within and the enemies without. What arms shall they
employ in war against the foreigners? Will the two enemy generals communicate to one another their campaign plans in order
that each shall be able to defend himself? Will they forbid themselves night attacks, snares, ambuscades, battles in which the
number of troops are unequal? Without doubt, they will not.
And such fighters would make one laugh. And these snares, these

artifices, all this strategy indispensable to warfare, you don't want them to be employed against the enemies within, against the disturbers of peace? No doubt, they will be used with less rigor; but, fundamentally, the rules will be the same. Is it possible to conduct by pure reason violent masses which are moved only by sentiment, passion and prejudice?

No matter whether the direction of affairs is placed in the hands of an autocrat, of an oligarchy or of the people itself, no war, no negotiation, no internal reform, could succeed without the help of these combinations which you seem to reprove, but which you would have been obliged to employ yourself if the king of France had given you charge of the smallest affair of state.

What a puerile reproach is that which attacked *The Prince!* Has politics anything to do with morals? Have you ever seen a single state conduct its affairs according to the principles that govern private morals? Then every war would be a sin, even when it would have just cause; every conquest having no other motive than glory, would be a heinous crime; every treaty in which one power would tip the balance to its side, would be an unworthy deception; every usurpation of sovereign power would be an act meriting death. Nothing would be legitimate but what is based on justice! but I told you just now, and I maintain even in the face of modern history: all sovereign powers have had force for an origin, or, what is the same thing, the negation of justice. Does that mean that I should outlaw it? No; but I regard it as an extremely limited application, as much in the relations of nations among themselves as in the relations of the governors with the governed.

This word "justice" itself, by the way, do you not see that it is infinitely vague? Where does it begin, where does it end? When will justice exist, when will it not exist? I take examples. Here is a State: bad organization of public powers, turbulence of democracy, impotence of laws to control discontented, disorder which reigns everywhere, will all precipitate it into ruin. A strong man thrusts himself from the ranks of the aristocracy or from the heart of the people; he breaks through all constituted power; he puts his hand on the laws, he alters all the institutions, and he gives twenty years of peace to his country. Did he have the right to do what he has done?

Pisistratus captures the citadel by a sudden attack and lays the ground for the age of Pericles. Brutus violates the monarchical constitution of Rome, expels the Tarquins, and with a stab founds a republic whose grandeur is the most imposing spectacle that has ever been presented to the universe. But the struggle between the patricians and the plebes, which, as long as it was carried on, made for the vitality of the republic, brought dissolution with it, and everything was about to perish. Cæsar and Augustus appear; they too are violators; but the Roman empire which succeeded the republic, thanks to them, lasts as long as did the republic, and failed only after covering the whole world with its debris. Well, was justice with these audacious men? No, according to you. And yet posterity has covered them with glory; in reality, they served and saved their country; they prolonged its existence through the centuries. You can easily see that among States the principle of justice is dominated by the principle of interest, and the thing that is made clear from these considerations is that *good can come from evil, that one arrives at good through evil,* as one heals through poison, as one saves life by cutting it with iron. I am less preoccupied by what is good and moral than by what is useful and necessary; I have taken societies as they are, and I have laid down rules in consequence.

Speaking abstractly, are violence and cunning an evil? Yes; but it is necessary to use them in governing men, so long as men are not angels.

Everything is good or evil, according to the use one makes of it and the fruit one harvests from it; the end justifies the means: and now, if you ask me why I, a republican, give preference everywhere to absolutist government, I will tell you that, as a witness in my homeland of the fickleness and the cowardice of the populace, of its innate taste for slavery, of its incapacity to conceive and to respect the conditions of free life; it is to my eyes a blind force which dissolves itself sooner or later, if it is not in the hands of a single man; I answer that the people, left to itself, would only be able to destroy itself; that it would never be able to administer, nor to judge, nor to make war. I will tell you that Greece never shone except in the eclipses of liberty; that without the despotism of the Roman aristocracy, and that, later, without the despotism of the emperors, the brilliant civilization of Europe would never have developed.

Shall I seek examples among modern States? They are so striking and so numerous that I take the nearest ones.

Under what institutions and under what men did the Italian republics shine? With what sovereigns did Spain, France and Germany constitute their power? Under Leo X, Julius II, Philip II, Barbarossa, Louis XIV, Napoleon, all men with heavy hands, placed more often on their swords than on the charters of their countries.

But I am surprised that I must talk so long to convince the illustrious writer who listens to me. Are not a part of these ideas, if I am not mistaken, in the *Esprit des Lois?* Has this discourse wounded the grave and calm man who meditated without passion on political problems? The *encyclopedists* were not Catos; the author of the *Persian Letters* was not a saint, nor even a fervent believer. Our school, which men call immoral, was perhaps more closely attached to the real God than the philosophers of the eighteenth century.

MONTESQUIEU. Your last words find me without anger, Machiavelli, and I have listened to you attentively. Will you listen to me, and will you let me speak to you with the same liberty?

MACHIAVELLI. I will be silent, and listen respectfully to the man who is called the *legislator of nations.*

SECOND DIALOGUE

MONTESQUIEU. Your doctrines are not new to me, Machiavelli; and if I find some difficulty in refuting them, it is, whether wrong or right, rather because they have no philosophical basis than because they disturb my thoughts. I readily understand that you are above all a man of politics, and that facts impress you more than ideas. But you will admit nevertheless that when it is a question of government, one must end up at certain principles. You give no place in your political system to morals, to religion, or to justice; you have in your mouth but two words: *force and cunning*. If your system reduces itself to the declaration that force plays a great rôle in human affairs, that cleverness is a necessary qualification for a statesman, you understand well that this is a truth that needs not be proved; but, if you elevate violence to a principle, cunning to a maxim of government, if you do not take into consideration in your calculations any of the laws of humanity, the code of tyranny is naught but the code of the brute, for animals, too, are adroit and strong, and, indeed, there is no justice among them but that of brute force. But I do not believe that even your fatalism will go so far, for you admit the existence of good and evil.

Your principle is that *good can come from evil*, and that it is permissible to do evil when it will result in good. Thus, you do not say: It is good in itself to go back on one's word; it is good to use corruption, violence and murder. But you do say: One can deceive when it is useful to do so, kill when that is necessary, take the property of others when that is advantageous. I hasten to add that, in your system, these maxims are applied only to principles, and when it is a question of their interests or of those of the State. Consequently, the prince has a right to violate his oaths; he can shed streams of blood to usurp power and to maintain himself; he can pillage those whom he proscribes, upset all the laws, make new ones, and violate these, too; he can squander

his finances, corrupt, compromise, punish and strike unceasingly.
MACHIAVELLI. But was it not you who said that in autocratic
states fear was necessary, virtue useless, honor dangerous; that
blind obedience was necessary, and that the prince would be lost
if for one instant he failed to lift his arm? *(Esprit des Lois,* pp.
24 and 25, Chap. IX, Book III.)
MONTESQUIEU. Yes, I said that; but when I discovered, as you
did, the frightful conditions upon which tyrannical power maintains itself, it was to disgrace it and not to build altars to it; it was
to inspire horror in my fatherland which never, luckily for her,
bowed her head beneath such a yoke. How is it you do not see
that force is only an accident in the progress of regular society, and
that the most arbitrary powers are obliged to seek their sanction
in considerations foreign to the theories of force? It is not only
in the name of interest, it is in the name of duty that all oppressors
act. They violate it, but they invoke it; the docrine of interest
is thus just as impotent by itself as are the means which it employs.
MACHIAVELLI. I interrupt you here; you take interest into account, that is enough to justify all the necessary policies which
are not in accord with justice.
MONTESQUIEU. It is a reason of state that you invoke. Notice,
then, that I cannot give as a basis of society just the thing that
destroys it. In the name of selfishness, princes and peoples, like
citizens, can only commit crimes. The selfishness of the State,
you say! But how am I to know if it is really profitable to commit
such-and-such an iniquity? Do we not know that the interests
of the state are more often the interests of the prince in particular,
or those of the corrupt favorites around him? I do not expose
myself to such consequences when I give justice as a basis for
the existence of society, because the idea of justice traces limits
which state interests cannot exceed.

And if you ask me what is the foundation of justice, I will tell
you that it is morality whose precepts have in them nothing doubtful or obscure, because they are written into all religions, and

they are imprinted in luminous characters on the conscience of man. It is this pure source from which should spring all laws, civil, political, economic, international.

Ex eodem jure, sive ex eodem fronte, sive ex eodem principio.

But here is where your inconsistency is conspicuous; you are Catholic, you are Christian; we worship the same God, you admit His commandments, you admit the existence of morality, you admit justice in the relations among human beings, and you throw to the ground all these rules when the question of the State or the prince arises. In a word, *politics, according to you, has nothing to do with morality.* You permit the monarch to do what you forbid the subject. According to whether the same actions are done by the weak or by the strong, you glorify them or you blame them; they are either crimes or virtues, according to the rank of the man who accomplishes them. You praise the prince for having done them, *and you send the subject to the galleys.* You do not dream that with such maxims, no society can last; you believe that the subject will keep his promises when he sees his sovereign break his; that he will respect the law when he knows that the man who handed it down to him has violated it and continually violates it; you believe he will hesitate to follow the road to violence, corruption and fraud when he sees those who are supposed to lead him following it at all times? Learn the truth; know that each usurpation of the prince in public affairs authorizes an equal infraction on the part of the subject; that every political perfidy engenders a social perfidy; that every violence on high legitimizes a violence lower down. That much for what concerns the citizens among themselves.

As for what concerns their relations with the governing powers, I need not tell you that it means civil war introduced in a state of ferment into the breast of society. The silence of the people is but the truce of the vanquished for whom complaint is a crime. Wait for him to awaken; you have invented the theory of force; rest assured that he has remembered it. At the first opportunity,

he will break his chains; he will break them perhaps under the
most futile pretext, and he will retake by force what force had
taken from him.

The maxim of despotism is the *perinde ac cadaver* of the
Jesuits; to kill or to be killed: that is its law: it is brutality today,
civil war tomorrow. It is thus, at least, that things come about
in European climes; in the Orient, the peoples sleep in peace amid
the degradation of servitude.

Princes cannot, therefore, permit themselves what private
morality does not permit; that is my conclusion; it is positive.
You thought you could embarrass me by giving examples of many
great men who, by bold acts accomplished in violation of the
laws, had given peace and sometimes glory to their country; and
from them you took your great argument: *good comes from
evil.* I am little moved; it has not been proven to me that these
daring men have done more good than evil; it is in no way established for me that their societies would not have been saved and
upheld without them. The methods of salvation which they bring
do not compensate for the germs of dissolution which they introduce into the States. Several years of anarchy are often less fatal
for a kingdom than many years of quiet despotism.

You admire the great men; I admire only the great institutions.
I believe that, to be happy, people have less need of men of genius
than of men of integrity; but I grant you, if you wish, that several
of the violent enterprises for which you are the apologist have
been capable of being turned to the advantage of certain States.
These acts could justify themselves in the ancient nations where
slavery and the dogma of fatality reigned. One finds them again
in the Middle Ages and even in modern times; but in proportion
as the customs are modified, as light is propagated among the
divers peoples of Europe, in proportion, especially, as the principles
of political science have become better known, justice has found
itself substituted for force in principle as well as in fact. No doubt,
the tempests of liberty will always exist, and a good number of
crimes will yet be committed in her name: but political fatalism

no longer exists. If you were able to say, in your times, that despotism was a necessary evil, you could not say it today, for, in the actual state of customs and political institutions among the principal peoples of Europe, despotism has become impossible.

MACHIAVELLI. Impossible . . . ? If you can manage to prove that to me, I agree to make a step in the direction of your ideas.

MONTESQUIEU. I will prove it to you very easily, if you still wish to listen.

MACHIAVELLI. Very willingly, but take care; I believe you are attempting a great deal.

THIRD DIALOGUE

MONTESQUIEU. A thick mass of shadows is coming toward this shore; the region we are in now will soon be invaded. Come to this side; otherwise we will soon be separated.

MACHIAVELLI. I did not find in your words just now the precision that characterized your language at the beginning of our conversation. I find that you have exaggerated the consequences of the principles which are comprised in the *Esprit des Lois*.

MONTESQUIEU. I expressly avoided, in that work, the making of long theories. If you knew it otherwise than by what has been reported to you, you would see that the particular developments that you give here spring without effort from the principles that I have laid down. Besides, I find no difficulty in admitting that the knowledge that I have acquired lately has modified or completed several of my ideas.

MACHIAVELLI. Do you really expect to maintain that despotism is incompatible with the political conditions of the peoples of Europe?

MONTESQUIEU. I have not said all the peoples; but I will cite, if you wish, those among whom the development of political science has brought great results.

MACHIAVELLI. What are those nations?

MONTESQUIEU. England, France, Belgium, a part of Italy, Prussia, Switzerland, the German Confederation, Holland, even Austria; that is, as you see, almost all that part of Europe over which once spread the Roman world.

MACHIAVELLI. I know a little about what has happened in Europe from 1527 to these times, and I assure you that I am very curious to hear you justify your position.

MONTESQUIEU. Well, listen to me, and I will succeed in convincing you, perhaps. It is not men but institutions that assure the reign of liberty and of good customs in the nations. On the perfection or the imperfection of the institutions depend all the benefits, as well necessarily as all the evils which could result for men in their union in a community; and, when I demand the best institutions, you understand that, according to the beautiful saying of Solon, I mean *the most perfect institutions that the people can support.* That is to say that I do not conceive of impossible conditions of existence for them, and that by that I separate myself from those deplorable reformers who pretend to construct governments on pure, rational hypotheses without taking into consideration climate, habits, customs and even prejudices.

At the beginning of a nation's history, institutions are what they can be. Antiquity has shown us marvelous civilizations, states in which the conditions of the free government were admirably understood. The peoples of the Christian era have had more difficulty in putting their constitutions in harmony with the movement of political life; but they have profited from the lessons of antiquity, and with civilizations infinitely more complicated, they have nevertheless arrived at more perfect results.

One of the primary causes of anarchy, as of despotism, has been the theoretical and practical ignorance in which the nations of Europe have been for so long of the principles which govern the organization of power. How, when the principle of sovereignty rested solely on the person of the prince, could the rights of the nation be affirmed? How, when the one charged with executing the laws was at the same time the legislator, could his power not be tyrannical? How could the citizens be guaranteed against arbitrary rule when the legislative and the executive power were already combined, and the judicial power also about to be united to it? (*Esprit des Lois*, p. 129, Book XI, Chap. VI.)

I know well that certain liberties, that certain public rights which are introduced sooner or later into the least advanced political customs, do not but permit the bringing of obstacles to the unlimited exercise of absolute royalty; that, on the other side, the fear of angering the people, the spirit of moderation among certain kings, have made them use with moderation the excessive powers with which they are invested; but it is not less true that such precarious guarantees were at the mercy of the monarch who possessed in principle the goods, the rights and the person of his subjects. The division of powers has realized in Europe the problem of free societies, and if something can sweeten for me the anxiety of the hours which precede the last judgment, it is the thought that my passage on earth was not foreign to this great emancipation.

You were born, Machiavelli, on the borders of the Middle Ages, and you saw, with the renaissance of art, the first dawning of modern times; but the society in the center of which you lived was, permit me to declare it, still imprinted with the manners of barbarity; Europe was a tournament. The ideas of war, domination and conquest filled the heads of the statesmen and the princes. Force was everything then, justice very little, I admit; kingdoms were as prey for the conquerors; within the states, the sovereigns fought with the great vassals; the great vassals wiped out the cities. Amid the feudal anarchy which placed all Europe in arms, the people, crushed to the ground, were in the habit of considering the great men and the princes as fatal divinities, to whom the human race had been delivered. You came into those tumultuous times, times full of grandeur, too. You saw intrepid captains, men of iron, audacious geniuses; and this world, filled with sombre beauties in its disorder, appeared to you as it would appear to an artist whose imagination is more struck than his moral sense; it is that which, to my eyes, explains *The Prince,* and you were not so far from the truth which you are willing to admit, when, a moment ago, by an Italian feint, it pleased you, in order to sound me, to attribute it to the caprice of a diplomat. But, since your time, the world has progressed; the peoples look upon themselves today as the arbiters of their destinies; they have, in fact as well as in law, destroyed privilege, destroyed aristocracy; they have established a principle which may be very new to you, a descendant of Marquis Hugo; they have established the principle of equality; they see in those who govern them only mandatories; they have realized the principle of equality by civil laws that nothing could take away from them. They hold to these laws as to their own blood, because they have in fact cost enough in the blood of their ancestors.

I spoke to you of wars just now: they rage always, I know; but, the first progress is that today they no longer give the conquerors the property of the vanquished states. A law that you hardly knew, international law, today guides the relations between the nations, just as civil law guides the relations of the subjects of every country.

After having assured their private rights by civil laws, their public rights by *treaties,* the peoples wanted to put themselves in order with their princes, and they assured their political rights by *constitutions.* Long in the hands of arbitrary rule by the confusion of powers, which permitted the princes *to make tyrannical laws and to exercise them tyrannically,* they separated the three powers, legislative, executive and judicial, by constitutional lines which cannot be crossed without an alarm being given to the political body.

By this single reform, which is an immense point, interior public justice was created, and the superior principles which constitute it are found to be redeemed. The person of the prince ceases to be confounded with that of the state; the sovereignty appears to have in part its source in the very heart of the nation, which makes for the distribution of powers between the prince and the

political bodies, independent of one another. I do not wish to the-
orize before the illustrious statesman who listens to me, upon the
régime which is called in England and France the *constitutional
régime;* it has today passed into the customs of the principal states
of Europe, not only because it is the expression of the highest
political science but mostly because it is the only practical method
of government in the presence of the ideas of modern civilization.

In all times, under the rule of liberty as under that of tyranny,
one cannot but govern by *laws*. It is, therefore, on *the manner
in which the laws are made* that are founded all the guarantees of
the citizens. If it is the prince who is the sole legislator, he will
only make tyrannical laws, and it would be fortunate if he did
not overthrow the state constitution in a few years; but, in any
case, it is full absolutism; if it is a senate, an oligarchy has been
constituted, a régime odious to the people, because it gives them
as many tyrants as masters; if it is the people, one runs to anarchy,
which is another way to end up in despotism; if it is an assembly
elected by the people, the first part of the problem is already resolved; for therein is the very basis of representative government,
today in power in the whole southern part of Europe.

But an assembly of representatives of the people which would
possess in itself the whole legislative sovereignty would not lose
time in abusing its power and in making the state run the greatest
perils. The régime definitely established is a happy compromise
between aristocracy, democracy and the monarchical establishment, having something of the nature of the three forms of
government at once, by means of a balance of powers which seem
to be the masterpiece of the human intellect. The person of the
sovereign remains sacred, inviolate; but, while conserving a mass
of capital privileges which, for the good of the state, must remain
in his power, his essential rôle is not more than that of *procurator
of the execution of the laws*. No longer having in his hand the
abundance of power, his responsibility lessens and passes to the
ministers whom he associates with his government. The law,
which he has either the exclusive power to propose or, together

with another state body, is prepared by a council composed of men experienced in government affairs, submitted to a high chamber, hereditary or elected for life, which examines whether these dispositions are not contrary to the constitution, voted by a legislative body emanating from national suffrage, applied by an independent magistracy. If the law is defective, it is rejected or amended by the legislative body; the upper chamber opposes its adoption if it is contrary to the principles upon which the constitution reposes.

The triumph of this system so profoundly conceived, and the mechanism of which, you understand, can be put together in a thousand ways, according to the temperament of the people to whom it is applied, has been to conciliate order with liberty, stability with movement, to make the entire citizenry participate in political life and to suppress the agitations in the public square. It is the country governing itself, by the alternative displacement of majorities, which influences in the chambers the naming of the directing ministers.

The relations between the prince and the subjects rest, as you see, on a vast system of guarantees, the unshakable basis of which is civil order. No one can be reached, body or goods, by an act of the administrative authority; individual liberty is under the protection of the magistrates; in criminal trials, the accused are judged by their peers; above all the jurisdictions, there is a supreme jurisdiction charged with revoking the decrees which are handed down in violation of the laws. The citizens themselves are armed, for the defense of their rights, by the institution of bourgeois militia which cooperates with the police in the cities; the humblest individual can, by means of petition, bring his complaint to the feet of the assembled sovereigns which represent the nation. The townships are administered by public officials named at the election. Each year, great provincial assemblies, also elected by suffrage, unite to express the needs and the wishes of the populations which surround them.

Such is the faint image, O Machiavelli, of some of the institutions which flourish today in modern countries, and especially in my beautiful fatherland; but as publicity is the essence of free nations, all these institutions could not live long if they did not function in broad daylight. A power still unknown in your century, and which was but born in my times, has come to give them the last breath of life. It is the *press,* long forbidden, still discredited by ignorance, but to which could be applied the beautiful words uttered by Adam Smith in speaking of credit: *It is a public voice.* It is by this voice, in fact, that is manifested the whole progress of ideas among modern nations. The press exercises the functions of the police on the state; it expresses needs, brings forth complaints, denounces abuses, arbitrary acts; it forces morality on all guardians of power; to bring this about, it is but necessary to draw public attention to them.

In societies ruled thus, O Machiavelli, what argument could you make for the ambition of princes and the enterprises of tyranny? I do not forget by what sorrowful convulsions this progress triumphed. In France, liberty, drowned in blood during the revolutionary period, only revived during the period of the restoration. There, new disturbances prepared themselves again; but already all the principles, all the institutions of which I have spoken, had passed into the tradition of France and of the people who gravitate about the sphere of her civilization. I have finished, Machiavelli. States, like sovereigns, are governed today only by the rules of justice. The modern minister who is inspired by your teachings would not stay in power one year; the monarch who put into practice the maxims of *The Prince* would rouse against him the reprobation of his subjects; he would be exiled from Europe.

MACHIAVELLI. You think so?

MONTESQUIEU. Will you pardon my frankness?

MACHIAVELLI. Why not?

MONTESQUIEU. Am I to believe that your ideas have been modified a little?

MACHIAVELLI. I propose to demolish, bit by bit, all the beautiful things you have just said, and to prove to you that it is my doctrines alone that hold good even today, in spite of the new ideas, in spite of the new customs, in spite of your pretended principles of public rights, in spite of all the institutions of which you have just spoken; but permit me, first, to ask you one question: How much do you know of contemporary history?

MONTESQUIEU. The facts that I have learned about the various states of Europe go up to the last days of the year 1847. The hazards of my wandering travels through infinite space and the confused multitude of souls which fill it, have not led me to encounter anyone who would have been able to inform me beyond the period I have just mentioned. Since I have descended into the resting place of the shades, I have passed about a half-century among the peoples of the ancient world, and it is only since the last quarter of a century that I have met the modern legions; besides, it must be said that most have arrived from the most distant corners of the universe. I do not even know exactly what year it is on earth.

MACHIAVELLI. Here, the last are the first, O Montesquieu! The statesman of the Middle Ages, the politician of barbarian times, finds that he knows more about the history of modern times than the philosopher of the eighteenth century. Human beings are in the year of our lord 1864.

MONTESQUIEU. Be kind enough, Machiavelli, to tell me now what has gone on in Europe since the year 1847.

MACHIAVELLI. Not, if you permit, before I have given myself the pleasure of throwing confusion into the heart of your theories.

MONTESQUIEU. As you please; but believe me, I do not feel any fear in that direction. Centuries are needed to change the principles and the form of governments under which people are in the habit of living. No new political teaching could have resulted in the fifteen years which have just passed; and, in any case, if that did happen, it would not be the doctrines of Machiavelli which could ever triumph.

MACHIAVELLI. You think not; then listen to me in my turn.

FOURTH DIALOGUE

MACHIAVELLI. In listening to your theories on the division of powers and on the benefits that the peoples of Europe owe it, I could not help admiring, Montesquieu, to what extent the illusion of the system can take hold of the greatest intellects.

Seduced by the institutions of England, you thought to be able to make of the constitutional régime the universal panacea for all states; but you have counted without the irresistible movement which today tears the nations from their old traditions. Two centuries will not pass before this form of government, which you admire, will be no more in Europe than a historic memory, something superannuated and decayed like Aristotle's rule of three unities.

First permit me to examine in itself your political mechanism: you balance the three powers, and you confine each one to its department; this one will make laws, this other will apply them, and this third will execute them: the prince will reign, the ministers will govern. What a marvelous thing is this constitutional seesaw! You have foreseen all, regulated all, save progress: the triumph of such a system would not be action; it would be immobility if the mechanism functioned with precision; but, in reality, things do not happen in this way. On the first occasion, movement will be produced by the rupture of one of the springs which you have so carefully forged. Do you believe that the powers will remain for a long time within the constitutional limits that you have assigned them, and that they will not attempt to go beyond them? Where is the independent legislative assembly that does not aspire to sovereignty? Where is the magistracy that will not bow to the weight of opinion? Where is the prince, above all, sovereign of a kingdom or chief of a republic, who will accept without reserve the passive rôle to which you would have him condemned; who, in his secret thoughts, will not meditate on the overthrow of the rival powers which disturb his action? In reality, you would have begun a struggle between all the opposing forces, roused all enterprises, given arms to all parties. You would have given strength to the assault of all ambitions, and made of the state an arena in which all factions would be unchained. In little time, there would be disorder everywhere; inexhaustible rhetoricians would transform the deliberating assemblies into oratorical jousts; audacious journalists, unbridled pamphleteers, would each day attack the person of the sovereign, would discredit the government, the ministers, the men of position. . . .

MONTESQUIEU. I have for a long time known these reproaches against liberal governments. They have no value in my eyes; the abuses do not condemn the institutions. I know of many states that live in peace, and have done so for a long time, under such laws; I pity those that cannot live thus.

MACHIAVELLI. Wait: In your calculations, you have not counted the social minorities. There are tremendous populations riveted to labor by poverty, as they were in other times by slavery. What difference, I ask you, do your parliamentary fictions make to their happiness? Your great political movement has after all only ended in the triumph of a minority privileged by chance as the ancient nobility was by birth. What difference does it make to the proletariat bent over its labor, weighted down by the heaviness of its destiny, that some orators have the right to speak, that some journalists have the right to write? You have created rights which will be purely academic for the mass of people, since it cannot make use of them. These rights, of which the law permits him the ideal enjoyment and necessity refuses him the actual exercise, are for the people only a bitter irony of destiny. I answer for it that one day they will capture them out of hatred, and that they will destroy them by their own hand to intrust themselves to despotism.

MONTESQUIEU. But what dislike has Machiavelli for humanity, and what idea has he of the baseness of modern nations? All-powerful God, I shall not believe that Thou hast created them so base. Machiavelli, no matter what he says, does not recognize the principles and the conditions of existence of modern civilization. Work is today the common law, as it is the divine law; and far from being a sign of servitude among men, it is the bond of their society, the instrument of their equality.

Political rights are in no way illusory to people in the lands where the law recognizes no privileges and where all careers are open to individual activity. No doubt, and in no society would it be otherwise, the inequality of intelligence and fortune brings about inevitable inequalities for individuals in the exercise of their rights; but does it not suffice that these rights exist so that the will of an enlightened philosophy shall be fulfilled, so that the emancipation of man shall be assured in such measure as it can be? Even for those whom chance has caused to be born into the most humble conditions, is it nothing to live in the realization of their independence and in their dignity as citizens? But that is only one facet of the question; for if the moral greatness of the races is attached to liberty, they are not less attached by their material interests.

MACHIAVELLI. I was expecting you to come to that. The school to which you belong has laid down principles of which it does not seem to realize the final consequences: you think that they lead to the reign of reason; I shall show you that they bring about the reign of force. Your political system, taken in its original purity, consists in giving a practically equal part of the action to different groups of forces of which nations are composed, to permit the social activities a justly proportionate competition; you do not wish the aristocratic element to surpass the democratic element. However, the temper of your institutions is to give more force to the aristocracy than to the people, more force to the prince than to the aristocracy, thus adjusting the powers to the political capacity of those who must exercise them.

MONTESQUIEU. You are right.

MACHIAVELLI. You make the different classes of society participate in the public functions according to their degree of aptitude and their enlightenment; you emancipate the bourgeoisie by the vote, you restrain the people by the amount of taxes conferring electoral rights; popular liberties create the power of opinion, aristocracy gives the prestige of grand manners, the throne throws over the nation the brilliance of the supreme rank; you keep all traditions, all the great memories, the culture of all great things. On the surface one sees a monarchical society, but all is fundamentally democratic; for, in reality, there is no barrier between the classes, and labor is the instrument of all fortunes. Is it not that, approximately?

MONTESQUIEU. Yes, Machiavelli; and you can at least understand the opinions which you do not share.

MACHIAVELLI. Well, all these fine things have passed or will pass like a dream; for you have a new principle with which all institutions undergo a change with a startling rapidity.

MONTESQUIEU. What is that principle?

MACHIAVELLI. It is that of popular sovereignty. Rest assured that the method of squaring a circle will be found long before the conciliation of balance of power with the existence of such a principle among nations in which it is admitted. The people, by an absolutely inevitable consequence, will one day or another take possession of all the powers which have been recognized as resting in it. Will it be to keep them? No. After several days of madness, it will throw them, out of weariness, to the first soldier of fortune who finds himself in its road. In your country, you saw, in 1793, how the French headsmen treated representative monarchy; the sovereign people asserted itself by the execution of its king, then made a litter of all its rights; it gave itself to Robespierre, Barras and Bonaparte.

You are a great thinker, but you do not know the unfathomable cowardice of humanity; I do not speak of those of my time, but of those of yours; servile in the face of force, pitiless in the face of weakness, implacable before blunders, indulgent before crimes, incapable of supporting the contrarieties of a liberal régime, and patient to the point of martyrdom before all the violences of bold despotism, upsetting thrones in its moments of anger, and giving itself rulers, whom it pardons for actions the least of which would have caused it to decapitate twenty constitutional kings.

Look then for justice; look for law, stability, order, respect of the so-complicated forms of your parliamentary mechanism with the violent, undisciplined, uncultivated masses to whom you have said: You are the law, you are the masters, you are the arbiters of the State! Oh, I know very well that the prudent Montesquieu, the circumspect politician, who laid down principles and reserved the consequences, did not write the dogma of popular sovereignty in the *Esprit des Lois;* but, as you said a moment ago, the consequences flow of themselves from the principles you have laid down. The affinity of your doctrines with those of the *Contrat Social* also makes itself felt. Thus, from the day the French revolutionaries wrote, swearing *in verba magistri:* "A government can only be the free work of a convention of associates," monarchical and parliamentary government was condemned to death in your homeland. Vainly was it attempted to restore the old principles, vainly did your king, Louis XVIII, on returning to France, attempt to make the powers return to their source by promulgating the declarations of '89 as a precedent for the royal grant; that pious fiction of aristocratic monarchy was in too flagrant contradiction with the past: it had to vanish at the sound of the revolution of 1830, like the government of 1830 in its turn. . . .

MONTESQUIEU. Finish.

MACHIAVELLI. Let us not anticipate. What you as well as I know of the past authorizes me until now to say that the principle of popular sovereignty is destructive of all stability, that it indefinitely perpetuates the right to revolution. It puts nations into open war against all human powers and even against God; it is the very incarnation of violence. It makes of the people a ferocious brute which sleeps when it is satiated with blood, and which is enchained; and this is the invariable progress which then follows the communities whose movement is ruled by this principle: popular sovereignty engenders demagogy, demagogy engenders anarchy, anarchy brings back despotism. Despotism, to you, is barbarity. Well, you see that the people returns to barbarity by way of civilization.

But that is not all, I assert that from still other points of view despotism is the sole form of government that is really appropriate to the social state of modern peoples. You have told me that their material interests bound them to liberty; here, you play too fine a game. What are, in general, the states which are in need of liberty? They are those which live by great sentiments, by great passions, by heroism, by faith, even by honor, as you would say in your times in speaking of the French monarchy. Stoicism can make a free people; Christianity, under certain conditions, could have the same privilege. I understand the necessities of liberty in Athens, in Rome, among the nations which breathed only by the glory of arms, all of whose expansions were satisfied by war, who, moreover, had need of all the energies of patriotism, of all civic enthusiasms to triumph over their enemies.

Public liberties were the natural patrimony of the states in which the servile and industrial functions were left to the slaves, in which man was useless if he was not a citizen. I include also liberty at certain epochs of the Christian era, and especially in the little states united to one another by systems of confederation analogous to those of the Hellenic republics, as in Italy and Germany. I find there a part of the natural causes which made liberty necessary. It would almost have been inoffensive in times when the principle of authority was not placed in question, in which religion had absolute authority over the spirit, in which the people, placed under the tutelar régime of the corporations, walked docilely under the hands of its pastors. If its political emancipation had been undertaken then, it would have been without danger; for it would have been accomplished in conformity with the principles on which rests the existence of all societies. But, with your great states, which exist only by means of industry; with your populations, Godless and faithless, in times when people are no longer satisfied by war, and when their violent activity is, of necessity, restricted to the homeland, liberty, with the principles which serve as its foundation, cannot but be a cause of dissolution and ruin. I add that it is no more necessary for the moral needs of the individual than it is for the states.

From the weariness of ideas and the shock of revolutions have come cold and disillusioned societies, which have achieved indifference in politics as in religion, which have no other stimulant than material satisfactions, which live only in their own interest, which have no other cult than that of gold, whose mercantile customs compete with those of the Jews whom they have taken for models. Do you believe that it is for love of liberty in itself that the inferior classes are trying to rise to the assault on power? It is by hatred of those who possess; in reality, it is to take away their riches, an instrument of enjoyment which they envy.

Those who possess invoke from all sides a strong arm, a forceful power; they demand only one thing, the protection of the state against the agitations which its weak constitution cannot resist, to give to themselves the necessary security so that they may enjoy and do business. What forms of government would you apply to societies in which corruption has stolen everywhere, in which morality has no guarantee save in repressive laws, in which the sentiment of patriotism itself is extinguished by I know not what universal cosmopolitanism?

I see no salvation in these societies, veritable giants with feet of clay, except in the institution of an extreme centralization, which puts all public force at the disposition of those who govern; in a hierarchic administration resembling that of the Roman empire, which rules mechanically all the movements of individuals; in a vast system of legislation which takes up in detail all the liberties that have been imprudently bestowed; in a tremendous despotism, in short, which could immediately and at all times strike at all who resist, all who complain. The Cæsarism of the Lower-Empire seems to me to realize quite well what I desire for the well-being of modern society. Thanks to these vast aparati which, I have been told, already function in more than one country of

Europe, they can live in peace, as in China, as in Japan, as in India. A common prejudice should not make us condemn these oriental civilizations, whose institutions we learn to appreciate more each day. The Chinese people, for example, is very commercial and very well administered.

FIFTH DIALOGUE

MONTESQUIEU. I hesitate in answering you, Machiavelli, for there is in your words I know not what satanic mockery, which gives me the inward suspicion that your discourse is not in complete accord with your secret thoughts. Yes, you have the fatal eloquence that loses the trace of truth, and you are the same sombre genius whose name is still the bogie of modern generations. Nevertheless, I readily recognize the fact that with such a powerful intellect one would lose too much in remaining quiet; I wish to hear you to the end, and I even wish to answer you, although, even now, I have little hope to convince you. You have just drawn a really sinister picture of modern society; I cannot know whether it is faithful, but it is at least incomplete, for in all things, besides the evil, there is the good, and you have only shown me the evil; moreover, you have not given me the means to verify how far you are right, for I know neither of what peoples nor of what states you wished to speak when you painted this dark picture of contemporary custom.

MACHIAVELLI. Well, let us admit that I have taken as an example that one of all the nations in Europe which is the most advanced in its civilization, and to which, I hasten to say, the picture that I have drawn could be least applied.

MONTESQUIEU. It is then of France that you wish to speak?

MACHIAVELLI. Well, yes.

MONTESQUIEU. You are right, for there the dark doctrines of materialism have penetrated least. It is France who has remained the home of the great ideas and the great passions whose source you believe exhausted, and it is from there that have come those great principles of public right to which you give no place in the government of nations.

MACHIAVELLI. You may add that it is the field of experiment consecrated to political theories.

MONTESQUIEU. I know of no experiment that has yet, by the establishment of despotism, proved of lasting benefit to contemporary nations and least of all to France, and it is this that in the very first place makes me find that your theories on the necessity of absolute power conform little to the reality of matters. I know at the present time of but two states in Europe completely deprived of the liberal institutions that have modified in all parts the purely monarchical element: they are Turkey and Russia, and still if you regard closely the interior movements which are operating in the heart of this latter power, perhaps you will find there the symptoms of an approaching transformation. You tell me, it is true, that in the more or less near future, the peoples, menaced by an inevitable dissolution, will return to despotism as to an ark of safety; that they will constitute themselves under the form of great absolute monarchies, similar to those of Asia; that is only a prediction: in how much time will that be accomplished?

MACHIAVELLI. Within a century.

MONTESQUIEU. You are a soothsayer; one century is always just so much gained; but let me tell you now why your prediction will not be fulfilled. Modern societies today must no longer be considered with the eyes of the past. Their customs, their habits, their needs, all have changed. One must not, therefore, put confidence without reserve in the inferences of historical analogy, when it comes to judging their destinies. One must beware above all of taking for universal laws facts which are but accidents, and of transforming into general rules the necessities of such a situation or the necessities of such a time. As for despotism occurring many times in history as a consequence of social disturbances, does it follow that it must be taken as a rule of government? As for its having served as a transition in the past, shall I conclude that it is calculated to settle the crises of modern times? Is it not more rational to say that other evils bring forth other remedies, other problems other solutions, other social customs other political customs? An invariable law of society is that it always tends toward perfection, toward progress; eternal wisdom has, if I may say so, condemned it; it has refused it movement in the opposite direction. It must achieve this progress.

MACHIAVELLI. Or it must die.

MONTESQUIEU. Let us not place ourselves at extremes; societies never die when they are about to give birth. When they are constituted in the manner which pleases them, their institutions can change, fall into decadence and perish; but they will have lasted for many centuries. It is thus that the different peoples of Europe have passed, by successive transformations, from the feudal system to the monarchical system, and from the monarchical system to the constitutional régime. This progressive development, the unity of which is so imposing, has nothing of fortuitousness about it; it has arrived as the necessary consequence of the movement which operated in ideas before being translated into fact.

Society cannot have forms of government other than those which are in agreement with its principles, and it is against this absolute law that you place yourself when you believe despotism compatible with modern civilization. As long as the peoples regarded sovereignty as a pure emanation of the divine will, they submitted without a murmur to absolute power; as long as their institutions were insufficient to assure their progress, they accepted arbitrariness. But, from the day their rights are recognized and solemnly declared, from the day more fertile institutions have been able to resolve through liberty all the functions of the social body, politics as an instrument of princes fell from its pedestal; power has become a dependency of the public domain; the art of government has changed into an affair of administration. Today things are ordained in such a way, in the various countries, that the directing power only appears as the motor of the organized forces.

Certainly, if you imagine these societies infected by all the corruptions, by all the vices of which you spoke to me only a moment ago, they will progress rapidly in the direction of decomposition: but how is it you do not see that the argument you draw from this is a veritable petition of principle? Since when does liberty abase the soul and degrade the character? Those are not the teachings of history; for it attests everywhere in characters of fire that the greatest peoples have been the most free. If customs were degraded, as you say, in some part of Europe that I do not know of, it is because despotism had passed through it; it is because liberty was extinguished there; it is, therefore, necessary to maintain it wherever it is, and to reestablish it where it no longer exists.

Do not forget that we are at this moment on the plane of principles; and if yours differ from mine, I expect them to be invariable; now, I no longer know where I am when I hear you praise liberty in antiquity and prohibit it in modern times, refusing or admitting it according to periods and places. These distinctions, supposing them justified, still do not leave the principle less intact, and it is to the principle alone that I hold.

MACHIAVELLI. I see that you avoid the reefs like an able pilot, keeping yourself to the high seas. Generalities are a great help in argument; but I confess that I am very impatient to know how the grave Montesquieu will extricate himself with the principle of popular sovereignty. I could not tell, until now, whether or not it was a part of your system. Do you or do you not admit it?

MONTESQUIEU. I cannot answer a question couched in those terms.

MACHIAVELLI. I knew that even your mind would be disturbed before this phantom.

MONTESQUIEU. You are wrong, Machiavelli; but, before answering you, I had to remind you what my writings were and what was the character of the mission which they were able to carry out. You have made my name jointly and severally responsible for the iniquities of the French revolution: it is a severe enough judgment for the philosopher who walked with such a prudent step in search of truth. Born in a century of intellectual effervescence, on the eve of a revolution which was to carry off the ancient forms of monarchic government in my native land, I can say that none of the subsequent consequences of progress of ideas then going on escaped my eyes from that time on. I could not fail to realize that the system of the division of power would one day necessarily displace the seat of sovereignty.

This principle, little known, poorly defined, above all, badly applied, could engender terrible equivocations, and overthrow French society from top to bottom. The perception of these perils became the rule for my words. Thus, while imprudent innovators, immediately attacking the source of power, unwittingly prepared a great catastrophe, I applied myself solely to the study of the forms of free government, to the extraction of clearly defined principles which preside over their establishment. Statesman rather than philosopher, lawyer rather than theologian, practical legislator, if the boldness of such a word is permitted me, I thought to do more for my country by teaching it to govern itself than by questioning the very principle of authority. God forbid, however, that I attempt to give myself purer merit at the expense of those who, like myself, sought truth in good faith! We have all made mistakes, but to each the responsibility for his deeds.

Yes, Machiavelli, and it is a concession that I do not hesitate to make to you, you were right just now when you said that it was necessary that the emancipation of the French people should be made in conformity with the superior principles which preside over the existence of human communities, and this reserve permits you to foresee the judgment that I will bring upon the principle of popular sovereignty.

First of all, I do not admit a designation which seems to exclude from sovereignty the most enlightened classes of society. This distinction is fundamental, because it makes of a state a pure democracy or a representative state. If sovereignty rests anywhere, it rests upon the entire nation; I will therefore in the first place call it national sovereignty. But the idea of this sovereignty is not an absolute truth, it is only relative. The sovereignty of human power corresponds to an idea profoundly subversive, the sovereignty of human rights; it is this materialist and atheistic doctrine that precipitated the French revolution into blood, and inflicted on it the disgrace of despotism after the delirium of independence. It is not correct to say that the nations are the absolute masters of their destinies, for their sovereign master is God Himself, and they will never be beyond His power. If they possessed absolute sovereignty, they could do everything, even contrary to eternal justice, even contrary to God; who would dare to go that far? But the principle of divine right, with the significance that is generally attached to it, is a no less fatal principle, for it links the people to obscurantism, to despotism, to the void; it reconstitutes logically the régime of castes, it makes of the people a herd of slaves, conducted, as in India, by the hand of the priests, and trembling beneath the whip of the master. How could it be otherwise? If the sovereign is the messenger of God, if he is the very representative of the Divinity on earth, he has every power over the human creatures subject to his empire, and this power will have a brake only in the general rules of equity, which it will always be easy to transgress.

It is in the field that separates these two extreme opinions that have been waged the furious battles of party spirit; some shout: No divine authority!; others: No human authority! O supreme Providence, my mind refuses to accept one or the other of these alternatives; they both appear to me equal blasphemies against Thy wisdom! Between divine right which excludes man and human right which excludes God, there lies the truth, Machiavelli; nations, like individuals, are free in the hands of God. They have all rights, all powers, charged with using them according to the rules of eternal justice. Sovereignty is human in the sense that it is given by men, and it is men who exercise it; it is divine in the sense that it is instituted by God, and that it can only be exercised in accordance with the precepts that He has established.

SIXTH DIALOGUE

MACHIAVELLI. I would like to come to definite conclusions. How far does the hand of God extend over humanity? Who makes the sovereigns?

MONTESQUIEU. The people.

MACHIAVELLI. It is written: *Per me reges regnant.* Which means literally: God makes kings. (Through me kings reign.)

MONTESQUIEU. That is a translation in the manner of *The Prince*, O Machiavelli, and it was given you in that century by one of your most illustrious partisans (Note: Machiavelli here evidently alludes to Joseph de Maistre, whose name, moreover, is again mentioned later on), but it is not from the Holy Scripture. God instituted sovereignty, he did not institute sovereigns. His all-powerful hand stopped there, because there begins the free human arbiter. "Kings reign according to My commandments, they must reign according to My law": such is the meaning of the divine Book. If it were otherwise, it would have to be said that the good as well as the evil princes are established by Providence: one would have to bow down before Nero as before Titus, before Caligula as before Vespasian. No, God did not wish that the most sacrilegious dominations should invoke His protection, that the vilest tyrannies should claim His investiture. To peoples as to kings, He left the responsibility for their acts.

MACHIAVELLI. I doubt very much whether that is orthodox. Whatever it is, according to you, it is the people who dispose of sovereign authority?

MONTESQUIEU. Be careful, in contesting it, of setting yourself up against a truth of pure common sense. That is not a novelty in history. In ancient times, in the middle ages, everywhere that power was established without invasion or conquest, sovereign power was born through the free will of the people, in the original form of election. To cite but one example, it was thus that in France the head of the Carlovingian race succeeded the descendants of Clovis, and the dynasty of Hugh Capet that of Charlemagne. *(Esprit des Lois,* p. 513, Book XXXI, ch. IV.) No doubt heredity became the substitute for election. The brilliance of services rendered, public gratitude, traditions, fixed the sovereignty on the principal families of Europe, and nothing was more legitimate. But the principle of entire national power is constantly rediscovered at the bottom of revolutions; it has always been invoked for the consecration of new powers. It is a prior and pre-existent principle, which has made itself only more strictly realized in the various constitutions of modern countries.

MACHIAVELLI. But if it is the people who choose their masters, cannot they, therefore, also overthrow them? If they have the right to establish the form of government which satisfies them, what will stop them from changing at the behest of their caprice? It will not be a régime of order and liberty that will come forth from your doctrines, it will be the indefinite era of revolutions.

MONTESQUIEU. You confound justice with the abuse that can result from its exercise, the principles with their application; those are fundamental distinctions, without which we cannot agree.

MACHIAVELLI. Do not hope to escape me, I demand of you logical deductions; refuse me them if you wish. I wish to know if, according to your principles, the people have the right to overthrow their sovereign?

MONTESQUIEU. Yes, in extreme cases and for just causes.

MACHIAVELLI. Who will be the judge of these extreme cases and of the justice of these extremes?

MONTESQUIEU. And who would you wish it to be, if not the people themselves? Have things happened otherwise since the beginning of world? That is a formidable sanction, no doubt, but beneficial and inevitable. How is it you do not see that the contrary doctrine, which commands of man respect for the most odious governments, would make them fall once more under the yoke of monarchical fatalism?

MACHIAVELLI. Your system has but one inconvenience, that it supposes the infallibility of reason among the people; but have they

not, like individuals, their passions, their mistakes, their injustices?
MONTESQUIEU. When the people will make mistakes, they will be punished as are individuals who have sinned against the moral law.
MACHIAVELLI. In what way?
MONTESQUIEU. They will be punished by the scourges of dissension, anarchy, even despotism. There is no other justice on earth, when awaiting that of God.
MACHIAVELLI. You have just uttered the word despotism, you see that one returns to it.
MONTESQUIEU. That objection is not worthy of your great mind, Machiavelli; I imagined the most extreme consequences of the principles which you oppose; that was sufficient for the real idea to be perverted. God did not give the people either the power or the will to change thus the forms of government which are the essential means of their existence. Among political societies as among organized beings, the nature of things limits of itself the expansion of free forces. The import of your argument must restrict itself to what is acceptable to reason.

You believe that, under the influence of modern ideas, revolutions would be more frequent. They will not be more, it is possible they will be less. Nations, indeed, as you said a moment ago, exist at the present time through industry, and what seems to you a cause for servitude is at the same time a principle of order and liberty. Industrial civilizations have sores that I do not forget, but one must not deny their benefits, nor distort their tendencies. Societies which live by labor, by exchange, by credit, are societies essentially Christian, no matter what one may say, for all these forms of industry, so powerful and so varied, are fundamentally but the application of several great moral ideas borrowed from Christianity, source of all strength as of all truth.

Industry plays such a considerable rôle in the progress of modern society that one cannot, from the point of view which you assume, make an exact calculation without taking into consideration its influence; and this influence is not all that you thought to charge it with. The science that seeks the relationships of industrial life and the maxims that are drawn therefrom are quite the most contrary to the principle of the concentration of powers. The tendency of political economy is to see in the political organism only a necessary but very costly mechanism, whose energy must be simplified, and it reduces the rôle of the government to functions so elementary that its greatest inconvenience is perhaps to destroy prestige. Industry is the born enemy of revolutions, for without social order it perishes and with it is arrested the vital progress of modern nations. It cannot do without liberty; and, note well, liberties in the question of industry necessarily engender political liberty, so much so that one could say that the people most advanced in industry are also the people most advanced in liberty. Leave India and China which exist under the blind destiny of absolute monarchy; look at Europe, and you will see.

You have just mentioned the word *despotism* again; well, Machiavelli, you whose sombre genius so profoundly assimilated all the subterranean passages, all the occult combinations, all the artifices of law and of government with the aid of which one can enchain the physical activity and the mental activity of the people; you who distrust man, you who dream of the terrible dominations of the Orient for them, you whose political doctrines are borrowed from frightful theories of Indian mythology, tell me, I beg of you, how you would go about organizing despotism amongst peoples whose public rights rest essentially on liberty, whose morals and religion develop all progress in the same direction, among Christian nations who live by commerce and industry, in states whose political bodies are in the presence of the publicity of the press which throws floods of light into the most obscure corners of power; call upon all the resources of your powerful imagination, seek, invent, and if you resolve the problem, I will say with you that the modern spirit is conquered.

MACHIAVELLI. Take care, you give me a fine chance, I may take you at your word.

MONTESQUIEU. Do so, I beseech you.

MACHIAVELLI. I do not expect to fail.

MONTESQUIEU. In a few hours we will perhaps be separated. These parts are not known to you, follow me in the twisting path that I shall take with you along this dark passage, we can yet escape for several hours the wave of shadows that you perceive over there.

SEVENTH DIALOGUE

MACHIAVELLI. We can stop here.

MONTESQUIEU. I am listening to you.

MACHIAVELLI. First I must tell you that you are wrong from beginning to end in the application of my principles. Despotism always presents itself before your eyes in the decayed forms of oriental monarchy, but it is not thus that I think of it; with new societies, new procedures must be employed. Today there is no question, in order to govern, of committing violent iniquities, decapitating one's enemies, stripping one's subjects of their possessions, spreading punishment; no, death, spoliation and physical torture cannot play a rôle secondary enough in the interior policies of modern states.

MONTESQUIEU. That is fortunate.

MACHIAVELLI. No doubt I have little admiration, I confess, for your civilizations of *cylinders and shafts;* but I advance with the centuries; the power of the doctrines to which my name is attached is that they accommodate themselves to all times and all situations. Machiavelli today *has grandchildren* who know the price of his lessons. I am believed very old, and every day I grow younger on earth.

MONTESQUIEU. You are jesting?

MACHIAVELLI. Listen to me and you shall judge. Today it is less a question of doing men violence than of disarming them, less of suppressing their political passions than of *wiping them out,* less of combating their instincts than of deceiving them, less of prohibiting their ideas than of changing them by appropriating them to oneself.

MONTESQUIEU. And how is that done? For I do not understand this language.

MACHIAVELLI. Permit me; that is the moral side of politics, we shall soon arrive at the applications. The principal secret of government consists in enfeebling the public spirit to the point of disinteresting it entirely in the ideas and the principles with which revolutions are made nowadays. In all times, peoples, like individuals, have been paid in words. Appearances nearly always are sufficient for them; they demand no more. One can, then, establish artificial institutions which correspond to a language and to ideas equally artificial; it is necessary to have the talent to strip the parties of *that liberal phraseology* with which they arm themselves against the government. It is necessary to satiate the people with it until they are weary, until they are disgusted. One speaks often today of the power of public opinion. I shall show you that it is made to express whatever one wants when one knows well the hidden resources of power. But before thinking of directing it, one must benumb it, strike it with uncertainty by astounding contradictions, work on it with incessant diversions, dazzle it with all sorts of different actions, mislead it imperceptibly in its pathways. One of the great secrets of the day is to know how to take possession of popular prejudices and passions, in such a way as to introduce a confusion of principles which makes impossible all understanding between those who speak the same language and have the same interests.

MONTESQUIEU. Where are you going with these words whose obscurity has in it something sinister?

MACHIAVELLI. If the wise Montesquieu means to put sentiment in the place of politics, I should perhaps stop here; I have not pretended to place myself on the terrain of morals. You have defied me to stop the progress in your societies unendingly tormented by the spirit of anarchy and revolt. Do you wish to let me say

how I would solve the problem? You can put aside your scruples
in accepting this thesis as a question of pure curiosity.

MONTESQUIEU. So be it.

MACHIAVELLI. I understand moreover that you would demand
more precise information of me; I will arrive at that. But permit
me to tell you first under what essential conditions the Prince can
hope today to consolidate his power. He will have to endeavor
above all to destroy the parties, to dissolve the collective forces
wherever they exist, to paralyze in all its manifestations individual
initiative; then the level of character would descend to himself,
and all knees will soon bend in servitude. Absolute power will no
longer be an accident, it will become a need. These political
precepts are not entirely new, but, as I said to you, it is the
processes that must be new. A large number of these results can
be obtained by simple regulations of the police and the administration. In your societies, so fine and so well organized, in the place
of absolute monarchies you have put a *monster which is called
the State*, a new Briareus whose arms extend everywhere, a
colossal organism of tyranny in whose shadow despotism is always
reborn. Well, under the invocation of the state, nothing will be
easier then to consummate the occult work of which I spoke to
you just now, and the most powerful methods of action will
perhaps be precisely those that one will have the talent to borrow
from this very industrial régime which calls forth your admiration.

With the aid of the sole regulating power, I would institute,
for example, huge financial monopolies, reservoirs of the public
wealth, on which depends so closely the fate of all the private
fortunes that they would be swallowed up with the credit of the
state the day after any political catastrophe. You are an economist,
Montesquieu, weigh the value of this combination.

Head of the government, all my edicts, all my ordinances
would constantly tend toward the same goal: to annihilate collective and individual forces; to develop excessively the preponderance of the state, to make of it the sovereign protector, promoter
and remunerator.

Here is another scheme borrowed from the industrial order: In modern times, the aristocracy, as a political force, has disappeared; but the landed bourgeoisie is still an element of dangerous resistance to governments, because it is independent in itself; it may be necessary to impoverish it or even to ruin it completely. It is enough, for this, to increase the charges which weigh on landed property, to maintain agriculture in a state of relative inferiority, to favor commerce and industry excessively, but speculation principally; for too great prosperity in industry can itself become a danger, in creating too large a number of independent fortunes.

The great industrialists and manufacturers will be reacted against advantageously by stimulation to a disproportionate luxury, by the elevation of taxes on salaries, by deep blows ably struck at the sources of production. I need not develop these ideas, you can readily understand in what circumstances and under what pretexts all this can be done. The interests of the people, and even a sort of zeal for liberty, for the great economic principles, will easily cover the true goal, if it is desired. It is useless to add that the perpetual upkeep of a large army continually exercised by foreign wars must be the indispensable complement of this system; it is necessary to arrive at the existence in the state only of proletarians, several millionaires, and soldiers.

MONTESQUIEU. Continue.

MACHIAVELLI. So much for the interior policies of the state. Outside, it is necessary to incite, from one end of Europe to the other, the revolutionary fermentation that is curbed at home. Two considerable advantages would result from that; the liberal agitation outside makes passable the repression within. Moreover, in this way one controls all the powers, among which one can create order or disorder at will. The important point is to entangle by cabinet intrigues all the threads of European politics in such a way as to play one against the other the Powers with whom one treats. Do not think that this duplicity, if it is well carried on, could become detrimental to a sovereign. Alexander VI practised only deception in his diplomatic negotiations and yet he always succeeded, so well did he know the science of cunning. (*The Prince*, p. 114, ch. XVII.) But for what you call today *the official language*, a striking contrast is necessary, and there one cannot affect too much the spirit of loyalty and conciliation; the people, who see only the outward appearance of things, will manufacture a reputation of wisdom for the ruler who can conduct his affairs in this way.

To all internal agitation, he must be able to respond with a foreign war; to any imminent revolution, with a general war; but since in politics words must never be in accord with deeds, it is necessary that, in these various crises, the prince be able enough to disguise his real designs under contrary design; he must always give the impression of acceding to public opinion while he does what his hands have secretly prepared.

To sum up the whole system in a word, revolution in the state is restrained on the one hand by the terror of anarchy, on the other, by bankruptcy, and, all things considered, by general war.

You have already been able to see, by means of the rapid outline I have just given you, what an important rôle the art of language is called upon to play in modern politics. I am far from disdaining the press, as you see, and I would be able in time of need to use the rostrum; what is essential is the use against one's enemies of all the arms they could employ against you. Not content with relying on the violent force of democracy, I would borrow of the subtleties of justice their most learned resources. When one makes decisions that could seem unjust or rash, it is essential to know how to express them in fine terms, to give them the highest reasons of morality and justice.

The power of which I dream, far, as you see, from having barbarian customs, must draw to itself all the forces and all the talents of the civilization in the heart of which it lives. It must surround itself with publicists, lawyers, jurisconsults, practical men and administrators, men who know thoroughly all the secrets, all the strength of social life, who speak all languages, who have studied man in all circles. They must be taken from anywhere and everywhere, for these men give surprising service through the ingenious procedures they apply to politics. With that, a whole world of economists is necessary, of bankers, of industrialists, of capitalists, of men of vision, of men with millions, for all fundamentally resolves itself into a question of figures.

As for the principal dignities, the principal dismemberment of power, one must so arrange as to give them to men whose antecedents and character place a gulf between them and other men, every one of whom has only to expect death or exile in case of a change in government and is in need of defending until his last breath all that exists.

Imagine for a moment that I have at my disposal the different moral and material resources which I have just sketched for you, and now give me any nation, do you hear! You regard it as a capital point, in the *Esprit des Lois, not to change the character of a nation (Esprit des Lois*, p. 252 et seq., book XIX, Chap. V) when one wishes it to conserve its original vigor. Well, I do not ask you twenty years to transform in the most complete way the most untamable European character and to make it as docile under tyranny as the smallest nation in Asia.

MONTESQUIEU. You have just added, in your jesting, another chapter to your treatise on *The Prince*. Whatever are your doctrines, I do not debate them; I make but one observation to you. It is evident that you have in no way held to the promise you had made; the use of these methods presupposes the existence of absolute power, and I have asked you precisely how you could establish it in political societies which rest upon liberal institutions.

MACHIAVELLI. Your observation is perfectly fair and I do not mean to escape it. This beginning was only a preface.

MONTESQUIEU. I put you in the presence of a state founded on representative institutions, monarchic or republic; I speak to you of a nation long familiar with liberty, and I ask you how, from there, you could return to absolute power.

MACHIAVELLI. Nothing could be easier.
MONTESQUIEU. Let us see!

EIGHTH DIALOGUE

MACHIAVELLI. I take the hypothesis which is most contrary to me; I take a state constituted as a republic. With a monarchy, the rôle that I propose to play would be too easy. I take a republic, because with such a form of government, I will encounter resistance almost insurmountable in appearance, in ideas, in custom, in laws. This hypothesis is not acceptable to you? I accept from your hands a state of no matter what form, great or small; I imagine it endowed with all the institutions that guarantee liberty, and I ask you this single question: Do you believe power is protected from a blow or from what is today called a coup d'état?

MONTESQUIEU. No, that is true; but you will at least admit that such an enterprise would be singularly difficult in the political society of our times, as it is organized.

MACHIAVELLI. And why? Are not these societies, as in all times, prey to factions? Are there not everywhere the elements of civil war, between parties, between pretenders?

MONTESQUIEU. That is possible; but I think I can make you understand in one word where your error lies. These usurpations, necessarily very rare because they are full of peril and they repudiate modern customs, supposing that they succeed, would in no way have the importance that you seem to attribute to them. A change of power would not bring about a change of institutions. A pretender will trouble the state; his party will triumph, I admit it; the power is in other hands, that is all; but the public rights and very foundation of the institutions remain upright. That is what concerns me.

MACHIAVELLI. Is it true that you have such an illusion?

MONTESQUIEU. Prove the contrary.

MACHIAVELLI. You grant me, for the moment, the success of an armed enterprise against the established power?

MONTESQUIEU. Yes.

MACHIAVELLI. Then note in what situation I find myself placed. I have for the moment suppressed all power other than my own. If the institutions still standing can erect some obstacle before me, it is pure form; in fact, the acts of my will can encounter no real resistance; at last I am in that extra-legal condition that the Romans called by a word so beautiful and so powerfully energetic: *dictatorship*. That is to say I can do all I wish at the present time; I am legislator, executive, judge, and, on horse-back, chief of the army.

Remember this. Now I have triumphed through the support of one faction, that is, this occurrence could only be accomplished in an atmosphere of deep internal dissension. One can tell at random, without being wrong, what were the causes. It will be an antagonism between the aristocracy and the people or between the people and the bourgeoisie. At the basis of things, it could not be otherwise; on the surface, there is a mixture of contrary ideas, opinions, influences and currents, as in all states where liberty has been unchained for a moment. There will be political elements of all kinds, fragments of parties once victorious, today defeated, unbridled ambitions, wild cupidity, implacable hatreds, terror everywhere, men of all opinions and all doctrines, would-be restorers of former régimes, demagogues, anarchists, utopians, all at work, all laboring equally from their side for the overthrow of the established order. What may be concluded from such a situation? Two things: first, that the country has great need of peace and that it will refuse nothing to him who can give it her; second, that in the middle of this division of parties, there is no real force or rather, there is only one, the people.

I myself am a victorious pretender; I bear, let us suppose, a great name in history, qualified to work on the imagination of the masses. Like Pisistratus, like Cæsar, like Nero even, I rely on the people; that is the *a b c* of all usurpers. There lies the blind power that gives the means to do everything with impunity, there lies authority, there the name that will cover all. The people indeed care much for your legal fictions and your constitutional guarantees!

I have brought quiet amid all the factions, and now you will see how I am going to proceed.

Perhaps you remember the rules I established in *The Prince* for the conservation of conquered provinces. The usurper in a state is in a situation similar to that of the conqueror. He is condemned to the renovation of everything, the dissolution of the state, the destruction of the city, the changing of the face of customs.

That is the goal, but in modern times one must aim at it only through roundabout ways, indirect means, cunning schemes and, as far as possible, without violence. Therefore, I will not destroy institutions directly, but I will reach them one by one by an unseen blow which will throw the mechanism into confusion. Thus I will reach, each in its turn, the judicial organization, the electorate, the press, individual liberty, education.

Above the primitive laws I will have passed a whole new legislation which, without exactly abrogating the old, will mask it first, and soon make it disappear completely. Such are my general conceptions, now you will see the details of execution.

MONTESQUIEU. Would that you were still in the gardens of Rucellai, O Machiavelli, to teach these fine lessons, and how sad it is that posterity could not hear you!

MACHIAVELLI. Rest assured; for those who can read, all this is in *The Prince*.

MONTESQUIEU. Well, you have arrived at the day after your coup d'état; what are you going to do?

MACHIAVELLI. One great thing, then a very little one.

MONTESQUIEU. Let us see the great one first.

MACHIAVELLI. After the success of a coup against the established power, all is not finished, and the parties do not generally consider themselves beaten. It is not yet exactly known how much the usurper's energy is worth, he will be tried, and they will rise against him with weapons in their hands. The moment has come to impress terror which will strike the entire city and will make the most intrepid souls shrink back.

MONTESQUIEU. What are you going to do? You told me that you repudiated bloodshed.

MACHIAVELLI. It is not a question of false humanity here. Society is menaced, it is in a state of lawful defense; the excess of strictness, even cruelty, will prevent more flowing of blood in the future. Do not ask me what will be done; it is necessary that the people be terrified once and for all and that fear soften them.

MONTESQUIEU. Yes, I remember; that is what you teach in *The Prince* in recounting the sinister execution of Borgia in Cesene (*The Prince*, p. 47, chap. VII). You are still the same.

MACHIAVELLI. No, no, you will see later; I only do this by necessity, and I suffer from it.

MONTESQUIEU. But who will start this blood flowing?

MACHIAVELLI. The army! that great justiciary of the state whose hand never dishonors its victims. Two results of the greatest importance will be obtained in the repression by the intervention of the army. From this time, on the one hand, it will find itself forever hostile to the civil population which it had punished without consideration, and on the other, it will attach itself in an indissoluble manner to the fate of its leader.

MONTESQUIEU. And you think that this blood will not fall back on you?

MACHIAVELLI. No, for in the eyes of the people, the sovereign, definitely, is a stranger to the excesses of a soldiery which is not always easy to hold back. Those who could be held responsible are the generals, the ministers who had executed my orders. These men, I assure you, will be devoted to me until their last breath, for they know very well what awaits them after me.

MONTESQUIEU. That is, therefore, your first act as sovereign? Now let us hear the second.

MACHIAVELLI. I do not know whether you have noticed what is, in politics, the power of little things. After what I have just told you, I will have all new coins struck with my effigy, and I will issue a considerable quantity.

MONTESQUIEU. But amid the first cares of the state, that would be a puerile measure.

MACHIAVELLI. You think so? You have not been in power. The human effigy on coins is the supreme sign of power. At the beginning there will be proud spirits who will shake with anger, but they will become accustomed to it; even the enemies of my power will be obliged to have my portrait in their purses. It is quite certain that the people will accustom themselves to seeing with a softer regard the features that are printed everywhere on the material token of our possessions. From the day my effigy is on the coins, I am king.

MONTESQUIEU. I confess that this notion is new to me; but let us continue. You have not forgotten that new peoples have the weakness of giving themselves constitutions that are guaranties of their rights? With your power emanating from force, with the projects that you explain to me, you will perhaps find yourself embarrassed in the presence of a fundamental charter whose every principle, every regulation, every plan, is contrary to your maxims of government.

MACHIAVELLI. I will make another constitution, that is all.

MONTESQUIEU. And you think that that will not be difficult?

MACHIAVELLI. Wherein will lie the difficulty? For the moment, there is no other will, no other force than mine and I have the popular element as a basis of action.

MONTESQUIEU. That is true. Still, I have one doubt: according to what you have been telling me, I imagine that your constitution will not be a monument of liberty. Do you think that a single crisis of strength, a single lucky violence will be sufficient to ravish all the rights of a nation, all her conquests, all her institutions, all the principles with which she has been in the habit of living?

MACHIAVELLI. Permit me! I don't go as fast as that. I said to

you, a few moments ago, that nations were like individuals, that
they attached more to appearances than to the reality of things;
in politics that is a rule the details of which I will follow scrupulously; if you will call to mind the principles to which you hold
the most, you will see that I am not as embarrassed by them as
you seem to think.

MONTESQUIEU. What are you going to do, O Machiavelli?

MACHIAVELLI. Don't be afraid, name them to me.

MONTESQUIEU. I don't trust myself, I confess it.

MACHIAVELLI. Then I will remind you myself. You would
not fail, no doubt, to speak to me of the principles of the separation
of powers, of liberty of speech and of the press, religious liberty,
individual liberty, the right to congregate, equality before the law,
the inviolability of property and of the home, the right of petition,
free consent to taxation, adequacy of punishment, the non-
retroactivity of the laws; is that enough and do you wish more?

MONTESQUIEU. I think that is much more than is necessary,
Machiavelli, to make your government uneasy.

MACHIAVELLI. There you are wrong, and this is so true that I
see no reason why I should not proclaim these principles; if you
wish, I will even make them the preamble to my constitution.

MONTESQUIEU. You have already proved to me that you are a
great magician.

MACHIAVELLI. There is no magic here, only political *savoir faire*.

MONTESQUIEU. But how, having inscribed these principles at the
head of your constitution, are you going to go about without
applying them?

MACHIAVELLI. Ah! take care, I have told you that I would proclaim these principles, but I have not said I would inscribe them
or even that I would expressly designate them.

MONTESQUIEU. What do you mean?

MACHIAVELLI. I will in no way sum up; I will take care to declare to the people that I recognize and confirm the great
principles of modern justice.

MONTESQUIEU. The import of this reticence escapes me.

MACHIAVELLI. You will see how important it is. If I expressly
enumerated these rights, my freedom of action will be chained to
those I have mentioned; that is what I do not want. In not
naming them, I seem to accord all and I do not specially accord
any; this permits me to set aside later, by means of exception,
those that I may judge dangerous.

MONTESQUIEU. I understand.

MACHIAVELLI. Of these principles, moreover, some belong to
political and constitutional law, others to civil law. That is a
distinction that must always serve as a rule in the exercise of
absolute power. It is to the civil rights that people hold most; I
will not touch them, if I can, and, in this way, one part of my
program at least will be fulfilled.

MONTESQUIEU. And as for the political rights . . . ?

MACHIAVELLI. I have written in my treatise on *The Prince* the
following maxim, which has never ceased to be true: "The governed will always be content with the prince, so long as he
touches neither their possessions nor their honor, and from that
time on he has only to combat the pretensions of a small number
of malcontents, whom he can finish off easily." That is my answer
to your question.

MONTESQUIEU. Strictly, one could find it insufficient; one could
answer you that political rights are also possessions; that it also
is of importance to the honor of the people to maintain it, and that
in disturbing it you are in reality striking at their possessions as
well as their honor. One could add still further that the maintenance of civil rights is linked with the maintenance of political
rights by a close solidarity. Who is to guarantee to the citizens
that if you strip them of political liberty today, you will not strip
them of individual liberty tomorrow; that if you attack their
liberty today, you will not attack their fortunes tomorrow?

MACHIAVELLI. It is certain that the argument has been presented
with much vivacity, but I believe that you also perfectly understand the exaggeration. You seem always to believe that people

of today are starved for liberty. Have you foreseen the case when
they wish no more of it, and can you demand of the princes
more passion for it than the people? Now, in your societies so
deeply liberated, in which the individual only lives in the sphere
of his egoism and his material interests, question the greatest
number, and you will see whether, from every side, you will not
be answered: What has politics to do with me? What has liberty
to do with me? Are not all governments the same? Must not a
government protect itself?

Note this well, moreover, it is not even the people who will
speak thus; it will be the bourgeois, the industrialists, the educated
men, the rich, the literati, all those who are in a position to appreciate your fine doctrines of public rights. They will bless me,
they will cry out that I have saved them, that they are in a
minority position, that they cannot help themselves. Look, the nations have I know not what secret love for the vigorous genius of
force. Of all violent actions marked by the talent of artifice, you
will hear said with an admiration that overcomes all blame: This
is not good, so be it, but it is clever, it is well done, it is strong!
MONTESQUIEU. You are, then, going to penetrate the professional
party with your doctrines?
MACHIAVELLI. No, we have arrived at the execution. I would
certainly have made several more steps if you had not obliged
me to digress. Let us continue.

NINTH DIALOGUE

MONTESQUIEU. You were at the day following a constitution
drawn up by yourself without the consent of the nation.
MACHIAVELLI. Here I stop you; I have not intended to offend
to this point the acknowledged ideas whose influence I am
aware of.
MONTESQUIEU. Really!

MACHIAVELLI. I speak very seriously.

MONTESQUIEU. You expect, then, to associate the nation with *the new fundamental work* that you are preparing?

MACHIAVELLI. Yes, no doubt. That surprises you? I will do much better; I will first have ratified by a popular vote the coup that I have carried against the state; I will say to the people, in suitable terms: All was going wrong; I have smashed everything, I have saved you, do you want me? You are free to condemn me or to absolve me by your vote.

MONTESQUIEU. Free, under the weight of terror and armed force.

MACHIAVELLI. I will be acclaimed.

MONTESQUIEU. I believe that.

MACHIAVELLI. And the popular vote, which I have as an instrument of my power, will become the very base of my government. I will establish a suffrage without distinction of class or tax, with which absolutism will be organized in a single blow.

MONTESQUIEU. Yes, for by one blow you crush at the same time the unity of the family, you lessen suffrage, you annul the preponderance of the enlightened, and you make numbers a blind power which operates at your will.

MACHIAVELLI. I bring about a progress ardently hoped for today by all peoples of Europe: I organize universal suffrage as did Washington in the United States, and the first use I make of it is to submit to it my constitution.

MONTESQUIEU. What! you are going to have it discussed in primary or secondary assemblies?

MACHIAVELLI. Oh! let us forget, I beg of you, your eighteenth century ideas; they are no longer of modern times.

MONTESQUIEU. Well, then in what manner will you have the acceptance of your constitution deliberated? How will the articles embodied in it be discussed?

MACHIAVELLI. But I do not intend that they shall be discussed at all, I thought I told you that.

MONTESQUIEU. I have only followed you on the terrain of the

principles it has pleased you to choose. You spoke to me of the United States; I do not know whether you are a new Washington, but what is certain is that the present constitution of the United States was discussed, deliberated and voted by representatives of the people.

MACHIAVELLI. I beg you, let us not confound the time, the place and the people; we are in Europe; my constitution is presented *en bloc*, it is accepted *en bloc*.

MONTESQUIEU. But in acting thus you are disguising nothing to anyone. How, in voting under these conditions, can the people know what they are doing and to what point it engages them?

MACHIAVELLI. And where have you ever seen that a constitution, really worthy of the name, really durable, has ever been the result of popular deliberation? A constitution must come forth fully armed from the head of one man alone, or it is nothing but a work condemned to oblivion. Without homogeneity, without linking of parties, without practical strength, it will necessarily bear the imprint of all the weakness of sight that have presided at its composition.

A constitution, once more, cannot but be the work of a single man; never have things been done otherwise; I prove it by the history of all the founders of empires, the example of Sesostris, of Solon, Lycurgus, Charlemagne, Frederick II, Peter I.

MONTESQUIEU. That is a chapter of one of your disciples that you are developing there.

MACHIAVELLI. Of whose?

MONTESQUIEU. Of Joseph de Maistre. There are therein certain general reflections that are not without truth but that I find without application. One would say, to hear you, that you are going to draw a people out of chaos or out of the deep night of their first origins. You do not seem to remember that, in the hypothetical nation in which we place ourselves, the country has attained the summit of its civilization, that its public rights are soundly entrenched, and that it is in possession of regular institutions.

MACHIAVELLI. I do not say no; therefore you will see that I need not destroy your institutions from top to bottom to arrive at my goal. It will suffice me to modify the arrangements and to change the methods.

MONTESQUIEU. Explain yourself.

MACHIAVELLI. Just now you gave me a discourse on constitutional politics, I intend to profit from it. I do not, by the way, know as little as is generally believed in Europe about all these ideas of seesaw politics; you can see that by my discourses on Titus-Livy. But let us return to the present problem. You noticed rightly, a moment ago, that in the parliamentary states of Europe the public powers were distributed almost everywhere in the same manner between a certain number of political bodies whose regular working constituted the government.

Thus one finds everywhere, under various names, but with practically uniform attributes, a ministerial organization, a senate, a legislative body, a council of state, a court of cassation; I must not exact from you any useless development of the respective mechanism of these powers, whose secret you know better than I; it is evident that each one of them corresponds to an essential function of the government. You will note *well* that it is the function that I call essential, not the institution. Thus it is necessary that there be a directing power, a moderating power, a legislative power, a regulating power; there can be no doubt of that.

MONTESQUIEU. But, if I understand you well, the various powers are but one in your estimation and you are ready to give it all to a single man by suppressing the institutions.

MACHIAVELLI. Once more it is that which deceives you. One could not act thus without danger . . . especially in France with the fanaticism which reigns there for what you call the principles of '89; but please listen to me carefully: in statics the displacement of a point of support changes the direction of the force, in mechanics the displacement of a spring changes the movement.

And yet in appearance it is the same apparatus, it is the same mechanism. It is equally true in physiology that the temperament depends on the state of the organs. If the organs are modified, the temperament changes. Well, the various institutions of which we have just spoken function, in governmental economics, like real organs of the human body. If I touch the organs, they remain, but the political complexion of the State will be changed. Do you understand that?

MONTESQUIEU. That is not difficult, and no periphrase was necessary for it. You keep names, you put aside things. That is what Augustus did at Rome when he destroyed the Republic. There was always a consulate, a prætorship, a censorship, a tribunal; but there were no longer consuls, prætors, censors, nor tribunes.

MACHIAVELLI. You must admit that one could choose worse models. Anything may be done in politics as long as one flatters public prejudices and respects appearances.

MONTESQUIEU. Don't go back into generalities; get to work, I am following you.

MACHIAVELLI. Don't forget from what personal convictions each one of my acts will spring. In my eyes your parliamentary governments are nothing but schools for dispute, nothing but centers of sterile agitations in the midst of which is exhausted the fertile activity of nations which the court and the press condemn to impotence. Consequently I have no remorse; I start from an elevated point of view and my aim justifies my acts.

For abstract theories I substitute practical reason, the experience of centuries, the example of men of genius who have done great things by the same means, I begin by returning to power its vital conditions.

My first reform at once dwells upon your claim of ministerial responsibility. In centralized countries, like yours, for instance, where opinion instinctively leaves everything to the head of the State, the good as well as the bad, to write at the top of a chart that the sovereign is irresponsible is to lie to public sentiment, is to establish a fiction which will always vanish at the sound of revolutions.

I begin, then, by striking out of my constitution the principle of ministerial responsibility; the sovereign that I institute will alone be responsible to the people.

MONTESQUIEU. Fortunately, there is no circumlocution there.

MACHIAVELLI. In your parliamentary system the representatives of the nation have, as you explained it to me, the initiative in projects of laws either alone or concurrently with executive power; well, that is the source of the most serious abuses, for in such an order of things each deputy could, at any time, substitute himself for the government in presenting laws insufficiently studied, insufficiently examined from all angles; why, with parliamentary initiative, the Chamber could, if it wished, overthrow the government. I strike out parliamentary initiative. The sovereign alone may propose laws.

MONTESQUIEU. I see that you are taking the best method of entering the course of absolute power; for in a State where the initiative of law belongs only to the sovereign, it is practically the sovereign who is the sole legislator; but before you go further, I should like to make an objection. You wish to establish yourself on a rock, and I find you seated on sand.

MACHIAVELLI. How?

MONTESQUIEU. Did you not take popular suffrage as the basis of your power?

MACHIAVELLI. Certainly.

MONTESQUIEU. Well, you are nothing but a representative to be recalled at the will of the people in whom alone resides the true sovereignty. You thought you could make use of this principle to support your authority; don't you see that you could easily be overthrown? On the other hand, you declared yourself solely responsible; do you, then, consider yourself an angel? But be so, if you wish; you will still be blamed for any evil which may arise, and you will perish at the first crisis.

MACHIAVELLI. You anticipate: the objection comes too soon, but I shall answer it at once since you force me to it. You are strangely mistaken if you believe that I have not foreseen your argument. If my power were threatened, it could be only because of factions. I am guarded against them by two basic rights which I have placed in my constitution.

MONTESQUIEU. And what are those rights?

MACHIAVELLI. The appeal to the people, the right to put the country in a state of siege. I am head of the army, I have the entire public force in my hands; at the first insurrection against my power, the bayonets would be an answer to resistance and I would again find in the ballot-box a new sanction of my authority.

MONTESQUIEU. You have unanswerable arguments; but let us get back to the legislative body which you have established. On this point I see complications; you have deprived this assembly of the parliamentary initiative, but it still has the right to vote the laws which you will present for its adoption. Undoubtedly you do not expect to permit it to exercise this right?

MACHIAVELLI. You are more suspicious than I, for I confess that I see nothing wrong with it. Since no one but myself may present the law, I have nothing to fear that anything may be done against my power. I have the key of the tabernacle. Besides, as I have already told you, it is a part of my plan to allow the institutions to exist—in appearance. Only I must state that I do not mean to allow to the Chamber what you call the right of amendment. It is evident that with the exercise of such a faculty, there is no law which could not be diverted from its original goal and the disposition of which is not capable of being changed. The law is accepted or rejected—no other alternative.

MONTESQUIEU. But no more is necessary to overthrow you: it would suffice merely that the legislative assembly systematically reject all your proposed laws or simply that it refuse to vote the taxes.

MACHIAVELLI. You know perfectly well that things cannot happen like that. Any chamber which would obstruct by such an act of temerity the movement of public affairs would commit suicide. Besides, I would have a thousand means of neutralising the power of such an assembly. I would reduce by half the number of representatives and I would, consequently, have half the amount of political passions to combat. I would reserve for myself the nominations of the presidents and vice-presidents who direct the deliberations. In place of permanent sessions, I would reduce them to several months. Above all I would do one thing which is of very great importance and the practice of which has already begun, I hear: I would abolish the free services of the legislative mandate; the deputies would receive a fee so that their duties would, to some extent, be salaried. I consider this innovation the most certain method of putting the representatives of the nation in power; I need not go into details about that for you; the efficacy of the method is self-evident. I may add that, as chief of the executive power, I have the right to call together or to dissolve the legislative body, and that in the event of dissolution, I would take advantage of the longest delay before calling together a new representation. I understand perfectly that the legislative assembly could not, without danger, remain independent of my power, but be reassured: we shall soon come across other practical means of linking it up. Do these constitutional details satisfy you? Or do you want more?

MONTESQUIEU. No, that is not at all necessary and you may go on now to the organisation of the Senate.

MACHIAVELLI. I see that you have very well understood that there lies the principal part of my work, the keystone of my constitution.

MONTESQUIEU. I really do not know what else you can do for, up to now, I consider you completely master of the Senate.

MACHIAVELLI. It pleases you to say that; but, in reality, sovereignty could not be established on such superficial bases. At the side of the ruler there must be bodies which impress by the brilliance of their titles and their dignities and by the personal example of those who compose them. It is not wise that the sovereign be seen to have a hand in everything; he must be able, if necessary, to cover his actions under the authority of the great judges who surround the throne.

MONTESQUIEU. It is easy to see that it is for this rôle that you destine the Senate and the Council of State.

MACHIAVELLI. It is impossible to conceal anything from you.

MONTESQUIEU. You speak of the throne: I see that you are king and we are just now in a republic. The transition has not been effected.

MACHIAVELLI. The illustrious French publicist cannot require me to stop for such details of execution: from the moment that I have full power, the hour when I shall have myself proclaimed king is no more than a question of opportunity. I shall be king before or after having promulgated my constitution—that is of little consequence.

MONTESQUIEU. That is true. Let us get back to the organisation of the Senate.

TENTH DIALOGUE

MACHIAVELLI. In the profound studies which you must have made for the composition of your memorable work on *The Causes of the Grandeur and of the Decadence of the Romans*, you must certainly have noticed the rôle played by the Senate in connection with the Emperors, starting from the reign of Augustus.

MONTESQUIEU. That, if you will permit me to say so, is a point which historical researches seem to me not yet to have completely clarified. This much is certain, that up until the last days of the Republic, the Roman Senate was an autonomous institution, vested with great privileges, having its own powers; that was the secret of its power, of the depth of its political traditions and of the grandeur which it impressed on the Republic. From the time of Augustus, the Senate is no more than an instrument in the hands of the Emperors, but it is not clear by what succession of acts they succeeded in stripping it of its power.

MACHIAVELLI. It is not precisely to elucidate this point of history that I beg you to return to this period of the Empire. This question for the moment does not interest me; all that I wished to tell you is that the Senate which I picture must fill, at the side of the prince, a political rôle analogous to that of the Roman Senate in the times which followed the fall of the Republic.

MONTESQUIEU. Well, but at this period the law was no longer voted in the popular comitia, but by senatorial decree; is that what you were thinking of?

MACHIAVELLI. Not at all: that would not conform at all to modern principles of constitutional law.

MONTESQUIEU. What thanks are due you for such a scruple!

MACHIAVELLI. Oh, I have no need of that to decree what I think necessary. No legislative order, you know, could go forth except at my suggestion, and besides I make decrees which have the force of laws.

MONTESQUIEU. That is true, you have forgotten that point which is by no means trivial; but I do not quite see for what purposes you are keeping the Senate.

MACHIAVELLI. Placed in the highest constitutional spheres, its direct intervention need appear only under solemn circumstances; if it were necessary, for instance, to alter the fundamental pact or if the sovereignty were placed in danger.

MONTESQUIEU. This language is prophetic. You like to prepare your effects.

MACHIAVELLI. The fixed idea of your modern constituents has been, up to the present, to wish to foresee all, to provide for all in the charters which they give to the people. I would not fall into such an error; I would not wish to enclose myself within an impassable circle; I would settle only that which it is impossible to leave uncertain; I would allow sufficient room for change so that, in great crises, there would be other means of safety than the disastrous expedient of revolution.

MONTESQUIEU. You speak wisely.

MACHIAVELLI. As for that which concerns the Senate, I would write into my constitution: "The Senate has the power to decide, by a senatus-consultum, everything which has not been foreseen by the constitution and which is necessary to its progress; it has the power to define the meaning of the articles of the constitution which may give rise to different interpretations; it has the power to maintain or to annul all the acts which are reported to it as unconstitutional by the government or denounced by the petition of the citizens; it has the power to lay the foundations of projects of law of a great national interest; it has the power to propose amendments to the constitution which will be enacted by a senatus-consultum."

MONTESQUIEU. That is all very fine and it is truly a Roman Senate. But I should like to make several remarks about your constitution: it will, I gather, be drawn up in very vague and ambiguous terms since you judge in advance that the articles which it contains will be capable of various interpretations.

MACHIAVELLI. No, but one must foresee everything.

MONTESQUIEU. I thought, on the contrary, that your principle in such a matter was to avoid foreseeing and providing for everything.

MACHIAVELLI. The illustrious president has not haunted the palace of Themis without profit, nor has he worn in vain the cap of president of a court of justice. My words had no other meaning than this: One must foresee what is essential.

MONTESQUIEU. Be good enough to tell me this: Has your Senate, which is the interpreter and guardian of the fundamental pact, a power of its own?

MACHIAVELLI. Decidedly not.

MONTESQUIEU. Then all that the Senate does will really be done by you?

MACHIAVELLI. I do not contradict that.

MONTESQUIEU. And all that it will interpret will really be interpreted by you; all that it will modify will really be modified by you; all that it will annul will really be annulled by you?

MACHIAVELLI. I admit it.

MONTESQUIEU. That is as much as to say that you reserve the right to destroy what you have done, to take away what you have given, to change your constitution, either for the worse or for the better, or even to make it disappear completely if you judge it necessary. I do not conjecture at your intentions or at the motives which might make you act in certain given circumstances; I only ask you where the citizens would find even the weakest guarantee in the midst of such despotism, and especially how they would ever agree to submit to it?

MACHIAVELLI. I see that your philosophic sensitiveness is returning. Rest assured, I would not bring any modification to the fundamental basis of my constitution without submitting these modifications to the acceptance of the people by means of universal suffrage.

MONTESQUIEU. But it would still be you who would be judge of the question as to whether the modification which you propose bears within it the fundamental character which would cause it to be submitted for the approval of the people. I still suppose that you would not pass by a decree or by a senatus-consultum what should be passed by a plebiscite. Would you surrender your constitutional amendments to general discussion? Would you allow them to be deliberated upon in the popular assembly?

MACHIAVELLI. By no means. If a debate over constitutional articles were ever engaged in before the popular assemblies, nothing could prevent the people from examining everything in virtue of its right of removal, and the next day there would be a revolution in the streets.

MONTESQUIEU. You are logical at least: then the constitutional amendments are to be presented in bulk and accepted in bulk?

MACHIAVELLI. Just so.

MONTESQUIEU. Well, then, I believe that we may pass on to the organization of the Council of State.

MACHIAVELLI. Really, you direct debates with the consummate precision of a President of a supreme court. I forgot to tell you that I would appoint the Senate as I appointed the legislative body.

MONTESQUIEU. That is understood.

MACHIAVELLI. And it is needless to add that I should also reserve to myself the right to nominate the Presidents and the Vice-Presidents of this assembly. Concerning the Council of State, I shall be more brief. Your modern institutions are instruments of centralisation so powerful that it is almost impossible to make use of them without exercising sovereign authority.

According to your own principles, what, in fact, is the Council of State? It is a sham political body destined to put a considerable power into the hands of the Prince, the customary power which is a sort of discretionary one which can serve at will to make real laws.

The Council of State is, I am told, invested in France with a special privilege perhaps even more excessive. In litigious matters, it may, I am assured, claim by right of evocation, and recover in its own authority, before the ordinary courts of justice, the knowledge of all litigations that seem to have an administrative character. Thus, to characterise briefly the exceptional in this latter privilege, the courts of justice must refuse to judge when it is a question of an act of the administrative authority, and the administrative authority may, in like case, take it out of the hands of the courts in order to leave the decision to the Council of State.

Now, once more, what is the Council of State? Has it any power of its own? Is it independent of the sovereign? Not at all. It is nothing but a Draughting Committee. When the Council of State makes a law, it is really the sovereign who makes it; when it renders a judgment, it is the sovereign who renders it, or, as you say nowadays, it is the administration, the administration which is judge and interested party in its own cause. Do you know anything stronger than that and do you believe that it would take much to place absolute power in those States where such institutions are already organized?

MONTESQUIEU. Your criticism is very just, I admit; but, since the Council of State is, in itself, an excellent institution, nothing is easier than to give it the necessary independence by isolating it, to a certain extent, from power. That, undoubtedly, is not what you will do.

MACHIAVELLI. Indeed, I shall maintain the type of unity in the institution where I find it and I shall bring it where it does not exist, by tightening the bonds of a solidarity which I regard as indispensable.

We have not wasted any time, you see, for here is my constitution finished.

MONTESQUIEU. Already?

MACHIAVELLI. A few contrivances wisely arranged are sufficient to change completely the progress of power. This part of my program is complete.

MONTESQUIEU. I thought you still had something to say about the highest court of appeal.

MACHIAVELLI. What I have to say to you can better be said at another time.

MONTESQUIEU. It is true that if we evaluate the sum of the powers which lie in your hands, you ought to begin to be satisfied.

To sum up:

You make laws:

1. In the form of propositions to the legislative body;
2. In the form of decrees;
3. In the form of senatorial decrees;
4. In the form of general regulations;
5. In the form of resolutions at the Council of State;
6. In the form of ministerial regulations;
7. And, finally, in the form of coups d'état.

MACHIAVELLI. You seem to have the idea that what still remains for me to do is not exactly the most difficult to accomplish.

MONTESQUIEU. That is, indeed, my idea.

MACHIAVELLI. Then you have not sufficiently noticed that my constitution was silent about a mass of acquired rights which would be incompatible with the new order of things that I have just established. There is, for instance, the freedom of the press; the right of association; the independence of the magistracy; the right of suffrage, of the election, by communes, of municipal officers; the institution of civic guards and many more things which will have to disappear or else be greatly modified.

MONTESQUIEU. But did you not recognize all these rights implicitly, since you solemnly recognized the principles of which they are but the application?

MACHIAVELLI. As I have told you, I recognized no principle and no right in particular; moreover, the measures which I shall take will only be the exceptions to the rule.

MONTESQUIEU. The exceptions which prove it—that is true.

MACHIAVELLI. But, to do that, I must be careful to choose the right moment, for an error there might ruin everything. I wrote in the treatise of *The Prince* a maxim which should serve as a rule of conduct in such cases: "The usurper of a state must commit, all at one time, the acts of severity which his safety necessitates, for later he will not be able to change either for the better or the worse; if it is for the worse that you have to act, you are too late once luck is against you; if it is for the better, your subjects will not be grateful for a change which they will consider forced on them."

The very next day after the promulgation of my constitution, I shall issue a succession of decrees, having the force of laws, which will suppress at a single stroke all the liberties and rights the exercise of which might be dangerous.

MONTESQUIEU. The moment would indeed be well chosen. The country would still be terror-stricken at your coup d'état. As for your constitution, nothing would be refused you, since you would be in a position to take everything; and as for your decrees, there would be nothing to grant you, since you ask for nothing and take all.

MACHIAVELLI. You have a quick tongue.

MONTESQUIEU. Not so quick as your action. In spite of your strength and penetration, I must admit that I have difficulty in believing that the country would not rise up in a second coup d'état prepared behind your back.

MACHIAVELLI. The country would voluntarily close its eyes; for, according to my hypothesis, it would be tired of strife, it would yearn for rest like the sand in the desert after the shower which follows the storm.

MONTESQUIEU. You are merely making beautiful figures of speech; it is too much.

MACHIAVELLI. I hasten to add that the liberties which I suppress I would promise solemnly to restore after the agitation dies down.

MONTESQUIEU. I believe they would have to wait forever.

MACHIAVELLI. That is possible.

MONTESQUIEU. It is certain, for your maxims permit the prince not to keep his word if he finds it to his interest.

MACHIAVELLI. Don't be in a hurry to speak; you shall see the use I expect to make of this promise; I should soon take it upon myself to pass for the most liberal man in my kingdom.

MONTESQUIEU. That would be a startling thing for which I am not in the least prepared; in the meanwhile, you would directly suppress all the liberties.

MACHIAVELLI. Directly is no word for a statesman; I would suppress nothing directly; it is just at this point that the fox's skin must be sewed on to the lion's skin. Of what use is politics if one could not reach by oblique means the goal which cannot be attained by a straight line? The foundations of my establishments are laid, the forces are ready, all that is necessary is to get them going. I shall do that with all the discretion which the new constitutional customs permit. It is here that one naturally places the stratagems of government and of legislation which prudence recommends to the prince.

MONTESQUIEU. I see that we are entering a new phase: I am prepared to listen.

ELEVENTH DIALOGUE

MACHIAVELLI. You wisely mention, in your *Esprit des Lois,* that the word liberty is a word to which one attaches greatly varied meanings. I am told that the following proposition may be found in your book: "Liberty is the right to do that which the laws permit." *(Esprit des Lois,* p. 123, book XI, chap. III.)

I am well pleased with that definition which I consider a good one, and I assure you that my laws will permit only what is necessary. Where would you like me to begin?

MONTESQUIEU. I should not mind seeing first of all how you will defend yourself against the press.

MACHIAVELLI. You have put your finger on the most delicate part of my task. The system which I conceive is, in this respect, as vast in its applications as it is diversified. Here, fortunately, I have full scope; I may decide and command with absolute security and almost without raising any discussion.

MONTESQUIEU. How so, if I may ask?

MACHIAVELLI. Because, in the majority of the parliamentary nations, the press has the faculty of making itself hated, since it is at the service only of violent, selfish, and exclusive passions, since it disparages through prejudice, since it is mercenary, since it is unjust, since it is without generosity and without patriotism; and, last but not least, since you will never be able to make the masses of the people understand of what value it may be.

MONTESQUIEU. Oh, if you are looking for grievances against the press, it is easy enough to amass a great many. If you ask of what value it may be, that is another thing. Briefly, it hinders the arbitrary use of power; it compels the government to act constitutionally; it forces the guardians of public authority to be honest, to be moderate, and to respect themselves and others. Finally, in a word, it gives to the oppressed the means of complaining and of being heard. One pardons much to an institution which, despite so many abuses, necessarily renders such services.

MACHIAVELLI. Yes, I am familiar with these pleadings, but make them understood, if you can, by the greatest number; count those who will be interested in the fate of the press, and you will see.

MONTESQUIEU. That is why it should be just as well for you to go on at once to the practical methods of *muzzling* the press; I believe that is the word for it.

MACHIAVELLI. Yes, it is just the word for it; besides, it isn't only journalism that I intend to repress.

MONTESQUIEU. It is printing itself.

MACHIAVELLI. You are beginning to use irony.

MONTESQUIEU. In just another moment you are going to take that away from me since you expect to shackle the press in all forms.

MACHIAVELLI. One is completely disarmed by such playfulness when it is so clever; but you will understand perfectly that it would hardly be worth while escaping from the attacks of journalism if one had to remain exposed to those of books.

MONTESQUIEU. Well, let us begin with journalism.

MACHIAVELLI. If I decided to suppress newspapers purely and simply, I would very imprudently shock public sensibility which it is always dangerous to oppose openly; I should proceed by a series of provisions which would seem to be simple measures of precaution and policy.

I would decree that in the future no newspaper could be founded except by authorization of the government; right there you have the danger arrested in its development; for, as you can easily understand, the newspapers which would be authorized would be only those organs devoted to the government.

MONTESQUIEU. But, since you are going into all details, allow me this question: the spirit of a newspaper changes with the personnel of its editorial staff; how would you get rid of a staff hostile to your power?

MACHIAVELLI. The objection is very weak, for, in the last analysis, if I so wished, I would not authorize the publication of any new sheet; but I have other plans, as you will see. You ask how I should counteract a hostile editorial staff? In the simplest manner; I would add that the authorization of the government is necessary for any changes made in the personnel of the chief or sub-editors of a newspaper.

MONTESQUIEU. But the old papers, which have remained enemies of your government, and whose staff has not changed, will speak aloud.

MACHIAVELLI. Wait! I would reach all newspapers, present or future, by fiscal measures which would check when needed all publicity enterprises; I would subject political journals to what you call nowadays the stamp and security. The business of the press would soon become so unremunerative, thanks to the raising of these taxes, that no one would go into it unknowingly.

MONTESQUIEU. The remedy is insufficient, because political parties spare no expenses.

MACHIAVELLI. Calm yourself—I have something with which to close their mouths: here come the repressive measures. There are some states in Europe where the knowledge of the misdemeanors of the press has been given over to the jury to decide upon. I know of no measure more deplorable than that, since it only stirs up opinion in connection with the most insignificant nonsense of journalists. The misdemeanors of the press have such an elastic character, the writer may disguise his attacks under such varied and subtle forms that it is not even possible to convey to the courts the knowledge of these offenses. The courts will always remain armed, that goes without saying, but the usual restraining force must be in the hands of the administration.

MONTESQUIEU. Then there are offenses which will not come under the jurisdiction of the courts, or, rather, which you will strike from both sides: from the courts of justice and from the administration?

MACHIAVELLI. Such a misfortune! What solicitude for a few wicked little journalists who insist on attacking and disparaging everything, who act with the government like the bandits that travelers meet on the road. They are always putting themselves beyond the law; what if one did outlaw them a little!

MONTESQUIEU. So it is upon them alone that your restrictions will fall?

MACHIAVELLI. I cannot undertake to do that, because these people are like the heads of the hydra of Lerna; when you cut ten, fifty more grow. I should put the blame principally on the newspapers as publicity undertakings. I would speak to them as follows: "I could have suppressed you all. I did not. I can still do it. I am going to let you exist, but naturally there is one condition, and that is that you do not obstruct my progress or diminish my power. I do not want to have to bring action against you every day, nor expound the law to restrain your infractions; neither can I have an army of censors whose duty it is to examine the night before what you print the next day. You have pens, write; but remember this: I claim, for myself and my representatives, the right to judge when I shall be attacked. No subtleties. When you attack me, I shall be aware of it and you yourselves will be well aware of it; in such a case, I will do justice myself, not at once, for I want to proceed circumspectly; I shall warn you once, twice; the third time your papers will be suppressed."

MONTESQUIEU. I see with astonishment that it is not exactly the journalist who is hit in this system; it is the newspaper, the ruin of which includes the interests that are grouped about it.

MACHIAVELLI. Let them group themselves elsewhere! We do not bother about such trifles. As I have just told you, my administration will not interfere with the sentences passed by the court. Two convictions in one year will automatically bring about the suppression of the paper. I would not rely on that alone, I would say to the newspapers, in a decree or a law: "Reduced to the greatest caution in matters that concern you, do not expect to arouse opinion by commentaries on the debates in my chambers; I forbid you to give an accurate account of legislative proceedings, I forbid you to give even an accurate account of the judiciary debates in connection with the press. Nor must you count on making an impression on the public by imaginary news from abroad; I shall punish false news by corporal punishment whether they are published in good or in bad faith."

MONTESQUIEU. That seems to me a little hard, since newspapers, being no longer able, without the greatest of dangers, to give themselves up to political valuations, will not be able to exist except by news. Now, when a paper publishes some news, it seems to me very difficult to insist on its veracity, since very often the paper can answer for it only to a certain extent, and when it is morally sure of its truth, material proof may be lacking.

MACHIAVELLI. Then they will look twice before stirring up the public—that is as it should be.

MONTESQUIEU. But I see something else. If you cannot be fought by newspapers in the country, they can fight you by papers abroad. All the dissatisfactions, all the hatred will be written at the gates of your kingdom; they will throw across the frontier fiery newspapers and pamphlets.

MACHIAVELLI. Ah, here you touch upon a point which I expect to take care of in the most rigorous manner, because the foreign press is indeed very dangerous. First of all, the introduction or circulation in the kingdom of unauthorized papers or pamphlets will be punished by imprisonment, and the sentence will be sufficiently severe to do away with any desire for it. Then, those of my subjects convicted of having written abroad anything against the government will be sought out, upon their return to the kingdom, and severely punished. It is really an infamy to write against the government when one is out of the country.

MONTESQUIEU. That depends. But the foreign press of the bordering states will have something to say.

MACHIAVELLI. You think so? We are supposing that I am reigning over a great kingdom. The little states which border my frontier will tremble before me, I assure you. In case of attack against my government, by the press or otherwise, I shall make them surrender the laws which cover their own nationals.

MONTESQUIEU. I see that I was right in saying, in the *Esprit des Lois,* that the frontiers of a despot ought to be laid waste. Civilization ought not penetrate. Your subjects, I am sure, will not know their history. According to Benjamin Constant, you will make of the kingdom an island where one will be ignorant of what goes on in Europe, and you will make of the capital another island where one will be ignorant of what goes on in the provinces.

MACHIAVELLI. I do not want my kingdom to be disturbed by noises from abroad. How could foreign news arrive? By a few agencies which centralize the news which is transmitted to them from the four quarters of the globe. Well, I suppose these agencies could be paid, and then they would give out no news except by order of the government.

MONTESQUIEU. That is a good idea; now you may go on to the regulation of books.

MACHIAVELLI. That bothers me very little, for in a period where journalism has assumed such tremendous proportions, hardly anyone reads books any more. But I don't by any means intend to give them a free hand. In the first place, I shall oblige those who wish to exercise the profession of printer, editor or librarian to secure a seal, that is, an authorization which the government may always withdraw, either directly or by decisions of the court.

MONTESQUIEU. But, in that case, these business people will be public officials. The instruments of thought will become the instruments of power!

MACHIAVELLI. You will not complain, I imagine, for things were like that in your time, too, under parliamentary rule; one must keep old customs when they are good. I will return to fiscal measures; I will extend to books the stamp which affects the newspapers, or rather I shall impose the burden of a stamp on those books which have not a certain number of pages. A book, for instance, which has not two or three hundred pages will not be a book, it will be only a brochure. I believe that you readily grasp the advantage of this scheme: on one hand I reduce, by this tax, the swarm of little writings which are like the appendages of journalism; on the other hand, I force those who wish to escape the tax to write long and costly compositions which will scarcely sell or which will barely be read in this form. Nowadays there are hardly any but a few poor devils who have the conscience to write books; they will give it up. The economic question will discourage literary vanity and penal law will disarm printing itself, for I shall make the publisher and the printer criminally responsible for the contents of the books. If there are writers daring enough to write books against the government, they must not be able to find anyone to publish them. The effects of this wholesome intimidation will indirectly re-establish a censor that the government itself could not exercise because of the disrepute into which this preventive measure has fallen. Before publishing new works, the printers and the publishers will consult one another, they will be informed; they will produce books which are in demand, and in this manner the government will always be usefully informed of the publications which are being prepared against it; it will bring about a preliminary attachment when it deems necessary and will report the authors to the courts.

MONTESQUIEU. You told me you would not touch civil rights. You do not seem to doubt that it is the freedom of industry that you have just hit by this legislation; the right of property, too, is involved—that will come in its turn.

MACHIAVELLI. These are but words.

MONTESQUIEU. Then you are through with the press, I gather.

MACHIAVELLI. Oh, not at all!

MONTESQUIEU. Why, what is there left?

MACHIAVELLI. The other half of the task.

TWELFTH DIALOGUE

MACHIAVELLI. Up to now I have showed you only the defensive part, so to speak, of the organic régime which I would impose on the press; now I must make you understand that I would know how to employ this institution to the advantage of my power. I dare say that no government, up to the present, has had a bolder conception than the one of which I am going to speak to you. In parliamentary countries, it is almost always because of the press that the governments fail; well, I foresee the possibility of counteracting the press by the press itself. Since journalism is such a great force, do you know what my government would do? It would turn journalist, it would become journalism incarnate.

MONTESQUIEU. Truly, you treat me to strange surprises! It is a panorama of infinite variety that you spread out before me; I am very curious, I must admit, to see how you will go about putting into effect this new program.

MACHIAVELLI. Much less effort of imagination is necessary than you think. I shall count the number of newspapers which represent what you call the opposition. If there are ten for the opposition, I shall have twenty for the government; if there are twenty, I shall have forty; if there are forty, I shall have eighty. You can readily understand now to what use I will put the faculty which I reserved for myself to authorize the creation of new political papers.

MONTESQUIEU. Really, that is very simple.

MACHIAVELLI. Not quite as simple as you think, though, because the masses must have no suspicion of these tactics; the scheme would lose its point, public opinion would shy at newspapers which openly defended my policies.

I shall divide in three or four categories the papers devoted to my power. In first rank I shall put a certain number of news-papers whose tone will be frankly official and which, at any encounter, will defend my deeds to the death. I tell you right from the start, these will not be the ones which will have the greatest influence on public opinion. In the second rank I shall place another series of newspapers the character of which will be no more than officious and the purposes of which will be to rally to my power that mass of luke-warm and indifferent persons who accept without scruple what is established but who do not go beyond that in their political faith.

It is in the newspaper categories which follow that will be found the most powerful supporters of my power. Here, the official or officious tone is completely dropped, in appearance, that is, for the newspapers of which I am going to speak will all be attached by the same chain to my government, a chain visible for some, invisible for others. I shall not attempt to tell you how many of them there will be, for I shall count on a devoted organ in each opinion, in each party; I shall have an aristocratic organ in the aristocratic party, a republican organ in the republican party, a revolutionary organ in the revolutionary party, an anarchist organ, if necessary, in the anarchist party. Like the god Vishnu my press will have a hundred arms, and these arms will stretch out their hands to all the possible shades of opinion over the whole surface of the country. Everyone will be of my party whether he knows it or not. Those who think they are speaking their own language will be speaking mine, those who think they are agitating their own party will be agitating mine, those who think they are marching under their own flag will be marching under mine.

MONTESQUIEU. Are these conceptions realizable or merely phantasmagoria? It is enough to make one dizzy.

MACHIAVELLI. Spare your strength, for you have not yet come to the end.

MONTESQUIEU. I am only wondering how you will be able to direct and rally all these military forces of publicity secretly hired by your government.

MACHIAVELLI. That is only a question of organization, you must understand; I shall institute, for instance, under the title of division of printing and the press, a center of operation to which one will come for orders. So, for those who will be only half in on the secret of this scheme, it will be a strange spectacle: they will see sheets, devoted to my government, which will attack me, which will shout, which will stir up a turmoil of confusion.

MONTESQUIEU. This is beyond me; I no longer follow.

MACHIAVELLI. And yet it is not too difficult to understand; you will notice that the foundation and the principles of my government will never be attacked by the newspapers of which I am speaking; they will never go in for anything more than a polemic skirmish, a dynastic opposition within the narrowest limits.

MONTESQUIEU. And what advantage do you find in that?

MACHIAVELLI. Your question is rather ingenuous. The result, considerable enough, will be to make the greatest number say: "But you see, one is free, one may speak under this régime, it is unjustly attacked; instead of repressing, as it might do, it tolerates these things!" Another result, not less important, will be to provoke, for instance, such observations as these: "You see to what point the foundations and principles of this government commands the respect of all; here are newspapers which allow themselves the greatest freedom of speech; well, they never attack the established institutions. They must be above the injustices of human passions, since the very enemies of the government cannot help rendering homage to them."

MONTESQUIEU. That, I confess, is truly machiavellian.

MACHIAVELLI. You do me a great honor, but something better is yet to come: With the aid of the secret loyalty of these public papers, I may say that I can direct at will the general opinion in all questions of internal or external politics. I arouse or lull the minds, I reassure or disturb them, I plead for and against, true and false. I have a fact announced and I have it refuted, according to the circumstances; in this way I plumb public thought, I gather the impression produced. I try combinations, projects, sudden decisions; in other words, I send out what you call in

France feelers. I fight my enemies as I please without ever compromising my power, since, after having the papers make certain statements, I may, when necessary, deny them most energetically; I solicit opinion on certain resolutions, I urge it on or I hold it back, I always have my finger on its pulse; it reflects, without knowing it, my personal impressions, and it occasionally is astonished at being so constantly in accord with its sovereign. Then they say that I have the feeling for the people, that there is a secret and mysterious sympathy which unites me to the movements of my people.

MONTESQUIEU. These various projects seem to be ideally perfect. Nevertheless I should like to comment on something, but very timidly this time: If you depart from the silence of China, if you permit, for the furthering of your designs, the provisional opposition which you have just spoken of on the part of your army of newspapers, I really do not understand how you can prevent the non-affiliated newspapers from answering, by overwhelming thrusts, the provocations the source of which they will guess. Do you not think that they will finally succeed in raising some of the veils which cover so many mysterious forces? When they will learn the secret of this comedy, will you be able to stop them from laughing at it? The game seems to me a little dangerous.

MACHIAVELLI. Not at all; I must tell you that I have spent a good part of my time at this point to examine the strength and the weakness of these schemes; I am well informed on all that has to do with the conditions of existence of the press in parliamentary countries. You must know that journalism is a sort of free-masonry; those who live by it are all more or less attached to one another by the bonds of professional discretion; like the ancient soothsayers, they do not readily divulge the secret of their oracles. They would gain nothing by betraying one another, for the majority of them have some more or less shameful secrets. It is quite probable, I agree, that at the heart of the capital, within a certain radius of people, these things will be no mystery; but, everywhere else, no one will suspect, and the great majority of the nation will follow, with the utmost confidence, the trail of the leaders which I will have given them.

What does it matter to me that, in the capital, a certain set will be aware of the tricks of my journalism? It is in the provinces that the greatest part of its influence will be felt. There I shall always have the barometer of opinion which is necessary for me, and there every one of my strokes will have the desired effect. The provincial press will belong to me entirely, there can be no contradiction nor discussion as to that; from the center of the administration where I shall hold court, they will transmit regularly to the governor of each province the order to have the newspapers speak in such and such a way, so that at the same moment, all over the country, such and such an influence will be produced, such and such an impulse will be given, often even before the capital becomes cognizant of it. You see by this that the opinion of the capital is not enough to preoccupy me. When necessary, it will learn too late about the external movement which would surround it without its knowledge.

MONTESQUIEU. The chain of your ideas carries everything away with such force that you make me lose the consciousness of a last objection which I wanted to refer to you. The fact still remains, in spite of all you have just said, that there still is in the capital a certain number of independent newspapers. It will be practically impossible for them to talk politics, that is certain, but they may still wage a war of details. Your administration will not be perfect; the development of absolute power brings with it a quantity of grievances of which even the sovereign is not the cause; for all the acts of your representatives which will touch private interests, you will be held guilty; they will complain, they will attack your representatives, you will necessarily be considered responsible for them, and esteem for you will decrease gradually.

MACHIAVELLI. I am not afraid of that.

MONTESQUIEU. It is true that you have increased to such an extent the means of repression that you have but to choose your method.

MACHIAVELLI. That is not what I was going to say; I do not even wish to be obliged to have ceaseless recourse to repression: I wish, through a simple injunction, to make it possible to put an end to any discussion on a subject concerning the administration.

MONTESQUIEU. And how do you expect to go about that?

MACHIAVELLI. I shall oblige the newspapers to put at the head of their columns the corrections which the government will impart to them; the representatives of the administration will give them notes in which they will be told categorically: "You have asserted such and such a fact, it is not exact; you made such and such a criticism, you were unjust, you were improper, you were wrong, do not forget it." That will be, as you see, a loyal and open censure.

MONTESQUIEU. To which, of course, there will be no reply.

MACHIAVELLI. Obviously not; discussion will be closed.

MONTESQUIEU. In this way you will always have the last word, and you will have it without the use of violence—it is very ingenious. You put it very well a short time ago when you said your government is journalism incarnate.

MACHIAVELLI. Just as I do not wish the country to be disturbed by rumors from abroad, so I do not wish it to be so by rumors from within, even the simplest private news. When there will be some extraordinary suicide, some big money question a little too suspicious, some misdeed by a public official, I shall forbid the papers to write of it. Silence about these things shows more respect for public honesty than does scandal.

MONTESQUIEU. And during this time you yourself will be a journalist with a vengeance?

MACHIAVELLI. I must. To make use of the press, to make use of it in all its forms: such is, today, the law of the powers which wish to exist. It is very singular, but it is so. And I shall engage in it to a much greater extent than you can imagine.

In order to understand the breadth of my system, it is neces-

sary to see how the language of my press is called to co-operate
with the official acts of my politics: I wish, suppose, to bring to
light the solution to a certain external or internal complication;
this solution, recommended by my newspapers which for several
months have been guiding public opinion each in its own way,
is brought forth one fine day as an official event. You know with
what discretion and what ingenious consideration authoritative
documents must be drawn up on important matters: the problem
to be solved in such a case is to give a certain amount of satisfaction to each party. Well, then, every one of my newspapers,
according to its tendency, will strive to persuade its party that
the resolution that has been made is the one which favors itself
most. That which will not be written in an official document, will
be brought to light by means of interpretation; that which is only
indicated, the officious newspapers will construe more openly,
and the democratic and revolutionary papers will shout from the
housetops; and while they are disputing and giving the most
varied interpretations to my acts, my government will always be
able to answer to one and all: "You are mistaken about my
intentions, you have misconstrued my declarations; I only meant
this or that." The main thing is never to be found in contradiction with oneself.

MONTESQUIEU. What! After what you have just told me, you
make such a claim?

MACHIAVELLI. Certainly, and your astonishment proves that you
did not understand me. It is necessary to make words, rather
than deeds, harmonize. How do you expect the masses of the
people to judge if it is reason which rules its government? It is
sufficient to tell it to them. I wish, then, that the various phases
of my policies be presented as the development of a single thought
clinging to an unchanging goal. Every event, foreseen or unforeseen, will be a result wisely brought about, the deviations of
direction will only be the different facets of the same question,
the various roads which lead to the same goal, the diversified
means to an identical solution pursued unceasingly in the face of

obstacles. The most recent event will be given as the logical conclusion to the previous ones.

MONTESQUIEU. In truth, you are admirable! What strength of mind! What activity!

MACHIAVELLI. Every day my newspapers will be filled with official speeches, with accountings, with references to the ministers and references to the sovereign. I shall not forget that I am living in a period where it is believed that all social problems may be settled by industry, and where the amelioration of the fate of the working classes is constantly being sought. I shall interest myself all the more in these questions inasmuch as they are a very fortunate counter-irritant to absorption in internal politics. When it comes to the peoples of the south, the governments must appear to be unceasingly occupied; the masses are satisfied to be inactive on condition that those who govern them give them the spectacle of a continual activity, a sort of fever; that they constantly attract their attention by novelties, surprises, theatrical strokes. That is strange, perhaps, but, once more, it is so.

I would comply with these indications, point by point; consequently, I would, in matters of commerce, industry, arts, and even adminstration, look into all sorts of projects, plans, combinations, changes, alterations, and improvements the fame of which in the press would cover the voices of the most numerous and most prolific publicists. Political economy has, it is said, made a fortune in France; well, I should leave to your theorists, to your utopians, to the most impassioned declaimers of your schools nothing to invent, nothing to publish, nothing even to say. The good of the people would be the sole and unchanging object of my public confidences. Whether I speak myself, or whether I have my ministers or my writers speak, one would never exhaust the subject of the grandeur of the country, of its prosperity, of the majesty of its purpose and of its destiny; one would never cease to support it for its great principles of modern law, for the great problems which arouse humanity. The most enthusiastic, the most universal liberalism would breathe through my writings. The people of the occident love the oriental style, and so the style of all official speeches, of all official manifestoes should always be adorned with images, always pompous, full of loftiness and reflections. The people do not like atheistic governments; in my communications with the public I should not fail to put my acts under the invocation of the Divinity, while tactfully associating my own star with that of the nation.

I should like the acts of my reign to be compared at every moment with those of past governments. It would be the best way to bring out my good deeds and to arouse the gratitude which they deserve.

It would be very important to place in relief the mistakes of those who preceded me, to show that I have always known how to avoid those mistakes. In this way, people would entertain toward the régimes which preceded my power a sort of antipathy, aversion even, which would end by becoming irreparable as an atonement.

Not only would I give to a certain number of newspapers the mission of continually exalting the glory of my reign, of throwing back upon governments other than mine the responsibility of the errors of European politics, but I should like most of these eulogies to appear to be echoes of foreign papers from which articles would be reproduced, true or false, which would render striking homage to my own policies. Besides, I would have, abroad, some paid newspapers whose support would be all the more efficacious since I would give them an appearance of opposition on several points of detail.

My principles, my ideas, my acts would be represented with the halo of youth, with the prestige of the new law in contrast to the decrepitude and decay of ancient institutions.

I realize that safety valves are necessary for public spirit, that intellectual activity, driven back at one point, is necessarily carried over to another. That is why I would not be afraid to throw the nation into all sorts of theoretical and practical speculations about the industrial régime.

Outside of politics, moreover, I assure you that I would be a very good prince, that I would peacefully allow the people to stir up philosophical or religious questions. Concerning religion, the doctrine of free examination has become a sort of monomania. One must not oppose this tendency, in fact, it could not be done without danger. In those countries of Europe which are furthest advanced in civilization, the invention of printing ended by giving birth to a literature that is insane, furious, unrestrained, almost unclean—it is a great misfortune. Well, it is sad to say, but, to satisfy this rage of writing which possesses your parliamentary countries, it is almost enough merely not to thwart it.

This pestiferous literature, the course of which cannot be obstructed, and the platitude of writers and political men who would be at the head of journalism, would not fail to form a shocking contrast to the dignity of the language which would fall from the steps of the throne, with the vivacious and colorful dialectic upon which care would be taken to rest all the manifestations of power. You understand, now, why I wished to surround the prince with this host of publicists, administrators, lawyers, business men and attorneys who are essential to the drawing up of this quantity of official communications of which I have spoken to you, and the impression of which on public opinion would always be very strong.

Such, in brief, is the general disposition of my régime concerning the press.

MONTESQUIEU. Then you are through with it?

MACHIAVELLI. Yes, and to my regret, for I was much more brief than I should have been. But our moments are counted and we must move rapidly.

THIRTEENTH DIALOGUE

MONTESQUIEU. I need to recover a little from the emotions which you have caused me to undergo. What fertility of resource, what strange conceptions! There is poetry in all that and a certain fatal beauty which the modern Byrons would not deny; one finds there the scenic talent of the author of Mandragore.

MACHIAVELLI. You think so, Monsieur de Decondat? Yet something tells me that you are not so certain in your irony; you are not sure that these things are impossible.

MONTESQUIEU. If it is my opinion which interests you, you shall have it; I await the conclusion.

MACHIAVELLI. I have not yet reached it.

MONTESQUIEU. Well, then, continue.

MACHIAVELLI. I am at your service.

MONTESQUIEU. At the outset, you outlined a formidable legislation concerning the press. You extinguished all voices, with the exception of your own. Here are the mute parties before you—do you fear no conspiracies?

MACHIAVELLI. No, for I should not be very foresighted if, with one twist of the hand, I did not disarm them all at once.

MONTESQUIEU. In that case, what are your methods?

MACHIAVELLI. I would begin by deporting by the hundreds those who, with gun in hand, greeted the accession of my power. I have been told that in Italy, in Germany and in France, it was through secret societies that the agitators who conspired against the government were recruited. I would tear to pieces the obscure threads which are woven like spider webs in dens.

MONTESQUIEU. And then?

MACHIAVELLI. The organization of a secret society, or affiliation with one, will be severely punished.

MONTESQUIEU. Good enough for the future; but the existing societies?

MACHIAVELLI. I shall expel, for public safety, all those who have

been definitely known to have been members. Those whom I
do not reach will remain under a continual threat, for I shall
put through a law which will permit the government to deport,
by administrative means, all who may have been affiliated with
such societies.

MONTESQUIEU. That is, without judgment.

MACHIAVELLI. Why do you say: without judgment? Is not the
decision of a government a judgment? You may rest assured
that there will be little pity for sedition-mongers. In countries
continually troubled by civil discord, peace must be brought
about by implacable acts of vigor; if there is a reckoning of
victims to be made in order to insure tranquillity, it will be made.
After that, the appearance of the one who commands becomes so
imposing that no one dares to make an attempt on his life.
After having covered Italy with blood, Sylla may reappear in
Rome as a private individual; no one would touch a hair of his
head.

MONTESQUIEU. I see that you are in a period of terrible execution; I hardly dare to make an observation. However, it seems to
me that, even in following your plans, you could be less severe.

MACHIAVELLI. If my clemency were called upon, I should see.
I can even confide to you that a portion of the severe provisions
which I shall write into the law will become purely comminatory,
on condition, however, that I am not forced to use them otherwise.

MONTESQUIEU. And that is what you call comminatory! Nevertheless your clemency reassures me a little; there are moments
when, if some mortal were to hear you, you would freeze his
blood.

MACHIAVELLI. Why? I lived very close to the Duke of Valentinois who left behind him a terrible reputation, which he well
deserved, for he had his pitiless moments; yet I assure you that
once the necessity for execution was passed, he was good-tempered
enough. The same could be said of almost all the absolute monarchs; at bottom they are good, especially so when it comes to
children.

MONTESQUIEU. I am not sure that I do not prefer you at the height of your wrath: your gentleness is more frightening. But to return. You have destroyed the secret societies.

MACHIAVELLI. Don't go so fast: I did not do that: you will cause some confusion.

MONTESQUIEU. What and how?

MACHIAVELLI. I prohibited secret societies the character and actions of which would escape the supervision of my government, but I did not mean to deprive myself of a means of information, a secret influence which can be considerable if one knows how to make use of it.

MONTESQUIEU. What can you be thinking of in that connection?

MACHIAVELLI. I foresee the possibility of giving to a certain number of these societies a sort of legal existence or, rather, to centralise them all under a single one the supreme head of which will be appointed by myself. In this way I shall hold in my hand the various revolutionary elements in the country. The people who make up these societies belong to all nations, to all classes, to all ranks; I shall be kept informed of the most obscure political intrigues. It will be like a branch of my police force about which I shall soon tell you.

This subterranean world of secret societies is filled with empty heads to which I shall not pay much attention, but there are directions to be given there, forces to move. If something is stirring, it is my hand which moves it; if a plot is being prepared, I am the head of it: I am the chief of the league.

MONTESQUIEU. And you believe that these hordes of democrats, these republicans, these anarchists, these terrorists will allow you to approach and break bread with them; you can believe that those who wish no human domination at all will accept a guide who will really be a master!

MACHIAVELLI. That is because you do not understand, Montesquieu! How much impotence and even simplicity is to be found among the majority of the men of European demagogism. These tigers have the souls of sheep, heads full of wind; one need only speak their language to be admitted to their ranks. Besides, almost all their ideas have an incredible affinity with the doctrines of absolute power. Their dream is the absorption of the individual into a symbolic unity. They demand the complete realization of equality by virtue of a power which can, after all, be in the hands of only a single man. You see that even here I am the head of their school! And then it must be said that they have no choice. Secret societies will exist under the conditions that I have just described to you or they will not exist at all.

MONTESQUIEU. The finale of *sic volo sic jubeo* is never long in coming, with you. I see definitely that you are well guarded against conspiracies.

MACHIAVELLI. Yes, for it is just as well to tell you that the legislation will not permit reunions or secret meetings which exceed a certain number of persons.

MONTESQUIEU. How many?

MACHIAVELLI. You insist upon details? No group of more than fifteen or twenty people, if that satisfies you.

MONTESQUIEU. What! Friends numbering more than fifteen or twenty will not be able to dine together?

MACHIAVELLI. You are already becoming alarmed, I see, in the name of gallic gayety. Well, yes, they may gather, for my rule will not be as savage as you think, but with one condition—that politics is not discussed.

MONTESQUIEU. They may discuss literature?

MACHIAVELLI. Yes, but on condition that under cover of literature they do not gather for a political purpose, for it is possible not to talk politics at all and still give to a banquet a character which will be understood by the public. That must not happen.

MONTESQUIEU. Alas! in such a system it is difficult for the citizens to live without being suspected by the government!

MACHIAVELLI. You are mistaken then; none but rebels will suffer from these restrictions; no one else will be aware of them.

It goes without saying that here I have nothing to do with acts of rebellion against my power, or of attempts to overthrow it, or of attacks either against the person of the prince or against his authority or his institutions. These are veritable crimes which are restrained by the common law of all legislations. They would be foreseen and punished in my kingdom according to classification and according to definitions which would not permit of the slightest direct or indirect attempt against the order of established things.

MONTESQUIEU. Permit me to have full confidence in you in this matter and not to inquire about your methods. Still it is not enough to establish a Draconian legislation; one must have a magistracy which is willing to apply it; that point is not without its difficulties.

MACHIAVELLI. There are no difficulties there.

MONTESQUIEU. Then you are going to destroy the judicial organization?

MACHIAVELLI. I destroy nothing: I modify and I initiate.

MONTESQUIEU. Then you are going to establish martial or provost's courts, exceptional tribunals?

MACHIAVELLI. No.

MONTESQUIEU. What then?

MACHIAVELLI. It is well for you to know first of all that I shall not need to decree a great many severe laws whose application I shall follow up. Many of them will already exist and will still be in force; for all governments, liberal or absolute, republican or royalist, come up against the same difficulties; they are obliged, in critical moments, to have recourse to rigorous laws some of which remain, others of which are weakened, depending on the needs which cause them. One must make use of both; concerning the latter, one must remember that they have not been explicitly abrogated, that they were perfectly good laws, and that the return of the abuses which they anticipated makes their application necessary. In this way the government seems to be performing nothing but an act of good administration, which is often the case.

You see that it is only a question of giving a little elasticity to the action of the courts, which is always easy in centralized countries where the magistracy is in direct contact with the administration, by means of the ministry upon which it depends.

As for the new laws which will be enacted under my reign and which, for the most part, will have been given out in the form of simple decrees, the application will perhaps not be quite so easy, because in those countries where the magistrate has a life-appointment, he may oppose by himself, in the interpretation of the law, the too direct action of power.

But I believe I have found a plan very ingenious, very simple, apparently perfectly lawful, which, without affecting the permanence of the magistracy, will modify what is too absolute in the consequences of the principle. I shall issue a decree that the magistrates must retire when they reach a certain age. I do not doubt that here, too, I shall have opinion on my side, for it is a painful spectacle to see, as is frequently the case, that the judge, who is called upon to decide the loftiest and most difficult questions, falls into a decrepitude of mind which renders him incapable.

MONTESQUIEU. But, if you will permit, I have some ideas about the things of which you speak. The fact which you bring out does not at all conform to experience. With those men who live by the continual exercise of the mind, the intelligence does not weaken as you mention; that, if I may say so, is the privilege of thought in those people where it becomes the principal element. If, in the case of some magistrates, the faculties become unsettled with age, in the case of the greater number, they are preserved and their light continually increases; there is no need to replace them, for death causes in their ranks the natural voids which are necessary; but even if there were, indeed, among them as many examples of decadence as you claim, it would still be a thousand times more worthwhile, in the interests of justice, to tolerate that evil than to accept your remedy.

MACHIAVELLI. I have reasons superior to yours.

MONTESQUIEU. Reasons of state?

MACHIAVELLI. Perhaps. You may be sure of one thing: in this

new organization the magistrates will not deviate more than formerly in purely civil questions.

MONTESQUIEU. How do I know? For, according to your words, I already see that they will deviate in political questions.

MACHIAVELLI. They will not deviate; they will do their duty as they must do it, for, in political matters, it is necessary, in the interest of order, that the judges be always on the side of power. It would be the worst thing in the world if a sovereign could be affected by seditious decrees against the government which the whole country would seize upon at once. Of what value would it be to have forced the press to be silent if the judgments of the courts were free?

MONTESQUIEU. Under a modest appearance, your method is quite powerful, is it not? Since you attach such importance to it.

MACHIAVELLI. Yes, for it causes this spirit of resistance to disappear, this *esprit de corps* which is always so dangerous in judiciary companies which have conserved the memory, perhaps the cult, of past governments. It introduces in their midst a mass of new elements the influence of which are wholly favorable to the spirit which animates my reign. Every year twenty, thirty, or forty posts of magistrates which become vacant by retirement bring about a change in the whole personnel of the courts which may in this way be renewed from top to bottom every six months. One single vacancy, you know, may entail fifty appointments by the successive effect of the heads of different ranks who are being moved up. You can imagine what will take place when there are thirty or forty vacancies at once. It is not only that the collective spirit disappears in what politics there may be, but one becomes more closely united to the government, with disposes of a greater number of places. There are young men who are desirous to start their careers, who are no longer stopped by the perpetuity of those who precede them. They know that the government likes order, that the country likes it also, and it becomes a question merely of serving the two, in doing justice, when order plays its part.

MONTESQUIEU. But, except for incredible blindness, you will be accused of arousing in the magistracy a spirit of competition fatal to the judiciary bodies. I shall not show you what are the consequences of this, since I know that that would not stop you.

MACHIAVELLI. I make no claim to escape criticism; it is of little importance to me, provided that I do not hear it. In all things I shall have for a principle the irrevocability of my decisions, in spite of murmurings. A prince who acts thus is always sure of gaining respect for his will-power.

FOURTEENTH DIALOGUE

MACHIAVELLI. I have already told you many times, and I repeat it once more, that I have no need to create and to organize everything; that I find in the institutions already existing a great many of the instruments of my power. Do you know what is the constitutional guarantee?

MONTESQUIEU. Yes, and I am sorry for your sake, because, without meaning to, I deprive you of a surprise which you would perhaps not have been angry to prepare for me, with the cleverness of setting which is your strong point.

MACHIAVELLI. Of what are you thinking?

MONTESQUIEU. I am thinking of what is true, at least, for France, of which you seem to be speaking; and that is, that it is a law of circumstance which must be modified, if not made to disappear completely, under a régime of constitutional liberty.

MACHIAVELLI. I consider you very moderate on this point. According to your ideas, it is simply one of the most tyrannical restrictions in the world. What! When private persons will be injured by representatives of the government in the exercise of their duties, and they will bring them before the courts, the judges will have to answer them: "We cannot decide for you, the door of the prætorium is closed; go to the administration to ask for the authorization to bring suit against its officials." But

that would be a veritable denial of justice. How often will it
happen that the government will authorize such suits?

MONTESQUIEU. What are you complaining of? It seems to me
that that would satisfy you very well.

MACHIAVELLI. I only told you that in order to show you that,
in states where justice comes across such obstacles, a government
has not much to fear from the tribunals. It is always as provisional agreements that such exceptions are inserted into the law,
but once the period of transition is passed, the exceptions remain,
and that is as it should be, for as long as order reigns, they disturb no one, and when times are troubled, they are necessary.

There is another modern institution which serves the operation
of central power with no less efficacy: that is the creation, in
connection with the tribunals, of a great magistracy which you
call the public ministry and which used to be called, with much
more reason, the ministry of the King, because this office is essentially removable and revocable at the will of the Prince. I have
no need to describe to you the influence of this magistrate over
the courts close to which he has his bench; suffice it to say that
it is considerable. Remember all this carefully. Now I am going
to speak to you of the highest court of appeal which plays a considerable rôle in the administration of justice.

The court of appeal is more than a judiciary body; it is, to a
certain extent, a fourth power in the state, because it has the last
word in the interpretation of the law. So I shall repeat what I
believe I told you concerning the Senate and the legislative assembly: such a court of justice which would be completely independent of the government would, in view of its sovereign and
almost discretionary power of interpretation, be able to overthrow it if it so wished. It would suffice merely to restrain or to
extend systematically, in the direction of liberty, the provisions of
laws which regulate the exercise of political rights.

MONTESQUIEU. And apparently it is just the contrary that you
are going to ask of it?

MACHIAVELLI. I shall ask nothing of it; it will itself do what is suitable for it to do. For it is here that the different causes of influence which I mentioned above will cooperate the most strongly. The nearer the judge is to power, the more it belongs to him. The conservative spirit of the reign will develop here to a greater degree than anywhere else, and the laws of strict police politics will receive, at the hands of this great assembly, an interpretation so favorable to my power, that I shall be relieved of a multitude of restrictive measures which, without that, would become necessary.

MONTESQUIEU. One would really say, to hear you, that laws are capable of the most fantastic interpretations. Are the legislative texts not clear and precise, that they lend themselves to extensions or restrictions such as you intimate?

MACHIAVELLI. Surely it is not to the author of the *Esprit des Lois,* to the experienced magistrate who must have rendered so many excellent decisions, that I can hope to teach the meaning of jurisprudence. There is no text, no matter how clear, which is not capable of receiving the most contrary interpretations, even in pure civil law; but I beg you to remember that we are talking of political matters. Now, it is a habit common to legislators of all times to draw up certain of their provisions in a manner elastic enough to regulate cases or, according to circumstances, to introduce exceptions which it would not have been prudent to explain more precisely.

I am well aware that I must give you examples, for without that my proposition would seem too vague to you. The difficulty for me is to find one of so general a character as to dispense with entering into long details. Here is one which I take by preference, since a short time ago we touched upon it.

In speaking of the constitutional guarantee, you were saying that this exceptional law should be modified in a free country.

Well, I am supposing that this law exists in the state which I govern, I am supposing that it was modified; therefore I imagine that before me a law was promulgated which, in electoral matters, permitted the prosecution of representatives of the government without the authorization of the Council of State.

The question comes up under my rule which, as you know, has introduced great changes in public equity. Someone wishes to bring suit against an official on the occasion of an electoral act; the magistrate of the public ministry rises and says: "The protection you wish to take advantage of can't be applied; it is no longer compatible with present institutions. The old law which dispenses with the authorization of the Council of State in such a case has been tacitly abrogated." The courts answer yes or no, in the end the discussion is brought before the court of appeals and this high tribunal thus defines public equity on this point: "The old law is tacitly abrogated; the authorization of the Council of State is necessary to prosecute public officials, even in electoral matters."

Here is another example, somewhat more special, it is borrowed by the police from the press: I have been told that in France there was a law which required, under penal sanction, that all those who made a living distributing and peddling pamphlets must be provided with an authorization given out by the public official who is, in each province, entrusted with the general administration. The law wished to regulate peddling and to subject it to strict supervision; that is the essential aim of this law; but the text of the provision reads, I suppose: "All distributors or peddlers must be provided with an authorization, etc."

Well, the court of appeals, if the question arises, will be able to say: "It is not only the professional act that the respective law had in view. It is any act whatsoever of distribution or peddling. Consequently, even the author of a pamphlet or of a work, several copies of which are distributed, even as gifts, without preliminary authorization, is party to distribution and peddling; therefore he comes under the threat of the penal provision."

You see at once what results from such an interpretation; instead of a simple police law, you have a law which restricts the right to publish one's thoughts by means of the press.

MONTESQUIEU. All you needed was to be a jurist.

MACHIAVELLI. That is absolutely necessary. How are governments overthrown these days? By legal distinctions, by the subtleties of constitutional law, by opposing to the ruling power all the means, all the weapons, all the contrivances which are not directly prohibited by law. And you expect that the ruling power would not make use of these stratagems of law which the parties employ with such obstinacy against the power? But then the struggle would not be equal, resistance would not even be possible; it would be necessary to abdicate.

MONTESQUIEU. You have so many stumbling-blocks to avoid that it would be a miracle if you anticipated all of them. The courts are not bound by their judgments. With a jurisprudence such as that which would be applied under your rule, you will have many lawsuits on your hands. The persons amenable to a tribunal will not weary of knocking at the door of the courts to demand other interpretations from them.

MACHIAVELLI. In the beginning that is possible; but when a certain number of arrests will have definitely put jurisprudence in its proper place, no one will continue to do what it forbids, and the source of the lawsuits will be exhausted. Public opinion would, in fact, be so much satisfied that when it came to a question of the meaning of laws, it would be referred to the official counsel of the administration.

MONTESQUIEU. And how, may I ask?

MACHIAVELLI. At certain critical times when there is fear that some difficulty may arise over such and such a point of legislation, the administration will declare, in the form of a notice, that such and such an act comes under the application of the law, that the law covers such and such a case.

MONTESQUIEU. But those are merely declarations which in no way bind the courts.

MACHIAVELLI. Undoubtedly, but these declarations have, none the less, a very great influence on the decisions of the courts of justice, coming as they do from an administration as powerful as the one I have organized. They will particularly have great control over individual resolutions and, in many cases (not to say always), they will forestall annoying lawsuits; people will refrain from them.

MONTESQUIEU. The farther we advance, the more I see that your government is becoming more and more paternal. What you are speaking of are judiciary customs almost patriarchal. It does indeed seem impossible that you should not be credited with a solicitude which displays itself under so many ingenious forms.

MACHIAVELLI. You must, nevertheless, realize that I am very far from the barbarous processes of government which you seemed to attribute to me at the beginning of this conversation. You see that violence plays no rôle; I take my point of support where everyone takes it nowadays—from the law.

MONTESQUIEU. From the law of the strongest.

MACHIAVELLI. The law which is obeyed is always the law of the strongest: I know of no exception to this rule.

FIFTEENTH DIALOGUE

MONTESQUIEU. Although we have surveyed a great sphere and you have organized almost everything, I need not conceal from you that there still remains much for you to do in order to reassure me completely as to the continuance of your power. That which astonishes me the most in the world is that you have based it on universal suffrage, that is, the most inconsistent element of its nature of which I am aware. Let us understand one another perfectly; you told me that you were king?

MACHIAVELLI. Yes, king.

MONTESQUIEU. For life, or hereditary?

MACHIAVELLI. I am king as one is king in all the kingdoms of the world, hereditary king with a succession from male to male, in order of issue, with the perpetual exclusion of women.

MONTESQUIEU. You are not gallant.

MACHIAVELLI. Pardon me, but I am prompted by the traditions of the Salian and Frankish monarchy.

MONTESQUIEU. You will, no doubt, explain to me how you expect to reconcile heredity with, for instance, the democratic suffrage of the United States?

MACHIAVELLI. Yes.

MONTESQUIEU. What! With this principle you hope to bind the will of future generations?

MACHIAVELLI. Yes.

MONTESQUIEU. For the present what I should like to see is the way you would manage with this suffrage when it is a question of applying it to the nomination of public officers.

MACHIAVELLI. What public officers? You know very well that, in monarchical states, it is the government which appoints the officials of all ranks.

MONTESQUIEU. That depends on which officials. Those which have to do with the administration of the townships are, in general, elected by the inhabitants, even under monarchical governments.

MACHIAVELLI. That will be changed by a law; in the future they will be appointed by the government.

MONTESQUIEU. And you will also appoint the representatives of the nation?

MACHIAVELLI. You know that that is not possible.

MONTESQUIEU. Then I pity you, for if you leave the voting to itself, if you do not arrange for some new plan, the assembly of the representatives of the people will not be long, under the influence of the parties, in filling up with deputies hostile to your power.

MACHIAVELLI. Just for that reason I had not the slightest intention of leaving the voting to itself.

MONTESQUIEU. I expected that. But what plan will you adopt?

MACHIAVELLI. The first point is to link to the government those who wish to represent the country. I shall impose upon the candidates the solemnity of the oath. Here it is not a question of an

oath to the nation, as your revolutionaries of '89 understood it; I
want an oath of loyalty to the prince himself and to his constitution.

MONTESQUIEU. But since in politics you do not fear to violate your
own, how can you expect that they should be more scrupulous than
yourself on this point?

MACHIAVELLI. I count little on the political conscience of men;
I count on the power of opinion: no one will dare to debase himself before it by openly proving false to his sworn oath. They
will dare still less since the oath which I shall place upon them
will precede the election instead of following it, and they will
be without any excuse for seeking votes, under these conditions, if
they are not decided in advance to serve me. Now it is necessary
to give to the government the means of resisting the influence of
the opposition, of preventing them from making deserters of those
who wish to defend it. At election time, the parties are in the
habit of announcing their candidates and placing them before
the government; I shall do as they do, I shall have candidates
announced and I shall place them before the parties.

MONTESQUIEU. If you were not all-powerful, the method would
be odious, for, while openly offering combat, you provoke blows.

MACHIAVELLI. I expect the agents of my government, from first
to last, to see to it that my candidates are successful.

MONTESQUIEU. That goes without saying.

MACHIAVELLI. Everything is of the greatest importance in this
matter. "The laws which establish suffrage are fundamental; the
manner in which suffrage is granted is fundamental; the law
which determines the manner of granting permits to vote is
fundamental." (Esprit des Lois, page 12 et seq., Book II, et seq.,
Chapter II, et seq.) Was it not you who said that?

MONTESQUIEU. I do not always recognize my language when it
passes through your lips; it seems to me that the words which you
cite were applied to democratic government.

MACHIAVELLI. Undoubtedly, and you have already been able to
see that my essential policy was to trust myself to the people, and

that although I wear a crown, my real and declared purpose is to represent it. Trustee of all the powers which it has delegated to me, I alone, after all, am its true representative. What I wish, it wishes; what I do, it does. Accordingly, it is indispensable that at the time of the elections the factions should not be able to substitute their influence for that of which I am the armed personification. Therefore I have found still other means to paralyze their efforts. You must know, for instance, that the law which forbids gatherings will naturally apply to those which might be formed in view of the elections. In this way, the parties will neither be able to plan together nor to make secret arrangements.

MONTESQUIEU. Why do you always put the parties first? Under pretext of putting shackles on them, do you not really put them on the voters themselves? The parties, in short, are only masses of voters; if the voters are not permitted to become enlightened through gatherings, through conferences, how will they be able to vote with a thorough knowledge of the matter?

MACHIAVELLI. I see that you do not know with what infinite art, with what guile, political passions frustrate prohibitive measures. Do not concern yourself with the voters—those who are animated by good intentions will always know for whom to vote. Besides, I shall use tolerance; not only shall I not forbid the gatherings which are formed in the interest of my candidates, but I shall go so far as to close my eyes to the actions of some popular candidates who will agitate noisily in the name of liberty; only I may as well tell you that those who shout the loudest will be my own men.

MONTESQUIEU. And how are you going to regulate the voting?

MACHIAVELLI. First of all, concerning the country people, I do not want the voters to go to vote in the great centers where they might come in contact with the spirit of opposition of the cities or towns and, from there, receive the pass-word which would come from the capital; I want them to vote by communes. The result of this plan, which seems so simple, will nonetheless be considerable.

MONTESQUIEU. That is easy to understand; you force the country vote to be divided among insignificant notorieties or, for lack of familiar names, to fall back on the candidates designated by your government. I should be very much surprised if, under this system, many capable or talented men were produced.

MACHIAVELLI. Public order has less need of talented men than of men devoted to the government. Great ability holds sway from the throne and among those who surround it—elsewhere it is useless; it is almost harmful even, for it can only act against the power.

MONTESQUIEU. Your aphorisms cut like a sword; I have no arguments to oppose you. Please let us go on with the rest of your electoral regulations.

MACHIAVELLI. For the reasons which I have just deduced for you I also do not want the vote by ticket which falsifies the election and which permits the coalition of men and of principles. Besides I shall divide the electoral colleges into a certain number of administrative districts in which there will be room for the election of but a single deputy and where, consequently, each voter will be able to place only one name on his voting paper.

In addition, there must be the possibility of neutralizing the opposition in the districts where it makes itself too strongly felt. Thus, let us suppose that in the previous elections a district has been noted for the majority of its hostile votes, or that one may reasonably suppose that it will declare itself against the government candidates, nothing is easier than to remedy that: if this district has only a small population, it may be attached to a district nearby or far away, but of greater expanse, in which its votes will be drowned and its political spirit lost. If the hostile district, on the contrary, has a large population, it may be divided up into several parts and annexed to neighboring districts in which it will be completely destroyed.

You understand that I am passing over a mass of details which are only accessories to the whole. Thus, when necessary, I divide the colleges into sections of colleges in order to give more opportunity for administrative action, and I have the colleges and the divisions of colleges presided over by municipal officers whose nominations depend upon the government.

MONTESQUIEU. I notice, with a certain surprise, that you are not making use of a measure which you recommended during the time of Leo X, and which consists of the substitution of votes by investigators after the elections.

MACHIAVELLI. That would perhaps be too difficult in these days, and I believe that this method should not be used except with the greatest caution. Besides, a clever government has so many other resources! Without directly buying the vote, with out-and-out money, nothing is easier than to influence the vote of the masses through administrative concessions, by promising here a port, there a market, further on a road, a canal; and inversely, by doing nothing for the cities and towns where the vote is unfavorable.

MONTESQUIEU. I have no objection to make to the profundity of these plans; but are you not afraid that people will say that sometimes you corrupt and sometimes you oppress popular suffrage? Are you not afraid of compromising your power in the struggles in which it will be so directly engaged? The slightest success obtained over your candidates will be a brilliant victory which will be a severe blow to your government. What keeps me constantly worried for you is that I see you always obliged to succeed in all things if you wish to avert a disaster.

MACHIAVELLI. You speak the language of fear, calm yourself. At the point to which I have arrived, I have succeeded in so many things that I cannot perish because of extremely small things. Bossuet's grain of sand is not made for true statesmen. I am so advanced in my career that I could, without danger, brave even storms; what, then, signify the minute difficulties of administration of which you speak? Do you believe that I claim to be perfect? Do I not know very well that more than one blunder will be committed around me? No, there is no doubt that I shall not be able to prevent a certain amount of pillage and scandal here and there. Is that sufficient to hinder the whole thing from progressing? The main thing is not so much to make no errors as to accept the responsibility with an attitude of energy which commands respect from the slanderers. And, what is more, if the opposition should succeed in introducing some orators into my chamber, what difference does it make to me? I am not one of those who wish to reckon without the necessity of their times.

One of my great principles is to oppose like to like. Just as I make use of the press by the press, I would make use of the courts by the courts; so I would have as many men as necessary ready and capable of speaking several hours without a stop. The chief thing is to have a compact majority and a reliable president. There is a particular art in conducting debates and carrying off the vote. And, besides, would I need to make use of the cunning of parliamentary strategy? Nineteen-twentieths of the Chamber would be my own men who would vote on orders, while I would pull the strings of an artificial and clandestinely recruited opposition; after that, let them make beautiful speeches: they will go into the ears of my deputies as the wind enters the keyhole of a lock. Now do you want me to speak to you of my Senate?

MONTESQUIEU. No, I know from Caligula what that will be like.

SIXTEENTH DIALOGUE

MONTESQUIEU. One of the salient points of your politics is the annihilation of parties and the destruction of collective forces. You have certainly not failed in this program; yet I see all around you some things which you have not even touched upon. You have not dealt with the clergy nor the University nor the bar nor the national militia nor the commercial corporations; and yet it seems to me that there is more than one dangerous element in all that.

MACHIAVELLI. I cannot tell everything at once. Let us turn at once to the national militia so that I need be bothered about it no further. Their dissolution was, of necessity, one of the first acts of my power. The organization of a civilian guard cannot be reconciled with the existence of a regular army, since citizens in arms may, at a given time, be transformed into rebels. Nevertheless, this point is not without its difficulty. The national guard is a useless institution, but it bears a popular name. In military states it flatters the puerile instincts of certain bourgeois classes which, by a rather ridiculous eccentricity, unites to commercial habits the taste for warlike demonstration. It is a harmless prejudice which it would be all the more ill-advised to go counter to, since the prince must never have the semblance of separating his interests from those of the city which thinks it has found a guarantee in the arming of its inhabitants.

MONTESQUIEU. But you mentioned that you would break up this militia.

MACHIAVELLI. I would break it up in order to reorganize it upon other lines. The main thing is to put it under the immediate orders of the agents of civil authority and to relieve it of the prerogative of recruiting its chiefs by means of elections; that is what I am going to do. Besides, I shall organize it only in the proper places, and I reserve the right to dissolve it again and to re-establish it upon still other lines, if circumstances require. I have nothing more to say to you on this point. As for the University, the present order of things is practically satisfactory. You are aware, of course, that these great bodies of instruction are no longer organized as they formerly were. I am assured that almost everywhere they have lost their autonomy and are no longer anything more than public services in care of the State. Now, as I have told you more than once, where the State is, the prince is; the moral direction of the public establishments is in his hands; it is his agents who inspire the spirit of youth. The heads as well as the members of the teaching body of all degrees are appointed by the government; they are attached to it, they depend upon it, that suffices; if here and there some traces of independent organization remain in any public school or academy whatsoever, it is easy to bring it back to the common center of unity and direction. It is only a question of a regulation or even of a simple ministerial order. At full speed I pass over the details which need no closer attention. Yet I must not leave this subject without telling you that I consider it very important to proscribe the studies of constitutional politics in the teaching of law.

MONTESQUIEU. Indeed you have good reasons for that.

MACHIAVELLI. My reasons are simple enough; I do not wish the young people, on leaving school, to busy themselves with politics at random; at the age of eighteen, one goes about making constitutions as one makes tragedies. Such teaching can only give false ideas to the youth and initiate it prematurely into matters which are beyond the limits of its reasoning. It is with these notions poorly digested and poorly understood that unsound statesmen are prepared, utopians the temerity of whose spirit is later translated into temerity of action.

The generations which are born under my reign must be brought up in the respect of established institutions, in the love of the prince; for this purpose I should make an ingenious use of the power of management of instruction: I believe that in general a great mistake is made in the school—contemporary history is neglected. It is at least just as essential to know one's own time as the time of Pericles; I should like to have the history of my reign, of myself while living, taught in the schools. That is how a new prince enters into the heart of a generation.

MONTESQUIEU. That would, of course, be a continual apology for all your deeds?

MACHIAVELLI. It is obvious that I would not have myself disparaged. The other method which I would use would have for a goal the reaction against free instruction, which cannot be directly proscribed. The universities contain armies of professors whose leisure time may be used for the propagation of good doctrines. I would have them give free courses in all the important towns, and in this way I would mobilize the education and the influence of the government.

MONTESQUIEU. In other words, you absorb, you confiscate for your profit even the last gleams of independent thought.

MACHIAVELLI. I confiscate nothing at all.

MONTESQUIEU. Are you going to permit professors other than your own to popularize science by the same methods, without license or authorization?

MACHIAVELLI. What! Do you expect me to sanction clubs?

MONTESQUIEU. No. Let us go on to something else.

MACHIAVELLI. Among the multitude of customary measures which the safety of my government requires, you have called my attention to the bar; that means going further than is necessary for the moment; besides, here I touch upon civil interests and you know that, in this matter, my rule of conduct is to abstain as much as possible. In the states where the bar is composed of a corporation, those amenable to a tribunal consider the independence of this institution as a guarantee inseparable from the right of the defense before the courts, and that it is a question of their honor, their interest, or their life. It is a serious thing to intervene here, for public opinion could be aroused at a cry which would not fail to cast aside the whole corporation. Nonetheless, I am aware that this order will be a center of influences constantly hostile to my power. This profession—and you know it better than I, Montesquieu—develops characters which are cold and stubborn in their principles, it develops spirits whose tendency is to seek in the acts of power the element of pure legality. The lawyer has not the lofty sense of social necessities to the same degree as has the magistrate; he sees the law from too near and from angles too petty to allow of just sentiment, whereas the magistrate. . . .

MONTESQUIEU. Spare me the apology.

MACHIAVELLI. Yes, for I am not forgetting that I am face to face with a descendant of the great magistrates who upheld the throne of the monarchy in France with such brilliance.

MONTESQUIEU. And who rarely lent themselves to the registration of decrees when they violated the law of the state.

MACHIAVELLI. That is how they ended by overthrowing the state itself. I do not want my courts of justice to be parliaments and the lawyers, under immunity of their gowns, to play politics there. The greatest man of the century to whom your country had the honor of giving birth, said: "I should like to cut the tongue of a lawyer who has anything to say against the government." Modern customs are milder; I should not go so far. On the first day, and in fitting circumstances, I shall limit myself to doing a very simple thing: I shall issue a decree which, while respecting the independence of the corporation, will nevertheless arrange for the lawyers to receive the investiture of their profession from the sovereign. In the exposé of the motives of my decree, it will not, I believe, be very difficult to show the people that they will find in this method of appointment a more weighty guarantee than when the corporation draws upon itself, that is, with the elements necessarily a little confused.

MONTESQUIEU. It is only too true that one may lend to the most detestable measures the language of reason! But look here, what are you going to do now in connection with the clergy? Here is an institution which depends on the state only on one side and which is set off by a spiritual power the seat of which is not with you. I know of nothing more dangerous to your power, I declare, than this power which speaks in the name of heaven and the roots of which are all over the earth: do not forget that the Christian word is a word of liberty. Undoubtedly the laws of the state have established a profound demarcation between religious and political authority; undoubtedly the word of the ministers of the cult cannot be heard except in the name of the Gospel; but the divine spiritualism which is evolved from it is the stumbling-block of political materialism. It is this book, so humble and so gentle, which has destroyed by itself the Roman empire and Cæsarism and its power. Those nations which are frankly Christian will always escape despotism, for Christianity raises the dignity of man too high for despotism to reach, since it develops moral forces upon which human power has no hold.

(*Esprit des Lois,* page 371, Book XXIV, Chapter I et seq.) Beware of the priest: he depends only upon God, and his influence is everywhere, in the sanctuary, in the family, in the school. You can do nothing to him: his hierarchy is not yours, he obeys a constitution which is decided neither by the law nor by the sword. If you reign over a Catholic nation and you have the clergy for enemy, you will perish sooner or later, even if all the people were for you.

MACHIAVELLI. I am not quite sure why you are pleased to make of the priest an apostle of liberty. I have never seen that, neither in ancient nor in modern times; I have always found in the priesthood a natural support of absolute power.

Note this: if, in the interests of my establishment, I had to make concessions to the democratic spirit of my epoch, if I took universal suffrage as the foundation of my power, it is only a stratagem required by the times. I claim the benefit of divine right nonetheless, I am king by the grace of God nonetheless. In view of this, the clergy must support me, for my principles of authority conform to their own. If, however, they show themselves rebellious, if they take advantage of their influence to carry on an underhand war against my government . . .

MONTESQUIEU. Well, what then?

MACHIAVELLI. You who speak of the influence of the clergy, do you not know to what point it was able to make itself unpopular in certain Catholic states? In France, for instance, journalism and the press defamed it to such an extent before the masses, they ruined its mission so greatly, that if I reigned in its kingdom, do you know what I could do?

MONTESQUIEU. What?

MACHIAVELLI. I could provoke a schism in the Church which would break all the bonds which attach the clergy to the court of Rome, for that is the Gordian knot. Through my press, through my publicists, through my statesmen I would have the following words circulated: "Christianity is independent of Catholicism; what Catholicism forbids, Christianity permits; the inde-

pendence of the clergy, its submission to the court of Rome, are
purely Catholic dogmas; such an order of things is a continual
menace to the safety of the state. The loyal subjects of the kingdom
should not have a foreign prince as their spiritual leader; that
is to leave internal order to the discretion of a power which might
become hostile at any moment; this hierarchy of the Middle
Ages, this protectorate of the people as children can no longer
be reconciled with the virile genius of modern civilization, with
its wisdom and its independence. Why go to Rome to seek a
director of conscience? Why should the head of the political
authority not be at the same time the head of the religious authority? Why should the sovereign not be pontiff?" Those are the
words I would have circulated by the press, especially by the
liberal press, and, what is very probable, the masses of the people
would hear them with joy.

MONTESQUIEU. If you can believe that and if you dared to attempt such an undertaking, you would learn promptly and terribly the power of Catholicism, even among the nations where it
seems to be weakened. (*Esprit des Lois*, Page 393, Book XXV,
Chapter XII.)

MACHIAVELLI. Attempt it, great God! But I ask pardon, on my
knees, of our divine master for having as much as described this
sacrilegious doctrine, inspired by the hatred of Catholicism; but
God, who has instituted human power, does not forbid it to protect
itself against the enterprises of the clergy, who violate the precepts of the Gospel when they show insubordination to the prince.
I know that they will not conspire except because of an imperceptible influence, but I would find the way to arrest the intention
which directs the influence, even at the heart of the court of
Rome.

MONTESQUIEU. How?

MACHIAVELLI. It would suffice for me to point out at the Holy
See the moral condition of my people, trembling under the yoke
of the Church, aspiring to cast it off, capable of detaching itself

from the Catholic unity and of throwing itself into the schism
of the Greek or Protestant Church.

MONTESQUIEU. Threat instead of action!

MACHIAVELLI. How mistaken you are, Montesquieu, and how
you disregard my respect for the pontifical throne! The only rôle
that I wish to play, the sole mission which belongs to me as
Catholic sovereign would be just that of defending the Church.
In the present day, you know, temporal power is gravely threatened, both by irreligious hate and by the ambition of the countries
north of Italy. Well, I would say to the Holy Father: "I shall
support you against all of them, I shall save you—it is my duty,
it is my mission. But at least do not attack me—support me with
your moral influence." Would that be too much to ask when
I would endanger my popularity by holding myself up to those
who are called the European democracy as defender of temporal
power which is, alas! completely discredited at present. This
danger would not stop me. Not only would I check any enterprise against the sovereignty of the Holy See on the part of the
neighboring states, but if, by misfortune, it were attacked, if the
Pope were to be driven out of the Papal States, as has already
happened, my bayonets alone would bring him back and would
keep him there always as long as I live.

MONTESQUIEU. That would indeed be a master stroke, for if you
kept a perpetual garrison at Rome, you would practically have
the Holy See at your command, as if it were in some province of
your kingdom.

MACHIAVELLI. Do you think that after such a service rendered
to the papacy, it would refuse to uphold my power; that the Pope
himself, at need, would refuse to come to consecrate me in my
capital? Are such events unexampled in history?

MONTESQUIEU. Yes, examples of everything can be found in
history. But if, instead of finding a Borgia or a Dubois on Saint
Peter's throne, as you seem to expect, you should find a pope
who resisted your intrigues and braved your anger, what would
you do?

MACHIAVELLI. In that case, under pretext of defending the temporal power, I would bring about his fall.

MONTESQUIEU. You have what is called genius!

SEVENTEENTH DIALOGUE

MONTESQUIEU. I said that you had genius; in truth, a certain type of it is necessary to conceive and to execute so many things. Now I understand the apologue of the god Vishnu; you have a hundred arms like the Hindu idol and each one of your fingers touches a spring. In the same way that you touch everything, are you also able to see everything?

MACHIAVELLI. Yes, for I shall make of the police an institution so vast that in the heart of my kingdom half of the people shall see the other half. May I give you some details on the organization of my police?

MONTESQUIEU. Go ahead.

MACHIAVELLI. I shall begin by creating a ministry of police which will be the most important of my ministries and which will centralize, as much for the exterior as for the interior, the numerous functions which I give over to that part of my administration.

MONTESQUIEU. But if you do that, your subjects will see immediately that they are caught in a prodigious net.

MACHIAVELLI. If this ministry incurs displeasure, I shall abolish it and I shall call it, if that pleases you better, the ministry of state. Besides, I shall organize in other ministries corresponding functions the greater part of which will be quietly blended in with what you call nowadays the ministry of the interior and the ministry of foreign affairs. You understand perfectly that here I am not interested in diplomacy but only in the proper means to assure my security against the factions, foreign as well as domestic. Well then, you may believe me that, in this connection, I shall find the majority of monarchs about in the same situation as myself, that is, very much disposed to second my views, which would consist in creating international police services in the interest of mutual safety. If, as I scarcely doubt, I succeed in attaining this result, here are some of the forms by which my police would manifest themselves abroad: Men of pleasure and good company in the foreign courts, to keep an eye on the intrigues of the princes and of the exiled pretenders; proscribed revolutionaries, some of whom I would not despair of being able to persuade, with money, to be of service to me as agents of transmission in regard to the secret practices of underhand demagogy; the establishment of political newspapers in the great capitals, printers and book stores placed in the same conditions and secretly subsidized in order to follow more closely, by means of the press, the direction of public thought.

MONTESQUIEU. It is no longer the factions of your kingdom but the very soul of humanity that you will end up by conspiring against.

MACHIAVELLI. You know that I do not take fright at big words. I want to arrange that every politician who goes abroad to plot can be observed, noted from one point to another, until his return to my kingdom, where he will be imprisoned for good and all so that he will no longer be in a position to plot again. In order to have well in hand the thread of revolutionary intrigues, I am dreaming of a plan which would, I think, be rather clever.

MONTESQUIEU. Good God, what may that be!

MACHIAVELLI. I should like to have a prince of my house, seated on the steps of my throne, who would play at being a malcontent. His mission would be to hold himself up as a liberal, a slanderer of my government and thus to rally (in order to observe them more closely) those who, in the highest ranks of my kingdom, might go in a little for demagogy. Riding above domestic and foreign intrigues, the prince to whom I would confide this mission would thus play the game of dupe to those who would not be in the secret of the comedy.

MONTESQUIEU. What! You would entrust to a prince of your house powers which you yourself class as befitting the police?

MACHIAVELLI. And why not? I know of reigning princes who,

while in exile, were attached to the secret police of certain cabinets.

MONTESQUIEU. If I continue to listen to you, Machiavelli, it is only to have the last word of this shocking wager.

MACHIAVELLI. Do not be so indignant, M. de Montesquieu; in the *Esprit des Lois* you called me a great man. (*Esprit des Lois*, Page 68, Book VI, Chapter V.)

MONTESQUIEU. You are making me atone dearly for that; it is to punish myself that I listen to you. Pass as quickly as you can over so many sinister details.

MACHIAVELLI. At home I am obliged to re-establish the black cabinet.

MONTESQUIEU. Re-establish . . .

MACHIAVELLI. Your best kings made use of it. The secrecy of letters must not be permitted to serve as a covering for plots.

MONTESQUIEU. It is that which makes you tremble; I understand it.

MACHIAVELLI. You are mistaken, for there will be plots under my reign; there must be.

MONTESQUIEU. What now?

MACHIAVELLI. There will perhaps be real plots, I cannot answer for that; but certainly there will be simulated plots. At certain times it may be an excellent method to arouse the sympathy of the people in favor of the prince, when his popularity is waning. In intimidating public spirit, certain severe measures may be obtained when necessary, or those which already exist may be maintained. False conspiracies which, of course, must be made use of only with the greatest caution, have still another advantage: they permit the discovery of real plots by giving rise to investigations which lead to a thorough search for traces of whatever one suspects.

Nothing is more precious than the life of the sovereign: it must be surrounded by innumerable guarantees, that is, innumerable agents, but at the same time it is necessary that this secret militia be concealed so cleverly that the sovereign seems to show no fear when he shows himself in public. I have been told that in Europe the precautions in this connection were so perfected that a prince who goes out into the streets might seem to be a simple citizen who is taking a walk, unguarded, among the crowd, whereas he is really surrounded by two or three thousand protectors.

In addition, I expect that my police will be interspersed in all ranks of society. There will be no secret meeting, no committee, no salon, no intimate hearth where there will not be an ear to hear what is said in every place, at every hour. Alas, for those who have wielded power it is an astonishing phenomenon with what facility men denounce one another. What is still more astonishing is the faculty of observation and of analysis which is developed in those who make up the political police; you have no idea of their ruses, their disguises, their instincts, the passion which they bring to their researches, their patience, their impenetrability; there are men of all ranks who go in for this profession through—how shall I say it?—a sort of love of the art.

MONTESQUIEU. Ah! Draw the curtain!

MACHIAVELLI. Yes, for at the very bottom of power there are secrets which terrify the eye. I spare you the description of more somber things which you have not heard. With the system that I shall organize, I shall be so completely informed that I shall be able to tolerate even guilty actions because at any moment of the day I will have the power to stop them.

MONTESQUIEU. Tolerate them? And why?

MACHIAVELLI. Because in European states the absolute monarch must not use force indiscreetly; because, in the depths of society, there are always secret activities about which nothing can be done when they are not formulated; because it is necessary to take the greatest care to avoid alarming public opinion concerning the security of power; because the parties are satisfied with murmurs, with harmless teasing, when they are reduced to impotence, and to claim to disarm them even of their temper would be folly. They will, then, be heard complaining here and there, in newspapers and books; they will attempt allusions against the government in speeches and addresses; under various pretexts, they will make some small manifestations of their existence; all that will be very timid, I swear to you, and the public, if informed, will be tempted only to laughter. I will be considered very good to support it, I shall pass for too good-natured; that is why I shall tolerate what seems to me to be without any danger: I do not even wish my government to be considered suspicious.

MONTESQUIEU. This language reminds me that you have left a gap, and a very serious one, in your decrees.

MACHIAVELLI. Which one?

MONTESQUIEU. You have not touched individual liberty.

MACHIAVELLI. I shall not touch it.

MONTESQUIEU. You think not? If you have reserved the faculty of toleration, you have also reserved the right to prevent all that appears dangerous to you. If the interest of the state, or even something slightly important, requires that a man be arrested in your kingdom at a particular moment, how can it be done if the law of habeas corpus exists in the legislation; if individual arrest is preceded by certain formalities, by certain guarantees? While the procedure is going on, time will be passing.

MACHIAVELLI. Allow me to state that even if I respect individual liberty, I did not forbid the judiciary organization to make some useful modifications in this regard.

MONTESQUIEU. I was well aware of that.

MACHIAVELLI. Oh! Do not be so superior, it will be the easiest thing in the world. Who is it who generally makes the laws on individual liberty in your parliamentary states?

MONTESQUIEU. It is a council of magistrates, the number and independence of whom are the guarantee of those brought before the courts.

MACHIAVELLI. It is certainly a vicious organization, for how do you expect that, with the slowness of the deliberations of a council, justice can have the necessary rapidity of apprehension of evil-doers?

MONTESQUIEU. Which evil-doers?

MACHIAVELLI. I am speaking of those who commit murder, robbery, crimes and misdemeanors which come under the common law. This tribunal must be given the unity of action which is necessary to it; I replace your council by a single magistrate, charged with making laws concerning the arrest of criminals.

MONTESQUIEU. But it is not a question now of criminals; with the aid of this regulation, you threaten the liberty of all the citizens. At least make a distinction in the cause of accusation.

MACHIAVELLI. That is just what I do not wish to do. Is the one who undertakes something against the government not as guilty as, if not more so than, the one who commits an ordinary crime or misdemeanor? Passion or misery mitigates many faults, but who forces people to busy themselves with politics? So I wish no distinction between the misdemeanors of common law and the political misdemeanors. Where, then, is the mentality of modern governments, to set up a sort of criminal court of justice for their slanderers? In my kingdom, the insolent journalist will mingle in the prisons with the plain thief and will appear at his side before the correctional jurisdiction. The conspirator will be seated before the criminal jury, side by side with the counterfeiter and the murderer. That is an excellent legislative modification, you must notice, for public opinion, seeing the conspirator treated as the equal of the ordinary criminal, will end up by confusing the two types in the same scorn.

MONTESQUIEU. You are ruining the very foundation of moral sense; but what does that matter to you? What surprises me is that you are keeping a criminal jury.

MACHIAVELLI. In those states which are centralized like mine, the public officials are the ones who appoint the members of the jury. In a question of a simple political misdemeanor, my minister of justice can always, when necessary, compose the chamber of judges who are well versed in such things.

MONTESQUIEU. Your internal legislation is irreproachable; it is time to pass to other matters.

EIGHTEENTH DIALOGUE

MONTESQUIEU. Up to now you have occupied yourself only with
the forms of your government and the rigorous laws necessary
to maintain it. That is a great deal, and yet it is nothing. There
still remains the most difficult of all problems for a sovereign
who wishes to exert absolute power in a European state accustomed to representative customs.
MACHIAVELLI. And what is this problem?
MONTESQUIEU. The problem of your finances.
MACHIAVELLI. That question has not been foreign to my calculations, for I remember having told you that everything resolved
itself into a question of figures.
MONTESQUIEU. All very well, but here it is the very nature of
the thing which will resist you.
MACHIAVELLI. You disturb me, I confess, for I date from a century of barbarism concerning political economy and I understand
very little of those things.
MONTESQUIEU. I am setting my mind at rest for you. In any case
allow me to ask you a question. I remember having written, in
the *Esprit des Lois*, that the absolute monarch was forced, by the
principle of his government, to impose only minor taxes on his
subjects. (*Esprit des Lois*, Page 80, Chapter X, Book XIII.)
Will you give your subjects at least this satisfaction?
MACHIAVELLI. I do not promise that and I know nothing, in
truth, more debatable than the proposition which you put forth
there. How do you expect the machinery of monarchical power,
the brilliance and the representation of a great court to exist without imposing heavy sacrifices on the nation? Your theory might
be true in Turkey, in Persia, heaven knows where! in small
countries without industry, where the people have no means to
pay the tax; but in European societies, where wealth overflows
the sources of labor and may be taxed in so many varied forms,
where luxury is a means of government, where the upkeep and

the expense of all the public services are centralized in the hands
of the state, where all the great posts, all the powers, are very
highly salaried, how do you expect one to limit himself to moderate
taxes, especially when one is sovereign master?

MONTESQUIEU. That is very true and I abandon my theory, the
real meaning of which seems to have escaped you. Your government, then, will be expensive; it is evident that it will cost more
than a representative government.

MACHIAVELLI. It is possible.

MONTESQUIEU. Yes, but it is just here that the difficulty begins.
I know how the representative governments provide for their
financial needs, but I have no idea of the means of existence of
absolute power in modern societies. If I question the past, I see
very clearly that it can exist only under the following conditions:
in the first place, the absolute monarch must be a military chief.
You undoubtedly understand that?

MACHIAVELLI. Yes.

MONTESQUIEU. In addition he must be a victor, for it is from
war that he must demand the principal resources which are necessary to maintain his pomp and his armies. If he demanded them
by taxation, he would crush his subjects. You see by this that it
is not because the absolute monarch spends less that he must
husband his resources, but because the law of his subsistence is
elsewhere. Now, today, war no longer brings in profits to those
who wage it: it ruins the victors as well as the vanquished. That
is a source of revenue which is out of your reach.

Taxes are left, but, of course, the absolute prince must be able
to do without the consent of his subjects in this regard. In the
despotic states, there is a legal fiction which permits them to tax
at will: in law, the sovereign is supposed to possess all the goods
of his subjects. When he takes something from them, he is only
taking back what belongs to him. Thus, no resistance.

And finally the prince must be able to dispose of the resources
procured for him by taxes without discussion as well as without
control. Such are the inevitable steps of absolutism; you must

agree that there would be much to do in order to achieve that. If the people of the present day are as indifferent as you say to the loss of their liberties, that does not mean that they will be so when it comes to their interests; their interests are bound to an economic régime exclusive of despotism: if you are not arbitrary in finances, you cannot be so in politics. Your whole reign will be overthrown because of the budget.

MACHIAVELLI. I am very calm on that point, as I am on all the rest.

MONTESQUIEU. That is what we shall have to see; let us come to the point. The vote on taxes, by the representatives of the nation, is the fundamental rule of modern states: will you accept the vote on taxation?

MACHIAVELLI. Why not?

MONTESQUIEU. Take care! This principle is the most express consecration of the sovereignty of the nation: for to grant it the right to vote taxes means also granting it the right to refuse them, to limit them, to reduce to nothing the prince's possibilities of action and consequently to destroy the prince himself, if need be.

MACHIAVELLI. You are categoric. Continue.

MONTESQUIEU. Those who vote the taxes are themselves taxpayers. Here their interests are strictly united to those of the nation, at a point where it will necessarily keep its eyes wide open. Thus you are going to find its representatives as little accommodating in connection with legislative credit as you found them yielding in connection with liberties.

MACHIAVELLI. It is here that the weakness of the argument is revealed; will you be good enough to note two considerations which you have forgotten. In the first place the representatives of the nation receive salaries; taxpayers or no, they are personally disinterested in the vote of taxes.

MONTESQUIEU. I agree that the idea is practical and the observation wise.

MACHIAVELLI. You see the disadvantage of considering the

things too systematically; the smallest, clever modification suffices to change everything. You would perhaps be right if I based my power on the aristocracy or on the bourgeois classes which might, at a given moment, refuse me their cooperation; but, in the second place, as a basis of action I have the proletariat of whom the mass possesses nothing. The burdens of the state scarcely weigh upon them and I would even arrange that these expenses should not touch them at all. Fiscal measures will trouble the working classes very little.

MONTESQUIEU. If I understand correctly, that is all very clear: the possessors will be forced to pay by the sovereign will of those who possess nothing. That is the ransom exacted of wealth by numbers and poverty.

MACHIAVELLI. Is that not just?

MONTESQUIEU. It is not even true, for in present-day society, from the economic point of view, there are neither rich nor poor. The artisan of yesterday is the bourgeois of tomorrow, by virtue of the labor law. If you strike at the territorial or industrial bourgeoisie, do you know what you are doing?

In reality you are making emancipation through labor more difficult, you are retaining a greater number of workers in the bonds of the proletariat. It is an aberration to believe that the proletariat can profit by blows struck at production. By impoverishing, through fiscal laws, those who have possessions, unnatural situations are created and, in time, even those who possess nothing become still poorer.

MACHIAVELLI. Those are pretty theories, but I have just as pretty ones to offer in contradiction, if you wish.

MONTESQUIEU. No, for you have not yet solved the problem which I placed before you. First you must obtain what you need to meet the expense of absolute sovereignty. It will not be as easy as you think, even with a legislative chamber in which you will have an assured majority, even with the omnipotence of popular mandate with which you are invested. Tell me, for instance, how you can bend the financial mechanism of the modern states to the demands of absolute power. I repeat, it is the very nature of things which is in opposition. The civilized peoples of Europe have surrounded the administration of their finances with guarantees so binding, so jealous, so multiple, that they leave no more room for collection than for the arbitrary use of public funds.

MACHIAVELLI. And what is this marvelous system?

MONTESQUIEU. That can be shown in few words.

The perfection of the financial system in modern times rests on two fundamental bases—*control* and *publicity*. In these essentials lies the guarantee of the taxpayers. A sovereign cannot meddle with it without saying indirectly to his subjects: "You have order, I wish disorder, I wish obscurity in the management of public funds; I need that because there is a mass of expenditures which I desire to be able to make without your approval, deficits which I desire to be able to conceal, receipts which I desire to have the means of disguising or of increasing according to circumstances."

MACHIAVELLI. Your beginning is good.

MONTESQUIEU. In free, industrial countries, everybody is familiar with the finances, by necessity, by interest and by trade, and your government can deceive no one in this regard.

MACHIAVELLI. Who told you that I wish to deceive anyone?

MONTESQUIEU. The entire work of the financial administration, no matter how vast and how complicated it may be in its details, in the last analysis comes down to two very simple operations—*receiving* and *spending*.

It is around these two kinds of financial acts that gravitate the multitude of laws and special regulations which, in themselves, have a very simple end in view: to act so that the taxpayer pays only the necessary and regularly established taxes, and to act so that the government cannot apply public funds to expenditures other than those approved by the nation.

I leave aside all that relates to the assessment and to the method of collecting the taxes, to the practical means of assuring the completeness of the collection, the order and the precision in the fluctuations of public funds; these are but accounting details which I have no intention of discussing with you. I only wish to show you how publicity moves along with control in the best organized systems of political finance in Europe.

One of the most important problems to be solved was to bring forth from obscurity, to make visible to all eyes, the elements of collection and expenses upon which is based the use of the public fortune in the hands of the government. This result has been attained by the creation of what is called in modern language the state budget, which is the estimate of the receipts and the expenses, anticipated not for a period of remote time, but each year for use the following year. The annual budget is, then, the main point and, in a way, the generator of the financial situation which improves or becomes worse in proportion to the established results. The items of which it is composed are prepared by the various administrators in the department, who are appointed for that purpose. As the foundation of their work they take the allocations of previous budgets, introducing the necessary modifications, additions and retrenchments. The whole is given to the minister of finance who centralizes the documents which are transmitted to him, and who presents to the legislative assembly what is called the plan of the budget. This great public work, printed, reproduced in a thousand newspapers, reveals to all eyes the internal and external politics of the state, the civil, judicial and military administration. It is examined, discussed and voted upon by the representatives of the country, after which it is executed in the same manner as the other laws of the state.

MACHIAVELLI. Allow me to admire with what clarity of deduction and what propriety of terms, completely modern, the illustrious author of the *Esprit des Lois* has been able, in financial matters, to get away from the somewhat vague theories and the occasionally rather ambiguous terms in the great work which has made him immortal.

MONTESQUIEU. The *Esprit des Lois* is not a financial treatise.

MACHIAVELLI. Your sobriety on this point deserves to be praised

 Be good enough to continue; I am listening with the greatest
interest.

NINETEENTH DIALOGUE

MONTESQUIEU. The creation of the budgetary system has brought
with it, one may say, all the other financial guarantees which are
today the share of well-regulated political societies.

Thus, the first law which the economy of the budget necessitates is that the funds required correspond with the existing resources. That is a balance which must always be openly expressed
by real and authentic figures, and recourse has been made to a
very wise measure in order better to assure this important result
and in order that the legislator who votes on the propositions
submitted to him should not be carried away by his ardor. The
general budget of the state is divided into two distinct budgets:
the budget of expenditures and the budget of revenue, which
must be voted upon separately, each by a special law.

In this way, the attention of the legislator is forced to concentrate, in turn, separately, on the active and passive situation, and
his decisions are not influenced in advance by the general balance
of revenue and expenses.

He scrupulously controls these two elements and it is, in the
last analysis, by their comparison, by their strict harmony, that
the general vote on the budget is produced.

MACHIAVELLI. That is all very well, but are the expenditures by
any chance impassably limited by the legislative vote? Is that possible? Can a chamber, without paralyzing the exercise of the
executive power, forbid its sovereign to provide for unforeseen
expenses through emergency measures?

MONTESQUIEU. I see that that disturbs you, but I cannot regret it.

MACHIAVELLI. Even in constitutional states is it not expressly
reserved for the sovereign to set up, through decrees, supple-

mentary or unusual credits in the interval between legislative sessions?

MONTESQUIEU. That is true, but on one condition, which is that these decrees are converted into laws at the meeting of the chambers. Their approval must intervene.

MACHIAVELLI. If it intervenes after the expenditure is pledged, in order to ratify what is done, I should not be averse to it.

MONTESQUIEU. I believe you; but, unfortunately, they do not stop there. The most advanced modern financial legislation forbids acting contrary to the normal anticipations of the budget, other than by laws leading to the opinion of supplementary and extraordinary credits. Expenses cannot be pledged without the intervention of the legislative power.

MACHIAVELLI. But in that case one can no longer even govern.

MONTESQUIEU. It seems that one can. The modern states have reflected that the legislative vote of the budget would end by becoming illusory, with the abuses of supplementary and extraordinary credits; that, in short, the expenses must be capable of being limited when the resources were so; that political events were not able to vary financial facts from one moment to another, and that the intervals between the sessions were not long enough to make it impossible to provide advantageously for them by an extra-budgetary vote.

They went still farther—they wished to arrange that once the resources were voted for such and such purposes, they might revert to the treasury if they were not used; they thought that the government, while remaining within the limits of allotted credits, must not be able to use the funds of one purpose to appropriate them for another, to cover this, to uncover that, by means of switching funds from one ministry to another through decrees; for that would be to evade their legislative destination and to return, by an ingenious detour, to arbitrary finance.

For this purpose they conceived what is called the *specifying of funds by subjects*, that is, that the vote of expenditures takes place through special subjects containing only correlative purposes and of the same nature for all the ministries. Thus, for instance, topic A will include, for all the ministries, expenditure A; topic B expenditure B; and so on. The result of this plan is that the funds which are not used must be annulled in the accounts of the various ministries and carried over as revenue in the budget of the following year. I need not tell you that the ministerial responsibility is the sanction of all these measures. The crown of the financial guarantees is the establishment of an accounting chamber, a sort of supreme court in its way, permanently charged with the exercise of the functions of jurisdiction and control over the accounts, the manipulation and the use of public funds, even having as its mission to point out those parts of financial administration which could be improved from the double point of view of expenditures and of revenue. These explanations are sufficient. Do you not find that with such an organization, absolute power would be in an embarrassing position?

MACHIAVELLI. I am still overwhelmed, I admit, by this financial inroad. You have taken me at my weak point: I told you that I understood very little of these matters but, you may believe me, I would have ministers who could refute all that and point out the danger of the majority of these measures.

MONTESQUIEU. Could not you yourself do that a little?

MACHIAVELLI. Yes, I could. I leave to my ministers the trouble of making pretty theories; that will be their principal occupation. As for myself, I shall talk finance to you rather as a statesman than an economist. There is one thing which you are too inclined to forget, and that is that the question of finances is, of all the divisions of politics, the one which most easily lends itself to the maxims of the treatise of *The Prince*. Those states which have budgets so methodically ordered and official writings so well regulated, impress me as do the business men who have their books perfectly kept and who are, after all, wholly ruined. Why, who has greater budgets than your parliamentary governments? What is it that costs more than the democratic republic of the United States, or than the royal republic of England? It is true

that the immense resources of this last-named power are used in
the service of the most profound and the most widespread politics.

MONTESQUIEU. You have gotten away from the question. What
are you trying to bring out?

MACHIAVELLI. This: the rules of the financial administration of
the states have no relation to those of domestic economy, which
seems to be the type of your conceptions.

MONTESQUIEU. Ah! the same distinction as between politics and
morals?

MACHIAVELLI. Well, yes; is it not universally recognized and
practiced? Were things not the same even in your time, although
much less advanced in this respect, and was it not you yourself
who said that the states permitted themselves certain financial
digressions which would put to shame even the most intemperate
gentleman's son?

MONTESQUIEU. It is true I said that, but if you draw from it an
argument favorable to your thesis, that is a real surprise for me.

MACHIAVELLI. You mean, no doubt, that one must not glory in
what is done but in what should be done.

MONTESQUIEU. Precisely.

MACHIAVELLI. I reply that one must desire the possible and that
what is done universally cannot but be done.

MONTESQUIEU. That is pure practice, I agree.

MACHIAVELLI. And I have an idea that if we were to balance
the accounts, as you say, my government, absolute as it is, would
cost less than yours; but let us drop this discussion which would
be without interest. You are really mistaken if you believe that I
am troubled by the perfection of the financial systems which you
have just explained to me. I rejoice with you over. the regularity
of the collection of the taxes, of the completeness of the revenue;
I rejoice over the exactitude of the accounts, I rejoice very sincerely. Do you really believe that I think it necessary that the
absolute sovereign must dip his hands into the state coffers, that
he must handle the public funds. . . . This luxury of precautions
is truly puerile. Is the danger there? Once more, all the better if

the funds are gathered, set in motion and circulated with the miraculous precision which you described. I am counting precisely on all these marvels of accounting, all these organic beauties of financial matter, to aid in the splendor of my reign.

MONTESQUIEU. You have the *vis comica*. The most astonishing thing to me about your financial theories is that they are directly opposed to what you say about them in the treatise of *The Prince*, where you strictly recommend not only economy in finance but even avarice. (*The Prince*, Page 106, Chapter XVI.)

MACHIAVELLI. If you are astonished, you have no reason to be, for times are no longer the same from this point of view, and one of the most important of my principles is to adjust myself to the times. Let us get back and for a while set a little aside what you told me of your department of accounts: does this institution belong to the judiciary order?

MONTESQUIEU. No.

MACHIAVELLI. Then it is a purely administrative body. I suppose it to be irreproachable. But when all the accounts are verified, it can make advances! Does that prevent funds from being voted, expenditures from being made? Its decisions of verification are no more informative of the situation than the budgets. It is a department of registry without remonstrance, it is an ingenious institution. I shall keep it up just as it is, without anxiety.

MONTESQUIEU. You will keep it up, you say! So you expect to touch upon the other parts of the financial organization?

MACHIAVELLI. You guessed as much, I suppose. After a political coup d'état, is not a financial coup d'état inevitable? Shall I not take advantage of power for that as well as for the rest? What is the magic virtue which would preserve your financial regulations? I am like that giant of some fairy tale or other whom the pigmies had bound with fetters during his sleep; on arising, he broke them without even noticing their existence. On the day following my accession, there will be no question of voting upon the budget; I shall issue a special decree, I shall dictatorially open the necessary accounts and I shall have them approved by my council of state.

MONTESQUIEU. And you expect to continue in this manner?

MACHIAVELLI. Not at all. Beginning with the following year I shall return to legality, for I do not intend to destroy anything directly, as I have already told you several times. Rules have been made before me, I shall make rules in my turn. You spoke to me of the vote of the budget by two distinct laws: I consider that a bad measure. One understands a financial situation much better when he votes the budget of revenue and the budget of expenditures at the same time. My government is a diligent government; the precious time of public deliberations must not be lost in useless discussions. Henceforth the budget of revenue and of expenditures will be included in a single law.

MONTESQUIEU. Good. And the law which forbids the appropriation of supplementary funds other than by a preliminary vote of the Chamber?

MACHIAVELLI. I abrogate it; you understand the reason for that.

MONTESQUIEU. Yes.

MACHIAVELLI. It is a law which would be inapplicable under any régime.

MONTESQUIEU. And the specifying of funds, the vote by topics?

MACHIAVELLI. It is impossible to maintain that: the budget of expenditures will no longer be voted by topics but by ministries.

MONTESQUIEU. That seems to me a mountainous undertaking, for the vote by ministry only gives each one of them a total to examine. It is like using a bottomless cask instead of a strainer to sift public expenditures.

MACHIAVELLI. That is not exact, for each account, as a whole, presents distinct elements, topics as you call them; if desired they will be examined, but they will be voted upon by ministries, with the right to change from one topic to another.

MONTESQUIEU. And from one ministry to another?

MACHIAVELLI. No, I do not go that far; I wish to remain within the limits of necessity.

MONTESQUIEU. Your moderation is faultless, and you believe that these financial innovations will not throw the country into a state of alarm?

MACHIAVELLI. Why should that alarm them more than my other political measures?

MONTESQUIEU. Why, because this touches the material interests of everyone.

MACHIAVELLI. Oh! those are very subtle distinctions.

MONTESQUIEU. Subtle! The word is well chosen. But do not put any subtlety into it yourself, and say frankly that a country which cannot defend its liberties cannot defend its money.

MACHIAVELLI. What can they complain of, since I have kept the essential principles of public law in financial matters? Are taxes not regularly established, regularly collected, funds regularly voted? Is it not true that here, as elsewhere, everything is based upon popular suffrage? No, without a doubt, my government is not reduced to indigence. The people who have acclaimed me not only easily tolerate the pomp of the throne, but they desire it, they seek it in a prince who is the expression of its power. The people really hate only one thing, and that is the wealth of their equals.

MONTESQUIEU. Do not escape once more; you have not yet come to the end; I lead you back inflexibly to the budget. No matter what you say, its very organization checks the development of your power. It is a frame the boundaries of which may be broken through, but not without risk and peril. It is published, its component parts are known, it remains as barometer of the situation.

MACHIAVELLI. Let us finish up this point, since you wish it.

TWENTIETH DIALOGUE

MACHIAVELLI. The budget is a frame, you say; yes, but it is an elastic frame which stretches as far as desired. I shall always be within it, never outside it.

MONTESQUIEU. What do you mean?

MACHIAVELLI. Is it for me to teach you how things come about, even in the states where the budgetary organization is pushed to its highest point of perfection? Perfection consists precisely in knowing how, by ingenious stratagems, to get out of a system of limitation which in reality is purely fictitious.

Just what is your annually voted budget? Nothing but a provisional regulation, an estimate of the principal financial occurrences. The situation is never definite until after the completion of expenditures made necessary during the course of the year. In your budgets there are I know not how many types of accounts which correspond to all the possible eventualities; complementary, supplementary, extraordinary, temporary, exceptional. And each one of these accounts by itself forms as many distinct budgets. Now, this is how things work out: the general budget, the one which is voted at the beginning of the year, comes to a total amount of, let us say, 800 millions. When half of the year is gone, the financial facts already no longer correspond to the first estimates; so what is called a rectifying budget is presented to the Chambers, and this budget adds 100 millions, 150 millions to the original figure. Then comes the supplementary budget: it adds 50 or 60 millions; finally comes the liquidation which adds 15, 20 or 30 millions. In short, in the general reckoning, the total of the unforeseen expenses forms one-third of the estimated expenditures. It is upon this last figure that the legislative vote of the Chambers falls as a form of confirmation. In this way, at the end of ten years the budget can be doubled and even tripled.

MONTESQUIEU. That this accumulation of expenditures could be the result of your financial improvements, I do not doubt, but no such thing will happen in the states where your proceedings are avoided. Moreover, you have not yet finished: after all, the expenditures must be in proportion to the revenues. How will you handle that?

MACHIAVELLI. Everything, it may be said, consists in the art of grouping figures and in certain distinctions of expenditures, by aid of which the necessary latitude is obtained. Thus, for instance, the distinction between the ordinary budget and the extraordinary budget may be of great help. Under cover of this word *extraordinary* one may easily pass off certain debatable expenditures and certain more or less problematic revenues. I have here, for instance, 20 millions in expenses; it must be met by 20 millions in revenue: I produce as revenue a war indemnity of 20 millions, not yet collected, but which will be later, or else I bring forth as revenue an increase of 20 millions in the proceeds of taxation which will be realized next year. So much for your revenues; I need not multiply the examples. As for the expenditures, one may have recourse to the opposite procedure: instead of adding, you subtract. Thus, for instance, you remove the cost of tax collection from the budget of expenses.

MONTESQUIEU. And under what pretext, may I ask?

MACHIAVELLI. One may say, and with reason, I believe, that it is not a state expense. And for the same reason it may also be arranged to omit from the budget of expenditures the cost of provincial and communal service.

MONTESQUIEU. As you see, I dispute nothing of all that; but what will you do with the revenues which are deficits, and the expenditures which you eliminate?

MACHIAVELLI. The big thing in this question is the distinction between the ordinary budget and the extraordinary budget. The expenditures which are absorbing you at present must be included in the extraordinary budget.

MONTESQUIEU. But after all these two budgets are finally totaled and the definite figure of expenditures is made known.

MACHIAVELLI. No total must be made; on the contrary. The ordinary budget appears alone; the extraordinary budget is an appendant which is provided for by other means.

MONTESQUIEU. And what are they?

MACHIAVELLI. Do not make me anticipate. You see first of all that there is a particular manner of presenting the budget, of concealing, if necessary, the growing increase. There is no government which is not forced to act thus; there are inexhaustible resources in industrial countries but, as you noticed, these countries are miserly and suspicious; they argue over the most necessary outlays. Financial politics cannot, any more than other politics, play with open cards: at every step one would be hindered; but after all and, I admit, thanks to the perfecting of the budgetary system, everything is found again, everything is classified, and if the budget has its mysteries, it also has its lights.

MONTESQUIEU. But only for the initiated, I have no doubt. I see that you will surround financial legislation with a formalism as impenetrable as the judiciary procedure among the Romans, at the time of the twelve tables. But let us go on. Since your expenditures increase, your resources must increase in the same proportion. Will you, like Julius Cæsar, find a value of two thousand million francs in the state coffers, or will you discover the Potosi mines?

MACHIAVELLI. Your darts are very ingenious; I shall do what all possible governments do, I shall borrow.

MONTESQUIEU. It is to this very point that I wished to lead you. It is certain that there are few governments who are not obliged to have recourse to borrowing; but it is also certain that they are obliged to make use of them sparingly; they could not, without immorality and without danger, encumber future generations with exorbitant burdens, out of all proportion to probable resources. How are loans made? By the issue of bonds containing an obligation on the part of the government to pay a yearly interest proportionate to the capital which has been deposited. If the loan is at 5 percent, for instance, the state, at the end of twenty years, has paid a sum equal to the capital borrowed; at the end of 40 years, a double amount; at the end of 60 years, a triple amount, and yet it always remains debtor for the total of the same capital. It may be added that if the state increased its debt indefinitely, doing nothing to diminish it, it would be driven either to the impossibility of further borrowing or to bankruptcy. These results are easy to comprehend; there is no country where they are not understood. The modern states wished to put a necessary limitation to the increase of taxes. So they conceived what is called the system of amortization, a scheme truly admirable for its simplicity and for its very practical method of execution. A special fund was created, the capitalized resources of which are meant to be a permanent redemption of the public debt by successive fractions; so that every time that the state borrows, it must endow the sinking fund with a certain capital for the purpose of liquidating the new debt at a given time. You see that this method of limitation is indirect and it is that which makes it so powerful. By means of amortization, the nation says to its government: "Borrow if you must, but you will have to find a way to meet the new obligation that you are contracting in my name." When one is continually obliged to amortize, one thinks twice before borrowing. If you amortize regularly, your loans will be passed.

MACHIAVELLI. And what makes you think that I expect to amortize? In which states is amortization a regular thing? Even in England it is suspended. Your example falls flat: what is done nowhere, cannot be done.

MONTESQUIEU. Then you would abolish amortization?

MACHIAVELLI. I did not say that, far from it; I shall allow this mechanism to function, and my government will make use of the funds which it produces; this plan presents a great advantage. At the presentation of the budget, from time to time the proceeds of the amortization of the following year may be made to figure as revenue.

MONTESQUIEU. And the following year it will figure as expenditures.

MACHIAVELLI. I do not know, that will depend on circumstances, for I will very much regret that this financial institution should not be able to continue regularly. My ministers will explain themselves in this connection in an extremely sorrowful manner. Great heavens, I do not claim that my administration will have nothing to be criticized from the financial point of view, but when the facts are properly presented, one gets by with many things. The

administration of finances is also largely a matter of the press,
it must not be forgotten.

MONTESQUIEU. How is that?

MACHIAVELLI. Did you not yourself say that the very essence
of the budget was publicity?

MONTESQUIEU. Yes.

MACHIAVELLI. Well, are budgets not accompanied by detailed
accounts, by reports, by all sorts of official documents? What resources do these public communications not give to the sovereign
if he is surrounded by clever men! I expect my minister of
finance to talk the language of numbers with an admirable clarity
and to have a literary style of impeccable purity.

It is well to repeat continually this truth, that "the management of public funds at the present time is handled in the open."

This incontestable statement must be presented in a thousand
forms; I intend to have written such phrases as the following:

"Our system of accounting, fruit of long experience, is distinguished by the clarity and the certitude of its procedures. It
obstructs abuses and gives to no one, from the smallest official
to *the chief of the state himself,* the means of diverting the least
sum from its original purpose, or of making irregular use of it."

Your language will be kept: could one do better? and I shall
have it said:

"The excellence of the financial system rests on two bases; control and publicity. Control which prevents a single farthing
from leaving the hands of the taxpayers to enter the public
treasury, to pass from one counting-house to another, and to be
given into the hands of a creditor of the state, without the legiti-
macy of its collection, the regularity of its movements, the right-
fulness of its use, being controlled by responsible agents, judicially
verified by permanent magistrates, and finally sanctioned in
the legislative accounts of the Chamber."

MONTESQUIEU. O Machiavelli! You are always jeering, but your
mockery has something infernal in it.

MACHIAVELLI. You forget where we are.

MONTESQUIEU. You defy heaven.

MACHIAVELLI. God fathoms the heart.

MONTESQUIEU. Continue.

MACHIAVELLI. At the beginning of the budgetary year, the comptroller of finances will declare:

"Up to now, nothing alters the provisions of the present budget. Without being the victim of illusions, there are serious reasons to hope that, for the first time in years, the budget, in spite of loans, will present a real balance. This desirable result, obtained in exceptionally difficult times, is the best proof that the upward movement of the public fortunes has never slowed down."

Is that properly done?

MONTESQUIEU. Go on.

MACHIAVELLI. In this connection there will be talk of this amortization which absorbed you a short time ago, and they will say: "Soon amortization will function. If the project which has been conceived in this connection will be realised, if the state revenues continue to progress, it is not impossible that, in the budget which will be presented in five years, the public accounts will be liquidated by a surplus of revenue."

MONTESQUIEU. Your hopes are long-dated; but à propos of the amortization, if, after having promised to start it functioning, nothing is done, what will you say?

MACHIAVELLI. If necessary, it will be boldly acknowledged. Such frankness does honor to the government and touches the people when it comes from a strong power. But, in return, my finance minister will use all his efforts to remove all significance from the heightened figure of expenses. He will say, and it will be true: "Actual practice in matters of finance shows that deficits are never entirely confirmed, that a certain quantity of new resources arise unexpectedly during the course of the year, notably through the increase of the proceeds of taxes; that, moreover, a considerable portion of funds which have been voted are put to no use and are annulled."

MONTESQUIEU. Will that happen?

MACHIAVELLI. Sometimes, you know, in finance there are words ready made, stereotyped phrases, which have a great effect on the public, calming and reassuring the people.

Thus, in artfully presenting such and such a debt, one says: *this figure is not at all exorbitant—it is normal, it conforms to previous budgets—the figure of the floating debt is very reassuring.* There is a host of similar locutions which I shall not mention because there are other more important practical stratagems to which I wish to call your attention.

First, in all official documents it is necessary to insist upon the development of prosperity, of commercial activity and of *the ever increasing progress of consumption.*

The taxpayer is less aroused by the disproportion of the budget when these things are repeated to him, and they may be repeated to satiety without his ever becoming suspicious, to such an extent do authentic accounts produce a magic effect upon the mind of bourgeois fools. When the budget can no longer be balanced and one wishes to prepare public spirit for some disappointment for the following year, one says in advance, in a report, *next year the deficit will only be so and so much.*

If the deficit is less than the estimate, it is a veritable triumph; if it is greater, one says: *"the deficit was greater than was estimated, but it was still higher last year;* altogether the situation is better, because less has been spent and yet we have gone through exceptionally difficult circumstances: war, poverty, epidemics, unforeseen subsistence crises, etc.

"But, next year, the increase of revenues will, in all probability, permit the attainment of a balance which has been so long sought: the debt will be reduced, the budget *suitably balanced.* This progress will continue, it may be hoped, and, save for extraordinary events, balance will become the custom of our finances, as it is the rule."

MONTESQUIEU. That is high comedy; the custom will be like the rule, it will never work, for I imagine that, under your reign, there will always be some extraordinary circumstance, a war, a crisis.

MACHIAVELLI. I do not know whether there will be subsistence crises; one thing is certain and that is that I shall hold the banner of national dignity very high.

MONTESQUIEU. That is the very least you could do. If you gather glory, one need not be grateful to you, for in your hands it is only a means of government; it is not that which will liquidate the debts of your state.

TWENTY-FIRST DIALOGUE

MACHIAVELLI. I am afraid that you are somewhat prejudiced against loans; they are valuable for more than one reason: they attach families to the government; they are excellent investments for private people, and modern economists today expressly recognize that, far from impoverishing the state, public debts enrich it. Will you allow me to explain how?

MONTESQUIEU. No, for I believe I know those theories. Since you are always talking of borrowing and never of repaying, I should first of all like to know from whom you will ask so much capital, and for what reason you will ask it.

MACHIAVELLI. For that, foreign wars are a great help. In the great states, they permit the borrowing of five or six hundred millions; one manages so as to spend only the half or two-thirds, and the rest finds its place in the treasury for domestic expenditures.

MONTESQUIEU. Five or six hundred millions, you say! And who are the bankers of modern times who can negotiate loans the amount of which would constitute the whole fortune of certain states?

MACHIAVELLI. Ah! You are still concerned with these rudimentary procedures of the loan? If you will permit me to say so, that is almost barbarian, in a matter of financial economy. Nowadays one no longer borrows of bankers.

MONTESQUIEU. Of whom, then?

MACHIAVELLI. Instead of striking bargains with capitalists who come to an agreement amongst themselves to frustrate any bidding and whose limited number destroys all competition, one appeals to all his subjects: to the rich, to the poor, to the artisans, to the business men, to whomever has a cent to dispose of; one opens what is called a public subscription, and so that each one can buy shares, it is divided into coupons of very small sums. They sell for from five to ten francs a share to 100,000, a million francs' worth of shares. The day after their issue the value of these shares is rising, is at a premium, as they say: everyone knows it, and they rush from all sides to buy; one would think them delirious. In several days the chests of the treasury are crammed; so much money is received that one hardly knows where to put it; however, arrangements are made to accept it, because if the subscription exceeds the capital of the stock issued, a great effect can be made upon public opinion.

MONTESQUIEU. Ah!

MACHIAVELLI. Defaulters are returned their money. That is done with much talk, with the help of the press. It is a striking event, carefully handled. Sometimes the surplus comes to two or three hundred millions: you may judge for yourself to what point public spirit is affected by this public confidence in the government.

MONTESQUIEU. Confidence which is mingled with a spirit of unrestrained stock-jobbing, as far as I can see. I have, indeed, already heard of this scheme, but everything, on your lips, is truly phantasmagoric. All right, then, let us say you have your hands full of money, but . . .

MACHIAVELLI. I would have even more than you think, because among the modern nations, there are great banking institutions which are able to lend directly to the state one or two hundred millions at the usual rate of interest; the large cities may also lend. Among these same nations there are other institutions which are called savings institutions: these are savings banks, sick funds, pensions. The state is accustomed to demand that their capital, which is immense, sometimes as much as five or six hundred millions, must be deposited in the public treasury where it operates with the common stock, allowing a small interest for those who deposit it.

Besides, governments may procure funds just as bankers do. They make out sight drafts on their treasury for the sum of two or three hundred millions, a sort of letter of exchange upon which they draw before they have entered into circulation.

MONTESQUIEU. Permit me to stop you: you speak of nothing but borrowing or of drawing on letters of exchange; are you never interested in paying something?

MACHIAVELLI. It is well to let you know that, in case of need, the domains of the state may be sold.

MONTESQUIEU. Ah, now you are selling! But will you never concern yourself with paying?

MACHIAVELLI. Without a doubt; now is a good time to tell you how to meet debts.

MONTESQUIEU. You say, *to meet debts;* I should like a more exact expression.

MACHIAVELLI. I use this expression because I consider it absolutely exact. It is not always possible to liquidate a debt, but it is always possible to meet it; the word is, in fact, very energetic, for a debt is a formidable enemy.

MONTESQUIEU. Well, how shall you meet it?

MACHIAVELLI. There are various methods: first of all is taxes.

MONTESQUIEU. That is, debt is used to pay the debt.

MACHIAVELLI. You speak to me as an economist and not as a financier. Do not confuse the two. One may really pay with the proceeds of a tax. I know that taxes cause talk; if the one that has been established is inconvenient, another may be found, or the same one re-established under another name. There is a great art, you know, in finding the weak points of taxable material.

MONTESQUIEU. You will soon have wiped them out, I imagine.

MACHIAVELLI. There are other ways: there is what is called conversion.

MONTESQUIEU. Ah!

MACHIAVELLI. This has to do with the debt which is called consolidated, that is, the one which accrues from the issue of loans. One says to the stockholders of the state, for instance: up till now I have paid you five percent on your money; that was the rate of interest on your shares. From now on I expect to pay no more than four or four and one-half percent. Agree to this reduction or be reimbursed for the capital which you loaned me.

MONTESQUIEU. But if the money is really returned, I consider the procedure quite honest so far.

MACHIAVELLI. Without a doubt it will be returned if requested; but very few will bother about that; stockholders have their habits; their funds are placed, they have confidence in the state; they prefer a smaller income and a certain investment. If everyone demanded his money it is evident that the treasury would be in a fix. That never happens and in this way one gets rid of a debt of several hundred millions.

MONTESQUIEU. That is an immoral measure, no matter what you say; a forced loan which lowers public confidence.

MACHIAVELLI. You do not know stockholders. Here is another plan which has to do with another type of debt. I was just saying to you that the state had at its disposition the funds of the savings institutions and that it made use of them by paying their interest, subject to returning them at the first request. If, after having handled them a long time, it is no longer prepared to return them, it consolidates the debt which fluctuates in its hands.

MONTESQUIEU. I know what that means; the state says to the depositors: "You want your money, I no longer have it; here is an annual income."

MACHIAVELLI. Exactly, and it consolidates in the same way all the debts to which it no longer feels equal. It consolidates treasury bonds, debts to the cities, to the banks, in short all those which compose what is so picturesquely called the floating debt, because it is made up of debts which have no definite assessment and which arrive at maturity at about the same time.

MONTESQUIEU. You have singular methods of freeing the state.

MACHIAVELLI. With what can you reproach me if I do only what the others are doing?

MONTESQUIEU. Oh! if everyone does it, one would, indeed, have to be very severe to reproach Machiavelli for it.

MACHIAVELLI. I am suggesting to you not even the thousandth part of the plans which may be used. Far from fearing the increase of perpetual stocks, I should like the entire public wealth to be in stocks; I would arrange that the towns, the communes, the public establishments convert into stocks their real estate or their personal capital. It is the very interest of my dynasty which would force me to these financial measures. There would not be in my kingdom a single farthing which would not be attached by a thread to my existence.

MONTESQUIEU. But even from this point of view, from this fatal point of view, will you reach your goal? Are you not marching in the most direct manner to your ruin across the ruin of the state? Do you not know that among all the nations of Europe there are huge markets of public funds where the prudence, the wisdom, the probity of the governments are auctioned off? According to the way in which you direct your finances, your funds would have the worst of it in foreign markets and would fall to the lowest market price, even on the Exchange of your own kingdom.

MACHIAVELLI. That is a flagrant error. A glorious government such as mine would be, cannot but enjoy great credit abroad. At home, its vigor would dominate all apprehensions. Besides, I do not intend that the credit of my state should depend upon the fears of a few candle-grease merchants; I would dominate the Exchange by the Exchange.

MONTESQUIEU. What now?

MACHIAVELLI. I would have gigantic establishments of credit

instituted apparently for the purpose of lending money to industry, but whose real function would be to uphold the stock. Capable of placing 400 or 500 millions of shares on the market, or of rarefying the market in the same proportions, these financial monopolies would always be masters of the Exchange. What do you think of this scheme?

MONTESQUIEU. A fine business your ministers, your favorites, your mistresses are going to do in these firms! So your government is going to play on the Exchange with the secrets of state?

MACHIAVELLI. What are you saying!

MONTESQUIEU. Then explain in some other way the existence of these firms. So long as you were only in the domain of doctrines, one might be mistaken about the true name of your politics; since you have arrived at the application, one can no longer be mistaken. Your government will be unique in history; one will never be able to slander it.

MACHIAVELLI. If someone in my kingdom presumed to say what you hint at, he would disappear as if by a thunderbolt.

MONTESQUIEU. A thunderbolt is fine evidence; you are fortunate to have it at your disposal. Have you finished with the financial aspects?

MACHIAVELLI. Yes.

MONTESQUIEU. Time is passing rapidly.

TWENTY-SECOND DIALOGUE

MONTESQUIEU. Before having heard you, I was not very familiar with either *the spirit of laws, or the spirit of finances.* I am indebted to you for having taught me both. You hold in your hands the greatest power of modern times, money. You are able to procure practically as much of it as you wish. With such prodigious resources you will undoubtedly do great things; here is finally an opportunity of showing that *good may come from evil.*

MACHIAVELLI. That is, indeed, what I expect to show you.

MONTESQUIEU. Well, let us see.

MACHIAVELLI. The greatest of my good deeds will be, first of all, that of having given domestic peace to my people. Under my reign the wicked passions are restrained, *the good people are reassured and the bad ones tremble.* I render liberty, dignity, strength to a country torn by factions before my time.

MONTESQUIEU. After having changed so many things, will you not end by changing the meaning of words?

MACHIAVELLI. Liberty does not consist in license, no more than dignity and strength consist in insurrection and disorder. My empire, peaceful at home, will be glorious abroad.

MONTESQUIEU. How?

MACHIAVELLI. I shall wage war in the four quarters of the globe. I shall cross the Alps, like Hannibal; I shall fight in India, like Alexander; in Libya, like Scipio; I shall go from the Atlas to the Taurus, from the shores of the Ganges to the Mississippi, from the Mississippi to the river Amur. The great wall of China will fall before my name; my victorious legions will defend the tomb of the Saviour in Jerusalem and the Pope in Rome; in Peru their feet will trample the dust of the Incas; in Egypt the ashes of Rameses; in Mesopotamia, of Nebuchadnezzar. Descending from Cæsar, from Augustus and from Charlemagne, on the shores of the Danube I shall avenge the defeat of Varus; on the shores of the Adige, the rout at Cannes; on the Baltic, the outrages of the Normans.

MONTESQUIEU. Be good enough to stop, I beg of you. If you thus avenge the defeats of all the great leaders, you will not be equal to it. I shall not compare you to Louis XIV, to whom Boileau said: *"Great king, cease conquering or I cease writing."* This comparison would humiliate you. I grant that no hero of ancient or of modern times could be compared to you.

But it is not at all a question of that: war in itself is an evil; it serves in your hands to support a still greater evil, slavery; but where in all this is the good which you promised me to do?

MACHIAVELLI. This is not the time to equivocate; glory is already a great good in itself; it is the most powerful of accumulated capitals; a sovereign who has glory has all the rest. He is the terror of the neighboring states, the arbiter of Europe. His credit forces itself insurmountably, for, in spite of what you have said of the sterility of victories, force never abdicates its rights. One pretends to a war of ideas, one makes a show of disinterestedness and, one fine day, one concludes by seizing a coveted province and by imposing a tribute of war upon the conquered.

MONTESQUIEU. In such a system it is the best thing to do, if one can; otherwise, the military career would be too foolish.

MACHIAVELLI. That's something like it! You see that our ideas are beginning to come a little closer together.

MONTESQUIEU. Yes, like the Atlas and the Taurus. Let us see the other great things of your reign.

MACHIAVELLI. I do not disdain as much as you seem to believe a parallel with Louis XIV. I would have more than one characteristic in common with this monarch; like him I would have gigantic constructions made; however, in this connection, my ambition would much exceed his and that of the most famous potentates; I should like to show to the people that the monuments whose construction used to require centuries, could be rebuilt by me in several years. The palaces of the kings my predecessors would fall under the hammer of the wreckers to rise again rejuvenated by new forms; I would overthrow whole towns to reconstruct them upon more regular plans, to obtain more beautiful perspectives. You cannot imagine to what point buildings attach the people to the monarch. One may say that people easily pardon the destruction of their laws on condition that houses are built for them. Besides, you will see in a moment that buildings serve particularly important objects.

MONTESQUIEU. After the buildings, what will you do?

MACHIAVELLI. You are going very rapidly: the number of great deeds is not boundless. Will you be good enough to tell me if, between Rameses II and Louis XIV, or Peter I, the two cardinal points of great reigns have not always been war and constructions.

MONTESQUIEU. It is true, and yet we have seen absolute sovereigns who have busied themselves with giving good laws, improving the customs, introducing simplicity and decency. We have seen some who have occupied themselves with order in finances, with economy; who have dreamed of leaving behind them order, peace, lasting institutions, sometimes even liberty.

MACHIAVELLI. Oh! all that will happen. You see that, according to yourself, absolute sovereigns have some good in them.

MONTESQUIEU. Alas! not too much. However, try to prove the contrary to me. Have you something good to tell me?

MACHIAVELLI. I would give prodigious scope to the spirit of enterprise; my reign would be the reign of business. I would launch speculation into directions new and hitherto unknown. My administration would even unlock some of its links. I would free a host of industries from regulations; the butchers, the bakers and the theatrical managers would be free.

MONTESQUIEU. Free to do what?

MACHIAVELLI. Free to make bread, free to sell meat and free to organize theatrical enterprises, without the permission of the authority.

MONTESQUIEU. I do not know what that signifies. Liberty of industry is a common right among modern peoples. Have you nothing better to tell me?

MACHIAVELLI. I would be constantly occupied with the condition of the people. My government would procure work for them.

MONTESQUIEU. Let the people find it themselves, that is much better. The political powers have not the right to become popular with the money of their subjects. Public revenues are nothing but a collective subscription the proceeds of which should be used only for general services; the working classes which have been accustomed to depend on the state fall into degradation; they lose their energy, their vigor, their funds of intellectual industry. Being paid by the state casts them into a sort of bondage from which they can never raise themselves except by destroying the state itself. Your constructions swallow up enormous sums in nonproductive expenditures; they make capital scarce, kill the small industry, destroy credit in the lower levels of society. Hunger is at the end of all your schemes. Make economies first, build afterward. Govern with moderation, with justice, govern the least possible and the people will have nothing to ask of you because they will have no need of you.

MACHIAVELLI. Ah! you look upon the miseries of the people so cold-bloodedly! The principles of my government are far different; I bear in my heart the suffering human beings, the little ones. I am indignant when. I see the wealthy ones procure pleasures inaccessible to the majority. I shall do all that I can to improve the material condition of the workers, the laborers, those who bow beneath the weight of social necessity.

MONTESQUIEU. Well, begin by giving them the resources which you are appropriating for the salaries of your grand dignitaries, your ministers, your consular personages. Set aside for them the bounties which you lavish recklessly upon your pages, your courtesans, your mistresses.

Still better, remove the purple, the sight of which is an affront to the equality of men. Get rid of your titles of Majesty, Highness, Excellency, which enter proud ears like pointed steel. Call yourself protector as Cromwell did, but do the deeds of the apostles; go to live in the hut of the poor, as Alfred the Great did, sleep in hospitals, stretch yourself on sickbeds like godly Louis. It is too easy to do evangelical charity when one passes his life in the midst of feasts, when one rests on sumptuous beds, with beautiful women, when, upon rising and upon going to sleep, one has great personages who rush to put on one's shirt. Be head of the family and not despot, patriarch and not prince.

If this rôle does not suit you, be the chief of a democratic republic, grant liberty, introduce it into the habits of the people, by force if that is your temperament. Be Lycurgus, be Agesilaus, be a Gracchus; but I do not know what it is in this soft civilization where everything bends, where everything fades near a prince, where every spirit is cast in the same mould, every soul in the same uniform; I can understand that one aspires to reign over men but not over automatons.

MACHIAVELLI. Here is a flood of eloquence I cannot stop. It is with such phrases that governments are overthrown.

MONTESQUIEU. Alas! You never have any other preoccupation than the one of maintaining your position. In order to put to the proof your love of the public welfare, one would have only to ask you to descend from the throne in the name of the safety of the state. The people, whose choice you are, would have only to express its will to you in this regard in order to know how you esteem its sovereignty.

MACHIAVELLI. What a strange question! Is it not for its own good that I would oppose it?

MONTESQUIEU. What do you know of that? If the people is above you, by what right do you subordinate its will to yours? If you are freely accepted, if you are not right but only necessary, why do you expect so much from force and nothing from reason? You are wise to tremble incessantly for your reign, for you are of those who last a single day.

MACHIAVELLI. A single day! I shall last all my life, and my descendants after me perhaps. You are acquainted with my political, economic and financial system. Do you wish to know the last means by the aid of which I shall shoot forth the roots of my dynasty to the deepest layers of the earth?

MONTESQUIEU. No.

MACHIAVELLI. You refuse to listen to me. Then you are vanquished, you, your principles, your school and your century.

MONTESQUIEU. Speak, since you insist, but let this talk be the last.

TWENTY-THIRD DIALOGUE

MACHIAVELLI. I am not answering any of your bursts of oratory. The enthusiasms of eloquence have nothing to do here. To say to a sovereign: "Will you be kind enough to descend from your throne for the happiness of your people?" Is that not madness? To say to him: "Since you are an emanation of popular suffrage, give yourself up to these fluctuations, let yourself be discussed." Is that possible? Is not the first law of all constituted power to defend itself not only in its own interest but also in the interest of the people which it governs? Have I not made the greatest sacrifice which it is possible to make to the principles of equality of modern times? After all, is not a government which has sprung from universal suffrage the expression of the will of the majority? You will tell me that this principle is destructive of public liberties; what can I do about it? When this principle has entered into the customs of the people, do you know how to tear it out? And, if it cannot be torn out, do you know how to realize it in the great European societies other than by the arm of a single man? You are severe in your judgment of the methods of government: point out to me another means of execution and, if there is no other than absolute power, tell me how this power can separate itself from the special imperfections to which its principle condemns it.

No, I am not a Saint Vincent de Paul, for my subjects need not an evangelical soul, but an arm; and I am not an Agesilaus, nor a Lycurgus, nor a Gracchus, for I am neither among the Spartans nor among the Romans; I am in the heart of voluptuous societies which ally the fury of pleasures to that of arms, the transports of force to those of the senses, which no longer desire divine authority, paternal authority, religious restraint. Is it I who have created the world in the midst of which I live? I am such because it is such. Would I have the power to stop its inclination? No, I can only prolong its life because it would dissolve still more quickly if it were left to itself. I take this society by its vices because it presents only vices to me; if it had virtues, I should take it by its virtues.

But if austere principles can affront my power, can they disregard the real services that I render, my genius and even my grandeur?

I am the arm, I am the sword of the Revolutions which the

harbinger breath of final destruction is leading astray. I contain insane forces which have no other motive power, at bottom, than the brutality of the instincts, which hunt plunder under the veil of principles. If I discipline these forces, if I arrest their expansion in my country, even for only a century, have I not deserved well of it? Can I not even claim the gratitude of the European states which turn their eyes toward me as toward Osiris who alone has the power to captivate these trembling crowds? Raise your eyes higher and bow before one who bears on his brow the fatal sign of human predestination.

MONTESQUIEU. Exterminating angel, grandson of Tamerlane, reduce the people to slavery, yet you will not prevent that somewhere there will be free souls who will brave you, and their disdain will suffice to safeguard the rights of the human conscience rendered imperceptible by God.

MACHIAVELLI. God protects the strong.

MONTESQUIEU. Please get to the last links of the chain which you have forged. Lock it well, use the anvil and the hammer, you can do all. God protects you, it is He Himself who guides your star.

MACHIAVELLI. I have difficulty in understanding the animation which now rules your words. Am I really so hard, I who have taken as final policy, not violence, but self-effacement? Calm yourself, I bring you more than one unexpected consolation. Only allow me to take a few more precautions which I consider necessary to my safety; you will see that with those with which I surround myself a prince has nothing to fear of circumstances.

Our writings have more than one resemblance, in spite of what you say, and I believe that a despot who wishes to be complete must certainly not dispense with reading you. For instance, you wisely remark in the *Esprit des Lois* that an absolute monarch must have a large prætorian guard *(Esprit des Lois,* Book X, Ch. XV, Page 127); the advice is good, I shall follow it. My guard would be about one-third of the strength of my army. I am a great lover of conscription which is one of the finest inventions of French genius, but I believe that this institution must be perfected by trying to retain in the army the greatest possible number of those who have completed their period of compulsory service. I would succeed, I believe, by resolutely taking possession of the kind of traffic which is carried on in some States, as in France for instance, in connection with voluntary service for money. I would suppress this shocking transaction and I myself would carry it on honestly in the form of a monopoly by creating an endowment fund for the army which would call to arms, by the enticement of money, those who would like to devote themselves exclusively to the military state, and would keep them there by the same means.

MONTESQUIEU. Then they would be types of mercenaries that you hope to form in your own country!

MACHIAVELLI. Yes, party hatred will say that, when I am moved only by the good of the people and by the interest, certainly very legitimate, of my preservation which is the common good of my subjects.

Let us go on to other subjects. What is going to astonish you is that I am returning to structures. I warned you that we would be led back to that. You are going to see the political idea which springs up from the vast system of construction that I have undertaken; through that I realize an economic theory which has caused many disasters in certain States of Europe, the theory of the organization of permanent work for the laboring classes. My reign promises them an indefinite salary. Myself dead, my system abandoned, no more work; the people are on strike and rise to assault the wealthy classes. They are in the midst of a peasant rising: industrial perturbation, overthrow of credit, insurrection in my State, revolt around it; Europe is aflame. I pause. Tell me if the privileged classes, which very naturally tremble for their fortunes, will not make common cause, very close cause, with the working classes to maintain me, me or my dynasty, if, on the other hand, the interest of European tranquillity does not attach to it all the powers of the first rank.

The question of building which seems slight is in reality, as you see, a colossal one. When it is a question of an object of this importance, no sacrifice must be spared. Have you noticed that almost all my political conceptions are lined with a financial plan? That is just what happens here, too. I shall institute a fund of public works which I shall endow with several hundred millions by the aid of which I shall invite constructions over the entire surface of my kingdom. You have guessed my aim: I shall support the rising of the working classes; that is the other army which I need against the factions. But this mass of proletarians which is in my hand must not be able to turn against me on the day when it will be without bread. I take care of that by the buildings themselves, for the unusual part of my plans is that each one at the same time furnishes its corollaries. The worker who builds for me at the same time builds the necessary means of defense against himself. Without knowing it, he drives himself from the great centers where his presence would disturb me; he makes forever impossible the success of revolutions which are made in the street. The result of great buildings is, indeed, to rarefy the space in which the artisan may live, to force him to the suburbs, and soon to cause him to leave even those; for living expenses increase with the increase in rent. My capital will hardly be habitable for those who live by their daily work except at the very outskirts. It certainly is not in the neighborhood of the seat of authority that insurrections can be formed. Undoubtedly, there will be an immense laboring population around the capital, formidable in a day of wrath; but the constructions that I would raise would all be conceived according to a strategic plan, that is, they would make way for great passages where, from one end to the other, cannons could circulate. The extremity of these great passages would be attached to a number of barracks, fortresses, so to speak, full of arms, soldiers and munitions. My successor would have to be a simple old man or a child to fall before an insurrection, for, at the motion of his hand, some bits of powder would sweep the uprising twenty leagues away from the capital. But the blood which courses in my veins is ardent and my race has all the signs of strength. Are you listening to me?

MONTESQUIEU. Yes.

MACHIAVELLI. But you understand that I do not expect to make material life difficult for the working population of the capital, and there I encounter an incontestable stumbling-block; but the fertility of resources that my government must have suggests an idea to me; that would be to build for the people huge cities where the rent would be very low and where the masses would find themselves reunited by bands as in great families.

MONTESQUIEU. Mouse-traps!

MACHIAVELLI. Oh! the spirit of disparagement, the unbridled hatred of the parties will not fail to vilify my institutions. They will say what you say. That matters little to me; if this method does not succeed another will be found.

I must not leave the chapter on constructions without mentioning a detail insignificant in appearance, but what is insignificant in politics? The innumerable edifices that I shall construct must be marked with my name, they must contain attributes, bas-reliefs, groups, which recall a theme of my history. My arms, my monogram, must be woven in everywhere. In one place, there will be angels who support my crown, in another, statues of justice and wisdom which bear my initials. These points are of the utmost importance, I consider them essentials.

It is by these signs, by these emblems that the person of the sovereign is always present; one lives with him, with his memory, with his thought. The feeling of his absolute sovereignty enters into the most rebellious spirits as the drop of water which falls unceasingly from the rock hollows out even granite. For the same reason I want my statue, my bust, my portraits to be in every public establishment, especially in the auditorium of the courts; I would be represented in royal costume or on horseback.

MONTESQUIEU. Beside the image of Christ.

MACHIAVELLI. Not at all, but opposite it; for sovereign power is an image of divine power. My image is thus allied with that of Providence and of justice.

MONTESQUIEU. Justice itself should wear your livery. You are not a Christian, you are a Greek emperor of the Lower Empire.

MACHIAVELLI. I am a Catholic, Apostolic and Roman emperor. For the same reasons as those which I have just pointed out to you, I wish my name, the name Royal, to be given to every public establishment. Royal Tribunal, royal Court, royal Academy, royal Legislative Body, royal Senate, royal Council of State; as often as possible this same term will be given to the officials, the agents, the official personnel which surrounds the government. Lieutenant of the king, archbishop of the king, comedian of the king, judge of the king, attorney of the king. In short, the name of royal will be imprinted on whatever will represent a sign of power, whether it be men or things. Only my birthday will be a national holiday and not a royal one. I must add that, whenever possible, streets, public places, squares, must bear names which recall historic memories of my reign. If one carefully follows these indications, whether he be Caligula or Nero, he is certain to impress himself forever upon the memory of the people and to transmit his prestige to the most distant posterity. How many things I have yet to add! I must limit myself.

For who could say everything without a mortal tedium? (This sentence is found in the preface of the *Esprit des Lois*, P. 1.— *Editor's note.*)

Here I am at petty means; I regret it, for these things are perhaps not worthy of your attention, but, for me, they are vital.

Bureaucracy is, they say, an evil of monarchic governments; I do not believe that. They are thousands of servants who are naturally attached to the order of existing things. I have an army of soldiers, an army of judges, an army of workers, I desire an army of employes.

MONTESQUIEU. You no longer take the pains to justify anything.

MACHIAVELLI. Have I time for that?

MONTESQUIEU. No, go on.

MACHIAVELLI. In the states which have been monarchic, and they all have been at least once, I have observed that there is a

veritable frenzy for decorations, for ribbons. These things cost the
prince scarcely anything and he can make happy people, and, even
better, loyal ones, by means of some pieces of stuff, some baubles
in silver or gold. In truth, I would need little persuasion to
decorate without exception those who would ask it of me. A man
decorated is a man bought. I would make of these marks of distinction a rallying sign for devoted subjects; I really believe I
would have, at this price, nine-tenths of my kingdom. In this way
I realize, as far as possible, the instincts of equality of the nation.
Note carefully: the more a nation in general sticks to equality, the
more the individual has a passion for distinctions. Here, then, is a
means of action which it would be too stupid to deprive oneself of.
Therefore far from giving up titles, as you advise me, I would
multiply them around me as often as I would the dignities. In my
court I want the etiquette of Louis XIV, the domestic hierarchy
of Constantine, a severe diplomatic formalism, an imposing cere-
monial; these are the infallible methods of government upon the
spirit of the masses. Against all that, the sovereign appears like
a God.

I am assured that in the states which seem most democratic
in ideas, the ancient monarchic nobility has lost practically nothing
of its prestige. I would have as chamberlains the gentlemen of
the oldest school. Many ancient names would no doubt be extinct;
by virtue of my sovereign power, I would bring them to life again
with titles, and the greatest names in history since Charlemagne
would be found at my court.

It is possible that these conceptions seem odd to you, but I
insist that they will do more for the consolidation of my dynasty
than the wisest laws. The cult of the prince is a sort of religion
and, like all possible religions, this cult prescribes contradictions
and mysteries beyond reason (Esprit des Lois, Book XXV, Chap.
II, p. 386). Each of my acts, inexplicable as it may seem,
proceeds from a calculation the sole object of which is my safety
and the safety of my dynasty. As I have mentioned in The Prince,
what is really difficult is to acquire power; but it is easy to keep

it, for all that is necessary is to remove that which is harmful and to establish that which protects. The essential characteristic of my policy, as you have been able to notice, was to make myself indispensable *(The Prince,* Chap. IX, p. 63); I have destroyed as many organized forces as was necessary so that nothing could proceed without me, so that even the enemies of my power would tremble at the thought of overthrowing it.

All that now remains for me to do consists only in the development of the moral methods which are sprouting in my institutions. My reign is a reign of pleasures; you will not forbid me to cheer my people by games, by festivals; that is how I expect to modify the customs. One cannot conceal that this century is a century of money; needs have doubled, luxury is ruining families; on every hand people aspire to material pleasures; a sovereign would have to be not of his times not to know how to turn to his profit this universal passion for money and this sensual ardor which consumes men nowadays. Misery clamps them as in a vice, luxury crushes them; ambition devours them, they are mine. But when I speak thus, at bottom it is the interest of my people which guides me. Yes, I shall call forth good from evil; I shall exploit materialism to the profit of concord and civilization; I shall extinguish the political passions of men by satisfying their ambitions, their desires and their needs. I claim to have as servants of my reign those who, under previous governments, will have made the most noise in the name of liberty. The most austere virtues are like that of the wife of Giocondo; all that is necessary is always to double the price of defeat. Those who resist money will not resist honors; those who resist honors will not resist money. In seeing those whom it believes the purest fall in their turn, public opinion will weaken so much that it will end up by abdicating completely. How could one complain after all? I shall not be severe except for that which has reference to politics; I shall persecute only this passion; I shall even secretly favor the others by the thousand underground ways which absolute power has at its disposal.

MONTESQUIEU. After having destroyed political conscience, you ought to undertake to destroy moral conscience; you have killed society, now you are killing man. May it please God that your words should resound to the very earth; never could a more striking refutation of your own doctrines strike human ears.

MACHIAVELLI. Allow me to finish.

TWENTY-FOURTH DIALOGUE

MACHIAVELLI. I have now only to indicate to you certain particulars concerning my method of action, certain habits of conduct which will give my government its final countenance.

In the first place, I wish my aims to be impenetrable even to those who are closest to me. I would be, in this manner, like Alexander VI and the Duke of Valentinois, of whom it was said proverbially in the court of Rome, of the former, "that he never did what he said"; of the latter, "that he never said what he did." I would only communicate my projects when I gave the command for execution and I would always give my orders at the very last moment. Borgia never acted otherwise; his ministers themselves knew nothing and everyone about him was always reduced to simple conjecture. I have the gift of immobility: there is my goal; I look to one side, and when it is within my reach, I turn suddenly and swoop upon my prey before it has time even to cry out.

You cannot believe what prestige such a power of dissimulation gives to the Prince. When it is combined with vigorous action, a superstitious respect surrounds him, his counsellors ask one another secretly what he will think of next, the people place their confidence only in him; he personifies in their eyes the Providence whose ways are inscrutable. When the people see him pass, they think with involuntary terror what he could do by a nod of his head; the neighboring States are always fearful and overwhelm him with marks of deference, for they never know if some enterprise already prepared will not descend on them from one day to the other.

MONTESQUIEU. You are powerful in the face of your people because you are holding them under your feet, but if you deceive the States with whom you have relations the way you deceive your subjects, you will soon be strangled in the arms of a coalition.

MACHIAVELLI. You force me to leave my subject, for I am interested here only in my interior policies; but if you wish to know one of the principal means by the aid of which I would keep in check the coalition of foreign hatred, here it is: I reign over a powerful kingdom, I have told you; well! I would seek among the surrounding States some great nation now decayed and attempting to recover itself; I would help it recover entirely by means of some general war, as has been done in Sweden, in Prussia, and as could be done from one day to another in Germany or in Italy; and this nation, which would only exist through me, which would be nothing but the work of my existence, would give me, as long as I am in power, three hundred thousand more men against an armed Europe.

MONTESQUIEU. And the welfare of your State by the side of which you would thus elevate a powerful rival and possible enemy after a given time?

MACHIAVELLI. Before all else I protect myself.

MONTESQUIEU. Thus you have nothing, not even a care for the destiny of your kingdom? (One cannot conceal the fact that here Machiavelli contradicts himself, for he says formally, Chap. IV, page 26, "that the Prince who makes another powerful works for his own ruin." *Editor's Note.*)

MACHIAVELLI. Who says that? If I watch out for my own welfare am I not at the same time watching out for the welfare of my kingdom!

MONTESQUIEU. Your royal aspect is standing out more and more; I would like to see it in its entirety.

MACHIAVELLI. Then please do not interrupt me.

It is quite necessary for a Prince, no matter what his force of intellect, always to find within himself the necessary mental resources. One of the greatest talents of a statesman is that of appropriating the advice that he hears around him. Very often one finds enlightening advice in his entourage. I would therefore assemble my council very often, I would make it argue, debate before me the most important questions. When the sovereign is not sure of his desires, or has not enough resources of language to veil his real thought, he must remain silent or must not speak except to prolong the discussion. It is very rare that, in a well-formed council, the real plan of action in a given situation is not formulated in one way or another. It is snatched up and very often one of these who had given his advice very obscurely is quite surprised to see it carried into action the next day.

You have been able to see in my institutions and my acts what attention I have always given to the creating of appearances; words are as necessary as actions. The height of cleverness is to create a belief in franchise, when one has a Punic faith. Not only will my aims be impenetrable, but my words will nearly always signify the opposite of what they will seem to indicate. Only the initiated will be able to penetrate the sense of the characteristic phrases that I will drop from the heights of my throne: when I will say: *My reign means peace*, it means there will be war; when I will say that I call upon *moral means*, it means I will use methods of force. Do you hear me?

MONTESQUIEU. Yes.

MACHIAVELLI. You have seen that my press has a hundred voices and that they speak incessantly of the grandeur of my reign, of the enthusiasm of my subjects for their sovereign; that at the same time they put into the mouths of the public the opinions, the ideas and even the formulas of phrase that must support their conversations; you have also seen that my ministers continually astonish the public by the incontestable testimony of their work. As for me, I will speak rarely, only once a year, besides occasional important situations. Thus each of my manifestations will be hailed, not only in my kingdom, but in the whole of Europe, as an event.

A Prince whose power is founded upon a democratic base, must speak carefully, albeit popularly. If necessary he must not fear to speak like a demagogue, for after all he is the people, and he must have its passions. There must be for him certain attentions, certain flatteries, certain demonstrations of tenderness which will have their place on occasion. It matters little that these methods may seem mean and puerile in the eyes of the world, the people will not look so closely and the effect will be produced.

In my book I recommend to the Prince to take for an example some great man of the past, in whose footsteps he must follow as much as possible. (*The Prince*, Chap. XIV, page 98.) The historical similarities have a great effect on the masses; one increases in their imagination, one is given in life the place that posterity is reserving for you. Besides, one finds in the biography of these great men certain comparisons, certain useful hints, sometimes identical situations, from which one can gather precious lessons, for all great political lessons rest in history. When one has found a great man with whom he has some likeness, he can do even better. You know that the people love a Prince who has a cultivated spirit, who has a taste for literature, who even has talent. Well, the Prince could not use his leisure to better advantage than to write, for instance, the biography of the great man of the past whom he has taken as a model. A severe philosophy could tax such things with weakness. When the sovereign is powerful he is pardoned, and is even endowed with I know not what grace.

Certain weaknesses, and even certain vices, moreover, serve the Prince as much as virtues do. You could recognize the truth of these observations according to the use I have had to make sometimes of duplicity, sometimes of violence. It must not be believed, for example, that the vindictive character of the sovereign could injure him; quite the contrary. If it is often opportune to employ clemency or magnanimity, it is necessary that at certain moments his anger should bear down in a terrible manner. Man is the image of God, and divinity has no less rigorous blows than mercy. When I would have resolved upon the loss of my enemies, I would therefore wipe them out until there remained only their dust. Men revenge themselves only for light injuries; they can do nothing for the great ones. *(The Prince,* Chap. III, page 17.) That is what I expressly say in my book. The Prince has only the choice of instruments which must serve his wrath; he will always find judges ready to sacrifice their conscience to projects of vengeance or hate.

Do not fear that the people will ever be moved by the things I do to it. First, it loves to feel the vigor of the arm that commands, and then it hates by nature whoever rises above it, and it instinctively rejoices when one strikes above it. Perhaps you do not know, moreover, with what facility one forgets. When the moment of rigorous action is past, hardly even those who have been struck remember. In Rome, during the time of the Lower Empire, Tacitus reports that the victims ran with joy to meet their tortures. You understand perfectly that there is no question of anything like that in modern times; customs have become far softer; several proscriptions, some imprisonments, the forfeiture of civic rights, those are rather light punishments. It is true that, to arrive at sovereign power, it was necessary to spill blood and to violate many rights; but, I repeat, everything will be forgotten. The least cajolery on the part of the Prince, several kind actions on the part of his ministers or his agents, will be accepted with the marks of the greatest gratitude.

If it is indispensable to punish with an inflexible ruthlessness, it is necessary to recompense with the same punctuality; that is what I shall never fail to do. Whoever renders a service to my government will be recompensed the very next day. Positions, distinctions, the highest dignities, will form so many certain steps for whoever will be occupied in serving my government usefully. In the army, in the magistrature, in all public works, advancement will be calculated upon the shade of opinion and the degree of zeal for my government. You are silent.

MONTESQUIEU. Continue.

MACHIAVELLI. I return to certain vices and even to certain whims which I think necessary for a Prince. The management of power is an enormous thing. However able the sovereign may be, however infallible his glance and however ruthless his decisions, there is still an immense *alea* in his existence. It is necessary to be superstitious. Do not think that this is of little consequence. There are, in the lives of Princes, situations so difficult, moments so grave, that human prudence counts for little. In such cases, one must almost cast the die to make decisions. The method that I refer to, and which I shall follow, consists, in certain critical moments, in becoming attached to historical dates, consulting happy anniversaries, making such and such a bold resolution under the auspices of a day on which one has won a victory, or made a lucky stroke. I must tell you that superstition has another very great advantage; the people know this tendency. These augural ideas often succeed; they must also be used when one is sure of success. The people, who only judge by results, accustom themselves to believe that each act of the sovereign corresponds to certain celestial signs, that historic coincidences force the hand of fortune.

MONTESQUIEU. The last word has been said; you are a gambler.

MACHIAVELLI. Yes, but I have unheard-of luck, and I have a hand so sure, a mind so fertile that fortune cannot turn against me.

MONTESQUIEU. Since you are painting your portrait, you must have still other vices and other virtues to exhibit.

MACHIAVELLI. I ask you to forgive luxury. The passion for women serves a sovereign far more than you think. Henri IV owed a part of his popularity to his incontinence. Men are so made that this propensity among those who govern them pleases them. Dissolute habits have at all times been a passion, a gallant career in which the Prince must surpass his equals, as he surpasses his soldiers before the enemy. These ideas are French, and I do not think that they are too displeasing to the illustrious author of the *Lettres Persanes*. I am not permitted to fall into reflections that are too vulgar, but nevertheless I cannot refrain from telling you that the most real result of the Prince's gallantry is to attract the sympathy of the more beautiful half of his subjects.

MONTESQUIEU. You are composing madrigals.

MACHIAVELLI. One can be serious and yet gallant: you have furnished the proof. I do not diminish my idea in any way. The influence of women on the public mind is considerable. In good politics, the Prince is condemned to be gallant, even when at heart he cares little for it; but that situation will be rare.

I can assure you that if I carefully follow the rules that I have just laid down, liberty will be little desired in my kingdom. They will have a strong sovereign, dissolute, filled with the spirit of chivalry, adroit in all the physical exercises: he will be loved. The austere will do nothing about it; they will follow the crowd; and more important, the independent men will be placed on the index: people will keep away from them. No one will believe either in their character or in their disinterest. They will pass for malcontents who wish to be bought. If, here and there, I do not encourage talent, it will be repulsed on all sides, and consciences will be walked on as would pavements. But at bottom, I shall be a moral Prince; I shall not permit people to go beyond certain limits. I will respect public modesty, in all places where I see that it wishes to be respected. Contaminations will not reach me, for I will give over to others the unpleasant parts of the administration. The worst that can be said of me is that I am a good Prince who has bad advisers, that I desire the good, that I desire it ardently, that I will always do what is right when it is pointed out to me.

If you knew how easy it is to govern when one has absolute power. There are no contradictions at all, no resistance; one can carry out one's designs at leisure, one has the time to correct one's mistakes. One can make the people happy without opposition, for that is what always preoccupies me. I can assure you that people will never be bored in my kingdom; minds will be always occupied with a thousand different things. I will give the people the spectacle of my equipages and the pomp of my Court; great ceremonies will be prepared; I will lay out gardens; I will offer my hospitality to Kings; I will have embassies from the most distant countries brought here. Sometimes there will be rumors of war, sometimes diplomatic complications which will be discussed for months; I will even go so far as to satisfy the monomania of liberty. The wars which will be waged during my reign will be undertaken in the name of the liberty of men and the independence of nations, and, while the people acclaim me on my travels, I will whisper secretly into the ears of the absolute monarchs: Fear nothing, I am with you, I wear a crown like you and I intend to conserve it: *I embrace European liberty, but only to strangle it.*

One thing alone could perhaps compromise my fortune at some moment; that will be the day when it is realized on every side that my policies are not honest, that my every act is marked by the stamp of cunning.

MONTESQUIEU. Who will be the blind who will not see that?

MACHIAVELLI. My entire people, excepting several groups of which I fear little. I have moreover formed about me a school of politicians of a very great relative strength. You cannot believe to what point Machiavellism is contagious, and how easy its precepts are to follow. In every branch of government there will be men of no consequence, or of very little consequence, who will be veritable Machiavellis in miniature who will scheme, who will dissimulate, who will lie with an imperturbable cold-bloodedness; truth will not be able to see light anywhere.

MONTESQUIEU. If you have not done anything but jest from one end to the other of this conversation, as I think you have, Machiavelli, I regard this irony as your most magnificent work.

MACHIAVELLI. Irony! You are deceiving yourself if you think that. Do you not understand that I have spoken without veiling my meaning, and that it is the terrible violence of truth that gives my words the color you think you see!

MONTESQUIEU. You have finished.

MACHIAVELLI. Not yet.

MONTESQUIEU. Then finish.

TWENTY-FIFTH DIALOGUE

MACHIAVELLI. I will reign for ten years under these conditions, without changing anything in my legislation; this is the only price of definite success. Nothing, absolutely nothing, must make me change during this period; the lid of the boiler must be of iron and lead; it is during this time that the phenomena of destruction of the dissatisfied spirit are elaborated. You think perhaps that the people will be unhappy, that they will complain. Ah! I would be inexcusable if that were so; but when the springs have been the most violently tensed, when I will weigh with the most terrible heaviness upon the chest of my people, this is what they will say: We have only what we deserve, let us suffer.

MONTESQUIEU. You are quite blind if you take that as an apology for your reign, if you do not understand that expression of these words is a violent regret of the past. That is a stoic saying that announces to you the day of chastisement.

MACHIAVELLI. You embarrass me. The hour has come to loosen the bonds, I will return the liberties.

MONTESQUIEU. A thousand times better the excess of your oppression. Your people will answer you: "Keep what you have taken."

MACHIAVELLI. Ah! How well I recognize implacable partisan hatred in that. To admit nothing to one's political adversaries, nothing, not even the benefits.

MONTESQUIEU. No, Machiavelli, nothing with you, nothing! The sacrificed victim receives no benefits from his executioner.

MACHIAVELLI. Ah! How easily I could penetrate the secret thought of my enemies in that matter. They flatter themselves, they hope that the force of expansion that I compress will sooner or later hurl me into space. The fools! They will only know me well at the end. In politics what is necessary to prevent any danger with the greatest possible repression? An imperceptible opening. And it will be found.

I will most certainly not return considerable liberty; well, see however to what point absolutism will have already penetrated into custom. I can wager that at the first noise of these liberties, there will be built around me rumors of alarm. My ministers, my councillors will cry that I am abandoning the rudder, that all is lost. I will be begged, in the name of the good of the State, in the name of the whole country, to do nothing about it; the people will say: "What is he thinking about? His genius is diminishing"; the indifferent will say: "He has come to the end of his tether"; the hateful will say: "He is dead."

MONTESQUIEU. And they will all be right, for a modern journalist (Benjamin Constant. *Editor's Note.*) has said with great truth: "Does one wish to despoil men of their rights? Nothing must be done by halves. Whatever is left will be of use to them to help regain what has been taken away. The hand that is still free unties the other from its bonds."

MACHIAVELLI. That is very well thought out; it is very true; I know that I am exposing myself very much. You see that people are unjust to me, that I love liberty more than they say. You asked me a moment ago if I knew self-denial, if I would sacrifice myself for my people, relinquish the throne if necessary: now you have my answer, I can relinquish it as a martyr.

MONTESQUIEU. You have become very tender-hearted. What liberties would you return?

MACHIAVELLI. I would permit my legislative chamber to inform me each year, at the new year, of their wishes in a petition.

MONTESQUIEU. But since the great majority of the chamber is devoted to you, what can you have if not thanks and messages of admiration and love?

MACHIAVELLI. Well, yes. Will not these messages be natural?

MONTESQUIEU. Are these all the liberties?

MACHIAVELLI. But this first concession is important, no matter what you say. Nevertheless I will not hold myself to that alone. There exists in Europe today a certain intellectual movement against centralization, not among the masses, but among the enlightened classes. I will decentralize, that is to say, I will give my governors of the provinces the right to decide on many of the little local questions hitherto submitted for the approval of my ministers.

MONTESQUIEU. You only make tyranny more insupportable if the municipal element counts for nothing in this reform.

MACHIAVELLI. That is the fatal precipitation of those who demand reforms: it is necessary to progress by prudent steps along the road of liberty. I do not, however, keep myself there: I will give commercial liberties.

MONTESQUIEU. You have already spoken of that.

MACHIAVELLI. It is because the industrial question always affects me: I do not wish it said of me that my legislation goes, by an excess of suspicion in the direction of the people, so far as to hinder it from providing for its own subsistence. It is for that reason that I will have presented to the chambers laws that have for their object to lessen a little the prohibitive resolutions of association. Besides, the tolerance of my government has rendered this measure quite useless, and since, in the final account, one must not disarm oneself, nothing will be changed in the law, except perhaps the form of its phrasing. We have today in the chambers deputies who lend themselves very well to these innocent strategies.

MONTESQUIEU. Is that all?

MACHIAVELLI. Yes, for it is a great deal, too much perhaps; but I think I can reassure myself; my army is enthusiastic, my magistrature faithful, and my penal legislation functions with the regularity and the precision of those all-powerful and terrible mechanisms that modern science has invented.

MONTESQUIEU. Thus, you will not touch the laws concerning the press?

MACHIAVELLI. You would not wish it.

MONTESQUIEU. Nor concerning municipal legislation?

MACHIAVELLI. Is that possible?

MONTESQUIEU. Nor your system of protectorate of the electorate?

MACHIAVELLI. No.

MONTESQUIEU. Nor the organization of the Senate, nor that of the legislative body, nor your interior system, nor your foreign policy, nor your economic régime, nor your financial régime?

MACHIAVELLI. I will not change anything besides what I have told you. To put it correctly, I have left the period of terror, and I am entering the way of tolerance; I can do it without danger; I could even give real liberties to the people, for one must be quite lacking in political sense not to realize that at this imaginary period my legislation has borne all its fruits. I have fulfilled the goal that I announced to you; the character of the nation has changed; the unimportant powers that I have given back have been for me the plumb with which I have measured the depth of the result. All is done, all is completed, there is no longer any possible resistance. There is no danger, there is nothing! And nevertheless I will return nothing. You have said that there lies practical truth.

MONTESQUIEU. Hasten to finish, Machiavelli. May my shadow never meet you again, and may God obliterate from my memory the last trace of all that I have just heard!

MACHIAVELLI. Take care, Montesquieu; before the moment that begins falls into eternity you will seek my footsteps with anguish and the memory of this conversation will desolate your soul through eternity.

MONTESQUIEU. Speak!

MACHIAVELLI. Let us return, then. I have done all that you know; by these concessions to the liberal spirit of my times, I have disarmed partisan hatred.

MONTESQUIEU. Ah! you will not drop this mask of hypocrisy with which you have covered heinous crimes that no human language has words for. You wish, then, that I leave the eternal night to disgrace you! Ah! Machiavelli! you yourself had not taught to degrade humanity to such a point! You did not conspire against conscience, you had not conceived the thought of making the human soul a mire in which the divine Creator Himself would recognize nothing.

MACHIAVELLI. That is true, I am surpassed.

MONTESQUIEU. Flee! do not prolong this talk one moment longer.

MACHIAVELLI. Before the shadows that advance tumultuously over there have reached this dark ravine which separates them from us, I will have finished; before they have arrived you will see me no longer and you will call me in vain.

MONTESQUIEU. Then finish, this will be the expiation of the sin I have committed in accepting this sacrilegious wager.

MACHIAVELLI. Ah! Liberty! So this is with what strength you hold some souls when the people scorn you or console themselves with baubles. Permit me to give you a very short defense of this subject:

Dion speaks of the Roman people being indignant against Augustus because of certain very harsh laws that he had promulgated, but, as soon as he had brought back the comedian Piladus, and the dissatisfied had been expelled from the city, discontent ceased.

That is my defense. Now here is the conclusion of the author, for it is an author whom I cite:

"Such a people felt tyranny more deeply when a dancer was exiled than when all its laws had been taken away." (*Esprit des Lois*, Book XIX, Chap. II, p. 253.)

Do you know who wrote that?

MONTESQUIEU. It makes little difference.

MACHIAVELLI. Recognize yourself, then, it was you. I can see only boors round about me, what can I do? Dancers will not be lacking in my reign, and they would have to be very bad before I decided to expel them.

MONTESQUIEU. I do not know whether you have quoted me exactly; but here is a citation that I can guarantee you: it will revenge through eternity the people you libel:

"The habits of the Prince contribute as much to liberty as the laws. He can, like them, make men beasts, and beasts men; if he loves free souls, he will have subjects, if he loves boors, he will have slaves." (Page 173, Chap. XXVII, Book XII.)

That is my reply, and if I had to add something to this quotation today, I would say:

"When public honesty is banished from the heart of the courts, when corruption spreads there without shame, yet it will never penetrate save in the hearts of those who have access to a bad Prince; love of virtue still lives in the hearts of the people, and the power of this principle is so great that the bad Prince has only to disappear in order that, by the very force of things, honesty will return in the practice of government at the same time as liberty."

MACHIAVELLI. That is very well written, in a very simple manner. There is only one thing wrong in what you have just said, that, in the mind as in the soul of my people, I personify virtue, and more, I personify *liberty*, do you hear, as I personify revolution, progress, the modern spirit, all that is good at the bottom of modern civilization. I do not say that I am respected, I do not say that I am loved, I say that I am venerated, I say that the people adore me; that if I wished it, I could have altars erected to me, for, explain it as you wish, I have the fatal gifts that work upon the masses. In your country Louis XVI was guillotined, he who wished only good for his people, who desired it with all the faith, all the ardor of a sincerely honest soul, and, several years before, altars had been erected to Louis XIV who cared less for the people than the least of his mistresses; who, at the slightest shake of a head, would have the mob cannonaded while he played dice with Lauzun. But I, I am much more than Louis XIV, with the popular suffrage that is the base of my government; I am Washington, I am Henri IV, I am Saint Louis, Charles-le-Sage, I take your best kings, to honor you. I am a king of Egypt and Asia at the same time, I am Pharaoh, I am Cyrus, I am Alexander, I am Sardanapalus; the soul of the people expands when I pass; it runs drunkenly in my footsteps; I am an object of idolatry; the father points me out to his son, the mother invokes my name in her prayers, the maiden looks at me with sighs and dreams that if my glance fell upon her by chance, she could perhaps lie for a moment on my couch. When the unhappy is oppressed, he says: *If the king but knew;* when someone desires revenge, when he hopes for help, he says, *The king will know.* Besides, I will never be approached without being found with my hands filled with gold. Those who surround me, it is true, are hard, violent, they deserve the stick at times, but it is necessary to have things thus; for their hateful despicable character, their cheap cupidity, their dissoluteness, their shameful wastefulness, their crass avarice make a contrast with the sweetness of my character, my simple bearing, my inexhaustible generosity. They will invoke my name, I tell you, like that of a god; in storms, in periods of want, in great fires, I hasten to them, the people throw themselves at my feet, they would carry me to the heavens in their arms, if God gave them wings.

MONTESQUIEU. All of which would not stop you from crushing it with cannonshot at the least sign of resistance.

MACHIAVELLI. That is true, but love does not exist without fear.

MONTESQUIEU. Has this frightful vision ended?

MACHIAVELLI. Vision! Ah! Montesquieu! you will shed tears for a long time: tear up the *Esprit des Lois,* beg God to give you forgetfulness for your part in heaven; for here is the terrible truth of which you already have the foreboding; there was no vision in what I have just told you.

MONTESQUIEU. What are you telling me?

MACHIAVELLI. What I have just described, this gathering of monstrous things before which the mind recoils in fright, this work that only hell itself could accomplish, all this is fact, all this exists, all this prospers in the face of the sun, at this very moment, in a part of the globe which we have left.

MONTESQUIEU. Where?

MACHIAVELLI. No, that would be to inflict upon you a second death.

MONTESQUIEU. Ah! Speak, in the name of heaven!

MACHIAVELLI. Well! . . .

MONTESQUIEU. What? . . .

MACHIAVELLI. The time has passed! Do you not see that the whirlwind is carrying me away?

MONTESQUIEU. Machiavelli!!

MACHIAVELLI. See those shadows which pass by not far from you, covering their eyes; do you recognize them? They are the glories that called forth the envy of the whole world. Now, they beseech the Lord to render them their fatherland! . . .

MONTESQUIEU. Eternal God, what have you permitted! . . .

ANALYTIC TABLE OF CONTENTS
OF "DIALOGUES IN HELL"

FIRST DIALOGUE.

Meeting of Machiavelli and Montesquieu in hell.

Machiavelli eulogizes posthumous life. He complains of the reprobation that posterity has attached to his name, and justifies himself.

His only crime has been to tell the truth to the people as to kings; *Machiavellism came before Machiavelli.*

His philosophical and moral system; theory of force. Negation of morality and justice in politics.

The great men do good in societies by violating all laws. *Good comes from evil.*

Causes for the preference given absolute monarchy. Incapacity of democracy. Despotism favorable to the development of great civilizations.

SECOND DIALOGUE.

Montesquieu answers. The doctrines of Machiavelli have no philosophical base. Force and cunning are not principles.

The most arbitrary powers are obliged to rest upon the law. State justice is but the particular interests of the Prince and his favorites.

Law and morality are the foundations of politics. Inconsequence of a contrary system. If the Prince goes beyond the rules of morality, the subjects will do the same.

The great men who violate the laws under the pretext of saving the State do more evil than good. Anarchy is often much less fatal than despotism.

Incompatibility of despotism with the actual state of the institutions among the principal peoples of Europe. Machiavelli invites Montesquieu to prove this statement.

THIRD DIALOGUE.

Development of Montesquieu's ideas. The confusion of powers is the primary cause of despotism and anarchy.

Influence of political customs under the sway of which *The Prince* was written. Progress of social science in Europe.

The vast system of guarantees with which nations surround themselves. Treaties, constitutions, civil laws.

Separation of the three powers, legislative, executive and judicial. That is the generating principle of political liberty, the principal obstacle of tyranny.

The representative régime is the most appropriate form of government in modern times. Conciliation of order and liberty.

Justice, the essential basis of government. The Monarch who would practice the maxims of *The Prince* today would be exiled from Europe.

Machiavelli maintains that his maxims have not ceased to prevail in the policies of princes. He offers to prove it.

FOURTH DIALOGUE.

Machiavelli criticizes the constitutional régime. The powers remain immobile or leave their orbit violently.

The mass of people indifferent to public liberties, the real enjoyment of which they cannot have.

The representative régime irreconcilable with the principle of popular sovereignty and the balance of power.

Revolutions. Popular sovereignty leads to anarchy, and anarchy to despotism.

Moral and social state of modern nations incompatible with liberty.

Salvation lies in centralization.

Cæsarism in the Lower-Empire. India and China.

FIFTH DIALOGUE.

The fatality of despotism is an idea that Montesquieu continues to combat.

Machiavelli took as universal laws, facts which are only accidents.

Progressive development of liberal institutions from the feudal system to representative government.

Institutions are corrupted only when liberty is lost. It is necessary, therefore, to maintain it with care in the regulation of power.

Montesquieu does not admit without reserve the principle of popular sovereignty. How he understands this principle. Divine right, human right.

SIXTH DIALOGUE.

Continuation of the same subject. Antiquity of the electoral principle. It is the primordial basis of sovereignty.

Extreme consequences of the sovereignty of the people. Revolutions will not be more frequent under the sway of this principle.

Important rôle of industry in modern civilization. Industry is as irreconcilable to revolutions as to despotism.

Despotism is so distant from customs of the more advanced nations of Europe that Montesquieu defies Machiavelli to find the means to bring it back.

Machiavelli accepts the challenge, and the dialogue centers on this question.

SEVENTH DIALOGUE.

Machiavelli first generalizes on the system which he proposes to employ.

His doctrines are for all time; even in this century he has grandchildren who know the price of his lessons.

It is only a question of putting despotism in harmony with modern customs. The principal rules which he lays down for arresting the movement in contemporary nations.

Internal policies, foreign policies.

New rules borrowed from the industrial régime.

How one can make use of the press, of the courts and of the subtleties of law.

To whom the power must be given.

By these various means one changes the character of the most untamable nation and renders it as docile in the face of tyranny as a little Asiatic nation.

Montesquieu invites Machiavelli to leave generalities; he places him in the presence of a State based on representative institutions and asks him how he could return from there to absolute power.

EIGHTH DIALOGUE. (The policies of Machiavelli in practice.)

One has power over the order of constituted things, by a coup d'état.

One depends on the people and during the dictatorship alters all legislation.

The necessity for impressing terror, the day after a coup d'état. Blood pact with the army. The usurper must have all coins struck with his effigy.

He will construct a new constitution and will not fear to give it as a basis the great principles of modern justice.

How he will take care not to apply these principles and will discard them successively.

NINTH DIALOGUE. (The Constitution.)

Continuation of the same subject. The coup d'état to be ratified by the people.

Universal suffrage established; absolutism results.

The constitution must be the work of one man; submitted to the electorate without discussion, presented as a whole, accepted as a whole.

To change the political complexion of the State, it suffices to change the disposition of the organs: the Senate, the legislative body, the Council of State, etc.

Of the legislative body. Suppression of ministerial responsibility and of parliamentary initiative. Only the Prince has power to propose laws.

He is guaranteed against the sovereignty of the people by the right of appeal to the people and the right to declare a state of siege.

Suppression of the right of amendment. Restriction of the number of deputies. Salary of the deputies. Shortening of the sessions. Discretionary power of convocation, of prorogation and of dissolution.

TENTH DIALOGUE. (The Constitution (Continued))

Of the Senate and its organization. The Senate must be only a sham political body destined to cover the actions of the Prince and to give him absolute and discretionary power over all laws.

Of the Council of State. It must play, in another sphere, the same rôle as the Senate. It transmits to the Prince the regulating and judiciary power.

The Constitution is completed. Recapitulation of the various ways in which the Prince makes this system law. He does so in seven ways.

Immediately after the Constitution, the Prince must decree a series of laws which will discard, by means of exception, the principles of public rights recognized en bloc in the constitution.

ELEVENTH DIALOGUE. (Of the laws.)

Of the press. The spirit of Machiavelli's laws. His definition of liberty is borrowed from Montesquieu.

Machiavelli first occupies himself with legislation of the Press in his kingdom. It extends over newspapers as well as books.

Authorization of the Government necessary to found a newspaper and for all changes in the editorial personnel.

Fiscal measures for restraining the Press. Abolition of jury in matters concerning the Press. Penalization by administrative and judiciary means. System of notices. Forbidding of detailed accounts of legislative procedure and of the trials of the Press.

Repression of false news, prohibition of foreign journals. Prohibition of the importing of unauthorized writings. Laws of the same type imposed on the small frontier States against their own nationals. Foreign correspondents must be in the pay of the government.

Means of controlling books. Licenses given by the government to printers, editors and publishers. Facultative retraction of these licenses. Penal responsibility of the printers. It obliges these latter to make themselves the police of the books and to refer them to agents of the administration.

TWELFTH DIALOGUE. (Of the Press. Continued)

How the government of Machiavelli will annihilate the Press in making itself the journalist.

Sheets devoted to the government will be twice as numerous as the independent papers. Official journals, semi-official, favorable, semi-favorable.

Liberal journals, democratic, revolutionary, all in the pay of the government unknown to the public. Method of organization and direction.

Handling of opinion. Tactics, managed, trial balloons.

Provincial journals. Importance of their rôle.

Administrative censorship of newspapers. Communiqués. Forbidding of reproduction of certain private news.

Official speeches, reports and accounts are an annex of the governmental press. Methods of language, artifices and style necessary for taking possession of public opinion.

Perpetual eulogy of the government. Reproduction of pretended articles in foreign papers which pay homage to the policies of the government. Criticism of the former governments. Tolerance in point of religious discussions and light literature.

THIRTEENTH DIALOGUE. (Of conspiracies.)

Reckoning of victims to be made in order to assure peace.

Of secret societies. Their danger. Deportation and proscription en masse of those who had taken part.

Facultative deportation of those who remain in the country.

Penal laws against those who affiliate themselves in the future.

Legal existence permitted certain secret societies, the chiefs of which to be named by the government, in order to know all and direct all.

Laws against the right to congregate and hold meetings.

Modification of the judiciary organization. Means of action on the magistracy without expressly abrogating the permanent tenure of judges.

FOURTEENTH DIALOGUE. (Of institutions already existing.)

Resources that Machiavelli borrows from them.

Constitutional guarantee. That it is an absolute immensity, but necessary, accorded to agents of the government.

Of the public ministry. What can be taken from this institution.

Court of Cassation: danger that this jurisdiction would present if it is too independent.

Of the resources that the art of jurisprudence presents in the application of laws that touch on the exercise of political rights.

How a text of law is supplemented by a decree. Examples.

Means of preventing as much as possible, in certain delicate cases, the recourse of citizens to the tribunals. Official declarations of the administration that the law applies to such and such case or in such and such way. Result of these declarations.

FIFTEENTH DIALOGUE. (Of suffrage.)

The difficulties to be avoided in the application of universal suffrage.

It is necessary to remove from elections the nomination of the heads of departments in all the councils of administration that issue from suffrage.

Universal suffrage would not, without the greatest peril, be abandoned to itself in the election of deputies.

The candidates must be bound by a preliminary oath. The government must place its candidates in the face of the electors, and have all its agents cooperate for their nomination.

The electors must not have the right to meet in order to vote in concert. One must avoid having them vote in the crowded points.

Suppression of the vote by ballot: Dismemberment of electoral districts where the opposition makes itself felt. How one can win over the electorate without directly buying it.

Opposition in the Chambers. Parliamentary strategy and the art of carrying off the vote.

SIXTEENTH DIALOGUE. (Certain corporations.)

Danger presented by collective forces in general.

National guard. Need for dissolving it. Organization and disorganization at will.

The University. It must depend entirely upon the State, in order that the government may direct the spirit of the youth. Suppression of the chairs of constitutional law. The teaching and the justification of modern history would be very useful to impress love and respect for the Prince in future generations. Mobilization of governmental influence by means of free courses given by professors at the university.

The Bar. Desirable reforms. The lawyers must exercise their profession under control of the government and be named by it.

The Clergy. The possibility for a Prince to combine spiritual sovereignty with political sovereignty. Danger which the independence of the priesthood would cause the State.

The policy carried on with the sovereign pontiff. Perpetual menace of a schism very useful to hold it.

The best means would be to be able to keep a garrison at Rome, unless it is decided to destroy the temporal power.

SEVENTEENTH DIALOGUE. (The Police.)

The great development that must be made in this institution.

Ministry of police. Change of name if the name is displeasing. Interior police, exterior police. Corresponding services in all the ministries. Services of the international police.

Rôle that a Prince of the blood can be made to play.

Reestablishment of the black cabinet necessary.

False conspiracies. Their usefulness. Means of exciting popularity of the Prince and of obtaining special State laws.

Invisible squads which must surround the Prince when he goes out. Improvements of modern civilization in this respect.

Distribution of the police in all classes of society.

It is proposed to make use of a certain tolerance when one has in one's hands all the power of armed force and the police.

With which the right of making rules for individual liberty must belong to a single magistrate and not to a council.

Assimilation of political misdemeanors with misdemeanors of common law. Salutary effect.

Lists of criminal jury composed by agents of the government. Jurisdiction in matters of simple political misdemeanors.

EIGHTEENTH DIALOGUE. (Finances and Financial ideas.)

Montesquieu's objections. Despotism can ally itself only with the system of conquest and military government.

Obstacles in the economic régime. Arbitrariness in politics implies arbitrariness in finance. The fundamental principle of vote on taxation.

Machiavelli's response. He relies on the proletariat, which is uninterested in financial combinations, and his deputies are salaried.

Montesquieu answers that the financial mechanism of modern States resists of itself the exigencies of absolute power. Budgets. The method of drawing them up.

NINETEENTH DIALOGUE. (The budgetary system.)

Guarantees presented by this system, according to Montesquieu. Necessary balance of receipts and expenditures. Separate vote on the budget for receipts and the budget for expenditures. Forbidding of opening supplementary and extraordinary credit. Vote on the budget by topic. Court of accounts.

Machiavelli's reply. Finance is of all phases of politics that which lends itself most to the doctrines of Machiavellism.

He will not touch the Court of acccounts, which he regards as an ingenious institution. He will enjoy the regularity of the collecting of public money and the marvels of bookkeeping.

He abrogates the laws guaranteeing the balance of the budget, the control and limiting of expenditures.

TWENTIETH DIALOGUE. (Continuation of the Same Subject.)

Budgets are only elastic frames which must expand at will. The legislative vote at bottom is nothing but a confirmation pure and simple.

The art of presenting the budget, of grouping the figures. Impor-

256 EXHIBIT A

tance of the distinction between the ordinary budget and the extraordinary budget. Artifices to mask expenditures and deficit. Financial formalism must be impenetrable.

Loans. Montesquieu explains that redemption is an indirect obstacle to expenditure. Machiavelli will do no redeeming; reasons that he gives for this.

The administration of finance is in large part an affair of the press. How detailed accounts and official reports can be turned into account.

Phrases, formulas and turns of language, promises, hopes, which must be used to give confidence to the tax-payers, either to prepare them in advance for a deficit, or to weaken its effect when it is produced.

At times it must be boldly admitted that one has undertaken too much, and announced resolutions of severe economy. How these declarations can be turned to accounts.

TWENTY-FIRST DIALOGUE. (Loans (Continued))

Machiavelli defends loans. New methods of borrowing by States. Public subscriptions.

Other means of procuring funds. Treasury bonds. Loans from public banks, by provinces and by cities. Mobilization in public funds of goods of communes and public establishments. Sale of national domains.

Institutions of credit and savings. They are a means of disposing of all the public wealth and of uniting the future of the citizens to the upholding of the established régime.

How to pay. Increase in taxes. Conversion. Consolidation. Wars.

How to uphold public credit. Great credit establishments whose ostensible mission is to lend to industry, whose hidden goal is to uphold the course of public funds.

TWENTY-SECOND DIALOGUE. (The Greatness of the Reign.)

The acts of Machiavelli are in proportion to the extent of the resources of which he can dispose. He will justify the theory *that good comes from evil.*

Wars in the four corners of the world. He will follow the trail of the greatest conquerors.

Within, huge constructions. Free play given to the spirit of speculation and enterprise. Industrial liberties. Amelioration of the lot of the working classes.

Reflections of Montesquieu on all these things.

TWENTY-THIRD DIALOGUE. (Of the various other means that Machiavelli will employ to consolidate his empire and perpetuate his dynasty.)

Establishment of a prætorian guard ready to pounce on the wavering parts of the empire.

Return from the constructions and their political utility. Realization of the idea of the organization of work. Insurrection prepared in case of overthrow of power.

Strategic roads, Bastilles, workers' cities in anticipation of insurrection. The people construct fortresses against themselves.

The little means. Trophies, emblems, images and statues which everywhere remind of the greatness of the Prince.

The name "Royal" given to all institutions and to all tax offices.

Streets, public squares and places must bear the historic names of the reign.

Bureaucracy. It is necessary to multiply the offices.

Decorations and their use. Means of making innumerable partisans at little cost.

Creation of titles and restoration of the greatest names since Charlemagne.

Usefulness of ceremonials and etiquette. Pomp and celebrations. Excitement to luxury and sensual pleasures as a diversion from political preoccupations.

Moral means. Impoverishment of characters. Moral misery and its utility.

With which moreover none of these means harms the reputation of the Prince and dignity of his reign.

TWENTY-FOURTH DIALOGUE. (Particulars of the aspect of the Prince as Machiavelli conceives him.)

Impenetrability of his designs. Prestige that this gives to the Prince. A word on Borgia and Alexander VI.

Means of preventing the coalition of foreign powers, each deceived in turn. Reconstitution of a fallen State which gives three hundred thousand more men against an armed Europe.

Councils and the use that the Prince must make of them.

Certain vices are a virtue in the Prince. Duplicity. How it is necessary. Everything consists in creating the appearance in all things.

Words that signify the opposite of what they seem to mean.

Language that the Prince must keep to in a State with a democratic base.

The Prince must take for himself the model of a great man of times gone by and write his biography.

With which it is necessary that the Prince be vindictive. With what facility victims forget: Saying of Tacitus.

Recompense must immediately follow services rendered.

Utility of superstition. It accustoms people to count on the lucky star of the Prince. Machiavelli is the luckiest of gamblers and his luck can never change.

Necessity of gallantry. It attracts the more beautiful half of his subjects.

How easy it is to govern with absolute power. Pleasures of all kinds that Machiavelli will give his people. Wars in the name of European independence. He will embrace the liberty of Europe, but only to strangle it.

School of men of politics formed by the efforts of the Prince. The State will be full of Machiavellis in miniature.

TWENTY-FIFTH AND LAST DIALOGUE. (The Last Word.)

Twelve years of reign under these conditions. The work of Machiavelli is consummated. Public spirit is destroyed. The character of the nation is changed.

Restitution of certain liberties. Nothing is changed in the system. The concessions are only in appearance. Only he has left the period of terror.

Stigma inflicted by Montesquieu. He does not wish to hear more. Anecdote of Dion about Augustus. Revengeful citation of Montesquieu.

Vindication of Machiavelli crowned. He is greater than Louis XIV, Henry IV, Washington. The people adore him.

Montesquieu declares that the system of government that Machiavelli has outlined are but visions and chimera.

Machiavelli replies that precisely all that he has just said exists on one point of the globe.

Montesquieu presses Machiavelli to tell him the name of the kingdom in which these things go on.

Machiavelli is about to speak; a whirlwind of souls carries him away.

EXHIBIT B

On August 16, 17 and 18, 1921, the London *Times* published
a series of articles from its Constantinople correspondent, revealing that the "Protocols of the Wise Men of Zion" had been
plagiarized from Maurice Joly's "Dialogues in Hell." Mr. Philip
P. Graves, the *Times* correspondent, described the discovery of
the plagiarism as follows:

"I must confess that when the discovery was communicated to me
I was at first incredulous. Mr. X., who brought me the evidence, was
convinced. 'Read this book through,' he said, 'and you will find
irrefutable proof that the "Protocols of the Learned Elders of Zion"
is a plagiarism.'

"Mr. X., who does not wish his real name to be known, is a
Russian landowner with English connections. Orthodox by religion, he
is in political opinion a Constitutional Monarchist. He came here as a
refugee after the final failure of the White cause in South Russia.
He had long been interested in the Jewish question as far as it
concerned Russia, had studied the 'Protocols,' and during the period of
Denikin's ascendancy had made investigations with the object of dis-
covering whether any occult 'Masonic' organization, such as the
'Protocols' speak of, existed in Southern Russia. The only such
organization was a Monarchist one. The discovery of the key to the
problem of the 'Protocols' came to him by chance.

"A few months ago he bought a number of old books from a former
officer of the Okhrana (Political Police) who had fled to Constantinople. Among these books was a small volume in French, lacking the
title-page with dimensions of 5½ by 3½ inches. It had been cheaply
rebound. On the leather back is printed in Latin capitals the word

Joli. The preface, entitled 'simple avertissement,' is dated Geneva, October 15, 1864. The book contains 324 pages, of which numbers 315-322 inclusive follow page 24 in the only copy known to Mr. X., perhaps owing to a mistake when the book was rebound. Both the paper and the type are characteristic of the 'sixties and seventies' of the last century. These details are given in the hope that they may lead to the discovery of the title of the book. *(The London Times,* in an editorial introductory note, wrote: 'The British Museum has a complete copy of book, which is entitled *Dialogue aux Enfers entre Machiavel et Montesquieu, ou la Politique de Machiavel au XIX. Siècle. Par un Contemporain,* and was published at Brussels in 1865. Shortly after its publication the author, Maurice Joly, a Paris lawyer and publicist, was arrested by the police of Napoleon III. and sentenced to 15 months' imprisonment.')

"Mr. X. believes it must be rare, since, had it not been so, the 'Protocols' would have speedily been recognized as plagiarism by anyone who had read the original.

"That the latter is a 'fake' could not be maintained for an instant by anyone who had seen it. Its original possessor, the old Okhrana officer, did not remember where he obtained it, and attached no importance to it. Mr. X., glancing at it one day, was struck by a resemblance between a passage which had caught his eye and a phrase in the French edition of the 'Protocols.' He followed up the clue, and soon realized that the 'Protocols' were to a very large extent as much a paraphrase of the Geneva original as the published version of a War Office or Foreign Office telegram is a paraphrase of the ciphered original.

"Before receiving the book from Mr. X. I was, as I have said, incredulous. I did not believe that Serge Nilus' 'Protocols' were authentic; they explained too much by the theory of a vast Jewish conspiracy. Professor Nilus' account of how they were obtained was too melodramatic to be credible, and it was hard to believe that real 'Learned Elders of Zion' would not have produced a more intelligent political scheme than the crude and theatrical subtleties of the Protocols. But I could not have believed, had I not seen, that the writer who supplied Nilus with his originals was a careless and shameless plagiarist.

"The Geneva book is a very thinly veiled attack on the despotism

of Napoleon III. in the form of a series of 25 dialogues divided into
four parts. The speakers are Montesquieu and Machiavelli. In the
brief preface to his book the anonymous author points out that it
contains passages which are applicable to all governments, 'but it particularly personifies a political system which has not varied in its
application for a single day since the fatal, and alas, too distant date
when it was enthroned.' Its references to the 'Haussmannisation' of
Paris, to the repressive measures of policy of the French Emperor, to
his wasteful financial system, to his foreign wars, to his use of secret
societies in his foreign policy (cf., his notorious relations with the
Carbonari), and his suppression of them in France, to his relations
with the Vatican, and to his control of the Press are unmistakable.

"The Geneva Book, or as it will henceforth be called, the Geneva
Dialogues, opens with the meeting of the spirits of Montesquieu and
Machiavelli on a desolated beach in the world of shades. After a
lengthy exchange of civilities, Montesquieu asks Machiavelli to explain
why from an ardent Republican he had become the author of 'The
Prince' and the 'founder of that sombre school of thought which has
made all crowned heads your disciples, but which is well fitted to
justify the worst crimes of tyranny.' Machiavelli replies that he is a
realist and proceeds to justify the teaching of 'The Prince,' and to
explain its applicability to the Western European States of 1864.

"In the first six 'Geneva Dialogues' Montesquieu is given a chance
of argument of which he avails himself. In the seventh, which corresponds to the fifth, sixth, seventh and part of the eighth 'Protocols'
he gives Machiavelli permission to describe at length how he would
solve the problem of stabilizing political societies 'incessantly disturbed
by the spirit of anarchy and revolution.' Henceforth Machiavelli, or,
in reality, Napoleon III., speaking through Machiavelli, has the lion's
share of the dialogue. Montesquieu's contributions thereto become
more and more exclamatory; he is profoundly shocked by Machiavelli-
Napoleon's defense of an able and ruthless dictatorship, but his counter-
arguments grow briefer and weaker. At times, indeed, the author of
L'Esprit des Lois is made to cut as poor a figure as—*parvum com-
ponere magno*—does Dr. Watson when he attempts to talk criminology
to Sherlock Holmes.

"The 'Protocols' follow almost the same order as the Dialogues. . . .

"In the last four 'Geneva Dialogues' Machiavelli's apotheosis of

the Second Empire, being based upon historical facts which took place
between 1852 and 1864, obviously furnished scanty material for the
plagiarist who wished to prove or, very possibly, had been ordered to
prove in the 'Protocols' that the ultimate aim of the leaders of Jewry
was to give the world a ruler sprung from the House of David. . . .

"It is amusing to find that the only subject with which the
'Protocols' deal on lines contrary to those followed by Machiavelli in
the 'Dialogues' is the private life of the Sovereign. The last words
of the 'Protocols' are 'Our Sovereign must be irreproachable.' The
Elders evidently propose to keep the King of Israel in great order.
The historical Machiavelli was, we know, rather a scandalous old
gentleman, and his shade insists that amorous adventures, so far from
injuring a Sovereign's reputation, make him an object of interest and
sympathy to 'the fairest half of his subjects.' "

AFFIDAVIT BY THE LONDON TIMES CORRESPONDENT

The affidavit by Philip P. Graves, of *The Times*, London,
submitted to the President of Court V, Berne, Switzerland, dated
October 24, 1934, follows:

5 HEREFORD SQUARE
LONDON, S. W. 7.
24th October, 1934.

To the President of Court V,
Amtehaus,
BERNE.
Sir,

In reply to your letter requesting me to appear in your Court as a
witness in the law suit concerning "The Protocols of the Elders of
Zion" I beg to make the following sworn statement:

I, PHILIP P. GRAVES, of 5 Hereford Square, London, S.W.7.
make oath and say as follows:

1. I am a journalist, and have for twenty-eight years been in
the service of the "Times" newspaper, Printing House Square,
London, E.C.4. I am at present a member of the Foreign Department thereof.

2. There has now been produced and shown to me, marked P G 1, a pamphlet entitled "The Truth about 'The Protocols'— a Literary Forgery," published by the "Times" newspaper at the price of one shilling, at Printing House Square, London, E.C.4., containing three articles from the "Times" newspaper of August 16th, 17th and 18th, 1921, together with a preface thereto.

3. I am the author of the articles which are contained in this pamphlet and of my own knowledge I say that the said pamphlet in respect of the said articles is a reproduction in all essentials of the said articles as they originally appeared on the said dates in the said newspaper.

4. For the purpose of the said articles I made a study of the document which is termed "The Protocols of the Learned Elders of Zion," and of the book entitled "Dialogue aux Enfers entre Machiavel et Montesquieu, ou la Politique de Machiavel au XIX Siècle. Par un Contemporain" by Maurice Joly, published at Brussels in 1865. The conclusions to which I have come in my said articles in the said "Times" newspaper represent my considered opinion in respect of the said Protocols.

5. I agree entirely with the last paragraph of the preface of the said pamphlet which summarises my opinion perfectly and runs as follows:—

"In the following three articles the Constantinople Correspondent of the 'Times' presents for the first time conclusive proof that the document is in the main a clumsy plagiarism. He has forwarded to the 'Times' a copy of the French book from which the plagiarism is made. The British Museum has a complete copy of the book, which is entitled 'Dialogue aux Enfers entre Machiavel et Montesquieu, ou la Politique de Machiavel au XIX. Siècle. Par un Contemporain,' and was published at Brussels in 1865. Shortly after its publication the author, Maurice Joly, a Paris lawyer and publicist, was arrested by the police of Napoleon III. and sentenced to 15 months' imprisonment."

I remain of the opinion that it is proper to describe the so-called Protocols of the Elders of Zion (which, as stated in the preface, were published in London in 1920 under the title of "The Jewish Peril") as a forgery and as a clumsy plagiarism designed in the first instance to excite hostility to the Jews and Liberals of Russia by false accusations, and used in its translations to excite hostility towards the Jews generally. Everything that has come to my notice—and I have endeavored to keep abreast with the material available—has strengthened the opinion expressed by me in the said articles.

6. I regret that owing to domestic causes I am unable to attend the Court and give my evidence in person.

SWORN at No. 5, Hereford
Square, South Kensington,
London, England, this
24th day of October 1934

PHILIP P. GRAVES

(Signature)

Before me—

H. PETER VENN

Not. Pub.

London

Vu à la Légation de Suisse à Londres
pour légalisation de la signature de Mr. H. Peter Venn,
notaire public à Londres, 24 Oct. 1934
Pour le Ministre de Suisse
et par ordre

EXHIBIT C

Here follows a translation from the Russian of the German novelette by the notorious Hermann Goedsche, who used the pseudonym of "Sir John Retcliffe." This product of "Retcliffe's fantastic imagination" tells its own story, clearly foreshadowing the Protocols, with all its accompaniment of melodrama, not even omitting the Devil himself. The Russian version was published in St. Petersburg in 1872.

THE JEWISH CEMETERY IN PRAGUE

AND

THE COUNCIL OF REPRESENTATIVES OF THE TWELVE TRIBES OF ISRAEL

The Jewish quarter of Prague represents a remarkable labyrinth of crooked and narrow streets; it is situated in the outskirts of Prague which witnessed numerous bloody episodes of Bohemian and German history. The dwellers of the dirty and dilapidated houses of this quarter are engaged in petty trading and profiteering in their own as well as in other parts of the city. Prague is the only city in Germany where the Jews live entirely isolated from the nation whose name they have taken in order to avail themselves of the privileges of the city population and to exploit it for their own purposes. The Jewish quarter in Prague is the same as the rag-fair in Vienna and the Temple in Paris. In these places deals amounting to thousands are transacted daily.

If you take a few steps along this dirty, foul market-place, you will suddenly come upon an old, high, decayed wall which surrounds a space of from two to three acres. Elder-trees and other wild shrubbery wind around this wall. Old Jewish houses are crowded all along near this wall, threatened with destruction at any moment. The strange circle formed by this wall has an unwelcome, puzzling appearance.

This is the city of the dead—the renowned Prague cemetery.

In this abode of rest may be seen the spirit of the nation, whose bones found shelter here after long wandering,—here is stamped all its history, full of sufferings, struggles and resistance.

It seems as though at any moment these tombs, overgrown with shrubbery, are ready to open, these stones growing for thousands of years are ready to raise themselves, and to let out into the world the restless wanderer with a pack upon his shoulder, with a staff in his hand, in order to go again to strange peoples,—to cheat and combat them and to seek a new Canaan—his dominion! The Jewish cemetery in Prague is the very oldest cemetery known. It was closed by order of the government a hundred years ago. For foreigners it is a historical landmark; for the Jews, it is a sacred place. The impression of this deserted spot is intensified by its surroundings. Amidst the closely crowded tombs and monuments, overgrown with moss, only a narrow passage remains which is almost entirely covered with shrubbery of thorn-bushes and mat-weed.

During the inspection, the watchman will tell the visitor the history of the death of Rabbi Ben Manasseh, the great conqueror of death, and Rabbi Loewe, the most learned Rabbi of the 17th century; he will speak of Simon the Just and of the Polish princess Anna Shmiless. He will then lead the visitor to the monument of Anna Kohn on which can be read the mysterious figure 606, which shows that the Jews, more than twelve hundred years ago, had buried their dead here, in the legendary times of Lyubush and her daughters.

If we are not to believe this figure, we must nevertheless agree with the opinion of the Jews that this is the oldest settlement and the first Jewish community in Europe.

Silently the Jewish guide and the curious foreigner go by one place where under an old lilac bush a heap of stone stands out, and when the foreigner asks, "What is this?" the guide gives an evasive an-swer——

"Beth Chaim—the house of life." Thus is the cemetery called. Yes, indeed, this place of rest is a house of life, for from here is given the mysterious impulse which makes the exiles masters of the earth and tyrants of nations,—the impulse which directs the golden calf to the chosen tribe.

The Jewish town has assumed a holiday aspect. The stands of the petty retailers have disappeared; Jewish boys and girls were strolling about in their holiday attire. The houses and windows were adorned with green branches. On the old benches sat men, talking seriously; in the alleys youths were chatting. From time to time men and women in their best Sabbath clothes were going to the synagogue, carrying prayer books in their hands; while poor Christian women whom need had forced to work in this quarter were running with keys and dishes in order to prepare for the feast.

It was the last day of the Feast of Booths, the day of Assembly, and dusk was gathering over the narrow streets, while the Christian part of the city was still brightly illumined by the last rays of the setting sun. Two men (the older wore a black silk mantle, with long earlocks, which showed that he was a Polish Jew; the other was middle aged, in modern clothes, with diamond studs in his shirt and a heavy golden chain on his vest) walked along the narrow streets, without paying any attention to the crowd.

The younger seemed to be the guide. Having come with his companion to the little house where the watchman of the cemetery lived, he knocked at the closed door, through a crevice of which the bright light of wax candles was seen, showing the watchman's holiday mood. It was a good summer—a large number of foreigners had visited the cemetery and were generous in their gifts.

In the doorway appeared the thin face of the watchman, whose short-sighted eyes began to look fixedly into the darkness.

"Come out into the street, Joel, somebody wants to talk to you!"

"O, God of Justice," said the watchman with amazement, as he came out of the door,—"One of the trustees! What is your pleasure to command me?"

"This Rabbi desires to make a brief prayer in the cemetery; he is leaving tomorrow morning by train."

"In the cemetery? This evening? But you know yourself, Mr. Banker, that I am forbidden to open the gates after sunset, and tonight is also the holy Sabbath."

"First of all, there is no need for you to shout here about my calling," replied the banker, displeased. "Every Jewish rag-picker will know that banker Rosenberg was here to see you. As for the permit to open the gates, I myself, as a trustee, authorize you to do it. I will wait here until he has completed his prayer. The company in your house must not know what we are doing here. Arrange it so that the curious crowd will not rush in there."

The watchman disappeared in the house, but soon returned with a bunch of keys and opened the gates of the cemetery. He took a lantern along and was about to light it.

"Don't!" said the Rabbi in a low voice. "I don't need any light. Lock the gates from the inside!"

"But, Herr von Rosenberg——"

"Lock it, I say!"

The watchman obeyed.

"Now lead me to the grave of the holy Rabbi Simeon-ben-Yehudah!"

"Hold on to my coat, esteemed sir," said the watchman. "It is dark and you may stumble over the old graves."

"I can see better at night than in the daytime, my son!" answered the learned Polish Jew.

"Here is the grave!"

The old Rabbi reverently leaned over the tombstone. The watchman heard him pronounce a prayer in Jewish. He used so many words of ancient Hebrew, or some other words of a language he did not understand, that he knew only a few separate expressions, although he himself had been in the past a teacher at the Bohemian community.

Having completed his prayer, the stranger turned to the watchman of the cemetery:

"When you accepted the position from your predecessor, did he not give you certain instructions?"

"Me?"

"Yes, you! It was so from the day the first person was buried in this place."

"Well, and what if he did give such instructions,—how does that concern you? This is the first time I am asked about this matter since I am employed here."

"Because this happens once in a hundred years, and human life rarely lasts as long as that."

"I see that you know about it, Rabbi," said the frightened watchman. "But I can obey you only if you mention the word which was given to me by my predecessor, because I took a sacred oath on the Bible."

The Polish Jew bent down and slowly pronounced a word of seven syllables.

The watchman bowed respectfully.

"You are the Rabbi!" he said. "All will be done as you command!"

"You will send away the friends who are feasting in your house before the clock strikes eleven. At the first stroke you will open the gates of the cemetery, and at the last stroke you will get into your house, lock the doors and windows, lie down in your bed and turn into a corpse together with the members of your household,—into a corpse that sees and hears nothing."

"I will neither look nor listen."

"The angel of death will leave your soul in your body and will force you to wander about among the graves to the end of time if you do not carry out my orders correctly. Now go, and remember that by virtue of your position you are the servant of the great Jerusalem synagogue. I need not tell you that you should not say anything to that vain, worldly man who brought me here."

Both returned to the gates, near which the banker was still on guard.

"Well," he said, "your desire is fulfilled, Rabbi, and you may inform my friend in Warsaw that Rosenberg and Son are always ready to do a favor to a guest recommended by such a personage. Now let us go home; my wife is waiting for us."

"Let us go, my son," replied the Rabbi. "But relieve me of worldly pleasures. I shall spend the night in prayer!"

The banker shrugged his shoulders and gave the watchman a gold coin.

"Joel," he said in a low voice, "the other trustees of the community must not know about this violation of the rule."

The watchman nodded, and the companion again disappeared in the dark streets, which had already become deserted, while in the houses people talked merrily and the sounds of holiday festivities were heard.

How poor, dirty and dark these little houses looked from outside! But it was quite different within! In the rear rooms of many of these houses the bright light of numerous wax candles was reflected in the splendid high mirrors, in expensive dishes and precious rugs. Girls and women, who in the morning perhaps walked with trays in their hands, now were seated at the tables in heavy silk gowns with golden chains and bracelets; their ornaments and diamonds were glittering.

The clock in the town-hall tower struck ten. In the chapel, near the statue of St. Nepomucenus, upon a stone bench, sat a large-sized man, with the pale serious face of Germanic type. Every physiognomist, looking at him, would have said that this man had devoted his youth to serious scientific work and that he had spent many sleepless nights over books.

The clock had just struck ten when upon the bridge appeared a man in a light summer coat, of about the same age as the young scientist. His face was pale, of waxen color, without the slightest natural red in his cheeks; his particularly prominent nose indicated his Jewish extraction; his forehead was high and large, his head was strongly developed. He walked straight over to the man who was waiting and who quickly arose.

"Good evening. I see you have received my letter. Have you it with you?"

"Yes, I know it by heart, I have read it so many times. My friend, it is written there, I have promised to give you the key to the Caballah, if I ever find the opportunity to do so. Although I am not always in the habit of fulfilling my vows, I am ready to fulfil this one, if you will wait for me in the evening of October 8, in Prague, on the old Moldau bridge, under the statue of Nepomucenus. Then follows your name."

"Yes, that is correct. Have you not yet given up your desire?"

"Less than ever before! You would render science an invaluable service."

"Listen, doctor, bend down a little over the rail; that of which we speak must not be heard even by the waves of the Moldau, if we wish to remain alive."

The young scientist looked in astonishment at his comrade, but did as he desired.

"Three years ago, in Rome, when I promised to acquaint you with the mysteries of Caballah, I did it more for the sake of boasting of a power and authority which, in reality, I did not possess. Although I had studied for some time the traditions of my nation, rather out of curiosity than because of the love of knowledge, I knew very well that I could hardly penetrate the corridor of those mysteries which I am still regarding as the sophistry and roguishness of exalted minds, invented for the purpose of holding fools in fear and subordination.

But several accidental discoveries, made by me since then, have changed my views and have aroused in me a sense of curiosity.

"You know, notwithstanding our brief acquaintance, that I am not the type of man who would abandon a clue or a conceived plan. What has caused me to make you my companion in satisfying my curiosity—that does not concern you. It is enough that now we have an opportunity to satisfy our mutual desire, and all depends on whether you will agree to accept the conditions upon which I can make you a partner in my investigation."

"If these are not against honor and conscience."

"In this respect you have nothing to risk, you are rather risking something else—your life. Do you feel that you are capable of facing a serious danger?"

"For the sake of science, yes!"

"Very well, in that case I must tell you that I will lead you to a place which we will not leave alive, if our presence is discovered. The slightest suspicion that we were uninvited witnesses of the secret will bring upon us persecution which will kill us sooner or later."

"You are whetting my curiosity, signor!"

"That is all I wanted to tell you. The other thing—you know that I am a Jew by birth. Although the Jews have driven me from their midst and cursed me according to their custom and traditions because I adopted Christianity,—still I have my own reasons for stipulating a condition—your word of honor that you will be silent about all you will see and hear, until I authorize you to speak."

"I swear by my honor."

"Very well. You will recall in your investigations of the Caballah that in the mysterious books mention is made of a meeting of the heads or chosen ones of the nation,—a meeting which takes place from time to time?"

"Yes, in the Yezire it is said very definitely, and if I understood correctly, such meetings take place every hundred years."

"Yes. The last meeting took place in 1760 and you recall that shortly afterward the movement of Judaism started. It is now 1787 years since the destruction of Jerusalem and this year is designated for a meeting of the Cabalistic Sanhedrim. This is the day of the meeting; the place is this city. I want to be present at this meeting in spite of the danger and am ready to take you along with me."

"But will it not be dishonest to listen, will it not be an unlawful interference with other people's secrets?"

"Per Bacco! as we Italians say; with such hesitations you must abandon once for all the idea of fulfilling your desire. Or do you think that the people who guard the secret of the Caballah will bring it to you on a tray? As far as I am concerned, I shall discover the secret, at any cost!"

After reflecting a few minutes, the scientist came to a decision.

"I shall go with you, come what may!"

"Very well. Now we have agreed. Let us go,—there is no time to lose."

The tower clock of the town-hall struck eleven. At the first stroke a key clicked in the lock of the cemetery gates. Then followed profound silence which indicated that the cemetery was open. The lights in the Jewish houses were gradually dying out, and at the same time the sounds of the merry feasting also subsided.

Mysterious silence reigned in that terrible place.

The gates creaked softly; the rustling of long coats was heard, touching the stones and shrubbery; finally a vague white figure appeared and slipped by like a shadow along the pathways.

This figure knelt before one of the tombstones; three times it touched the stone with its forehead and softly whispered a prayer.

Along the path leading from the gates came an old man, bent, limping, sighing and coughing. He came over to the ancient tombstone, and lowered himself on his knees near the white figure that had entered before him, and he, too, whispered a prayer.

Then heavy footsteps were heard, and a tall, impressive figure appeared on the road, clad in a white mantle, and he, too, fell down on his knees, as though unwillingly, in front of the tombstone.

Thirteen times this was repeated. Thirteen old men came over to the tombstone. The doctor counted them, but he could not understand whether they were alive or dead. A shiver crept down his back, his heart began to beat faster from fright. He involuntarily recalled the terrible legend of the Day of Atonement in the tenth month, Tishri, in the synagogue of Posen when, during the prayer of Kol Nidrei, the congregation kept growing larger and larger; unknown people, pushing one another, wrapped in prayer shawls, came in, one hundred after another, until the terrified Rabbi lifted his hand as if to curse and exclaimed: "He who has flesh in his cheeks, let him throw off the prayer shawl!" Hundreds remained covered, and when the prayer shawls were torn away from them, all saw the skulls of the dead who had come out of the graves to celebrate the Day of Atonement with the rest of the congregation.

As there, it seemed to him that the prayer shawls had fallen off the heads of the praying old men, and a row of dead skulls appeared. At that moment the clock struck twelve. A sharp metallic sound rang out on the grave, after which a blue flame appeared and illumined the thirteen kneeling figures.

"I greet you, Roshe beth Aboth (heads) of the twelve tribes of Israel," announced a dull voice.

"We greet you, son of the accursed."

"A hundred years have already passed. Where have the Nesiyim (princes of the tribes) come from?"

"From the lands where the nation of Adonai has been scattered by the orders of our forefathers."

"Are you ready to fulfil the promise during the coming century?"

"We are ready!"

"Then say, whose representatives are you, and where do you come from? Tribe of Judah?"

"From Amsterdam," replied a strong, loud voice.

"Tribe of Benjamin?"

"Toledo!" came the dull answer.

"Tribe of Levi?"

"Worms!"

"Tribe of Manasseh?"

"Budapest!"

"Tribe of Gad?"

"Cracow!"

"Tribe of Simeon?"

"Rome!"

"Tribe of Zebulun?"

"Paris!"

"Tribe of Dan?"

"Constantinople!"

"Tribe of Asher?"

"London!"

"Tribe of Issachar?"

The answer came in a faint voice and could not be heard distinctly.

"Tribe of Naphtali?"

"Prague!"

"And I am the representative of the unfortunate and exiles," said the man who asked the questions in a dull voice. "I am myself wandering about all over the world in order that I may unite you for the sake of the cause of redemption which has been promised to the seed of Abraham and which was taken from them by the sons of him who was crucified! Who is here of the house of Aaron, let him rise, scrutinize the heads of the tribes and gather the council."

The man who was the first to arrive rose and then seated himself upon the tombstone. One by one the others came over to him and whispered in his ear a seven-syllabled word, and each time he nodded in approval. After that all returned to their former places. "Brethren," said the Levite, "our fathers formed a union which compels all those chosen as representatives of the tribes to gather every hundred years at the grave of the great teacher of Caballah whose doctrines give the chosen ones power on earth and supremacy over all the descendants of Ishmael. Eighteen hundred years the struggle has been conducted by the nation of Israel for supremacy which was promised to Abraham and which was taken away from us by the Cross. Trampled under foot by our enemies, under the terror of death and all kinds of humiliation and violence, the nation of Israel, nevertheless, has not abandoned this struggle, and as they are scattered all over the earth, the whole earth must belong to them! Our learned men are conducting this struggle for hundreds of years; the nation is gradually rising from its fall; its power is growing and spreading. To us belong the earthly god, which was made for us with such sorrow by Aaron in the desert . . . the Golden Calf which the backsliders are worshipping!"

"We hear!" they whispered on all sides.

"When all the gold on earth will be ours, the power will go over to us. Then will be fulfilled the promise made to Abraham. Gold is the ruler of the earth. Gold is power, reward, pleasure . . . all that human beings fear and desire. This is the mystery of the Caballah . . . the teachings concerning the spirit which rules the world, and about the future! Eighteen centuries we have belonged to our enemies. The future belongs to us. For the fifth time in the course of the thousand-year-old struggle to which we have consecrated ourselves, those who know of the existence of the secret union have gathered here to take counsel as to the means which are afforded us by the sins of our enemies, and each time, for five hundred years, a new Sanhedrim, ordered the fiercest struggle. But, excepting Russia, not a single century has been crowned with such success as this one. Therefore we may think that the time for which we are striving is near, and we may say, 'The Future is ours!' "

"Yes, if persecutions against the Jews will not take place in the meantime!" pointed out one of the men with a bitter smile.

"The dark days of such a danger are passed. The success of so-called civilization among the Christian nations may serve as the best protection for our endeavors. Before listening to the individual opinions, let us examine the material means, the pure capital possessed by the nation of Israel. . . ."

"But against the three and a half million Jews with their money there are 265 million enemies in Europe, or rather 500 million fists," remarked one of those present.

"The head will protect us against the fists, as in the past. Labor is the slave of speculation, and violence is the slave of wisdom. Who will deny that cunning is the distinctive trait of our nation?

"Our nation is ostentatious and greedy, arrogant and pleasure-loving.

"Where there is light there is also shadow. It is not in vain that Adonai our God gave his chosen people the tenacity of a snake, the cunning of a fox, the look of a falcon, the memory of a dog, the diligence of an ant, and the sociability of a beaver. We were in captivity on the rivers of Babylon, and have become powerful! Our temple was destroyed, but we have built a thousand new temples! For eighteen hundreds years we were slaves; now we have grown head and shoulders above all other nations."

All the twelve pronounced the concluding words——

"Brethren," said the Levite, "the time has come when, in accordance with the laws of the founder of our union, we must determine ways and means by which the Jews shall attain their goal as soon as possible; our experience of a hundred years will help us in this. We who know must direct and guide the masses which are blind. We, the builders, will combine the dead stones into a pillar which must reach the sky."

"The Tower of Babel was destroyed by the hand of Him whose name I dare not pronounce," said the sceptic.

"Our structure rests upon the foundation of the promise made to Abraham. It is your turn to speak, representative of the tribe of Reuben! By what means will the Jewish nation achieve power and supremacy over all other nations on earth?"

A shrill, unpleasant voice then spoke:

"All the princes and the lands of Europe are at present in debt. The stock exchange regulates these debts. But such things are done only by movable capital; therefore all the movable capital must go over to the hands of the Jews. The foundation for this is already laid, judging from what we have heard here. If we will be supreme in the stock exchange, we will attain the same supremacy in the governments. Therefore it is necessary to facilitate loans in order to get them into our hands all the more. Wherever possible, we must take in exchange for capital, mortgages on railroads, taxes, mines, jewels and domains. Furthermore, the stock exchange is a means for the transfer of the belongings of the small people to the hands of the capitalists, by drawing them into stock gambling. Transactions in securities are a splendid invention of our nation. Although the stock exchange members cheat one another sometimes, it is the outsider who always pays in the end."

The voice which resounded on the Paris Bourse became silent.

"Do the zekenim agree with the opinion of our brother?" asked the Levite.

A whisper of approbation was the answer to this question.

"Representative of the tribe of Simeon, it is your turn now!"

A serious, dull voice resounded after this order. Each word was pronounced slowly and thoughtfully:

"Ownership of land is always the iron-clad, everlasting possession of every country. This in itself gives power, respect and influence. Therefore, the Jews should secure the possibility of acquiring real estate. It will not be hard to accomplish this, if we acquire movable capital. Therefore it is necessary to facilitate loans on land. Under the fear of scandal we will destroy land wealth and minimize its importance. Ownership of land should be mobilized, if lands are sold as other commodities. The more we help in the breaking up of estates, the more easily will they fall into our hands. Under the pretext of relieving the poor classes, it is necessary to levy all taxes of states and communities on the land owners. When the land is in our hands, the labor of the Christian workers and farmers will give us a tenfold income."

He who did not belong to any tribe laughed sneeringly.

"This advice is good, but not new. Ask in Paris and Vienna, who owns the houses there?"

A whisper of approbation was heard again.

"Tribe of Judah, your turn!"

The voice that resounded was marked with conviction and reminded one of the sound of the Thaller.

"Industry, the power of the burgher, which hinders the Jewish nation, must be paralyzed even as agriculture. The manufacturer should be no better than an ordinary worker. The means to accomplish this may be the unlimited freedom of trade. The manufacturer will take the place of the artisan as he does not have to work, only to speculate. The children of Israel can adapt themselves to all branches of work. Their capital and dexterity will be the substitute for right. Transforming the artisans into our factory workers, we will be in a position to direct the masses for our political purposes. Whoever resists this system will be destroyed by competition. The senseless and ungrateful masses will not support the artisans in this struggle, if commodities are reduced in price to a certain extent."

A noisy approbation of the new Sanhedrim showed that the soundness of this advice had long been appreciated and even applied in practice.

"Now it is my turn," said the representative of Levi—"I speak in the name of the tribe of Aaron. The natural enemy of the Jews is the Christian church. Therefore we must try to humiliate it, we must instill into it free-thinking, scepticism, and conflicts. Therefore we will, first of all, start a war on the clergy, we will try to arouse suspicion against it and ridicule it. The main pillar of the church is the school. Therefore we must gain influence over the young. Under the guise of progress and the equal rights of all religions, we will destroy the study of religion in Christian schools. Then the Jews may become teachers in all schools; then religion will be taught at home. And as there is little time left for that, the spirit of religion will gradually decline, and eventually it will be destroyed altogether. Agitation for the appropriation of property belonging to the churches and schools, the transfer of church property to the state, or (what is the same) into the hands of the Jews, will be our reward!"

Again approbation followed the words of the man who had spoken. Nobody contradicted him and he announced:

"Representative of the tribe of Issachar, it is your turn!"

Now an old, trembling voice spoke:

"Let our brethren strive for the abolition of armed force. The coarse military art is not for the sons of Israel. Not everyone can be a Gideon! The army is for the defense of the throne and the school of narrow patriotism. Not the sword, but reason and money must rule. Therefore at every opportune instance, it is necessary to help the downfall of the military class, to arouse suspicion in the masses against it, and to incite animosity against one another. It is enough for the soldiers to do police duty and to protect the wealthy from those who have nothing."

"The Lion of Judah has spoken," said the stranger angrily. "David conquered Goliath. The nations will soon wear long coats instead of military armour. A slap on the bourse will be equivalent to a lost battle."

It looked as though a storm was arising against this arrogant sarcasm, but one word from the eldest restored them all to calm.

"This is the son of Baal! He may say whatever he pleases. But he will do whatever is decided by the council of the tribes."

"The tribe of Zebulun may speak!"

A dull voice, like a storm in the distance, said as follows:

"Our nation is conservative to its very root, and clings fast to what is old. But our interest demands that we participate, or, rather, direct the movements of nations. It is indisputable that ours is a time of many reforms, whose main purpose is the amelioration of the material condition of the needy classes. But for this the propertied classes must sacrifice their capitals. Capital is in the hands of the Jews. Therefore they must outwardly take part in the movement and try to divert it from social and political reforms. The masses themselves are blind and foolish, and permit the shouters to rule over them. Who shouts more loudly and more shrewdly than the Jews? Therefore our nation has been the first on the platform, in the press, and in all Christian communities! The more communities and meetings, the more dissatisfaction and idleness. From this it follows inevitably that the people grow poorer, that they become subjected to those who have money, leading to the enrichment of the latter. Besides, every movement makes us richer, for the smaller people are ruined and are contracting debts. The unstability of the foundation increases our power and our influence. Therefore the support of every kind of dissatisfaction, every revolution, increases our capital and brings us nearer to our goal."

This terrible speech was followed by prolonged silence. Every member of this secret Sanhedrim seemed to be thinking of its terrible meaning. The son of Baal again laughed hoarsely.

"Are you afraid of blood? It isn't yours."

Then one member of the gathering expressed his approval, and all others followed his example.

"Son of the tribe of Dan, your turn!"

The answer bore the stamp of a Jew of the lower order:

"Every business in which there is speculation and profit must be in our hands. That is our natural right. First of all, we must get control of the traffic in liquor, butter, wool, and bread. Then we shall have in our hands agriculture, farming. We can prepare bread everywhere, and if dissatisfaction and want should arise, we can easily throw the blame on the government. Petty things which give a great deal of trouble and yield very little profit, we can leave in the hands of the Christians. Let them work hard and suffer as the chosen people suffered for several centuries."

This speech scarcely needed approval. The Levite called on the next one.

"Tribe of Naphtali?"

The following words rang out shrilly and with assurance:

"All governmental positions should be open to us. Once this principle is established, the cunning and flattery of the Jewish employees will help them to penetrate even there, and they will have real influence. I am speaking only of the posts which bring honor, power, and pre-eminence. Positions which require work and knowledge may remain for the Christians. Therefore the Jews may neglect positions of secondary importance. Justice is very important for us, the law is a great step forward. This occupation is suited to the cunning and skill of our people and gives us influence and power against our natural enemies. Why can't a Jew be Minister of Education as he has already been more than once Minister of Finance?"

"Remember the scaffold of Haman, the fate of Shushan and Leopold!" said a warning voice.

"Why does the raven croak about the past which is so distant and almost forgotten? More than one of our people has been a Minister in France and respected by the King himself."

Approval was expressed in a tone of satisfied pride; then the orator continued:

"Our people must be among the legislators of the governments. The laws of the goyim against the children of Israel must be abolished. We will maintain the laws of our Fathers. We need no longer any laws that would protect us. No. We must concern ourselves about laws that will give us privileges. A mild law respecting bankruptcy, promulgated in the interests of humanity, would be a golden mountain in our hands. First of all we must see to it that the law regarding usury is abolished in all countries under the pretext that money would thereby become cheaper. Money is just such a commodity as others, and the law should give us the right to regulate its price according to our desire."

"Now is the turn for the tribe of Benjamin."

"What can I add to the counsel of such wise men? The Jew should also make use of honors, and should be at the head of all organizations that may give him honor without risks, and he should engage in science and the arts which are more adapted to the character of our people and which we can master more easily. We can become good actors and philosophers, because there is room for speculation in these domains. In the arts our people will look after the receptions and will burn incense to ourselves. In science we will take up medicine and philosophy. These afford opportunities for theories and speculation. A physician penetrates the secrets of families and holds their lives in his hands."

"Tribe of Asher, your turn!"

"We must demand free marriage between Jews and Christians. Israel will only be the gainer, even though there be an admixture of impure blood to a certain degree. Our sons and daughters will marry into renowned and powerful Christian families. We give money and thus have influence. The Christian relationship cannot have a bad influence on us, while we can exert a strong influence over them. That is one thing. Another thing is that we respect the Jewish woman and

THE JEWISH CEMETERY IN PRAGUE 281

we enjoy the forbidden pleasure with the women of our enemies. We have money, and for money we can get everything. A Jew must never make a daughter of his own race his mistress. If he should desire to sin against the Seventh Commandment he should content himself with Christian girls."

"What is the use of employing the beautiful girls of the goyim in our stores if not for this?" angrily interposed the representative of the evil spirit. "Whoever will not want to satisfy our desire will get no work, consequently no bread. Go to the large cities and you will see that they are not waiting for your wise men's orders. Substitute a contract for sacrament in the marriage of Christians and their wives and daughters will come to you still more readily."

The terrible cynicism of these words, touching such a delicate subject, must have produced a profound impression, especially since the views of the ancient doctrines were so strict on the topic of moral purity.

"What does the law say?" asked one of the twelve.

"For adultery with a woman of our own people—death; for seducing a girl—a fine, if she was not betrothed; if she was betrothed—death. But the law is not so rigorous with regard to one who lives with a slave—her body belongs to her master."

"Are the goyim better than our slaves?"

This explanation was followed by a whisper of approval.

"The tribe of Manasseh may speak now!"

The last of the orators lifted his hand and during his speech he raised and lowered it, as if desiring thus to make a stronger impression by his words. His voice was hoarse and unpleasant, but he spoke skilfully and with assurance.

"If gold is the first power in the world, the press is the second. Of what value are all the opinions and advice given here without the aid of the press? We will attain our aim only when the press is in our hands. Our people must direct the daily publications. We are cunning, shrewd, and we possess money which we know how to utilize for our purposes. We need great political newspapers which mold public opinion—criticism, the literature of the streets and the stage. In this way we will crowd out the Christians step by step, and will dictate to the world what it should believe in, what it should respect, and what it should curse. We will repeat the sorrowful cry of Israel and the complaints against the persecutions which are directed against us. Then, even though each individual may be against us, the masses, in their stupidity, will always be for us. With the press in our hands, we can turn wrong into right, dishonesty into honesty. We can shake all foundations, and separate families. We can destroy faith in all that our enemies, until now, have believed. We can ruin credits and arouse passions. We can declare war; we can award fame or disgrace. We can uplift or ruin talent.

"When Israel shall have gold and the press in his hands, we will be able to ask: 'On what day will it please you to *put on Atarah* (crown) which belongs to us by right, to erect Shisse (?) and extend the Shebet (sceptre) over the nations of the earth?'"

A noisy greeting followed these words and the agitated men who listened hardly understood for some time what was being said at the meeting. At last the voice of the Levite called upon all to be silent.

"The Roshe-Bate-Aboth of the twelve tribes have uttered words of wisdom. These words will be as pillars for the times to come, if the son of him 'who has not rest' will write these words upon his memory and spread the seeds among the nation of Israel in order that it may grow to be a mighty tree. They will be the sword with which Israel will strike down his enemies. Our posterity must share among themselves happiness, wealth and power as it shared misfortune and dangers. They must help one another. Wherever one of them places his foot, he must drag another—his brother—along with him. If one of them is unfortunate, others must help him, if he but lives according to the law of our nation.

"He who was in prison for ten years, may become a rich man to whom princes will bow, if only our people will not forsake him. Where everybody is against us, all will be for us. After forty years of wandering in the desert, the hand of Jehovah brought us to power in the land of Canaan; the same hand will lead us after forty-five times forty years from our misfortune and miseries to rule over lands which are forty-five times vaster than Canaan. If Israel shall obey the decision here adopted by the Sanhedrim of the Caballah, our grand-children, coming a hundred years hence to the grave of the founder of our union, will announce to him that they have indeed become the princes of the world and that the promise made to the nation of Israel has been fulfilled. Other nations will become his slaves! Renew our oath, sons of the golden calf, and go to all lands of the world."

The blue flame flared up brightly upon the grave of the Rabbi; each of the thirteen threw upon the tomb a stone which each carried under his cloak.

It seemed to the doctor that on the top of the tombstone, in the bluish flame, there appeared a monstrous golden figure of an animal.

Then he heard the same metallic sound that he had heard when the light first appeared. Then impenetrable darkness covered the cemetery.

The white figures again slipped by among the tombstones. The gates creaked softly.

The clock in the tower struck two past midnight. The last of the mysterious visitors knocked at the window and a hoarse voice said (as though the speaker knew that the watchman was not asleep):

"Close the house of life, watchman of those who are awaiting the resurrection, and may your lips be sealed with the seal of Solomon for a hundred years."

The scholar still lay motionless; he was afraid to stir; all he had heard had made upon him such a dreadful impression.

A noise near him indicated that his companion was rising.

"To concentrate in their hands all the capital of the nations of all lands; to secure possession of all the land, railroads, mines, houses; to be at the head of all organizations, to occupy the highest governmental posts, to paralyze commerce and industry everywhere, to seize the press, to direct legislation, public opinion and national movements—and all for the purpose of subjugating all nations on earth to their power! No! I shall struggle against the golden calf and shall smash it to pieces as Moses smashed it in the desert."

"What we heard is a threat against all society. Here is my hand, I will be your comrade in this struggle against the power of gold."

The Italian shook his head, but accepted the extended hand. "No," he said, "I want to act alone. There is a force which, if properly directed, is not weaker than gold. That force is poverty and her companion, labor. I shall call them out and lead them into battle. Proud Israel! Beware! I shall put against you the *Artel* (union) and Labor."

"And I," said the scholar, with animation, "all that is lofty and noble,—science, idealism, faith—I shall lead these against this materialism."

His comrade laughed:

"Your ideals will crumble as clay striking against metal. Only the forces of poverty and hunger can be the fighters that will defeat the golden calf. Our ways part here; you will go one way, and I another. My promise is fulfilled; but remember your vow—be silent as to all that you have heard and seen here!"

EXHIBIT D

This is the mythical speech alleged by the German novelist, Hermann Goedsche ("Sir John Retcliffe"), to have been delivered by an unnamed Rabbi at an imaginary Jewish Congress in Lemberg. The author of the absurdly fantastic story, "The Jewish Cemetery in Prague," vouched for the authenticity of the "Rabbi's Speech" which he himself had composed, along the lines of his own story. The explanatory note is by G. V. Butmi, the Russian anti-Semitic writer who brought out one of the early versions of the Protocols in Russia.

The paragraphs which are indented and parts in italics were omitted in the Butmi version, but are given in the French publication "Le Péril Judéo Maçonnique—I. Les Protocols des Sages de Zion," by Jouin, Paris, 1920.

THE RABBI'S SPEECH TO THE JEWISH PEOPLE*

Our fathers ordained the chosen ones in Israel to gather, without fail, once every century, at the grave of our great Master Caleb, the

* NOTE. (Toward the end of the last century there appeared a book in London by Retcliffe entitled "A Review of Political and Historical Events During the Past Ten Years." This work was translated into French. The French periodical press, without waiting for the complete translation of the book, reproduced certain parts of it because they were of special interest. Thus the French newspapers and magazines published translations from the English of an intensely interesting speech (from the Hebrew), most edifying for Russia, delivered by one of the Rabbis, THE AUTHENTICITY OF WHICH SPEECH IS VOUCHED FOR BY THE ABOVE-MENTIONED AUTHOR. This inimitable gem must in the eyes of Russians assume all the more importance since it is brought out by that "highly civilized" humane and practical country, England, which has given protection to the Russian Jews against the unsuccessfully invented persecutions on the part of the Russian government and people. This monstrous document was sent at the time in printed form, in the French language, to the editorial office of the Odessa newspaper "Novorosisk

285

sainted Rabbi Simeon Ben Judah, whose great knowledge is imparted to the elect of each generation to gain the power over the whole world and authority over all the descendants of Israel. . . .

It is already eighteen centuries that the war of Israel is being waged with the power which had been promised to Abraham but which had been snatched away from him by the *Cross.* Trampled under foot, humiliated by his enemies, ceaselessly under threats of death, of persecution, of rapine and violence of every sort, Israel has not succumbed; and if he is dispersed over the whole world it is because the whole world should belong to him.

It has been for a few [eighteen] centuries now that our learned men have been fighting against the Cross with courage and persistence which nothing can break. Our people is rising gradually and, with each day, its forces are growing. *It is to us that this God of the day belongs, which was erected by Aaron in the wilderness, this golden calf, this universal deity of the epoch.*

When we become, at last, the sole possessors of all the gold to be found on earth, the true power will practically be transferred to our hands, and the promises made to Abraham will be fulfilled. *Gold— is the greatest power on earth; it is might, reward, the instrument of every authority, it is all man, both fears and desires. This is the sole mystery, the most profound science of that spirit with the aid of which the entire world is ruled.* This is what the future holds in store. Eighteen centuries have belonged to our enemies; this century and the following must belong to us, the People of Israel, and will be ours, without fail. Here, for the tenth time during a thousand years of cruel and incessant struggle with our enemies, have assembled at this cemetery; at the grave of the great Master, Caleb, the sainted Rabbi Simeon Ben Judah, the elect of each of the tribes of the Israelite people, in order to discuss and agree upon, the means of making use, in the interests of our cause, of all the tremendous mistakes and errors, which our enemies—the Christians—have not ceased to commit. Every

Telegraph" for those who might want to examine the accuracy of the translation published in No. 4996 of that newspaper, dated January 15, 1891, and reprinted in No. 21 of the Petersburg newspaper "Znamya," dated January 22, 1904. THE SPEECH RELATES TO THE TIME OF THE SANHEDRIN OF 1869.)

time the new Sanhedrin (assembly) proclaimed and preached merciless warfare against our enemies, but not once during the past centuries did our forefathers succeed in concentrating in our hands such an enormous quantity of gold [*and consequently of power*] as the nineteenth century has given us. We are therefore able, without any senseless illusions, to flatter ourselves with the hope of attaining our goal before long, and we can look forward with assurance into the very eyes of the future.

Persecutions and insults,—these sombre and tortuous times, which the people of Israel bore with heroic patience,—have fortunately come to an end, owing to the progress of civilization among the Christians, and this progress is the best shield under which we can hide and scheme, in order that we may cover quickly and decisively the last span of that distance which divides us from our supreme aim. Let us cast a cursory glance at the economic situation of Europe and analyze the resources which fell to the Israelites from the beginning of the present century, owing to the concentration in their hands of the tremendous capital which is in their possession at the present time. It turns out that in Paris, London, Vienna, Berlin, Amsterdam, Hamburg, Rome, Naples, etc. [*and in all lands—the Rothschilds*], that everywhere, the Israelites are the masters of the financial situation, being as they are possessors of many billions, not to mention localities of the second and third class where all the financial funds are in their hands and not mentioning that, without their direct influence, no financial operation, no work of any importance, could be carried out anywhere at any time. At present, all the emperors, kings and ruling princes are burdened with tremendous debts incurred in order to be able to maintain numerous standing armies [*to sustain their tottering thrones*]. The Bourse quotes and regulates these moneys, and we are the full masters of the Bourse in all the centres of the globe. The problem before us now is to facilitate even to a greater extent the means of contracting these loans and thus to become the sole managers of all valuables, after which the exploitation of all their railroads, mines, forests, large factories and industrial plants, as well as of all other (real property) including duties and taxes, will fall into our hands, as a security for the capital lent by us to the various States.

Agriculture will forever remain the principal source of a country's wealth. The possession of large plots of land will pave for us even a broader way to honors and will strengthen our influence (over the highest officials of the country). From this follows, that our efforts will be directed towards inducing our brethren in Israel to make large agricultural purchases. We must, therefore, do our utmost to break up large estates into small parcels, in order to be able to purchase them in the easiest and quickest way. Under the pretext of trying to help the working classes, it is necessary to oppress the large landowners with taxation in all its severity. When these possessions will thus gradually be transferred into our hands, the whole labor of the Christian proletariat will become for us a new source of tremendous profits. *Since the Christian Church is one of our most dangerous enemies, we must work tirelessly to weaken its influence, and in order to accomplish this, it is necessary to use all our efforts to implant in the Christian intellectual class ideas of atheism, scepticism, dissension and to call forth religious disputes among the newly formed groups and sects of Christendom.*

Logically, we must begin by depreciating the ministers of this religion. Let us declare open war on them, let us provoke suspicions on their devotion, on their private conduct, and by ridicule and persiflage we shall be right in the consideration attached to the state and the costume of the priest.

Every war, every revolution, every political and religious upheaval brings nearer the moment when we shall attain the great end for which we have been striving so long. Commerce and speculation—these branches, most plentiful in their fruits,—must never be suffered to slip out of the hands of the Israelites.

. . . and once these branches have become identified with us, we shall, through the flattery and perspicacity of our executives, know how to penetrate to the prime source of true influence and power. It is understood that we are concerned only with those pursuits that entail honors, power or privileges, for all those that require knowledge, labor or disagreeable conditions, these can and should be left to the Christians. The magistrature is an institution of prime importance for us. The legal profession develops most the faculty of civilization and initiates one furthest in the affairs of our natural enemies, the Christians, and it is through it that we can subject them to our mercy. Why should not the Jews become Ministers of Instruction when they have so often been Ministers of Finance? The Jews must also aspire to the rank of legislators with the object of abrogating the laws made by the Goyim, faithless sinners, against the sons of Israel, the true believers, in their invariable attachment to the holy laws of Abraham.

Moreover, on this point, our plan is nearing the most complete realization, for progress has nearly everywhere recognized and accorded to us the same civic rights as to Christians, but that which it is of importance to obtain, that which must be the object of our ceaseless efforts, is a law less severe on bankruptcy. We shall make of it a gold mine more rich than were ever the mines of California.

With this object in view the people of Israel must direct its ambition towards those high offices of authority which have the power to distribute honors and esteem. The most assured way of attaining such offices is to have weight and importance in the various industrial enterprises, financial and commercial operations, and to be on guard for all pitfalls and temptations which may lead to the prosecution of the sons of Israel in the country's courts.

Our people, in deciding upon one operation or another, must be guided by wisdom and tact, which are the distinguishing traits of its natural gifts. We must not remain passive to anything that may aid us in gaining a place of honor in society; philosophy, medicine, law, political economy—in other words, all branches of science, art, literature—represent a wide field where even our smallest successes, developing our abilities, will be of great benefit to our cause.

These vocations are inseparable from speculation. Thus the production of a musical composition, even though it be very mediocre, will furnish to our co-religionists a plausible reason for elevating on a pedestal and surrounding with a halo the Jew who will be the author of it. As for the sciences, medicine and philosophy, they must equally be a part of our intellectual domain.

To the physician are usually confided the most intimate secrets of the family and he, therefore, holds in his hands the health and life of our ancient enemies—the Christians. We are obliged to encourage matrimonial unions between Israelites and Christians, for the people of Israel, risking no loss whatsoever from such contact, will only gain from such unions.

. . . The introduction of a certain quantity of impure blood into our God-chosen race will not corrupt it. Our daughters will furnish us through these marriages alliances with Christian families that possess influence and power. In exchange for the money that we give, it is just that we obtain influence over everything that surrounds us.

Our relationship with the Christians will not make us deviate from the path we have always been following; on the contrary, with a certain degree of artfulness and cunning, this relationship will gradually make us full masters of their destinies. *It is desirable, that the Israelites refrain from keeping concubines of our holy faith and rather select Christian girls for the part.* The substitution of the simple formality of a contract before some civil power for the church ceremony is of the greatest importance to us, because on this condition Christian women will overflow our camp.—If gold is the first power on this earth, then the second power is undoubtedly the press. But of what significance is the latter without the former? Since we cannot realize all the above-stated aims without the assistance of the press, *it is absolutely necessary that the management of all the newspapers and magazines of all the countries, be in our hands. The possession of gold, of the press and of sufficient means for the satisfaction of certain qualities of its soul, will make us masters of public opinion and will subjugate to us the masses.*

Following this method on every step of our way with a persistence which is one of our highest qualities, we will push the Christians aside and reduce their influence to zero. We will dictate to the world what it should believe, what it must revere or despise. It is possible that persons will be found who will arise against us; arming themselves, they will hurl insults and curses at us; but the docile, ignorant masses will harken to us and will take our part. *Once we become absolute masters of the press, we will easily be able to refashion the ideas of honor, of virtue, of faithfulness—and to deal the first blow to the family-conception which is considered to this day as the most sacred institution and which must be reduced to a state of decay. We shall then be able to uproot the belief in that which our enemies, the Christians, shall have worshipped until that time and instead of that, having brought up the army in a spirit of infatuation with the various passions, we shall openly declare war upon everything that the gentiles are at present revering and worshipping.*

May all this be understood and noted, and let every child of Israel become imbued with its true principles. Then our might will grow like a gigantic tree the branches of which will bear fruits, known as riches, pleasure, power.

. . . as a compensation for that hideous condition which for long centuries has been the unique lot of the people of Israel.

When one of us makes a step forward let the next one follow him. If his foot slips let his co-religionists hasten to support him. If an Israelite is trapped by the court of the country in which he resides, his brethren in faith should use all their efforts to get him out of trouble or to help him otherwise, but on the condition that the Israelite in question acted according to the laws which Israel observes strictly and guards for so many centuries, and the precepts of our religion.

Our people is conservative, faithful to the religious ceremonies and usages which our ancestors have bequeathed to us.

It is very important for us to pretend to be expounders and protagonists of social questions prevalent at the time in a country, especially of those whose aim it is to better the fate of the workingman; but, in reality, our efforts must gravitate towards possession and rule over the movements of public opinion.

The blindness of the masses and the tendency of their leaders to yield to oratory, as empty as it is loud, make them easy prey for us and a double weapon for our popularity and credit. With the aid of oratory, our speakers will be able to make people believe our artificial enthusiasm which Christians usually attain through the medium of genuine sentiment.

It is necessary to support, as much as possible, the Proletariat and to subjugate it to those in charge of the finances. Acting in this manner, it will be for us to incite the masses, whenever we shall need them. We will use them as weapons for upheavals and revolutions and each of these catastrophes will move our cause forward with gigantic strides and will bring us, with a quick pace, nearer our goal—to reign over the entire world, as it was promised by our Father Abraham.

EXHIBIT E

This is a translation of Sergius Nilus' Epilogue taken from the copy of the "Protocols" in the British Museum.

THE NILUS EPILOGUE, 1917

According to secret Jewish Zionism, a political plan was devised in theory for the peaceful conquest of the world for Zion, by Solomon and other sages already 929 years before the birth of Christ. In the course of historical developments, the plan was elaborated and augmented by their followers initiated in this affair. These sages decided to conquer the world peacefully for Zion, by the cunning of the symbolic snake, whose head should constitute the government of the Jews initiated in the plans of the sages (always masked even from their own people) and the body—the Judean nation. Penetrating the bosoms of the governments encountered on the way, this snake has undermined and eaten away (overthrowing) all governments, non-Jewish forces according to their growth.

This it should also do in the future, carefully following the outlined plan, until the cycle of the road travelled by it is completed by the return of the head of the snake to Zion, and until the snake will thus include and concentrate in the sphere of its circle the whole of Europe, and through Europe the rest of the world, utilizing all forces of conquest and by economic means in order to subject also the other continents to its influence, to the influence of its cycle. The return of the head of the snake could be accomplished only over the razed plains of the governmental power of all the European countries,—that is through economic disorganization and ruin, introduced by Zion everywhere by means of spiritual decadence and moral turpitude, chiefly, with the aid of Jewish women under the guise of French, Italian and Spanish women, the best introducers of immorality into the conduct of the rulers of nations. Women in the hands of Zion serve as bait for those, who owing to them are always in need of money, and therefore barter their conscience in order to get money at any cost. This money, in fact, is only loaned to them, for it quickly comes back to the hands of bribing Zion through these very women, and at the same time they have secured slaves for Zion.

EXHIBIT F

Here is "The Britons" translation of the complete text of the notorious Nilus "Protocols of the Wise Men of Zion."

PROTOCOLS OF THE MEETINGS OF THE LEARNED ELDERS OF ZION
PROTOCOL NO. 1

. . . Putting aside fine phrases we shall speak of the significance of each thought: by comparisons and deductions we shall throw light upon surrounding facts.

What I am about to set forth, then, is our system from the two points of view, that of ourselves and that of the *goyim* (*i.e.*, non-Jews).

It must be noted that men with bad instincts are more in number than the good, and therefore the best results in governing them are attained by violence and terrorisation, and not by academic discussions. Every man aims at power, everyone would like to become a dictator if only he could, and rare indeed are the men who would not be willing to sacrifice the welfare of all for the sake of securing their own welfare.

What has restrained the beasts of prey who are called men? What has served for their guidance hitherto?

In the beginnings of the structure of society they were subjected to brutal and blind force; afterwards—to Law, which is the same force, only disguised. I draw the conclusion that by the law of nature right lies in force.

Political freedom is an idea but not a fact. This idea one must know how to apply whenever it appears necessary with this bait of an idea to attract the masses of the people to one's party for the purpose of crushing another who is in authority. This task is rendered easier if the opponent has himself been infected with the idea of freedom, *so-called liberalism*, and, for the sake of an idea, is willing to yield some of his power. It is precisely here that the triumph of our theory appears: the slackened reins of government are immediately, by the law of life, caught up and gathered together by a new hand, because the blind might of the nation cannot for one single day exist without guidance, and the new authority merely fits into the place of the old already weakened by liberalism.

In our day the power which has replaced that of the rulers who were liberal is the power of Gold. Time was when Faith ruled. The idea of freedom is impossible of realisation because no one knows how to use it with moderation. It is enough to hand over a people to self-government for a certain length of time for that people to be turned into a disorganised mob. From that moment on we get internecine strife which soon develops into battles between classes, in the midst of which States burn down and their importance is reduced to that of a heap of ashes.

Whether a State exhausts itself in its own convulsions, whether its internal discord brings it under the power of external foes—in any case it can be accounted irretrievably lost: *it is in our power*. The despotism of Capital, which is entirely in our hands, reaches out to it a straw that the State, willy-nilly, must take hold of: if not—it goes to the bottom.

Should anyone of a liberal mind say that such reflections as the above are immoral I would put the following questions:—If every State has two foes and if in regard to the external foe it is allowed and not considered immoral to use every manner and art of conflict, as for example to keep the enemy in ignorance of plans of attack and defence, to attack him by night or in superior numbers, then in what way can the same means in regard to a worse foe, the destroyer of the structure of society and the commonweal, be called immoral and not permissible?

Is it possible for any sound logical mind to hope with any success to guide crowds by the aid of reasonable counsels and arguments, when any objection or contradiction, senseless though it may be, can be made and when such objection may find more favour with the people, whose powers of reasoning are superficial? Men in masses and the men of the masses, being guided solely by petty passions, paltry beliefs, customs, traditions and sentimental theorism, fall a prey to party dissension, which hinders any kind of agreement even on the basis of a perfectly reasonable argument. Every resolution of a crowd depends upon a chance or packed majority, which, in its ignorance of political secrets, puts forth some ridiculous resolution that lays in the administration a seed of anarchy.

The political has nothing in common with the moral. The ruler who is governed by the moral is not a skilled politician, and is therefore unstable on his throne. He who wishes to rule must have recourse both to cunning and to make-believe. Great national qualities, like frankness and honesty, are vices in politics, for they bring down rulers from their thrones more effectively and more certainly than the most powerful enemy. Such qualities must be the attributes of the kingdoms of the *goyim*, but we must in no wise be guided by them.

Our right lies in force. The word "right" is an abstract thought and proved by nothing. The word means no more than:—Give me what I want in order that thereby I might have a proof that I am stronger than you.

Where does right begin? Where does it end?

In any State in which there is a bad organisation of authority, an impersonality of laws and of the rulers who have lost their personality amid the flood of rights ever multiplying out of liberalism, I find a new right—to attack by the right of the strong, and to scatter to the winds all existing forces of order and regulation, to reconstruct all institutions and to become the sovereign lord of those who have left to us the rights of their power by laying them down voluntarily in their liberalism.

Our power in the present tottering condition of all forms of power will be more invincible than any other, because it will remain invisible until the moment when it has gained such strength that no cunning can any longer undermine it.

Out of the temporary evil we are now compelled to commit will emerge the good of an unshakeable rule, which will restore the regular course of the machinery of the national life, brought to naught by liberalism. The result justifies the means. Let us, however, in our plans, direct our attention not so much to what is good and moral as to what is necessary and useful.

Before us is a plan in which is laid down strategically the line from which we cannot deviate without running the risk of seeing the labour of many centuries brought to naught.

In order to elaborate satisfactory forms of action it is necessary to have regard to the rascality, the slackness, the instability of the mob, its lack of capacity to understand and respect the conditions of its own life, or its own welfare. It must be understood that the might of a mob is blind, senseless and unreasoning force ever at the mercy of a suggestion from any side. The blind cannot lead the blind without bringing them into the abyss; consequently, members of the mob, upstarts from the people even though they should be as a genius for wisdom, yet having no understanding of the political, cannot come forward as leaders of the mob without bringing the whole nation to ruin.

Only one trained from childhood for independent rule can have understanding of the words that can be made up of the political alphabet.

A people left to itself, *i.e.*, to upstarts from its midst, brings itself to ruin by party dissensions excited by the pursuit of power and honours and disorders arising therefrom. Is it possible for the masses of the people calmly and without petty jealousies to form judgments, to deal with the affairs of the country, which cannot be mixed up with personal interests? Can they defend themselves from an external foe? It is unthinkable, for a plan broken up into as many parts as there are heads in the mob, loses all homogeneity, and thereby becomes unintelligible and impossible of execution.

It is only with a despotic ruler that plans can be elaborated extensively and clearly in such a way as to distribute the whole properly among the several parts of the machinery of the State: from this the conclusion is inevitable that a satisfactory form of government for any country is one that concentrates in the hands of one responsible person. Without an absolute despotism there can be no existence for civilisation which is carried on not by the masses but by their guide, whosoever that person may be. The mob is a savage and displays its savagery at every opportunity. The moment the mob seizes freedom in its hands it quickly turns to anarchy, which in itself is the highest degree of savagery.

Behold the alcoholised animals, bemused with drink, the right to an immoderate use of which comes along with freedom. It is not for us and ours to walk that road. The peoples of the *goyim* are bemused with alcoholic liquors; their youth has grown stupid on classicism and from early immorality, into which it has been inducted by our special agents—by tutors, lackeys, governesses in the houses of the wealthy, by clerks and others, by our women in the places of dissipation frequented by the *goyim*. In the number of these last I count also the so-called "society ladies," voluntary followers of the others in corruption and luxury.

Our countersign is—Force and Make-believe. Only force conquers in political affairs, especially if it be concealed in the talents essential to statesmen. Violence must be the principle, and cunning and make-believe the rule for governments which do not want to lay down their crowns at the feet of agents of some new power. This evil is the one and only means to attain the end, the good. Therefore we must not stop at bribery, deceit and treachery when they should serve towards the attainment of our end. In politics one must know how to seize the property of others without hesitation if by it we secure submission and sovereignty.

Our State, marching along the path of peaceful conquest, has the right to replace the horrors of war by less noticeable and more satisfactory sentences of death, necessary to maintain the terror which tends to produce blind submission. Just but merciless severity is the greatest factor of strength in the State: not only for the sake of gain but also in the name of duty, for the sake of victory, we must keep to the programme of violence and make-believe. The doctrine of squaring accounts is precisely as strong as the means of which it makes use. Therefore it is not so much by the means themselves as by the doctrine of severity that we shall triumph and bring all governments into subjection to our super-government. It is enough for them to know that we are merciless for all disobedience to cease.

Far back in ancient times we were the first to cry among the masses of the people the words "Liberty, Equality, Fraternity," words many times repeated since those days by stupid poll-parrots who from all sides round flew down upon these baits and with them carried away the well-being of the world, true freedom of the individual, formerly so well guarded against the pressure of the mob. The would-be wise men of the *goyim*, the intellectuals, could not make anything out of the uttered words in their abstractness; did not note the contradiction of their meaning and inter-relation: did not see that in nature there is no equality, cannot be freedom: that Nature herself has established

inequality of minds, of characters, and capacities, just as immutably
as she has established subordination to her laws: never stopped to think
that the mob is a blind thing, that upstarts elected from among it to
bear rule are, in regard to the political, the same blind men as the
mob itself, that the adept, though he be a fool, can yet rule, whereas
the non-adept, even if he were a genius, understands nothing in the
political—to all these things the *goyim* paid no regard; yet all the time
it was based upon these things that dynastic rule rested: the father
passed on to the son a knowledge of the course of political affairs in
such wise that none should know it but members of the dynasty and
none could betray it to the governed. As time went on the meaning
of the dynastic transference of the true position of affairs in the political was lost, and this aided the success of our cause.

In all corners of the earth the words "Liberty, Equality, Fraternity"
brought to our ranks, thanks to our blind agents, whole legions who
bore our banners with enthusiasm. And all the time these words were
canker-worms at work boring into the well-being of the *goyim*, putting
an end everywhere to peace, quiet, solidarity and destroying all the
foundations of the *goy* States. As you will see later, this helped us
to our triumph; it gave us the possibility, among other things, of
getting into our hands the master card—the destruction of the privileges, or in other words of the very existence of the aristocracy of
the *goyim*, that class which was the only defence peoples and countries
had against us. On the ruins of the natural and genealogical aristocracy
of the *goyim* we have set up the aristocracy of our educated class
headed by the aristocracy of money. The qualifications for this aristocracy we have established in wealth, which is dependent upon us,
and in knowledge, for which our learned elders provide the motive
force.

Our triumph has been rendered easier by the fact that in our relations with the men whom we wanted we have always worked upon
the most sensitive chords of the human mind, upon the cash account,
upon the cupidity, upon the insatiability for material needs of man;
and each one of these human weaknesses, taken alone, is sufficient to
paralyse initiative, for it hands over the will of men to the disposition
of him who has bought their activities.

The abstraction of freedom has enabled us to persuade the mob in
all countries that their government is nothing but the steward of the

people who are the owners of the country, and that the steward may be replaced like a worn-out glove.

It is this possibility of replacing the representatives of the people which has placed them at our disposal, and, as it were, given us the power of appointment.

PROTOCOL NO. 2

It is indispensable for our purpose that wars, so far as possible, should not result in territorial gains: war will thus be brought on to the economic ground, where the nations will not fail to perceive in the assistance we give the strength of our predominance, and this state of things will put both sides at the mercy of our international *agentur;* which possesses millions of eyes ever on the watch and unhampered by any limitations whatsoever. Our international rights will then wipe out national rights, in the proper sense of right, and will rule the nations precisely as the civil law of States rules the relations of their subjects among themselves.

The administrators, whom we shall choose from among the public, with strict regard to their capacities for servile obedience, will not be persons trained in the arts of government, and will therefore easily become pawns in our game in the hands of men of learning and genius who will be their advisers, specialists bred and reared from early childhood to rule the affairs of the whole world. As is well known to you, these specialists of ours have been drawing to fit them for rule the information they need from our political plans, from the lessons of history, from observations made of the events of every moment as it passes. The *goyim* are not guided by practical use of unprejudiced historical observation, but by theoretical routine without any critical regard for consequent results. We need not, therefore, take any account of them—let them amuse themselves until the hour strikes, or live on hopes of new forms of enterprising pastime, or on the memories of all they have enjoyed. For them let that play the principal part which we have persuaded them to accept as the dictates of science (theory). It is with this object in view that we are constantly, by means of our press, arousing a blind confidence in these theories. The intellectuals of the *goyim* will puff themselves up with their knowledge and without any logical verification of it will put into effect all the information available from science, which our *agentur* specialists have cunningly pieced together for the purpose of educating thèir minds in the direction we want.

Do not suppose for a moment that these statements are empty words: think carefully of the successes we arranged for Darwinism, Marxism, Nietzsche-ism. To us Jews, at any rate, it should be plain to see what a disintegrating importance these directives have had upon the minds of the *goyim*.

It is indispensable for us to take account of the thoughts, characters, tendencies of the nations in order to avoid making slips in the political and in the direction of administrative affairs. The triumph of our system, of which the component parts of the machinery may be variously disposed according to the temperament of the peoples met on our way, will fail of success if the practical application of it be not based upon a summing up of the lessons of the past in the light of the present.

In the hands of the States of to-day there is a great force that creates the movement of thought in the people, and that is the Press. The part played by the Press is to keep pointing out requirements supposed to be indispensable, to give voice to the complaints of the people, to express and to create discontent. It is in the Press that the triumph of freedom of speech finds its incarnation. But the *goyim* States have not known how to make use of this force; and it has fallen into our hands. Through the Press we have gained the power to influence while remaining ourselves in the shade; thanks to the Press we have got the *gold* in our hands, notwithstanding that we have had to gather it out of oceans of blood and tears. But it has paid us, though we have sacrificed many of our people. Each victim on our side is worth in the sight of God a thousand *goyim*.

PROTOCOL NO. 3

To-day I may tell you that our goal is now only a few steps off. There remains a small space to cross and the whole long path we have trodden is ready now to close its cycle of the Symbolic Snake, by which we symbolise our people. When this ring closes, all the States of Europe will be locked in its coil as in a powerful vice.

The constitution scales of these days will shortly break down, for we have established them with a certain lack of accurate balance in order that they may oscillate incessantly until they wear through the pivot on which they turn. The *goyim* are under the impression that they have welded them sufficiently strong and they have all along kept on expecting that the scales would come into equilibrium. But the pivots—the kings on their thrones—are hemmed in by their representatives, who play the fool, distraught with their own uncontrolled and irresponsible power. This power they owe to the terror which has been breathed into the palaces. As they have no means of getting at their people, into their very midst, the kings on their thrones are no longer able to come to terms with them and so strengthen themselves against seekers after power. We have made a gulf between the far-seeing Sovereign Power and the blind force of the people so that both have lost all meaning, for like the blind man and his stick, both are powerless apart.

In order to incite seekers after power to a misuse of power we have set all forces in opposition one to another, breaking up their liberal tendencies towards independence. To this end we have stirred up every form of enterprise, we have armed all parties, we have set up authority as a target for every ambition. Of States we have made gladiatorial arenas where a host of confused issues contend. . . . A little more, and disorders and bankruptcy will be universal. . . .

Babblers inexhaustible have turned into oratorical contests the sittings of Parliament and Administrative Boards. Bold journalists and unscrupulous pamphleteers daily fall upon executive officials. Abuses of power will put the final touch in preparing all institutions for their overthrow and everything will fly skyward under the blows of the maddened mob.

All people are chained down to heavy toil by poverty more firmly than ever they were chained by slavery and serfdom; from these, one way and another, they might free themselves, these could be settled with, but from want they will never get away. We have included in the constitution such rights as to the masses appear fictitious and not actual rights. All these so-called "People's Rights" can exist only in idea, an idea which can never be realised in practical life. What is it to the proletariat labourer, bowed double over his heavy toil, crushed by his lot in life, if talkers get the right to babble, if journalists get the right to scribble any nonsense side by side with good stuff, once the proletariat has no other profit out of the constitution save only those pitiful crumbs which we fling them from our table in return for their voting in favour of what we dictate, in favour of the men we place in power, the servants of our *agentur*. . . . Republican rights for a poor man are no more than a bitter piece of irony, for the necessity he is under of toiling almost all day gives him no present use of them, but on the other hand robs him of all guarantee of regular and certain earnings by making him dependent on strikes by his comrades or lockouts by his masters.

The people under our guidance have annihilated the aristocracy, who were their one and only defence and foster-mother for the sake of their own advantage which is inseparably bound up with the wellbeing of the people. Nowadays, with the destruction of the aristocracy, the people have fallen into the grips of merciless money-grinding scoundrels who have laid a pitiless and cruel yoke upon the necks of the workers.

We appear on the scene as alleged saviours of the worker from this oppression when we propose to him to enter the ranks of our fighting forces—Socialists, Anarchists, Communists—to whom we always give support in accordance with an alleged brotherly rule (of the solidarity of all humanity) of our *social masonry*. The aristocracy, which enjoyed by law the labour of the workers, was interested in seeing that the workers were well fed, healthy and strong. We are interested in just the opposite—in the diminution, the *killing out of the* GOYIM. Our power is in the chronic shortness of food and physical weakness of the worker because by all that this implies he is made the slave of our will, and he will not find in his own authorities either strength or energy to set against our will. Hunger creates the right of capital to rule the worker more surely than it was given to the aristocracy by the legal authority of kings.

By want and the envy and hatred which it engenders we shall move the mobs and with their hands we shall wipe out all those who hinder us on our way.

When the hour strikes for our Sovereign Lord of all the World to be crowned it is these same hands which will sweep away everything that might be a hindrance thereto.

The *goyim* have lost the habit of thinking unless prompted by the suggestions of our specialists. Therefore they do not see the urgent necessity of what we, when our kingdom comes, shall adopt at once, namely this, that *it is essential to teach in national schools one simple, true piece of knowledge, the basis of all knowledge—the knowledge of the structure of human life, of social existence, which requires division of labour, and, consequently, the division of men into classes and conditions.* It is essential for all to know that *owing to difference in the objects of human activity there cannot be any equality,* that he who by any act of his compromises a whole class cannot be equally responsible before the law with him who affects no one but only his own honour. The true knowledge of the structure of society, into the secrets of which we do not admit the *goyim,* would demonstrate to all men that the positions and work must be kept within a certain circle, that they may not become a source of human suffering, arising from an education which does not correspond with the work which individuals are called upon to do. After a thorough study of this knowledge the peoples will voluntarily submit to authority and accept such position as is appointed them in the State. In the present state of knowledge and the direction we have given to its development the people, blindly believing things in print—cherishes—thanks to promptings intended to mislead and to its own ignorance——a blind hatred towards all conditions which it considers above itself, for it has no understanding of the meaning of class and condition.

This hatred will be still further magnified by the effects of an *economic crisis,* which will stop dealings on the exchanges and bring industry to a standstill. We shall create by all the secret subterranean methods open to us and with the aid of gold, which is all in our hands, *a universal economic crisis whereby we shall throw upon the streets whole mobs of workers simultaneously in all the countries of Europe.* These mobs will rush delightedly to shed the blood of those whom, in the simplicity of their ignorance, they have envied from their cradles, and whose property they will then be able to loot.

"Ours" they will not touch, because the moment of attack will be known to us and we shall take measures to protect our own.

We have demonstrated that progress will bring all the *goyim* to the sovereignty of reason. Our despotism will be precisely that; for it will know how by wise severities to pacificate all unrest, to cauterise liberalism out of all institutions.

When the populace has seen that all sorts of concessions and indulgences are yielded it in the name of freedom it has imagined itself to be sovereign lord and has stormed its way to power, but, naturally, like every other blind man it has come upon a host of stumbling blocks, *it has rushed to find a guide, it has never had the sense to return to the former state* and it has laid down its plenipotentiary powers at *our* feet. Remember the French Revolution, to which it was we who gave the name of "Great": the secrets of its preparations are well known to us for it was wholly the work of our hands.

Ever since that time we have been leading the peoples from one disenchantment to another, so that in the end they should turn also from us in favour of that *King-Despot of the blood of Zion, whom we are preparing for the world.*

At the present day we are, as an international force, invincible, because if attacked by some we are supported by other States. It is the bottomless rascality of the *goyim* peoples, who crawl on their bellies to force, but are merciless towards weakness, unsparing to faults and indulgent to crimes, unwilling to bear the contradictions of a free social system but patient unto martyrdom under the violence of a bold despotism—it is those qualities which are aiding us to independence. From the premier-dictators of the present day the *goyim* peoples suffer patiently and bear such abuses as for the least of them they would have beheaded twenty kings.

What is the explanation of this phenomenon, this curious inconsequence of the masses of the peoples in their attitude towards what would appear to be events of the same order?

It is explained by the fact that these dictators whisper to the peoples through their agents that through these abuses they are inflicting injury on the States with the highest purpose—to secure the welfare of the peoples, the international brotherhood of them all, their solidarity and equality of rights. Naturally they do not tell the peoples that this unification must be accomplished only under our sovereign rule.

And thus the people condemn the upright and acquit the guilty, persuaded ever more and more that it can do whatsoever it wishes. Thanks to this state of things the people are destroying every kind of stability and creating disorders at every step.

The word "freedom" brings out the communities of men to fight against every kind of force, against every kind of authority, even against God and the laws of nature. For this reason we, when we come into our kingdom, shall have to erase this word from the lexicon of life as implying a principle of brute force which turns mobs into bloodthirsty beasts.

These beasts, it is true, fall asleep again every time when they have drunk their fill of blood, and at such times can easily be riveted into their chains. But if they be not given blood they will not sleep and continue to struggle.

PROTOCOL NO. 4

Every republic passes through several stages. The first of these is comprised in the early days of mad raging by the blind mob, tossed hither and thither, right and left: the second is demagogy, from which is born anarchy, and that leads inevitably to despotism—not any longer legal and overt, and therefore responsible despotism, but to unseen and secretly hidden, yet nevertheless sensibly felt despotism in the hands of some secret organisation or other, whose acts are the more unscrupulous inasmuch as it works behind a screen, behind the backs of all sorts of agents, the changing of whom not only does not injuriously affect but actually aids the secret force by saving it, thanks to continual changes, from the necessity of expending its resources on the rewarding of long services.

Who and what is in a position to overthrow an invisible force? And this is precisely what our force is. *Gentile* masonry blindly serves as a screen for us and our objects, but the plan of action of our force, even its very abiding-place, remains for the whole people an unknown mystery.

But even freedom might be harmless and have its place in the State economy without injury to the well-being of the peoples if it rested upon the foundation of faith in God, upon the brotherhood of humanity, unconnected with the conception of equality, which is negatived by the very laws of creation, for they have established subordination. With such a faith as this a people might be governed by a wardship of parishes, and would walk contentedly and humbly under the guiding hand of its spiritual pastor submitting to the dispositions of God upon earth. This is the reason why *it is indispensable for us to undermine all faith, to tear out of the minds of the* GOYIM *the very principle of Godhead and the spirit, and to put in its place arithmetical calculations and material needs.*

In order to give the *goyim* no time to think and take note, their minds must be diverted towards industry and trade. Thus, all the nations will be swallowed up in the pursuit of gain and in the race for it will not take note of their common foe. But again, in order that freedom may once for all disintegrate and ruin the communities of the *goyim*, we must put industry on a speculative basis: the result of this will be that what is withdrawn from the land by industry will slip through the hands and pass into speculation, that is, to our classes.

The intensified struggle for superiority and shocks delivered to economic life will create, nay, have already created, disenchanted, cold and heartless communities. Such communities will foster a strong aversion towards the higher political and towards religion. Their only guide is gain, that is Gold, which they will erect into a veritable cult, for the sake of those material delights which it can give. Then will the hour strike when, not for the sake of attaining the good, not even to win wealth, but solely out of hatred towards the privileged, the lower classes of the *goyim* will follow our lead against our rivals for power, the intellectuals of the *goyim*.

PROTOCOL NO. 5

What form of administrative rule can be given to communities in which corruption has penetrated everywhere, communities where riches are attained only by the clever surprise tactics of semi-swindling tricks; where looseness reigns: where morality is maintained by penal measures and harsh laws but not by voluntary accepted principles: where the feelings towards faith and country are obliterated by cosmopolitan convictions? What form of rule is to be given to these communities if not that despotism which I shall describe to you later? We shall create an intensified centralisation of government in order to grip in our hands all the forces of the community. We shall regulate mechanically all the actions of the political life of our subjects by new laws. These laws will withdraw one by one all the indulgences and liberties which have been permitted by the *goyim*, and our kingdom will be distinguished by a despotism of such magnificent proportions as to be at any moment and in every place in a position to wipe out any *goyim* who oppose us by deed or word.

We shall be told that such a despotism as I speak of is not consistent with the progress of these days, but I will prove to you that it is.

In the times when the peoples looked upon kings on their thrones as on a pure manifestation of the will of God, they submitted without a murmur to the despotic power of kings: but from the day when we insinuated into their minds the conception of their own rights they began to regard the occupants of thrones as mere ordinary mortals. The holy unction of the Lord's Anointed has fallen from the heads of kings in the eyes of the people, and when we also robbed them of their faith in God the might of power was flung upon the streets into the place of public proprietorship and was seized by us.

Moreover, the art of directing masses and individuals by means of cleverly manipulated theory and verbiage, by regulations of life in common and all sorts of other quirks, in all which the *goyim* understand nothing, belongs likewise to the specialists of our administrative brain. Reared on analysis, observation, on delicacies of fine calculation, in this species of skill we have no rivals, any more than we have either in the drawing up of plans of political actions and solidarity. In this respect the Jesuits alone might have compared with us, but we have contrived to discredit them in the eyes of the unthinking mob as an overt organisation, while we ourselves all the while have kept our secret organisation in the shade. However, it is probably all the same to the world who is its sovereign lord, whether the head of Catholicism or our despot of the blood of Zion! But to us, the Chosen People, it is very far from being a matter of indifference.

For a time perhaps we might be successfully dealt with by a coalition of the GOYIM *of all the world:* but from this danger we are secured by the discord existing among them whose roots are so deeply seated that they can never now be plucked up. We have set one against another the personal and national reckonings of the *goyim,* religious and race hatreds, which we have fostered into a huge growth in the course of the past twenty centuries. This is the reason why there is not one State which would anywhere receive support if it were to raise its arm, for every one of them must bear in mind that any agreement against us would be unprofitable to itself. We are too strong—there is no evading our power. *The nations cannot come to even an inconsiderable private agreement without our secretly having a hand in it.*

Per Me reges regnant. "It is through Me that Kings reign." And it was said by the prophets that we were chosen by God Himself to rule over the whole earth. God has endowed us with genius that we may be equal to our task. Were genius in the opposite camp it would still struggle against us, but even so a newcomer is no match for the old-established settler: the struggle would be merciless between us, such a fight as the world has never yet seen. Aye, and the genius on their side would have arrived too late. All the wheels of the machinery of all States go by the force of the engine, which is in our hands, and that engine of the machinery of States is—Gold. The science of political economy invented by our learned elders has for long past been giving royal prestige to capital.

Capital, if it is to co-operate untrammelled, must be free to establish a monopoly of industry and trade: this is already being put in execution by an unseen hand in all quarters of the world. This freedom will give political force to those engaged in industry, and that will help to oppress the people. Nowadays it is more important to disarm the peoples than to lead them into war: more important to use for our advantage the passions which have burst into flames than to quench their fire: more important to catch up and interpret the ideas of others to suit ourselves than to eradicate them. *The principal object of our directorate consists in this: to debilitate the public mind by criticism; to lead it away from serious reflections calculated to arouse resistance; to distract the forces of the mind towards a sham fight of empty eloquence.*

In all ages the peoples of the world, equally with individuals, have accepted words for deeds, for *they are content with a show* and rarely pause to note, in the public arena, whether promises are followed by performance. Therefore we shall establish show institutions which will give eloquent proof of their benefit to progress.

We shall assume to ourselves the liberal physiognomy of all parties, of all directions, and we shall give that physiognomy a voice *in orators who will speak so much that they will exhaust the patience of their hearers and produce an abhorrence of oratory.*

In order to put public opinion into our hands we must bring it into a state of bewilderment by giving expression from all sides to so many contradictory opinions and for such length of time as will suffice to make the GOYIM *lose their heads in the labyrinth and come to see that the best thing is to have no opinion of any kind in matters political,* which it is not given to the public to understand, because they are understood only by him who guides the public. This is the first secret.

The second secret requisite for the success of our government is comprised in the following: To multiply to such an extent national failings, habits, passions, conditions of civil life, that it will be impossible for anyone to know where he is in the resulting chaos, so that the people in consequence will fail to understand one another. This measure will also serve us in another way, namely, to sow discord in all parties, to dislocate all collective forces which are still unwilling to submit to us, and to discourage any kind of personal initiative which might in any degree hinder our affair. *There is nothing more dangerous than personal initiative;* if it has genius behind it, such initiative can do more than can be done by millions of people among whom we have sown discord. We must so direct the education of the *goyim* communities that whenever they come upon a matter requiring initiative they may drop their hands in despairing impotence. The strain which results from freedom of action saps the forces when it meets with the freedom of another. From this collision arise grave moral shocks, disenchantments, failures. *By all these means we shall so wear down the goyim that they will be compelled to offer us international power of a nature that by its position will enable us without any violence gradually to absorb all the State forces of the world and to form a Super-Government.* In place of the rulers of to-day we shall set up a bogey which will be called the Super-Government Administration. Its hands will reach out in all directions like nippers and its organisation will be of such colossal dimensions that it cannot fail to subdue all the nations of the world.

PROTOCOL NO. 6

We shall soon begin to establish huge monopolies, reservoirs of colossal riches, upon which even large fortunes of the *goyim* will depend to such an extent that they will go to the bottom together with the credit of the States on the day after the political smash. . . .

You gentlemen here present who are economists, just strike an estimate of the significance of this combination! . . .

In every possible way we must develop the significance of our Super-Government by representing it as the Protector and Benefactor of all those who voluntarily submit to us.

The aristocracy of the *goyim* as a political force, is dead—we need not take it into account; but as landed proprietors they can still be harmful to us from the fact that they are self-sufficing in the resources upon which they live. It is essential therefore for us at whatever cost to deprive them of their land. This object will be best attained by increasing the burdens upon landed property—in loading lands with debts. These measures will check land-holding and keep it in a state of humble and unconditional submission.

The aristocrats of the *goyim*, being hereditarily incapable of contenting themselves with little, will rapidly burn up and fizzle out.

At the same time we must intensively patronise trade and industry, but, first and foremost, speculation, the part played by which is to provide a counterpoise to industry: the absence of speculative industry will multiply capital in private hands and will serve to restore agriculture by freeing the land from indebtedness to the land banks. What we want is that industry should drain off from the land both labour and capital and by means of speculation transfer into our hands all the money of the world, and thereby throw all the *goyim* into the ranks of the proletariat. Then the *goyim* will bow down before us, if for no other reason but to get the right to exist.

To complete the ruin of the industry of the *goyim* we shall bring to the assistance of speculation the luxury which we have developed among the *goyim*, that greedy demand for luxury which is swallowing up everything. *We shall raise the rate of wages which, however, will not bring any advantage to the workers, for, at the same time, we shall produce a rise in prices of the first necessaries of life, alleging that it arises from the decline of agriculture and cattle-breeding: we shall further undermine artfully and deeply sources of production, by accustoming the workers to anarchy and to drunkenness and side by side therewith taking all measure to extirpate from the face of the earth all the educated forces of the* GOYIM.

In order that the true meaning of things may not strike the GOYIM

*before the proper time we shall mask it under an alleged ardent desire
to serve the working classes and the great principles of political economy about which our economic theories are carrying on an energetic
propaganda.*

PROTOCOL NO. 7

The intensification of armaments, the increase of police forces—
are all essential for the completion of the aforementioned plans.
What we have to get at is that there should be in all the States of the
world, besides ourselves, only the masses of the proletariat, a few
millionaires devoted to our interests, police and soldiers.

Throughout all Europe, and by means of relations with Europe,
in other continents also, we must create ferments, discords and hostility. Therein we gain a double advantage. In the first place we keep
in check all countries, for they well know that we have the power
whenever we like to create disorders or to restore order. All these
countries are accustomed to see in us an indispensable force of coercion.
In the second place, by our intrigues we shall tangle up all the threads
which we have stretched into the cabinets of all States by means of
politics, by economic treaties, or loan obligations. In order to succeed
in this we must use great cunning and penetration during negotiations and agreements, but, as regards what is called the "official
language," we shall keep to the opposite tactics and assume the mask
of honesty and compliancy. In this way the peoples and governments
of the *goyim*, whom we have taught to look only at the outside of whatever we present to their notice, will still continue to accept us as the
benefactors and saviours of the human race.

We must be in a position to respond to every act of opposition by
war with the neighbours of that country which dares to oppose us:
but if these neighbours should also venture to stand collectively together
against us, then we must offer resistance by a universal war.

The principal factor of success in the political is the secrecy of its
undertakings: the word should not agree with the deeds of the diplomat.

We must compel the governments of the *goyim* to take action in
the direction favoured by our widely conceived plan, already approaching the desired consummation, by what we shall represent as
public opinion, secretly prompted by us through the means of that

so-called "Great Power"—*the Press, which, with a few exceptions that may be disregarded, is already entirely in our hands.*

In a word, to sum up our system of keeping the governments of the goyim in Europe in check, we shall show our strength to one of them by terrorist attempts and to all, if we allow the possibility of a general rising against us, we shall respond with the guns of America or China or Japan.

PROTOCOL NO. 8

We must arm ourselves with all the weapons which our opponents might employ against us. We must search out in the very finest shades of expression and the knotty points of the lexicon of law justification for those cases where we shall have to pronounce judgments that might appear abnormally audacious and unjust, for it is important that these resolutions should be set forth in expressions that shall seem to be the most exalted moral principles cast into legal form. Our directorate must surround itself with all these forces of civilisation among which it will have to work. It will surround itself with publicists, practical jurists, administrators, diplomats and, finally, with persons prepared by a special super-educational training *in our special schools.* These persons will have cognisance of all the secrets of the social structure, they will know all the languages that can be made up by political alphabets and words; they will be made acquainted with the whole underside of human nature, with all its sensitive chords on which they will have to play. These chords are the cast of mind of the goyim, their tendencies, shortcomings, vices and qualities, the particularities of classes and conditions. Needless to say that the talented assistants of authority, of whom I speak, will be taken not from among the goyim, who are accustomed to perform their administrative work without giving themselves the trouble to think what its aim is, and never consider what it is needed for. The administrators of the goyim sign papers without reading them, and they serve either for mercenary reasons or from ambition.

We shall surround our government with a whole world of economists. That is the reason why economic sciences form the principal subject of the teaching given to the Jews. Around us again will be a whole constellation of bankers, industrialists, capitalists and—*the*

main thing—millionaires, because in substance everything will be set-
tled by the question of figures.

For a time, until there will no longer be any risk in entrusting
responsible posts in our States to our brother-Jews, we shall put them
in the hands of persons whose past and reputation are such that
between them and the people lies an abyss, persons who, in case of
disobedience to our instructions, must face criminal charges or disappear—this in order to make them defend our interest to their last
gasp.

PROTOCOL NO. 9

In applying our principles let attention be paid to the character of
the people in whose country you live and act; a general, identical
application of them, until such time as the people shall have been
re-educated to our pattern, cannot have success. But by approaching
their application cautiously you will see that not a decade will pass before
the most stubborn character will change and we shall add a new
people to the ranks of those already subdued by us.

The words of the liberal, which are in effect the words of our
masonic watchword, namely, "Liberty, Equality, Fraternity," will,
when we come into our kingdom, be changed by us into words no
longer of a watchword, but only an expression of idealism, namely,
into: "The right of liberty, the duty of equality, the ideal of brotherhood." That is how we shall put it,—and so we shall catch the bull
by the horns. . . . *De facto* we have already wiped out every kind of
rule except our own, although *de jure* there still remain a good many
of them. Nowadays, if any States raise a protest against us it is only
pro forma at our discretion and by our direction, for *their anti-*
Semitism is indispensable to us for the management of our lesser
brethren. I will not enter into further explanations, for this matter has
formed the subject of repeated discussions amongst us.

For us there are no checks to limit the range of our activity. Our
Super-Government subsists in extra-legal conditions which are described
in the accepted terminology by the energetic and forcible word—
Dictatorship. I am in a position to tell you with a clear conscience that
at the proper time we, the law-givers, shall execute judgment and
sentence, we shall slay and we shall spare, we, as head of all our

troops, are mounted on the steed of the leader. We rule by force of will, because in our hands are the fragments of a once powerful party, now vanquished by us. *And the weapons in our hands are limitless ambitions, burning greediness, merciless vengeance, hatreds and malice.*

It is from us that the all-engulfing terror proceeds. We have in our service persons of all opinions, of all doctrines, restorating monarchists, demagogues, socialists, communists, and utopian dreamers of every kind. We have harnessed them all to the task: *each one of them on his own account is boring away at the last remnants of authority, is striving to overthrow all established form of order.* By these acts all States are in torture; they exhort to tranquillity, are ready to sacrifice everything for peace: *but we will not give them peace until they openly acknowledge our international Super-Government*, and with submissiveness.

The people have raised a howl about the necessity of settling the question of Socialism by way of an international agreement. *Division into fractional parties has given them into our hands, for, in order to carry on a contested struggle one must have money, and the money is all in our hands.*

We might have reason to apprehend a union between the "clear-sighted" force of the *goy* kings on their thrones and the "*blind*" force of the *goy* mobs, but we have taken all the needful measure against any such possibility: between the one and the other force we have erected a bulwark in the shape of a mutual terror between them. In this way the blind force of the people remains our support and we, and we only, shall provide them with a leader and, of course, direct them along the road that leads to our goal.

In order that the hand of the blind mob may not free itself from our guiding hand, we must every now and then enter into close communion with it, if not actually in person, at any rate through some of the most trusty of our brethren. When we are acknowledged as the only authority we shall discuss with the people personally on the market places, and we shall instruct them on questions of the political in such wise as may turn them in the direction that suits us.

Who is going to verify what is taught in the village schools? But what an envoy of the government or a king on his throne himself may say cannot but become immediately known to the whole State, for it will be spread abroad by the voice of the people.

In order not to annihilate the institutions of the *goyim* before it

is time we have touched them with craft and delicacy, and have taken
hold of the ends of the springs which move their mechanism. These
springs lay in a strict but just sense of order; we have replaced them
by the chaotic license of liberalism. We have got our hands into the
administration of the law, into the conduct of elections, into the press,
into liberty of the person, *but principally into education and training
as being the corner-stones of a free existence.*

We have fooled, bemused and corrupted the youth of the GOYIM
*by rearing them in principles and theories which are known to us to
be false although it is by us that they have been inculcated.*

Above the existing laws without substantially altering them, and
by merely twisting them into contradictions of interpretations, we have
erected something grandiose in the way of results. These results found
expression first in the fact that the *interpretations masked the laws:*
afterwards they entirely hid them from the eyes of the governments
owing to the impossibility of making anything out of the tangled web
of legislation.

This is the origin of the theory of course of arbitration.

You may say the *goyim* will rise upon us, arms in hand, if
they guess what is going on before the time comes; but in the West
we have against this a manœuvre of such appalling terror that the
very stoutest hearts quail—the undergrounds, metropolitains, those
subterranean corridors which, before the time comes, will be driven
under all the capitals and from whence those capitals will be blown
into the air with all their organisations and archives.

PROTOCOL NO. 10

To-day I begin with a repetition of what I said before, and *I beg
you to bear in mind that governments and peoples are content in the
political with outside appearances.* And how, indeed, are the *goyim* to
perceive the underlying meaning of things when their representatives give the best of their energies to enjoying themselves? For our
policy it is of the greatest importance to take cognisance of this detail;
it will be of assistance to us when we come to consider the division
of authority, freedom of speech, of the press, of religion (faith),
of the law of association, of equality before the law, of the inviolability of property, of the dwelling, of taxation (the idea of concealed

taxes), of the reflex force of the laws. All these questions are such as ought not to be touched upon directly and openly before the people. In cases where it is indispensable to touch upon them they must not be categorically named, it must merely be declared without detailed exposition that the principles of contemporary law are acknowledged by us. The reason of keeping silence in this respect is that by not naming a principle we leave ourselves freedom of action, to drop this or that out of it without attracting notice; if they were all categorically named they would all appear to have been already given.

The mob cherishes a special affection and respect for the geniuses of political power and accepts all their deeds of violence with the admiring response: "rascally, well, yes, it is rascally, but it's clever! . . . a trick, if you like, but how craftily played, how magnificently done, what impudent audacity!" . . .

We count upon attracting all nations to the task of erecting the new fundamental structure, the project for which has been drawn up by us. This is why, before everything, it is indispensable for us to arm ourselves and to store up in ourselves that absolutely reckless audacity and irresistible might of the spirit which in the person of our active workers will break down all hindrances on our way.

When we have accomplished our coup d'état we shall say then to the various peoples: "Everything has gone terribly badly, all have been worn out with sufferings. We are destroying the causes of your torment—nationalities, frontiers, differences of coinages. You are at liberty, of course, to pronounce sentence upon us, but can it possibly be a just one if it is confirmed by you before you make any trial of what we are offering you." . . . Then will the mob exalt us and bear us up in their hands in a unanimous triumph of hopes and expectations. Voting, which we have made the instrument which will set us on the throne of the world by teaching even the very smallest units of members of the human race to vote by means of meetings and agreements by groups, will then have served its purposes and will play its part then for the last time by a unanimity of desire to make close acquaintance with us before condemning us.

To secure this we must have everybody vote without distinction of classes and qualifications, in order to establish an absolute majority, which cannot be got from the educated propertied classes. In this way, by inculcating in all a sense of self-importance, we shall destroy among the *goyim* the importance of the family and its educational value and remove the possibility of individual minds splitting off, for the mob, handled by us, will not let them come to the front nor even give them a hearing; it is accustomed to listen to us only who pay it for obedience and attention. In this way we shall create a blind, mighty force which will never be in a position to move in any direction without the guidance of our agents set at its head by us as leaders of the mob. The people will submit to this régime because it will know that upon these leaders will depend its earnings, gratifications and the receipt of all kinds of benefits.

A scheme of government should come ready made from one brain, because it will never be clinched firmly if it is allowed to be split into fractional parts in the minds of many. It is allowable, therefore, for us to have cognisance of the scheme of action but not to discuss it lest we disturb its artfulness, the interdependence of its component parts, the practical force of the secret meaning of each clause. To discuss and make alterations in a labour of this kind by means of numerous votings is to impress upon it the stamp of all ratiocinations and misunderstandings which have failed to penetrate the depth and nexus of its plottings. We want our schemes to be forcible and suitably concocted. Therefore WE OUGHT NOT TO FLING THE WORK OF GENIUS OF OUR GUIDE to the fangs of the mob or even of a select company.

These schemes will not turn existing institutions upside down just yet. They will only affect changes in their economy and consequently in the whole combined movement of their progress, which will thus be directed along the paths laid down in our schemes.

Under various names there exists in all countries approximately one and the same thing. Representation, Ministry, Senate, State Council, Legislative and Executive Corps. I need not explain to you the mechanism of the relation of these institutions to one another, because you are aware of all that; only take note of the fact that each of the above-named institutions corresponds to some important function of the State, and I would beg you to remark that the word "important" I apply not to the institution but to the function, consequently it is not the institutions which are important but their functions. These institutions have divided up among themselves all the functions of government— administrative, legislative, executive, wherefore they have come to operate as do the organs in the human body. If we injure one part in the machinery of State, the State falls sick, like a human body, and will die.

When we introduced into the State organism the poison of Liberalism its whole political complexion underwent a change. States have been seized with a mortal illness—blood-poisoning. All that remains is to await the end of their death agony.

Liberalism produced Constitutional States, which took the place of what was the only safeguard of the *goyim*, namely, Despotism; and *a constitution, as you well know, is nothing else but a school of discords,* misunderstandings, quarrels, disagreements, fruitless party agitations, party whims—in a word, a school of everything that serves to destroy the personality of State activity. *The tribune of the "talkeries" has, no less effectively than the Press, condemned the rulers to inactivity and impotence,* and thereby rendered them useless and superfluous, for which reason indeed they have been in many countries deposed. *Then it was that the era of republics became possible of realisation; and then it was that we replaced the ruler by a caricature of a government—by a president, taken from the mob, from the midst of our puppet creatures, our slaves.* This was the foundation of the mine which we have laid under the *goy* people, I should rather say, under the *goy* peoples.

In the near future we shall establish the responsibility of presidents.

By that time we shall be in a position to disregard forms in carrying through matters for which our personal puppet will be responsible. What do we care if the ranks of those striving for power should be thinned, if there should arise a deadlock from the impossibility of finding presidents, a deadlock which will finally disorganize the country?

In order that our scheme may produce this result we shall arrange elections in favour of such presidents as have in their past some dark, undiscovered stain, some "Panama" or other—then they will be trustworthy agents for the accomplishment of our plans out of fear of revelations and from the natural desire of everyone who has attained power, namely, the retention of privileges, advantages and honour connected with the office of president. The chamber of deputies will provide cover for, will protect, will elect the president, but we shall take from it the right to propose new, or make changes in existing laws, for this right will be given by us to the responsible president, a puppet in our hands. Naturally, the authority of the president will then become a target for every possible form of attack, but we shall provide him with a means of self-defence in the right of an appeal to the people, for the decision of the people over the heads of their representatives, that is to say, an appeal to that same blind slave of ours— the majority of the mob. Independently of this we shall invest the president with the right of declaring a state of war. We shall justify this last right on the ground that the president as chief of the whole army of the country must have it at his disposal, in case of need for the defence of the new republican constitution, the right to defend which will belong to him as the responsible representative of this constitution.

It is easy to understand that in these conditions the key of the shrine will lie in our hands, and no one outside of ourselves will any longer direct the force of legislation.

Besides this we shall, with the introduction of the new republican constitution, take from the Chamber the right of interpellation on government measures, on the pretext of preserving political secrecy, and, further, we shall by the new constitution reduce the number of representatives to a minimum, thereby proportionately reducing political passions and the passion for politics. If, however, they should, which is hardly to be expected, burst into flame, even in this minimum, we shall nullify them by a stirring appeal and a reference to the majority of the whole people. . . . Upon the president will depend the appointment of presidents and vice-presidents of the Chamber and the Senate. Instead of constant sessions of Parliaments we shall reduce their sittings to a few months. Moreover, the president, as chief of the executive power, will have the right to summon and dissolve Parliament, and, in the latter case, to prolong the time for the appointment of a new parliamentary assembly. But in order that the consequences of all these acts which in substance are illegal, should not, prematurely for our plans, fall upon the responsibility established by us of the president, *we shall instigate ministers and other officials of the higher administration about the president to evade his dispositions by taking measures of their own*, for doing which they will be made the scapegoats in his place. . . . This part we especially recommend to be given to be played by the Senate, the Council of State, or the Council of Ministers, but not to an individual official.

The president will, at our discretion, interpret the sense of such of the existing laws as admit of various interpretation; he will further annul them when we indicate to him the necessity to do so, besides this, he will have the right to propose temporary laws, and even new departures in the government constitutional working, the pretext both for the one and other being the requirements for the supreme welfare of the State.

By such measures we shall obtain the power of destroying little by little, step by step, all that at the outset when we enter on our rights, we are compelled to introduce into the constitutions of States to prepare for the transition to an imperceptible abolition of every kind of constitution, and then the time is come to turn every form of government into *our despotism*.

The recognition of our despot may also come before the destruction of the constitution; the moment for this recognition will come when the peoples, utterly wearied by the irregularities and incompetence— a matter which we shall arrange for—of their rulers, will clamour: "Away with them and give us one king over all the earth who will unite us and annihilate the causes of discords—frontiers, nationalities, religions, State debts—who will give us peace and quiet, which we cannot find under our rulers and representatives."

But you yourselves perfectly well know that *to produce the possibility of the expression of such wishes by all the nations it is indispensable to trouble in all countries the people's relations with their governments so as to utterly exhaust humanity with dissension, hatred, struggle, envy and even by the use of torture, by starvation, BY THE INOCULATION OF DISEASES, by want, so that the* GOYIM *see no other issue than to take refuge in our complete sovereignty in money and in all else.*

But if we give the nations of the world a breathing space the moment we long for is hardly likely ever to arrive.

PROTOCOL NO. 11

The State Council has been, as it were, the emphatic expression of the authority of the ruler: it will be, as the "show" part of the Legislative Corps, what may be called the editorial committee of the laws and decrees of the ruler.

This, then, is the programme of the new constitution. We shall make Law, Right and Justice (1) in the guise of proposals to the Legislative Corps, (2) by decrees of the president under the guise of general regulations, of orders of the Senate and of resolutions of the State Council in the guise of ministerial orders, (3) and in case a suitable occasion should arise—in the form of a revolution in the State.

Having established approximately the *modus agendi* we will occupy ourselves with details of those combinations by which we have still to complete the revolution in the course of the machinery of State in the direction already indicated. By these combinations I mean the freedom of the Press, the right of association, freedom of conscience, the voting principle, and many another that must disappear for ever from the memory of man, or undergo a radical alteration the day after the promulgation of the new constitution. It is only at that moment that we shall be able at once to announce all our orders, for, afterwards, every noticeable alteration will be dangerous, for the following reasons: if this alteration be brought in with harsh severity and in a sense of severity and limitations, it may lead to a feeling of despair caused by fear of new alterations in the same direction; if, on the other hand, it be brought in in a sense of further indulgences it will be said that we have recognised our own wrongdoing and this will destroy the prestige of the infallibility of our authority, or else it will be said that we have become alarmed and are compelled to show a yielding disposition, for which we shall get no thanks because it will be supposed to be compulsory. . . . Both the one and the other are injurious to the prestige of the new constitution. What we want is that from the first moment of its promulgation, while the peoples of the world are still stunned by the accomplished fact of the revolution, still in a condition of terror and uncertainty, they should recognise once for all that we are so strong, so inexpugnable, so superabundantly filled with power, that in no case shall we take any account of them, and so far from paying any attention to their opinions or wishes, we are ready and able to crush with irresistible power all expression or manifestation thereof at every moment and in every place, that we have seized at once everything we wanted and shall in no case divide our power with them. . . . Then in fear and trembling they will close their eyes to everything, and be content to await what will be the end of it all.

The *goyim* are a flock of sheep, and we are their wolves. And you know what happens when the wolves get hold of the flock? . . .

There is another reason also why they will close their eyes: for we shall keep promising them to give back all the liberties we have taken away as soon as we have quelled the enemies of peace and tamed all parties. . . .

It is not worth while to say anything about how long a time they will be kept waiting for this return of their liberties. . . .

For what purpose then have we invented this whole policy and insinuated it into the minds of the *goys* without giving them any chance to examine its underlying meaning? For what, indeed, if not in order to obtain in a roundabout way what is for our scattered tribe unattainable by the direct road? It is this which has served as the basis for our organisation of SECRET MASONRY WHICH IS NOT KNOWN TO, AND AIMS WHICH ARE NOT EVEN SO MUCH AS SUSPECTED BY, THESE *GOY* CATTLE, ATTRACTED BY US INTO THE "SHOW" ARMY OF MASONIC LODGES IN ORDER TO THROW DUST IN THE EYES OF THEIR FELLOWS.

God has granted to us, His Chosen People, the gift of the dispersion, and in this which appears in all eyes to be our weakness, has come forth all our strength, which has now brought us to the threshold of sovereignty over all the world.

There now remains not much more for us to build up upon the foundation we have laid.

PROTOCOL NO. 12

The word "freedom," which can be interpreted in various ways, is defined by us as follows:—

Freedom is the right to do that which the law allows. This interpretation of the word will at the proper time be of service to us, because all freedom will thus be in our hands, since the laws will abolish or create only that which is desirable for us according to the aforesaid programme.

We shall deal with the press in the following way: What is the part played by the press to-day? It serves to excite and inflame those passions which are needed for our purpose or else it serves selfish ends of parties. It is often vapid, unjust, mendacious, and the majority of the public have not the slightest idea what ends the press really serves. We shall saddle and bridle it with a tight curb: we shall do the same also with all productions of the printing press, for where would be the sense of getting rid of the attacks of the press if we remain targets for pamphlets and books? The produce of publicity, which nowadays is a source of heavy expense owing to the necessity of censoring it, will be turned by us into a very lucrative source of income to our State: we shall lay on it a special stamp tax and require deposits of caution-money before permitting the establishment of any organ of the press or of printing offices; these will then have to guarantee our government against any kind of attack on the part of the press. For any attempt to attack us, if such still be possible, we shall inflict fines without mercy. Such measures as stamp tax, deposit of caution-money and fines secured by these deposits, will bring in a huge income to the government. It is true that party organs might not spare money for the sake of publicity, but these we shall shut up at the second attack upon us. No one shall with impunity lay a finger on the aureole of our government infallibility. The pretext for stopping any publication will be the alleged plea that it is agitating the public mind without occasion or justification. *I beg you to note that among those making attacks upon us will also be organs established by us, but they will attack exclusively points that we have pre-determined to alter.*

Not a single announcement will reach the public without our control. Even now this is already being attained by us inasmuch as all news items are received by a few agencies, in whose offices they are focused from all parts of the world. These agencies will then be already entirely ours and will give publicity only to what we dictate to them.

If already now we have contrived to possess ourselves of the minds of the *goy* communities to such an extent that they all come near looking upon the events of the world through the coloured glasses of those spectacles we are setting astride their noses: if already now there is not a single State where there exist for us any barriers to admittance into what *goy* stupidity calls State secrets: what will our position be then, when we shall be acknowledged supreme lords of the world in the person of our king of all the world. . . .

Let us turn again to the *future of the printing press*. Every one desirous of being a publisher, librarian, or printer, will be obliged to provide himself with the diploma instituted therefor, which, in case of any fault, will be immediately impounded. With such measures *the instrument of thought will become an educative means in the hands of our government, which will no longer allow the mass of the nation to be led astray in by-ways and fantasies about the blessings of progress.* Is there any one of us who does not know that these phantom blessings are the direct roads to foolish imaginings which give birth to anarchical relations of men among themselves and towards authority, because progress, or rather the idea of progress, has introduced the conception of every kind of emancipation, but has failed to establish its limits. . . . All the so-called liberals are anarchists, if not in fact, at any rate in thought. Every one of them is hunting after phantoms of freedom, and falling exclusively into license, that is, into the anarchy of protest for the sake of protest. . . .

We turn to the periodical press. We shall impose on it, as on all printed matter, stamp taxes per sheet and deposits of caution-money, and books of less than 30 sheets will pay double. We shall reckon them as pamphlets in order, on the one hand, to reduce the number of magazines, which are the worst form of printed poison, and, on the other, in order that this measure may force writers into such lengthy productions that they will be little read, especially as they will be costly. At the same time what we shall publish ourselves to influence mental development in the direction laid down for our profit will be cheap and will be read voraciously. The tax will bring vapid literary ambitions within bounds and the liability to penalties will make literary men dependent upon us. And if there should be any found who are desirous of writing against us, they will not find any person eager to print their productions. Before accepting any production for publication in print the publisher or printer will have to apply to the authorities for permission to do so. Thus we shall know beforehand of all tricks preparing against us and shall nullify them by getting ahead with explanations on the subject treated of.

Literature and journalism are two of the most important educative forces, and therefore our government will become proprietor of the majority of the journals. This will neutralise the injurious influence of the privately owned press and will put us in possession of a tremendous influence upon the public mind. . . . If we give permits for ten journals, we shall ourselves found thirty, and so on in the same proportion. This, however, must in nowise be suspected by the public.

For which reason all journals published by us will be of the most opposite, in appearance, tendencies and opinions, thereby creating confidence in us and bringing over to us our quite unsuspicious opponents, who will thus fall into our trap and be rendered harmless.

In the front rank will stand organs of an official character. They will always stand guard over our interests, and therefore their influence will be comparatively insignificant.

In the second rank will be the semi-official organs, whose part it will be to attract the tepid and indifferent.

In the third rank we shall set up our own, to all appearance, opposition, which, in at least one of its organs, will present what looks like the very antipodes to us. Our real opponents at heart will accept this simulated opposition as their own and will show us their cards.

All our newspapers will be of all possible complexions—aristocratic, republican, revolutionary, even anarchical—for so long, of course, as the constitution exists. . . . Like the Indian idol Vishnu they will have a hundred hands, and every one of them will have a finger on any one of the public opinions as required. When a pulse quickens these hands will lead opinion in the direction of our aims, for an excited patient loses all power of judgment and easily yields to suggestion. Those fools who will think they are repeating the opinion of a newspaper of their own camp will be repeating our opinion or any opinion that seems desirable for us. In the vain belief that they are following the organ of their party they will in fact follow the flag which we hang out for them.

In order to direct our newspaper militia in this sense we must take especial and minute care in organising this matter. Under the title of central department of the press we shall institute literary gatherings at which our agents will without attracting attention issue the orders and watchwords of the day. By discussing and controverting, but always superficially, without touching the essence of the matter, our organs will carry on a sham fight fusillade with the official newspapers solely for the purpose of giving occasion for us to express ourselves more fully than could well be done from the outset in official announcements, whenever, of course, that is to our advantage.

These attacks upon us will also serve another purpose, namely, that our subjects will be convinced of the existence of full freedom of speech and so give our agents an occasion to affirm that all organs which oppose us are empty babblers, since they are incapable of finding any substantial objections to our orders.

Methods of organisation like these, imperceptible to the public eye but absolutely sure, are the best calculated to succeed in bringing the attention and the confidence of the public to the side of our government. Thanks to such methods we shall be in a position as from time to time may be required, to excite or to tranquillise the public mind on political questions, to persuade or to confuse, printing now truth, now lies, facts or their contradictions, according as they may be well or ill received, always very cautiously feeling our ground before stepping upon it. . . . *We shall have a sure triumph over our opponents since they will not have at their disposition organs of the press in which they can give full and final expression to their views* owing to the aforesaid methods of dealing with the press. We shall not even need to refute them except very superficially.

Trial shots like these, fired by us in the third rank of our press, in case of need, will be energetically refuted by us in our semi-official organs.

Even nowadays, already, to take only the French press, there are forms which reveal masonic solidarity in acting on the watchword: all organs of the press are bound together by professional secrecy; like the augurs of old, not one of their numbers will give away the secret of his sources of information unless it be resolved to make announcement to them. Not one journalist will venture to betray this secret, for not one of them is ever admitted to practise literature unless his whole past has some disgraceful sore or other. . . . These sores would be immediately revealed. So long as they remain the secret of a few the prestige of the journalist attracts the majority of the country—the mob follows after him with enthusiasm.

Our calculations are especially extended to the provinces. It is indispensable for us to inflame there those hopes and impulses with which we could at any moment fall upon the capital, and we shall represent to the capitals that these expressions are the independent hopes and impulses of the provinces. Naturally, the source of them will be always one and the same—ours. *What we need is that, until such time as we are in the plenitude of power, the capitals should find themselves stifled by the provincial opinion of the nation*, i.e., of *a majority arranged by our agentur.* What we need is that at the psychological moment the capitals should not be in a position to discuss an accomplished fact for the simple reason, if for no other, that it has been accepted by the public opinion of a majority in the provinces.

When we are in the period of the new régime transitional to that of our assumption of full sovereignty we must not admit any revelations by the press of any form of public dishonesty; it is necessary that the new régime should be thought to have so perfectly contented everybody that even criminality has disappeared. . . . Cases of the manifestation of criminality should remain known only to their victims and to chance witnesses—no more.

PROTOCOL NO. 13

The need for daily bread forces the *goyim* to keep silence and be our humble servants. Agents taken on to our press from among the *goyim* will at our order discuss anything which it is inconvenient for us to issue directly in official documents, and we meanwhile, quietly amid the din of the discussion so raised, shall simply take and carry through such measures as we wish and then offer them to the public as an accomplished fact. No one will dare to demand the abrogation of a matter once settled, all the more so as it will be represented as an improvement. . . . And immediately the press will distract the current of thought towards new questions (have we not trained people always to be seeking something new?). Into the discussions of these new questions will throw themselves those of the brainless dispensers of fortunes who are not able even now to understand that they have not the remotest conception about the matters which they undertake to discuss. Questions of the political are unattainable for any save those who have guided it already for many ages, the creators.

From all this you will see that in securing the opinion of the mob we are only facilitating the working of our machinery, and you may remark that it is not for actions but for words issued by us on this or that question that we seem to seek approval. We are constantly making public declaration that we are guided in all our undertakings by the hope, joined to the conviction, that we are serving the commonweal.

In order to distract people who may be too troublesome from discussions of questions of the political we are now putting forward what we allege to be new questions of the political, namely, questions of industry. In this sphere let them discuss themselves silly! The masses are agreed to remain inactive, to take a rest from what they suppose to be political activity (which we trained them to in order to use them as a means of combating the *goy* governments) only on condition of being found new employments, in which we are prescribing them something that looks like the same political object. In order that the masses themselves may not guess what they are about *we further distract them with amusements, games, pastimes, passions, people's palaces. . . . Soon we shall begin through the press to propose competitions in art, in sport of all kinds:* these interests will finally distract their minds from questions in which we should find ourselves compelled to oppose them. Growing more and more disaccustomed to reflect and form any opinions of their own, people will begin to talk in the same tone as we, because we alone shall be offering them new directions for thought . . . of course through such persons as will not be suspected of solidarity with us.

The part played by the liberals, utopian dreamers, will be finally played out when our government is acknowledged. Till such time they will continue to do us good service. Therefore we shall continue to direct their minds to all sorts of vain conceptions of fantastic theories, new and apparently progressive: for have we not with complete success turned the brainless heads of the *goyim* with progress, till there is not among the *goyim* one mind able to perceive that under this word lies a departure from truth in all cases where it is not a question of material inventions, for truth is one, and in it there is no place for progress. Progress, like a fallacious idea, serves to obscure truth so that none may know it except us, the Chosen of God, its guardians.

When we come into our kingdom our orators will expound great problems which have turned humanity upside down in order to bring it at the end under our beneficent rule.

Who will ever suspect then that ALL THESE PEOPLES WERE STAGE-MANAGED BY US ACCORDING TO A POLITICAL PLAN WHICH NO ONE HAS SO MUCH AS GUESSED AT IN THE COURSE OF MANY CENTURIES? . . .

PROTOCOL NO. 14

When we come into our kingdom it will be undesirable for us that there should exist any other religion than ours of the One God with whom our destiny is bound up by our position as the Chosen People and through whom our same destiny is united with the destinies of the world. We must therefore sweep away all other forms of belief. If this gives birth to the atheists whom we see to-day, it will not, being only a transitional stage, interfere with our views, but will serve as a warning for those generations which will hearken to our preaching of the religion of Moses, that, by its stable and thoroughly elaborated system, has brought all the peoples of the world into subjection to us. Therein we shall emphasise its mystical right, on which, as we shall say, all its educative power is based. . . . Then at every possible opportunity we shall publish articles in which we shall make comparisons between our beneficent rule and those of past ages. The blessings of tranquillity, though it be a tranquillity forcibly brought about by centuries of agitation, will throw into higher relief the benefits to which we shall point. The errors of the *goyim* governments will be depicted by us in the most vivid hues. We shall implant such an abhorrence of them that the peoples will prefer tranquillity in a state of serfdom to those rights of vaunted freedom which have tortured humanity and exhausted the very sources of human existence, sources which have been exploited by a mob of rascally adventurers who know not what they do. . . . *Useless changes of forms of government to which we instigated the* GOYIM *when we were undermining their state structures, will have so wearied the peoples by that time that they will prefer to suffer anything under us rather than run the risk of enduring again all the agitations and miseries they have gone through.*

At the same time we shall not omit to emphasise the historical mistakes of the *goy* governments which have tormented humanity for so many centuries by their lack of understanding of everything that constitutes the true good of humanity in their chase after fantastic schemes of social blessings, and have never noticed that these schemes kept on producing a worse and never a better state of the universal relations which are the basis of human life. . . .

The whole force of our principles and methods will lie in the fact that we shall present them and expound them as a splendid contrast to the dead and decomposed old order of things in social life.

Our philosophers will discuss all the shortcomings of the various beliefs of the *goyim*, BUT NO ONE WILL EVER BRING UNDER DISCUSSION OUR FAITH FROM ITS TRUE POINT OF VIEW SINCE THIS WILL BE FULLY LEARNED BY NONE SAVE OURS, WHO WILL NEVER DARE TO BETRAY ITS SECRETS.

In countries known as progressive and enlightened we have created a senseless, filthy, abominable literature. For some time after our entrance to power we shall continue to encourage its existence in order to provide a telling relief by contrast to the speeches, party programme, which will be distributed from exalted quarters of ours. . . . Our wise men, trained to become leaders of the *goyim*, will compose speeches, projects, memoirs, articles, which will be used by us to influence the minds of the *goyim*, directing them towards such understanding and forms of knowledge as have been determined by us.

PROTOCOL NO. 15

When we at last definitely come into our kingdom by the aid of *coups d'état* prepared everywhere for one and the same day, after the worthlessness of all existing forms of government has been definitely acknowledged (and not a little time will pass before that comes about, perhaps even a whole century) we shall make it our task to see that against us such things as plots shall no longer exist. With this purpose we shall slay without mercy all who take arms (in hand) to oppose our coming into our kingdom. Every kind of new institution of anything like a secret society will also be punished with death; those of them which are now in existence, are known to us, serve us and have served us, we shall disband and send into exile to continents far removed from Europe. *In this way we shall proceed with those* GOY *masons who know too much*; such of these as we may for some reason spare will be kept in constant fear of exile. We shall promulgate a law making all former members of secret societies liable to exile from Europe as the centre of our rule.

Resolutions of our government will be final, without appeal.

In the *goy* societies, in which we have planted and deeply rooted discord and protestantism, the only possible way of restoring order is to employ merciless measures that prove the direct force of authority: no regard must be paid to the victims who fall, they suffer for the well-being of the future. The attainment of that well-being, even at the expense of sacrifices, is the duty of any kind of government that acknowledges as justification for its existence not only its privileges but its obligations. The principal guarantee of stability of rule is to confirm the aureole of power, and this aureole is attained only by such a majestic inflexibility of might as shall carry on its face the emblems of inviolability from mystical causes—from the choice of God. *Such was, until recent times, the Russian autocracy, the one and only serious foe we had in the world, without counting the Papacy.* Bear in mind the example when Italy, drenched with blood, never touched a hair of the head of Sulla* who had poured forth that blood: Sulla enjoyed an apotheosis for his might in the eyes of the people, though they had been torn in pieces by him, but his intrepid return to Italy ringed him round with inviolability. The people do not lay a finger on him who hypnotises them by his daring and strength of mind.

Meantime, however, until we come into our kingdom, we shall act in the contrary way: we shall create and multiply free masonic lodges in all the countries of the world, absorb into them all who may become or who are prominent in public activity, for in these lodges we shall find our principal intelligence office and means of influence. All these lodges we shall bring under one central administration, known to us alone and to all others absolutely unknown, which will be composed of our learned elders. The lodges will have their representatives who will serve to screen the above-mentioned administration of *masonry* and from whom will issue the watchword and programme. In these lodges we shall tie together the knot which binds together all revolutionary and liberal elements. Their composition will be made up of all strata of society. The most secret political plots will be known to us and will fall under our guiding hands on the very day of their conception. *Among the members of these lodges will be al-*

---

* Some versions of the "Protocols" followed Joly's "Dialogues" so closely that Joly's mistaken spelling of Sulla's name as "Sylla" was also copied. In the translation of the "Protocols" here used, however, the mistake was rectified.—H. B.

most all the agents of international and national police since their service is for us irreplaceable in the respect that the police is in a position not only to use its own particular measures with the insubordinate, but also to screen our activities and provide pretexts for discontents, *et cetera.*

The class of people who most willingly enter into secret societies are those who live by their wits, careerists, and in general people, mostly light-minded, with whom we shall have no difficulty in dealing and in using to wind up the mechanism of the machine devised by us. If this world grows agitated the meaning of that will be that we have had to stir it up in order to break up its too great solidarity. *But if there should arise in its midst a plot, then at the head of that plot will be no other than one of our most trusted servants.* It is natural that we and no other should lead *masonic* activities, for we know whither we are leading, we know the final goal of every form of activity whereas the *goyim* have knowledge of nothing, not even of the immediate effect of action; they put before themselves, usually, the momentary reckoning of the satisfaction of their self-opinion in the accomplishment of their thought without even remarking that the very conception never belonged to their initiative but to our instigation of their thought. . . .

The *goyim* enter the lodges out of curiosity or in the hope by their means to get a nibble at the public pie, and some of them in order to obtain a hearing before the public for their impracticable and groundless fantasies: they thirst for the emotion of success and applause, of which we are remarkably generous. And the reason why we give them this success is to make use of the high conceit of themselves to which it gives birth, for that insensibly disposes them to assimilate our suggestions without being on their guard against them in the fullness of their confidence that it is their own infallibility which is giving utterance to their own thoughts and that it is impossible for them to borrow those of others. . . . You cannot imagine to what extent the wisest of the *goyim* can be brought to a state of unconscious naïveté in the presence of this condition of high conceit of themselves, and at the same time how easy it is to take the heart out of them by the slightest ill-success, though it be nothing more than the stoppage of the applause they had, and to reduce them to a slavish submission for the sake of winning a renewal of success. . . .

By so much as ours disregard success if only they can carry through their plans, by so much the GOYIM *are willing to sacrifice any plans only to have success.* This psychology of theirs materially facilitates for us the task of setting them in the required direction. These tigers in appearance have the souls of sheep and the wind blows freely through their heads. We have set them on the hobby-horse of an idea about the absorption of individuality by the symbolic unit of *collectivism.* . . . They have never yet and they never will have the sense to reflect that this hobby-horse is a manifest violation of the most important law of nature, which has established from the very creation of the world one unit unlike another and precisely for the purpose of instituting individuality. . . .

If we have been able to bring them to such a pitch of stupid blindness is it not a proof, and an amazingly clear proof, of the degree to which the mind of the *goyim* is undeveloped in comparison with our mind? This it is, mainly, which guarantees our success.

And how far-seeing were our learned elders in ancient times when they said that to attain a serious end it behoves not to stop at any means or to count the victims sacrificed for the sake of that end. . . . We have not counted the victims of the seed of the *goy* cattle, though we have sacrificed many of our own, but for that we have now already given them such a position on the earth as they could not even have dreamed of. The comparatively small numbers of the victims from the number of ours have preserved our nationality from destruction.

Death is the inevitable end for all. It is better to bring that end nearer to those who hinder our affairs than to ourselves, to the founders of this affair. *We execute masons in such wise that none save the brotherhood can ever have a suspicion of it, not even the victims themselves of our death sentence, they all die when required as if from a normal kind of illness.* . . . Knowing this, even the brotherhood in its turn dare not protest. By such methods we have plucked out of the midst of *masonry* the very root of protest against our disposition. While preaching liberalism to the *goyim* we at the same time keep our own people and our agents in a state of unquestioning submission.

Under our influence the execution of the laws of the *goyim* has been reduced to a minimum. The prestige of the law has been exploded by the liberal interpretations introduced into this sphere. In

the most important and fundamental affairs and questions judges
decide as we dictate to them, see matters in the light wherewith we
enfold them for the administration of the *goyim*, of course, through
persons who are our tools though we do not appear to have anything
in common with them—by newspaper opinion or by other means. . . .
Even senators and the higher administration accept our counsels. The
purely brute mind of the *goyim* is incapable of use for analysis and
observation, and still more for the foreseeing whither a certain manner
of setting a question may tend.

In this difference in capacity for thought between the *goyim* and
ourselves may be clearly discerned the seal of our position on the
Chosen People and of our higher quality of humanness, in contra-
distinction to the brute mind of the *goyim*. Their eyes are open, but
see nothing before them and do not invent (unless, perhaps, material
things). From this it is plain that nature herself has destined us to
guide and rule the world.

When comes the time of our overt rule, the time to manifest its
blessings, we shall remake all legislatures, all our laws will be brief,
plain, stable, without any kind of interpretations, so that anyone will
be in a position to know them perfectly. The main feature which
will run right through them is submission to orders, and this principle
will be carried to a grandiose height. Every abuse will then disappear
in consequence of the responsibility of all down to the lowest unit
before the higher authority of the representative of power. Abuses of
power subordinate to this last instance will be so mercilessly punished
that none will be found anxious to try experiments with their own
powers. We shall follow up jealously every action of the administration on which depends the smooth running of the machinery of
the State, for slackness in this produces slackness everywhere; not a
single case of illegality or abuse of power will be left without exemplary punishment.

Concealment of guilt, connivance between those in the service of
the administration—all this kind of evil will disappear after the very
first examples of severe punishment. The aureole of our power demands suitable, that is, cruel, punishments for the slightest infringe-
ment, for the sake of gain, of its supreme prestige. The sufferer,
though his punishment may exceed his fault, will count as a soldier
falling on the administrative field of battle in the interest of au-

thority, principle and law, which do not permit that any of those who hold the reins of the public coach should turn aside from the public highway to their own private paths. *For example: our judges will know that whenever they feel disposed to plume themselves on foolish clemency they are violating the law of justice which is instituted for the exemplary edification of men by penalties for lapses and not for display of the spiritual qualities of the judge.* . . . Such qualities it is proper to show in private life, but not in a public square which is the educational basis of human life.

Our legal staff will serve not beyond the age of 55, firstly because old men more obstinately hold to prejudiced opinions, and are less capable of submitting to new directions, and second because this will give us the possibility by this measure of securing elasticity in the changing of staff, which will thus the more easily bend under our pressure: he who wishes to keep his place will have to give blind obedience to deserve it. In general, our judges will be elected by us only from among those who thoroughly understand that the part they have to play is to punish and apply laws and not to dream about the manifestations of liberalism at the expense of the educational scheme of the State, as the *goyim* in these days imagine it to be. . . . This method of shuffling the staff will serve also to explode any collective solidarity of those in the same service and will bind all to the interests of the government upon which their fate will depend. The young generation of judges will be trained in certain views regarding the inadmissibility of any abuses that might disturb the established order of our subjects among themselves.

In these days the judges of the *goyim* create indulgences to every kind of crime, not having a just understanding of their office, because the rulers of the present age in appointing judges to office take no care to inculcate in them a sense of duty and consciousness of the matter which is demanded of them. As a brute beast lets out its young in search of prey, so do the *goyim* give their subjects places of profit without thinking to make clear to them for what purpose such place was created. This is the reason why their governments are being ruined by their own forces through the acts of their own administration.

Let us borrow from the example of the results of these actions yet another lesson for our government.

We shall root out liberalism from all the important strategic posts of our government on which depends the training of subordinates for our State structure. Such posts will fall exclusively to those who have been trained by us for administrative rule. To the possible objection that the retirement of old servants will cost the Treasury heavily, I reply, firstly, they will be provided with some private service in place of what they lose, and, secondly, I have to remark that all the money in the world will be concentrated in our hands, consequently it is not our government that has to fear expense.

Our absolutism will in all things be logically consecutive and therefore in each one of its decrees our supreme will will be respected and unquestionably fulfilled: it will ignore all murmurs, all discontents of every kind and will destroy to the root every kind of manifestation of them in act by punishment of an exemplary character.

We shall abolish the right of cassation, which will be transferred exclusively to our disposal—to the cognisance of him who rules, for we must not allow the conception among the people of a thought that there could be such a thing as a decision that is not right of judges set up by us. If, however, anything like this should occur, we shall ourselves cassate the decision, but inflict therewith such exemplary punishment on the judge for lack of understanding of his duty and the purpose of his appointment as will prevent a repetition of such cases. . . . I repeat that it must be borne in mind that we shall know every step of our administration which only needs to be closely watched for the people to be content with us, for it has the right to demand from a good government a good official.

Our government will have the appearance of a patriarchal paternal guardianship on the part of our ruler. Our own nation and our subjects will discern in his person a father caring for their every need, their every act, their every inter-relation as subjects one with another, as well as their relations to the ruler. They will then be so thoroughly imbued with the thought that it is impossible for them to dispense with this wardship and guidance, if they wish to live in peace and quiet, *that they will acknowledge the autocracy of our ruler with a devotion bordering on* APOTHEOSIS, especially when they are convinced that those whom we set up do not put their own in place of his authority, but only blindly execute his dictates. They will be rejoiced that we have regulated everything in their lives as is done by wise parents who desire to train their children in the cause of duty and submission. For the peoples of the world in regard to the secrets of our polity are ever through the ages only children under age, precisely as are also their governments.

As you see, I found our despotism on right and duty: the right to compel the execution of duty is the direct obligation of a government which is a father for its subjects. It has the right of the strong that it may use it for the benefit of directing humanity towards that order which is defined by nature, namely, submission. Everything in the world is in a state of submission, if not to man, then to circumstances or its own inner character, in all cases, to what is stronger. And so shall we be this something stronger for the sake of good.

We are obliged without hesitation to sacrifice individuals, who commit a breach of established order, for in the exemplary punishment of evil lies a great educational problem.

When the King of Israel sets upon his sacred head the crown offered him by Europe he will become patriarch of the world. The indispensable victims offered by him in consequence of their suitability will never reach the number of victims offered in the course of centuries by the mania of magnificence, the emulation between the *goy* governments.

Our King will be in constant communion with the peoples, making to them from the tribune speeches which fame will in that same hour distribute over all the world.

PROTOCOL NO. 16

In order to effect the destruction of all collective forces except ours we shall emasculate the first stage of collectivism—the *universities*, by re-educating them in a new direction. *Their officials and professors will be prepared for their business by detailed secret programmes of action from which they will not with immunity diverge, not by one iota. They will be appointed with especial precaution, and will be so placed as to be wholly dependent upon the Government.*

We shall exclude from the course of instruction State Law as also all that concerns the political question. These subjects will be taught to a few dozens of persons chosen for their pre-eminent capacities from among the number of the initiated. *The universities must no longer send out from their halls milksops concocting plans for a con-*

stitution, like a comedy or a tragedy, busying themselves with questions of policy in which even their own fathers never had any power of thought.

The ill-guided acquaintance of a large number of persons with questions of polity creates utopian dreamers and bad subjects, as you can see for yourselves from the example of the universal education in this direction of the *goyim.* We must introduce into their education all those principles which have so brilliantly broken up their order. But when we are in power we shall remove every kind of disturbing subject from the course of education and shall make out of the youth obedient children of authority, loving him who rules as the support and hope of peace and quiet.

Classicism, as also any form of study of ancient history, in which there are more bad than good examples, we shall replace with the study of the programme of the future. We shall erase from the memory of men all facts of previous centuries which are undesirable to us, and leave only those which depict all the errors of the government of the *goyim.* The study of practical life, of the obligations of order, of the relations of people one to another, of avoiding bad and selfish examples, which spread the infection of evil, and similar questions of an educative nature, will stand in the forefront of the teaching programme, which will be drawn up on a separate plan for each calling or state of life, in no wise generalising the teaching. This treatment of the question has special importance.

Each state of life must be trained within strict limits corresponding to its destination and work in life. The *occasional genius has always managed and always will manage to slip through into other states of life, but it is the most perfect folly for the sake of this rare occasional genius to let through into ranks foreign to them the untalented who thus rob of their places those who belong to those ranks by birth or employment. You know yourselves in what all this has ended for the* GOYIM *who allowed this crying absurdity.*

In order that he who rules may be seated firmly in the hearts and minds of his subjects it is necessary for the time of his activity to instruct the whole nation in the schools and on the market places about his meaning and his acts and all his beneficent initiatives.

We shall abolish every kind of freedom of instruction. Learners of all ages will have the right to assemble together with their parents in the educational establishments as it were in a club: during these assemblies, on holidays, teachers will read what will pass as free lectures on questions of human relations, of the laws of examples, of the limitations which are born of unconscious relations, and, finally, of the philosophy of new theories not yet declared to the world. These theories will be raised by us to the stage of a dogma of faith as a transitional stage towards our faith. On the completion of this exposition of our programme of action in the present and the future I will read you the principles of these theories.

In a word, knowing by the experience of many centuries that people live and are guided by ideas, that these ideas are imbibed by people only by the aid of education provided with equal success for all ages of growth, but of course by varying methods, we shall swallow up and confiscate to our own use the last scintilla of independence of thought, which we have for long past been directing towards subjects and ideas useful for us. The system of bridling thought is already at work in the so-called system of teaching by *object lessons*, the purpose of which is to turn the *goyim* into unthinking submissive brutes waiting for things to be presented before their eyes in order to form an idea of them. . . . In France, one of our best agents, Bourgeois, has already made public a new programme of teaching by object lessons.

PROTOCOL NO. 17

The practice of advocacy produces men cold, cruel, persistent, unprincipled, who in all cases take up an impersonal, purely legal standpoint. They have the inveterate habit to refer everything to its value for the defence and not to the public welfare of its results. They do not usually decline to undertake any defence whatever, they strive for an acquittal at all costs, cavilling over every petty crux of jurisprudence and thereby they demoralise justice. For this reason we shall set this profession into narrow frames which will keep it inside this sphere of executive public service. Advocates, equally with judges, will be deprived of the right of communication with litigants; they will receive business only from the court and will study it by notes of report and documents, defending their clients after they have been interrogated in court on facts that have appeared. They will receive an honorarium without regard to the quality of the defence.

This will render them mere reporters on law-business in the interests of justice and as counterpoise to the proctor who will be the reporter in the interests of prosecution; this will shorten business before the courts. In this way will be established a practice of honest unprejudiced defence conducted not from personal interest but by conviction. This will also, by the way, remove the present practice of corrupt bargain between advocates to agree only to let that side win which pays most. . . .

We have long past taken care to discredit the priesthood of the GOYIM, and thereby to ruin their mission on earth which in these days might still be a great hindrance to us. Day by day its influence on the peoples of the world is falling lower. *Freedom of conscience* has been declared everywhere, *so that now only years divide us from the moment of the complete wrecking of that Christian religion:* as to other religions we shall have still less difficulty in dealing with them, but it would be premature to speak of this now. We shall set clericalism and clericals into such narrow frames as to make their influence move in retrogressive proportion to its former progress.

When the time comes finally to destroy the papal court the finger of an invisible hand will point the nations towards this court. When, however, the nations fling themselves upon it, we shall come forward in the guise of its defenders as if to save excessive bloodshed. By this diversion we shall penetrate to its very bowels and be sure we shall never come out again until we have gnawed through the entire strength of this place.

The King of the Jews will be the real Pope of the Universe, the patriarch of an international Church.

But, *in the meantime,* while we are re-educating youth in new traditional religions and afterwards in ours, *we shall not overtly lay a finger on existing churches, but we shall fight against them by criticism calculated to produce schism.* . . .

In general, then, our contemporary press will continue *to convict* State affairs, religions, incapacities of the *goyim,* always using the most unprincipled expressions in order by every means to lower their prestige in the manner which can only be practised by the genius of our gifted tribe. . . .

Our kingdom will be an apologia of the divinity Vishnu, in whom is found its personification—in our hundred hands will be, one in each, the springs of the machinery of social life. We shall see everything without the aid of official police which, in that scope of its rights which we elaborated for the use of the *goyim*, hinders governments from seeing. In our programme *one-third of our subjects will keep the rest under observation* from a sense of duty, on the principle of volunteer service to the State. It will then be no disgrace to be a spy and informer, but a merit: unfounded denunciations, however, will be cruelly punished that there may be no development of abuses of this right.

Our agents will be taken from the higher as well as the lower ranks of society, from among the administrative class who spend their time in amusements, editors, printers and publishers, booksellers, clerks, and salesmen, workmen, coachmen, lackeys, etcetera. This body, having no rights and not being empowered to take any action on their own account, and consequently a police without any power, will only witness and report: verification of their reports and arrests will depend upon a responsible group of controllers of police affairs, while the actual act of arrest will be performed by the gendarmerie and the municipal police. Any person not denouncing anything seen or heard concerning questions of polity will also be charged with and made responsible for concealment, if it be proved that he is guilty of this crime.

Just as nowadays our brethren are obliged at their own risk to denounce to the kabal apostates of their own family or members who have been noticed doing anything in opposition to the *kabal, so in our kingdom over all the world it will be obligatory for all our subjects to observe the duty of service to the State in this direction.*

Such an organisation will extirpate abuses of authority, of force, of bribery, everything in fact which we by our counsels, by our theories of the superhuman rights of man, have introduced into the customs of the *goyim.* . . . But how else were we to procure that increase of causes predisposing to disorders in the midst of their administration? . . . Among the number of those methods one of the most important is—agents for the restoration of order, so placed as to have the opportunity in their disintegrating activity of developing and displaying their evil inclinations—obstinate self-conceit, irresponsible exercise of authority, and, first and foremost, venality.

PROTOCOL NO. 18

When it becomes necessary for us to strengthen the strict measures of secret defence (the most fatal poison for the prestige of authority) we shall arrange a simulation of disorders or some manifestation of discontents finding expression through the co-operation of good speakers. Round these speakers will assemble all who are sympathetic to his utterances. This will give us the pretext for domiciliary perquisitions and surveillance on the part of our servants from among the number of the *goyim* police. . . .

As the majority of conspirators act out of love for the game, for the sake of talking, so, until they commit some overt act we shall not lay a finger on them but only introduce into their midst observation elements. . . . It must be remembered that the prestige of authority is lessened if it frequently discovers conspiracies against itself: this implies a presumption of consciousness of weakness, or, what is still worse, of injustice. You are aware that we have broken the prestige of the *goy* kings by frequent attempts upon their lives through our agents, blind sheep of our flock, who are easily moved by a few liberal phrases to crimes provided only they be painted in political colours. *We have compelled the rulers to acknowledge their weakness in advertising overt measures of secret defence and thereby we shall bring the promise of authority to destruction.*

Our ruler will be secretly protected only by the most insignificant guard, because we shall not admit so much as a thought that there could exist against him any sedition with which he is not strong enough to contend and is compelled to hide from it.

If we should admit this thought, as the *goyim* have done and are doing, we should *ipso facto* be signing a death sentence, if not for our ruler, at any rate for his dynasty, at no distant date.

According to strictly enforced outward appearances our ruler will employ his power only for the advantage of the nation and in no wise for his own or dynastic profits. Therefore, with the observance of this decorum, his authority will be respected and guarded by the subjects themselves, it will receive an apotheosis in the admission that with it is bound up the well-being of every citizen of the State, for upon it will depend all order in the common life of the pack. . . .

Overt defence of the king argues weakness in the organisation of his strength.

Our ruler will always among the people be surrounded by a mob of apparently curious men and women, who will occupy the front ranks about him, to all appearance by chance, and will restrain the ranks of the rest out of respect as it will appear for good order. This will sow an example of restraint also in others. If a petitioner appears among the people trying to hand a petition and forcing his way through the ranks, the first ranks must receive the petition and before the eyes of the petitioner pass it to the ruler, so that all may know that what is handed in reaches its destination, that, consequently, there exists a control of the ruler himself. The aureole of power requires for its existence that the people may be able to say: "If the king knew of this," or: "the king will hear of it."

With the establishment of official secret defence the mystical prestige of authority disappears: given a certain audacity, and everyone counts himself master of it, the sedition-monger is conscious of his strength, and when occasion serves watches for the moment to make an attempt upon authority. . . . For the *goyim* we have been preaching something else, but by that very fact we are enabled to see what measures of overt defence have brought them to. . . .

Criminals with us will be arrested at the first more or less well-grounded *suspicion;* it cannot be allowed that out of fear of a possible mistake an opportunity should be given of escape to persons suspected of a political lapse or crime, for in these matters we shall be literally merciless. If it is still possible, by stretching a point, to admit a reconsideration of the motive causes in simple crimes, there is no possibility of excuse for persons occupying themselves with questions in which nobody except the government can understand anything. . . . And it is not all governments that understand true policy.

PROTOCOL NO. 19

If we do not permit any independent dabbling in the political we shall on the other hand encourage every kind of report or petition with proposals for the government to examine into all kinds of projects for the amelioration of the condition of the people; this will reveal to us the defects or else the fantasies of our subjects, to which we shall respond either by accomplishing them or by a wise rebutment to prove the short-sightedness of one who judges wrongly.

Sedition-mongering is nothing more than the yapping of a lap-dog at an elephant. For a government well organised, not from the police but from the public point of view, the lap-dog yaps at the elephant in entire unconsciousness of its strength and importance. It needs no more than to take a good example to show the relative importance of both and the lap-dogs will cease to yap and will wag their tails the moment they set eyes on an elephant.

In order to destroy the prestige of heroism for political crime we shall send it for trial in the category of thieving, murder, and every kind of abominable and filthy crime. Public opinion will then confuse in its conception this category of crime with the disgrace attaching to every other and will brand it with the same contempt.

We have done our best, and I hope we have succeeded, to obtain that the *goyim* should not arrive at this means of contending with sedition. It was for this reason that through the press and in speeches, indirectly—in cleverly compiled schoolbooks on history, we have advertised the martyrdom alleged to have been accepted by sedition-mongers for the idea of the commonweal. This advertisement has increased the contingent of liberals and has brought thousands of *goyim* into the ranks of our livestock cattle.

PROTOCOL NO. 20

To-day we shall touch upon the financial programme, which I put off to the end of my report as being the most difficult, the crowning and the decisive point of our plans. Before entering upon it I will remind you that I have already spoken before by way of a hint when I said that the sum total of our actions is settled by the question of figures.

When we come into our kingdom our autocratic government will avoid, from a principle of self-preservation, sensibly burdening the masses of the people with taxes, remembering that it plays the part of father and protector. But as State organisation costs dear it is necessary nevertheless to obtain the funds required for it. It will, therefore, elaborate with particular precaution the question of equilibrium in this matter.

Our rule, in which the king will enjoy the legal fiction that everything in his State belongs to him (which may easily be translated into fact), will be enabled to resort to the lawful confiscation of all sums of every kind for the regulation of their circulation in the State. From this follows that taxation will best be covered by a progressive tax on property. In this manner the dues will be paid without straitening or ruining anybody in the form of a percentage of the amount of property. The rich must be aware that it is their duty to place a part of their superfluities at the disposal of the State since the State guarantees them security of possession of the rest of their property and the right of honest gains, I say honest, for the control over property will do away with robbery on a legal basis.

This social reform must come from above, for the time is ripe for it—it is indispensable as a pledge of peace.

The tax upon the poor man is a seed of revolution and works to the detriment of the State which in hunting after the trifling is missing the big. Quite apart from this, a tax on capitalists diminishes the growth of wealth in private hands in which we have in these days concentrated it as a counterpoise to the government strength of the *goyim*—their State finances.

A tax increasing in a percentage ratio to capital will give a much larger revenue than the present individual or property tax, which is useful to us now for the sole reason that it excites trouble and discontent among the *goyim*.

The force upon which our king will rest consists in the equilibrium and the guarantee of peace, for the sake of which things it is indispensable that the capitalists should yield up a portion of their incomes for the sake of the secure working of the machinery of the State. State needs must be paid by those who will not feel the burden and have enough to take from.

Such a measure will destroy the hatred of the poor man for the rich, in whom he will see a necessary financial support for the State, will see in him the organiser of peace and well-being since he will see that it is the rich man who is paying the necessary means to attain these things.

In order that payers of the educated classes should not too much distress themselves over the new payments they will have full accounts given them of the destination of those payments, with the exception of such sums as will be appropriated for the needs of the throne and the administrative institutions.

He who reigns will not have any properties of his own once all in the State represents his patrimony, or else the one would be in contradiction to the other; the fact of holding private means would destroy the right of property in the common possessions of all.

Relatives of him who reigns, his heirs excepted, who will be maintained by the resources of the State, must enter the ranks of servants of the State or must work to obtain the right of property; the privilege of royal blood must not serve for the spoiling of the treasury.

Purchase, receipt of money or inheritance will be subject to the payment of a stamp progressive tax. Any transfer of property, whether money or other, without evidence of payment of this tax which will be strictly registered by names, will render the former holder liable to pay interest on the tax from the moment of transfer of these sums up to the discovery of his evasion of declaration of the transfer. Transfer documents must be presented weekly at the local treasury office with notifications of the name, surname and permanent place of residence of the former and the new holder of the property. This transfer with register of names must begin from a definite sum which exceeds the ordinary expenses of buying and selling of necessaries, and these will be subject to payment only by a stamp impost of a definite percentage of the unit.

Just strike an estimate of how many times such taxes as these will cover the revenue of the *goyim* States.

The State exchequer will have to maintain a definite complement of reserve sums, and all that is collected above that complement must be returned into circulation. On these sums will be organised public works. The initiative in works of this kind, proceeding from State sources, will bind the working class firmly to the interests of the State and to those who reign. From these same sums also a part will be set aside as rewards of inventiveness and productiveness.

On no account should so much as a single unit above the definite and freely estimated sums be retained in the State treasuries, for money exists to be circulated and any kind of stagnation of money acts ruinously on the running of the State machinery, for which it is the lubricant; a stagnation of the lubricant may stop the regular working of the mechanism.

The substitution of interest-bearing paper for a part of the token of exchange has produced exactly this stagnation. The consequences of this circumstance are already sufficiently noticeable.

A court of account will also be instituted by us and in it the ruler will find at any moment a full accounting for State income and expenditure, with the exception of the current monthly account, not yet made up, and that of the preceding month, which will not yet have been delivered.

The one and only person who will have no interest in robbing the State is its owner, the ruler. This is why his personal control will remove the possibility of leakages of extravagances.

The representative function of the ruler at receptions for the sake of etiquette, which absorbs so much invaluable time, will be abolished in order that the ruler may have time for control and consideration. His power will not then be split up into fractional parts among time-serving favourites who surround the throne for its pomp and splendour, and are interested only in their own and not in the common interests of the State.

Economic crises have been produced by us for the *goyim* by no other means than the withdrawal of money from circulation. Huge capitals have stagnated, withdrawing money from States, which were constantly obliged to apply to those same stagnant capitals for loans. These loans burdened the finances of the State with the payment of interest and made them the bond slaves of these capitals. . . . The concentration of industry in the hands of capitalists out of the hands of small masters has drained away all the juices of the peoples and with them also of the States. . . .

The present issue of money in general does not correspond with the requirements per head, and cannot therefore satisfy all the needs of the workers. The issue of money ought to correspond with the growth of population and thereby children also must absolutely be reckoned as consumers of currency from the day of their birth. The revision of issue is a material question for the whole world.

You are aware that the gold standard has been the ruin of the States which adopted it, for it has not been able to satisfy the demands for money, the more so that we have removed gold from circulation as far as possible.

With us the standard that must be introduced is the cost of workingman power, whether it be reckoned in paper or in wood. We shall make the issue of money in accordance with the normal requirements of each subject, adding to the quantity with every birth and subtracting with every death.

The accounts will be managed by each department (the French administrative division), each circle.

In order that there may be no delays in the paying out of money for State needs the sums and terms of such payments will be fixed by decree of the ruler; this will do away with the protection by a ministry of one institution to the detriment of others.

The budgets of income and expenditure will be carried out side by side that they may not be obscured by distance one to another.

The reforms projected by us in the financial institutions and principles of the *goyim* will be closed by us in such forms as will alarm nobody. We shall point out the necessity of reforms in consequence of the disorderly darkness into which the *goyim* by their irregularities have plunged the finances. The first irregularity, as we shall point out, consists in their beginning with drawing up a single budget which year after year grows owing to the following cause: this budget is dragged out to half the year, then they demand a budget to put things right, and this they expend in three months, after which they ask for a supplementary budget, and all this ends with a liquidation budget. But, as the budget of the following year is drawn up in accordance with the sum of the total addition, the annual departure from the normal reaches as much as 50 per cent. in a year, and so the annual budget is trebled in ten years. Thanks to such methods, allowed by the carelessness of the *goy* States, their treasuries are empty. The period of loans supervenes, and that has swallowed up remainders and brought all the *goy* States to bankruptcy.

You understand perfectly that economic arrangements of this kind, which have been suggested to the *goyim* by us, cannot be carried on by us.

Every kind of loan proves infirmity in the State and a want of understanding of the rights of the State. Loans hang like a sword of Damocles over the heads of rulers, who, instead of taking from their subjects by a temporary tax, come begging with outstretched palm of our bankers. Foreign loans are leeches which there is no possibility of removing from the body of the State until they fall off of themselves or the State flings them off. But the *goy* States do not tear them off; they go on in persisting in putting more on to themselves so that they must inevitably perish, drained by voluntary blood-letting.

What also indeed is, in substance, a loan, especially a foreign loan? A loan is—an issue of government bills of exchange containing a percentage obligation commensurate to the sum of the loan capital. If the loan bears a charge of 5 per cent., then in twenty years the State vainly pays away in interest a sum equal to the loan borrowed, in forty years it is paying a double sum, in sixty—treble, and all the while the debt remains an unpaid debt.

From this calculation it is obvious that with any form of taxation per head the State is baling out the last coppers of the poor taxpayers in order to settle accounts with wealthy foreigners, from whom it has borrowed money instead of collecting these coppers for its own needs without the additional interest.

So long as loans were internal the *goyim* only shuffled their money from the pockets of the poor to those of the rich, but when we bought up the necessary person in order to transfer loans into the external sphere all the wealth of States flowed into our cash-boxes and all the *goyim* began to pay us the tribute of subjects.

If the superficiality of *goy* kings on their thrones in regard to State affairs and the venality of ministers or the want of understanding of financial matters on the part of other ruling persons have made their countries debtors to our treasuries to amounts quite impossible to pay it has not been accomplished without on our part heavy expenditure of trouble and money.

Stagnation of money will not be allowed by us and therefore there will be no State interest-bearing paper, except a one per cent. series, so that there will be no payment of interest to leeches that suck all the strength out of the State. The right to issue interest-bearing paper will be given exclusively to industrial companies who will find no difficulty in paying interest out of profits, whereas the State does not make interest on borrowed money like these companies, for the State borrows to spend and not to use in operations.

Industrial papers will be bought also by the government which from being as now a payer of tribute by loan operations will be transformed into a lender of money at a profit. This measure will stop the stagnation of money, parasitic profits and idleness, all of which were useful for us among the *goyim* so long as they were independent but are not desirable under our rule.

How clear is the undeveloped power of thought of the purely brute brains of the *goyim*, as expressed in the fact that they have been borrowing from us with payment of interest without ever thinking that all the same these very moneys plus an addition for payment of interest must be got by them from their own State pockets in order to settle up with us. What could have been simpler than to take the money they wanted from their own people?

But it is a proof of the genius of our chosen mind that we have contrived to present the matter of loans to them in such a light that they have even seen in them an advantage for themselves.

Our accounts, which we shall present when the time comes, in the light of centuries of experience gained by experiments made by us on the *goy* States, will be distinguished by clearness and definiteness and will show at a glance to all men the advantage of our innovations. They will put an end to those abuses to which we owe our mastery over the *goyim*, but which cannot be allowed in our kingdom.

We shall so hedge about our system of accounting that neither the ruler nor the most insignificant public servant will be in a position to divert even the smallest sum from its destination without detection or to direct it in another direction except that which will be once fixed in a definite plan of action.

And without a definite plan it is impossible to rule. Marching along an undetermined road and with undetermined resources brings to ruin by the way heroes and demi-gods.

The *goy* rulers, whom we once upon a time advised should be distracted from State occupations by representative receptions, observances of etiquette, entertainments, were only screens for our rule. The accounts of favourite courtiers who replaced them in the sphere of affairs were drawn up for them by our agents, and every time gave satisfaction to short-sighted minds by promises that in the future economies and improvements were foreseen. . . . Economies from what? From new taxes?—were questions that might have been but were not asked by those who read our accounts and projects. . . .

You know to what they have been brought by this carelessness, to what a pitch of financial disorder they have arrived, notwithstanding the astonishing industry of their peoples. . . .

To what I reported to you at the last meeting I shall now add a detailed explanation of internal loans. Of foreign loans I shall say nothing more, because they have fed us with the national moneys of the *goyim*, but for our State there will be no foreigners, that is, nothing external.

We have taken advantage of the venality of administrators and the slackness of rulers to get our moneys twice, thrice and more times over, by lending to the *goy* governments moneys which were not at all needed by the States. Could anyone do the like in regard to us? . . . Therefore, I shall only deal with the details of internal loans.

States announce that such a loan is to be concluded and open subscriptions for their own bills of exchange, that is, for their interest-bearing paper. That they may be within the reach of all the price is determined at from a hundred to a thousand; and a discount is made for the earliest subscribers. Next day by artificial means the price of them goes up, the alleged reason being that everyone is rushing to buy them. In a few days the treasury safes are as they say overflowing and there's more money than they can do with (why then take it?). The subscription, it is alleged, covers many times over the issue total of the loan; in this lies the whole stage effect—look you, they say, what confidence is shown in the government's bills of exchange.

But when the comedy is played out there emerges the fact that a debit and an exceedingly burdensome debit has been created. For the payment of interest it becomes necessary to have recourse to new loans, which do not swallow up but only add to the capital debt. And when this credit is exhausted it becomes necessary by new taxes to cover, not the loan, but only the interest on it. These taxes are a debit employed to cover a debit. . . .

Later comes the time for conversions, but they diminish the payment of interest without covering the debt, and besides they cannot be made

without the consent of the lenders; on announcing a conversion a pro-
posal is made to return the money to those who are not willing to
convert their paper. If everybody expressed his unwillingness and demanded his money back, the government would be hooked on their
own flies and would be found insolvent and unable to pay the
proposed sums. By good luck the subjects of the *goy* governments,
knowing nothing about financial affairs, have always preferred losses
on exchange and diminution of interest to the risk of new investments
of their moneys, and have thereby many a time enabled these governments to throw off their shoulders a debit of several millions.

Nowadays, with external loans, these tricks cannot be played by the
goyim for they know that we shall demand all our moneys back.

In this way an acknowledged bankruptcy will best prove to the
various countries the absence of any means between the interests of the
peoples and of those who rule them.

I beg you to concentrate your particular attention upon this point
and upon the following: nowadays all internal loans are consolidated
by so-called flying loans, that is, such as have terms of payment more
or less near. These debts consist of moneys paid into the savings banks
and reserve funds. If left for long at the disposition of a government
these funds evaporate in the payment of interest on foreign loans, and
are replaced by the deposit of equivalent amount of *rentes*.

And these last it is which patch up all the leaks in the State treasuries of the *goyim*.

When we ascend the throne of the world all these financial and
similar shifts, as being not in accord with our interests, will be swept
away so as not to leave a trace, as also will be destroyed all money
markets, since we shall not allow the prestige of our power to be
shaken by fluctuations of prices set upon our values, which we shall
announce by law at the price which represents their full worth without
any possibility of lowering or raising. (Raising gives the pretext for
lowering, which indeed was where we made a beginning in relation
to the values of the *goyim*.)

We shall replace the money markets by grandiose government credit
institutions, the object of which will be to fix the price of industrial
values in accordance with government views. These institutions will
be in a position to fling upon the market five hundred millions of
industrial paper in one day, or to buy up for the same amount. In this

way all industrial undertakings will come into dependence upon us. You may imagine for yourselves what immense power we shall thereby secure for ourselves. . . .

PROTOCOL NO. 22

In all that has so far been reported by me to you, I have endeavoured to depict with care the secret of what is coming, of what is past, and of what is going on now, rushing into the flood of the great events coming already in the near future, the secret of our relations to the *goyim* and of financial operations. On this subject there remains still a little for me to add.

In our hands is the greatest power of our day—gold: in two days we can procure from our storehouses any quantity we may please.

Surely there is no need to seek further proof that our rule is pre-destined by God? Surely we shall not fail with such wealth to prove that all that evil which for so many centuries we have had to commit has served at the end of ends the cause of true well-being—the bringing of everything into order? Though it be even by the exercise of some violence, yet all the same it will be established. We shall contrive to prove that we are benefactors who have restored to the rent and mangled earth the true good and also freedom of the person, and there-with we shall enable it to be enjoyed in peace and quiet, with proper dignity of relations, on the condition, of course, of strict observance of the laws established by us. We shall make plain therewith that freedom does not consist in dissipation and in the right of unbridled licence any more than the dignity and force of a man do not consist in the right for everyone to promulgate destructive principles in the nature of freedom of conscience, equality and the like, that freedom of the person in no wise consists in the right to agitate oneself and others by abominable speeches before disorderly mobs, and that true freedom consists in the inviolability of the person who honourably and strictly observes all the laws of life in common, that human dignity is wrapped up in consciousness of the rights and also of the absence of rights of each, and not wholly and solely in fantastic imaginings about the subject of one's *ego*.

Our authority will be glorious because it will be all-powerful, will rule and guide, and not muddle along after leaders and orators shrieking themselves hoarse with senseless words which they call great principles and which are nothing else, to speak honestly, but utopian. . . . Our authority will be the crown of order, and in that is included the whole happiness of man. The aureole of this authority will inspire a mystical bowing of the knee before it and a reverent fear before it of all the peoples. True force makes no terms with any right, not even with that of God: none dare come near to it so as to take so much as a span from it away.

<h2 style="text-align:center">PROTOCOL NO. 23</h2>

That the peoples may become accustomed to obedience it is necessary to inculcate lessons of humility and therefore to reduce the production of articles of luxury. By this we shall improve morals which have been debased by emulation in the sphere of luxury. We shall reestablish small master production which will mean laying a mine under the private capital of manufacturers. This is indispensable also for the reason that manufacturers on the grand scale often move, though not always consciously, the thoughts of the masses in directions against the government. A people of small masters knows nothing of unemployment and this binds him closely with existing order, and consequently with the firmness of authority. Unemployment is a most perilous thing for a government. For us its part will have been played out the moment authority is transferred into our hands. Drunkenness also will be prohibited by law and punishable as a crime against the humanness of man who is turned into a brute under the influence of alcohol.

Subjects, I repeat once more, give blind obedience only to the strong hand which is absolutely independent of them, for in it they feel the sword of defence and support against social scourges. . . . What do they want with an angelic spirit in a king? What they have to see in him is the personification of force and power.

The supreme lord who will replace all now existing rulers, dragging on their existence among societies demoralised by us, societies that have denied even the authority of God, from whose midst breaks out on all sides the fire of anarchy, must first of all proceed to quench this all-devouring flame. Therefore he will be obliged to kill off those existing societies, though he should drench them with his own blood, that he may resurrect them again in the form of regularly organised troops fighting consciously with every kind of infection that may cover the body of the State with sores.

This Chosen One of God is chosen from above to demolish the senseless forces moved by instinct and not reason, by brutishness and not humanness. These forces now triumph in manifestations of robbery and every kind of violence under the mask of principles of freedom and rights. They have overthrown all forms of social order to erect on the ruins the throne of the King of the Jews; but their part will be played out the moment he enters into his kingdom. Then it will be necessary to sweep them away from his path, on which must be left no knot, no splinter.

Then will it be possible for us to say to the peoples of the world: "Give thanks to God and bow the knee before him who bears on his front the seal of the predestination of man, to which God Himself has led his star that none other but He might free us from all the before-mentioned forces and evils."

PROTOCOL NO. 24

I pass now to the method of confirming the dynastic roots of King David to the last strata of the earth.

This confirmation will first and foremost be included in that in which to this day has rested the force of conservatism by our learned elders of the conduct of all the affairs of the world, in the directing of the education of thought of all humanity.

Certain members of the seed of David will prepare the kings and their heirs, selecting not by right of heritage but by eminent capacities, inducting them into the most secret mysteries of the political, into schemes of government, but providing always that none may come to knowledge of the secrets. The object of this mode of action is that all may know that government cannot be entrusted to those who have not been inducted into the secret places of its art. . . .

To these persons only will be taught the practical application of the aforenamed plans by comparison of the experiences of many centuries, all the observations on the politico-economic moves and social sciences—in a word, all the spirit of laws which have been unshakably established by nature herself for the regulation of the relations of humanity.

Direct heirs will often be set aside from ascending the throne if in their time of training they exhibit frivolity, softness and other qualities that are the ruin of authority, which render them incapable of governing and in themselves dangerous for kingly office.

Only those who are unconditionally capable for firm, even if it be to cruelty, direct rule will receive the reins of rule from our learned elders.

In case of falling sick with weakness of will or other form of incapacity, kings must by law hand over the reins of rule to new and capable hands. . . .

The king's plans of action for the current moment, and all the more so for the future, will be unknown, even to those who are called his closest counsellors.

Only the king and the three who stood sponsor for him will know what is coming.

In the person of the king who with unbending will is master of himself and of humanity all will discern as it were fate with its mysterious ways. None will know what the king wishes to attain by his dispositions, and therefore none will dare to stand across an unknown path.

It is understood that the brain reservoir of the king must correspond in capacity to the plan of government it has to contain. It is for this reason that he will ascend the throne not otherwise than after examination of his mind by the aforesaid learned elders.

That the people may know and love their king it is indispensable for him to converse in the market-places with his people. This ensures the necessary clinching of the two forces which are now divided one from another by us by the terror.

This terror was indispensable for us till the time comes for both these forces separately to fall under our influence.

The King of the Jews must not be at the mercy of his passions, and especially of sensuality: on no side of his character must he give brute instincts power over his mind. Sensuality worse than all else disorganises the capacities of the mind and clearness of views, distracting the thoughts to the worst and most brutal side of human activity.

The prop of humanity in the person of the supreme lord of all the world of the holy seed of David must sacrifice to his people all personal inclinations.

Our supreme lord must be of an exemplary irreproachability.

EXHIBIT G

Translation of an article by Count A. M. du Chayla, a Frenchman by birth, who lived many years in Russia and who knew Sergius Nilus intimately. The article appeared in Paris, in 1921.

NILUS AND THE PROTOCOLS

Towards the end of January, 1909, in my eagerness for religious research, I followed the advice of the late Metropolitan of St. Petersburg, Monseigneur Anthony, and betook myself to the renowned monastery "Optina Pustina."

This monastery is situated about six versts from the town Kozelsk, in the district of Kaluga, between a large pine forest and the left bank of the river Jizdra. Near the monastery were a number of villas in which resided laymen who desired to lead a monastic life. At that time the community comprised about 400 monks who busied themselves with agricultural labors and led a life of religious contemplation under the spiritual guidance of three Elders. In those days, the monastery at Optina was the source of a remarkable influence on Russian thought. It was frequently visited by the great Russian writers, such as Gogol, Tolstoy, and Dostoyevski, the latter of whom took one of the Elders of the Monastery as a model for one of the characters in his "Brothers Karamazoff."

The day following my arrival, the head of the monastery, Archimandrite Xenophon, proposed to introduce me to Mr. S. A. Nilus, a religious writer living near the monastery. In Petersburg I had already heard of Nilus from Mr. W. A. Ternawtseff, in charge of special missions for the Procurator General of the Holy Synod and a member of the Society of Religious Philosophy. He had told me that Nilus was an interesting man, though very eccentric.

After dinner I was introduced to Nilus in the rooms of the Archimandrite. He was a man of about 45, of the true Russian type, big and broad, with a gray beard and deep blue eyes, which, however, seemed to be veiled with a troubled shadow. He wore boots and a Russian blouse, girdled with an embroidered ribbon.

S. A. Nilus spoke French very well, which was very useful to me. We were both very glad to make one another's acquaintance, and I did not hesitate to accept his invitation to visit him. He lived in a large villa of about ten rooms where formerly lived pensioned priests. Nilus and his family, in all three people, occupied only four rooms. The other rooms formed a sort of asylum paid for by a pension which the minister of the court had granted to Nilus' wife. This asylum sheltered all sorts of degenerates, idiots and lunatics, awaiting miraculous cures.

The ancestors of Nilus were Swiss émigrés who had come to Russia during the reign of Peter I. Nilus assured me that he was a direct descendant of Maliouta Skouratoff, a special executioner under Ivan the Terrible. Nilus himself was a ruined proprietor from the district of Orel. His brother Dimitry Alexandrovitch Nilus was a judge in Moscow. The two brothers were enemies. Sergey Alexandrovitch regarded his brother as an atheist, while the latter looked upon Sergey as a madman.

Nilus was undoubtedly a man of excellent education. He had successfully graduated from the courses of law at the Moscow University. He knew perfectly French, German, and English, and was well acquainted with contemporary European literature. But, as I later learned, Nilus could not get along with anyone. His tumultuous character and capricious temperament had forced him to give up his post at the Ministry of Justice which had appointed him judge in Trans-Caucasia on the Persian frontier. He was a great admirer of Nietzsche's philosophy with its theoretical anarchism and radical negation of actual civilization.

With such a temperament Nilus found it impossible to stay in Russia. He went abroad with a certain Madame K. and lived a long time in France and especially in Biarritz, until he was informed that his property in Orel had become worthless. It was then, about 1900, that Nilus underwent a spiritual crisis which moved him to mysticism.

Nilus presented me to his wife, Helena Alexandrovna Ozerov, a former lady-in-waiting at the court of the Queen Alexandra Fiodorovna.

She was the daughter of Ozerov, former Russian minister to Athens. Mme. Nilus was a good-natured and submissive woman subordinate to her husband in every respect. So submissive was she in fact that she was in good relations with the former friend of Nilus, Mme. K. who, also ruined, had been given shelter in their house.

My friendly relations with Nilus lasted during the nine months of my stay at Optina until November 10th, 1909. When I later returned to Russia I again called on Nilus but his intolerance forced me to break off relations with him.

In 1918, Nilus lived in Kiev at the convent known as Protection of the Holy Virgin. I later learned that in the winter of 1918-1919 after the fall of Hetman (Skoropadsky) he escaped to Germany and lived in Berlin. This information was confirmed by Mme. Kartzeva, a nurse at the hospital of the White Cross in Crimea.

From the very beginning, my relations with Nilus were marked with endless discussions on religious questions, in which he made all efforts to convert me to his point of view. On the third or fourth day after our acquaintance, during a discussion on the relationship between civilization and Christianity, Nilus asked me if I was acquainted with the Protocols of the Wise Men of Zion which he was editing. I replied that I knew nothing about them.

Nilus picked up a book and began to translate in French the most remarkable passages of the text and his commentaries on them. At the same time he was watching the expression on my face, imagining that I would be thunderstruck by his revelations. He was very much troubled when I declared that I could see nothing in the document that differed greatly from the pamphlets of Edouard Drumont and the mystifications of Leo Taxil. Nilus objected to this, saying that my knowledge of the Protocols was of a superficial and fragmentary character and that the verbal translation tends to weaken the effect. He said that it would be easy for me to acquaint myself with the Protocols inasmuch as the original was written in French.

Later I learned that the portfolio containing the Protocols was kept until January, 1909, at the home of the monk, Daniel Bolotoff, a portrait painter well known in Petersburg. Nilus did not keep the manuscript of the Protocols with him fearing that the Jews would steal it. I remember my amusement and his fear when a Jewish druggist from Kozelsk had wandered in Nilus' garden in the course of a walk through the forest near the monastery. Nilus was for a long time convinced that this Jewish druggist was a spy sent to watch on his movements.

A few days after our first conversation concerning the Protocols, about four o'clock in the afternoon, I received a note in which Nilus asked me to call at once about important business. I found Nilus alone in his study. His wife and Mme. K. had gone to attend vespers. I noticed on his desk a large envelope of a black material with a large three-branched cross with the inscription "By this sign thou shalt conquer." A small ikon of the Archangel Michael was placed on the envelope. The whole thing bore the character of exorcism.

Nilus, after some signs before a large ikon, opened the envelope and took out a note-book bound in leather. I later learned that both the envelope and the leather binding had been prepared in the monastery under the personal supervision of Nilus. The cross and the other symbols had been executed by Mme. Nilus under the direction of her husband.

"This," said Nilus, "is the map of the Kingdom of the Antichrist."

He opened the note book. On the first page I noticed a large blue spot as if some one had over-turned an inkwell and that the ink had been removed to some extent. The paper was thick and yellowish. The text was written in French in several handwritings and, it seemed to me, even with different inks.

"The reason for this," said Nilus, "is that at the sessions of the Kahal different persons filled each time the duties of secretary. This accounts for the different handwritings."

Apparently Nilus regarded this detail as a proof that the manuscript was an original text. Yet I remember that he told me another time that the manuscript was only a copy.

After having shown me the manuscript, Nilus placed it before me on the desk, opened the first page and said "Now, read!" In reading the manuscript I was struck by certain peculiarities of the text. There were many mistakes in spelling and especially idioms that were not French. There was no doubt that the manuscript had not been prepared by a Frenchman. I read for two hours and one half. When I had finished, Nilus took the note book, replaced it in its envelope, and locked it in a drawer of his desk. While I was reading Mme.

Nilus and Mme. K. returned from church. I did not know whether Mme. K. was a party to the secret of the manuscript. I therefore said nothing about it. Nilus, however, was eager to know my opinion and seeing my discomfiture, guessed exactly the cause of my silence.

"Come, you doubting Thomas," he said laughingly, "do you believe now after you have touched, seen, and read the Protocols? Tell us what you think of them. There are no strangers here. My wife knows all about them and as far as Mme. K. is concerned, it is thanks to her that the schemes of the enemies of Christ have been discovered."

I was greatly interested. Could it be that Nilus obtained the Protocols through Mme. K.? I was wondering how a woman so obese as to be almost immobile and who, moreover, suffered from disease, could have penetrated the "Secret Kahal of the Wise Men of Zion."

"Yes," said Nilus, "Mme. K. lived abroad for a long time. In Paris, she received from the hands of a Russian General this manuscript which she transmitted to me. This General had removed the manuscript from the archives of the Freemasons."

I asked Nilus whether the name of this General was a secret.

"Not at all," replied Nilus, "it is General Ratchkovsky, a very brave and active man who has done much in his day to counteract the activities of the enemies of Christ."

I recalled that while in France, when I was taking lessons in Russian from a student called Ezopoff, the latter had told me that the Russian political police did not leave Russian political offenders in peace even when the latter had escaped to France. He said that General Ratchkovsky was at the head of this police. I asked Nilus if this General Ratchkovsky was not the head of the Russian political police in France. My question seemed to surprise and displease Nilus. He replied in a vague manner that Ratchkovsky fought against Freemasonry and Satanic sects.

Nilus was anxious to know the impression left on me by the Protocols. I told him plainly that I adhered to my former statement that the Protocols belong to the class of cheap mystifications such as "The Devil Unmasked" and "The Devil During the 19th Century," etc. Nilus' face clouded.

"You are indeed under the influence of the Devil," he said. "The greatest trick of the Devil is that he can make people deny not only his influence on human events but even his very existence. What will you say when I show you how everything contained in the Protocols has come true and how the mysterious sign of the Antichrist appears everywhere as an announcement of his approaching reign?"

Nilus arose and we all followed him into his study. He picked up his book and brought in from his own room a small chest which I later called the museum of the Antichrist. He began to read further in the text and the commentaries which he was preparing for the edition. He then passed on to the "evidence." He opened the chest and I saw amidst indescribable disorder a number of objects made of rubber, some household utensils, insignia of technical schools, even the cipher of the Queen Alexandra Fiodorovna and the cross of the Legion of Honor. On each of these objects his hallucination showed him the "seal of the Antichrist" in the guise of a triangle or a pair of crossed triangles. It was enough for any object to bear on it a figure resembling somewhat a triangle for his inflamed imagination to see in it the sign of the Antichrist and the seal of the Wise Men of Zion. All these observations entered into the edition of the Protocols, published in 1911.

With increasing restlessness under the influence of a sort of mystic terror Nilus explained to me that the sign of the "Son of Iniquity" has contaminated everything, and that it flourishes even amidst the designs and ornaments of churches and in the decorations of the holy ikons. It was midnight. The appearance, the voice, and the weird gestures of Nilus showed that his mind was on the brink of a precipice, and that his reason would at any moment dissolve into madness.

I tried to calm Nilus and to show him that even in the Protocols nothing is said of sinister signs. I did my best to convince him that he had discovered nothing new, since the mystic sign of which he spoke has been noted in every work on occultism from those of Hermes Triamegistus and Paracelsus, who surely were not Wise Men of Zion, down to our contemporaries, Papus, Stanislas de Guaita etc., who surely are not Jews. Nilus noted carefully my arguments, but instead of calming him, as I hoped they would, they only aggravated to their utmost limit his morbid sensations.

A few days later, he sent to the bookseller Gautheir at Moscow a large order for all the books on the hermetic sciences which I had mentioned to him. In the third edition of the Protocols which appeared two years later, in 1911, he inserted many extracts and illustrations which he had borrowed from the books which I had mentioned to him.

A little later when General Ratchkovsky was involved in some political scandal I asked Nilus, "Don't you believe that your General Ratchkovsky has been duped by some one and that in taking his Protocols as gospel truth you are following a false trail?"

"You know," replied Nilus, "my favorite citation from St. Paul is 'The will of God is accomplished through human weakness.' Let us admit that the Protocols are false, but is it not possible that God should make use of them in order to expose the iniquity which is approaching? Did not the ass of Balaam utter prophecy? Cannot God transform the bones of a dog into sacred miracles? If He can do these things, He can also make the announcement of truth come from the mouth of a liar."

Before exposing the circumstances which brought Nilus into possession of the Protocols, I wish to call to the attention of the reader a peculiarity in the 1917 edition of the Protocols. I refer to the statement by Nilus that the manuscript of the Protocols had been transmitted to him by a nobleman named Alexey Nikolaievitch Soukhotin. This statement is a direct contradiction of what Nilus had previously told me, namely, that the manuscript had been given to him by Mme. K., who had obtained it from General Ratchkovsky.

Being well acquainted with the intimate life of Nilus I can readily understand why, in a public document, he could not speak of Mme. K. . . . I am convinced that this A. N. Soukhotin is not a mythical person but, in all probability, the intermediary between Mme. K., who was then in Paris, and Nilus who was in Russia. For intimate reasons Soukhotin thus became the veil, hiding from the reader the mysterious lady, Mme. K.

The translation of the document took place under the following circumstances:

In 1900 Nilus returned to Russia and wandered in poverty from monastery to monastery. It was then that he wrote "Notes of an Orthodox, or the Great and the Little," a small volume in which he described the conversion of an intellectual atheist to religious mysticism. This booklet elicited some very warm reviews in the Russian religious periodicals which eventually reached the Grand Duchess Elizabeta Fiodorovna who thus became interested in Nilus.

The Grand Duchess had always fought against the adventurers who surrounded the Czar and especially a certain Philipp of Lyons. She was greatly dissatisfied with the confessor of the royal family, Archpriest Yamyscheff, whose duty it was to preserve the Czar from malign influences. The Grand Duchess thought that Nilus, a Russian mystic and orthodox, would exert a favorable influence on the Czar.

Major General Michael Petrovitch Stepanoff was greatly attached to the Grand Duchess, and it was through him that Nilus was sent to Tsarskoye Sielo and there introduced to Helena Alexandrovna Ozerov, who was later to become his wife. This took place in 1901.

When Nilus left France, there remained in Paris a person very dear to him, namely, Mme. K. This woman, who had lost her entire fortune and who was greatly saddened by her separation from Nilus, became interested in mysticism and frequented all the occult circles in Paris. It was thus that she encountered Ratchkovsky who moved in the same circles, and received from him the manuscript of the Protocols of the Wise Men of Zion which she transmitted to Nilus. It is quite possible that Ratchkovsky, who was then intent on removing the influence of Philipp on the Czar, wished to make use of the Protocols in order to gain the good will of Nilus, who he thought would be the successor of Philipp.

Nilus produced a very good impression on Helena Ozerov and the rest of the Court who were opposed to Philipp. Thanks to the aid of these persons, he was enabled to publish in 1902 the first edition of the Protocols with an appendix on his own religious experiences. The book was entitled "The Great in the Little and the Antichrist as a Near Political Possibility." A copy of it was presented to the Czar and Czarina. At the same time the adversaries of Philipp arranged the marriage between Nilus and Mlle. Ozerov and the ordination of Nilus into the priesthood. Arrangements were also being made to establish Nilus as the confessor of the Czar. Things looked so promising that Nilus had already ordered priestly garments.

However, Philipp and his followers trumped up a canonical prohibition against the induction of Nilus into the priesthood. As soon as this prohibition was called to the attention of the ecclesiastical authorities, Nilus fell into disgrace and was forced to leave Tsarskoye Sielo. Again penniless except for the meagre honorarium which he received from the *Feuillets de la Trinité*, he again wandered from monastery to monastery. Marriage was impossible, for Mlle. Ozerov possessed nothing beyond the pension which she was receiving while at Court and which would have been withdrawn had she married Nilus.

In 1905, however, Philipp had ceased to exert any influence on the Czar. The friends of Nilus obtained the Imperial consent to grant Mlle. Ozerov her pension even if she married. It was also through the influence of Mlle. Ozerov that Nilus was enabled to publish a second edition of the Protocols with new material concerning St. Seraphin de Saroff. I remember that this edition bore a title different from the first and was published in Tsarskoye Sielo under the auspices of the Red Cross.

Nilus married Mlle. Ozerov but the canonical prohibition still held good and it was impossible for him to enter the priesthood or to exert any spiritual influence on the Czar.

The first two editions of the Protocols passed almost unnoticed in Russia. In fact, only one newspaper reviewed the books. The theological reviews did not even mention them, and it is doubtful whether they knew of their existence since the edition was a small one and was bought by very few people. Most of the authorities of the Russian Church with whom I spoke concerning Nilus and his work had a very poor opinion of Nilus whom they regarded as a crazed fanatic. In 1911, Nilus addressed a letter to the patriarchs of the Orient, to the Holy Synod, and to the Pope, asking them to call together the 8th Oecumenical Council in order to take measures to protect Christianity against the coming of the Antichrist. At the same time Nilus preached this doctrine of preparedness to the monks at Optina. The monastic peace was so troubled by Nilus that the authorities asked him never again to appear at the cloister.

The first indications of public interest in the Protocols became apparent in 1918. A new edition of the Protocols was published by Ismailoff, a Moscow lawyer. The *Sentinel*, a publication marked for its constant pogrom agitation, was advertising the new edition. In February, 1919, however, the Diet of the Don ordered the suppression of this publication. The center of anti-Semitic propaganda was then transferred to Rostoff, the seat of the Department of Propaganda for the army of General Denikine. From Rostoff the Protocols were sent out in great numbers and distributed among the units of the volunteers and among the Cossack troops at Kouban. They served as fuel to a violent agitation in favor of pogroms and brought lurid and pernicious results. This propaganda demoralized the troops and gave them a justification for the pillages which were a cause of their eventual defeat. A circular against this propaganda was sent to all the chaplains at the front by Archpriest George Schavelsky, head of the military clergy, but the effects of this circular were paralyzed by the attitude of the commanding officers.

During the summer of 1918 Malakhoff, formerly a professor at the Moscow Academy, arrived at Rostoff and began a violent anti-Semitic agitation based on the Protocols. The Protocols were of special importance in the pogroms in the Ukraine. One of my friends, Colonel Dzougaeff, told me this characteristic anecdote: He was in Kiev during the fighting between the Hetman Skoropadsky and Petlioura. He escaped in disguise but was later arrested by the soldiers of Petlioura who mistook him for a Jew and wished to shoot him. One of the chiefs whom he asked the reason for this said, "You wish to give us a king with a head of gold. So it was stated at the sessions of your Wise Men of Zion." . . .

Crimea, during the régime of General Wrangel, was especially noted for anti-Semitic propaganda based on the Protocols. Professor Malakhoff, the priest Vostokoff and some journalists subsidized by the government, announced at the top of their voices the danger of the Protocols and the universal Judeo-Masonic plot.

EXHIBIT H

THE "DIALOGUES" AND THE "PROTOCOLS" IN PARALLEL PAGES

The following selections from Joly's "Dialogues in Hell" (1864) and the "Protocols of the Wise Men of Zion" (1895-1905), in parallel pages, prove beyond any doubt whatever that the "Protocols" were plagiarized from the "Dialogues." The similarity is all the more striking when we bear in mind the fact that both documents are here presented in translation—the "Dialogues" from the original French and the "Protocols" from the Russian, after having passed through the plagiarism of the German novelist Goedsche. The close resemblance of the ideas and phrases in these documents constitutes incontrovertible proof of the falsification. Only a few of the selections showing the striking similarity of the two documents are reproduced here.

The fabricators of the "Protocols" based their entire cynical political structure upon that of Machiavelli in the "Dialogues." In several instances they even paraphrased Montesquieu to suit their needs. Most of the ideas in the first part of Joly's "Dialogues" are lifted entirely with but slight modifications, sometimes reproduced almost word for word and sentence for sentence. The only differences lie in the substitution of an alleged Jewish dislike for Gentiles, for Machiavelli's distrust and contempt for humanity as a whole, and in the substitution of a mythical Jewish organization for the imperial government of Napoleon III.

Since Joly's last dialogues develop into a lengthy discussion of the financial activities and transactions of the French imperial government, the fabricators of the "Protocols" departed somewhat from their textbook toward the end, retaining fewer passages. Because the "Protocols" were intended to be a form of prophecy and a plan for the future, fewer allusions to transitory questions were appropriated from the original "Dialogues."

371

Dialogues

The evil instinct in man is more powerful than the good. Man leans more toward the evil than the good; fear and power have more control over him than reason. . . . All men seek power, and there is none who would not be an oppressor if he could; all, or nearly all, are ready to sacrifice the rights of others to their own interests.

What restrains these ravenous animals that we call men? In the beginnings of society, it is brute force, without control; later, it is law, that is, force again, ruled by certain forms. You have consulted all the sources of history; everywhere force appears before justice.

Political liberty is only a relative idea. . . .

Dialogues

States, once constituted, have two kinds of enemies; the enemies within and the enemies without. What arms shall they employ in war against the foreigners? Will the two enemy generals communicate to one another their campaign plans in order that each shall be able to defend himself? Will they forbid themselves night attacks, snares, ambuscades, battles in which the number of troops are unequal? Without doubt, they will not. And such fighters would make one laugh. And these snares, these artifices, all this strategy indispensable to warfare, you don't want them to be employed against the enemies within, against the disturbers of peace? . . . Is it possible to conduct by pure reason violent masses which are moved only by sentiment, passion and prejudice?

Dialogues

Has politics anything to do with morals?

Dialogues

This word "justice" itself, by the way, do you not see that it is infinitely vague?

Protocols

It must be noted that men with bad instincts are more in number than the good, and therefore the best results in governing them are attained by violence and terrorisation, and not by academic discussions. Every man aims at power, everyone would like to become a dictator if only he could, and rare indeed are the men who would not be willing to sacrifice the welfare of all for the sake of securing their own welfare.

What has restrained the beasts of prey who are called men? What has served for their guidance hitherto?

In the beginnings of the structure of society they were subjected to brute and blind force; afterwards—to Law, which is the same force, only disguised. I draw the conclusion that by the law of nature right lies in force.

Political freedom is an idea but not a fact.

Protocols

If every State has two foes and if in regard to the external foe it is allowed and not considered immoral to use every manner and art of conflict, as for example to keep the enemy in ignorance of plans of attack and defence, to attack him by night or in superior numbers, then in what way can the same means in regard to a worse foe, the destroyer of the structure of society and the commonweal, be called immoral and not permissible?

Is it possible for any sound logical mind to hope with any success to guide crowds by the aid of reasonable counsels and arguments, when any objection or contradiction, senseless though it may be, can be made and when such objection may find more favour with the people, whose powers of reasoning are superficial?

Protocols

The political has nothing in common with the moral.

Protocols

The word "right" is an abstract thought and proved by nothing.

Dialogues

Where does it begin, where does it end? When will justice exist, when will it not exist? I take examples. Here is a State: bad organization of public powers, turbulence of democracy, impotence of laws to control, discontented, disorder which reigns everywhere, will all precipitate it into ruin. A strong man thrusts himself from the ranks of the aristocracy or from the heart of the people; he breaks through all constituted power; he puts his hand on the laws, he alters all the institutions, and he gives twenty years of peace to his country. Did he have the right to do what he has done?

Dialogues

I am less preoccupied by what is good and moral than by what is useful and necessary.

Dialogues

. . . you have in your mouth but two words: force and cunning. If your system reduces itself to the declaration that force plays a great rôle in human affairs, that cleverness is a necessary qualification for a statesman, you understand well that this is a truth that need not be proved; but, if you elevate violence to a principle, cunning to a maxim of government, if you do not take into consideration in your calculations any of the laws of humanity, the code of tyranny is naught but the code of the brute. . . .

Your principle is that good can come from evil, and that it is permissible to do evil when it will result in good. Thus, you do not say: It is good in itself to go back on one's word; it is good to use corruption, violence and murder. But you do say: One can deceive when it is useful to do so, kill when that is necessary, take the property of others when that is advantageous.

Dialogues

I spoke to you of wars just now: they rage always, I know; but, the first progress is that today they no longer give the conquerors the property of the vanquished states. A law that you hardly know, international law, today guides the relations between the nations, just as civil law guides the relations of the subjects of every country.

Protocols

Where does right begin? Where does it end?

In any State in which there is a bad organisation of authority, an impersonality of laws and of the rulers who have lost their personality amid the flood of rights ever multiplying out of liberalism, I find a new right—to attack by the right of the strong, and to scatter to the winds all existing forces of order and regulation, to reconstruct all institutions and to become the sovereign lord of those who have left to us the rights of their power by laying them down voluntarily in their liberalism.

Protocols

Let us, however, in our plans, direct our attention not so much to what is good and moral as to what is necessary and useful.

Protocols

Our countersign is—Force and Make-believe. Only force conquers in political affairs, especially if it be concealed in the talents essential to statesmen. Violence must be the principle, and cunning and make-believe the rule for governments which do not want to lay down their crowns at the feet of agents of some new power. This evil is the one and only means to attain the end, the good. Therefore we must not stop at bribery, deceit and treachery when they should serve towards the attainment of our end. In politics one must know how to seize the property of others without hesitation if by it we secure submission and sovereignty.

Protocols

It is indispensable for our purpose that wars, so far as possible, should not result in territorial gains: war will thus be brought on to the economic grounds, where the nations will not fail to perceive in the assistance we give the strength of our predominance, and this state of things will put both sides at the mercy of our international *agentur*;

EXHIBIT H

Dialogues

In reality, you would have begun a struggle between all the opposing forces, roused all enterprises, given arms to all parties. You would have given strength to the assault of all ambitions, and made of the state an arena in which all factions would be unchained. In little time, there would be disorder everywhere; inexhaustible rhetoricians would transform the deliberating assemblies into oratorical jousts; audacious journalists, unbridled pamphleteers, would each day attack the person of the sovereign, would discredit the government, the ministers, the men of position. . . .

There are tremendous populations riveted to labor by poverty, as they were in other times by slavery. What difference, I ask you, do your parliamentary fictions make to their happiness? Your great political movement has after all only ended in the triumph of a minority privileged by chance as the ancient nobility was by birth. What difference does it make to the proletariat bent over its labor, weighted down by the heaviness of its destiny, that some orators have the right to speak, that some journalists have the right to write? You have created rights which will be purely academic for the mass of the people, since it cannot make use of them. These rights, of which the law permits him the ideal enjoyment and necessity refuses him the actual exercise, are for the people only a bitter irony of destiny.

which possesses millions of eyes ever on the watch and unhampered by any limitations whatsoever. Our international rights will then wipe out national rights, in the proper sense of right, and will rule the nations precisely as the civil law of States rules the relations of their subjects among themselves.

Protocols

In order to incite seekers after power to a misuse of power we have set all forces in opposition one to another, breaking up their liberal tendencies towards independence. To this end we have stirred up every form of enterprise, we have armed all parties, we have set up authority as a target for every ambition. Of States we have made gladiatorial arenas where a host of confused issues contend. . . . A little more, and disorders and bankruptcy will be universal. . . .

Babblers inexhaustible have turned into oratorical contests the sittings of Parliament and Administrative Boards. Bold journalists and unscrupulous pamphleteers daily fall upon executive officials. Abuses of power will put the final touch in preparing all institutions for their overthrow and everything will fly skyward under the blows of the maddened mob.

All people are chained to heavy toil by poverty more firmly than ever they were chained by slavery and serfdom; from these, one way and another, they might free themselves, these could be settled with, but from want they will never get away. We have included in the constitution such rights as to the masses appear fictitious and not actual rights. All these so-called "People's Rights" can exist only in idea, an idea which can never be realized in practical life. What is it to the proletariat labourer, bowed double over his heavy toil, crushed by his lot in life, if talkers get the right to babble, if journalists get the right to scribble any nonsense side by side with good stuff, once the proletariat has no other profit out of the constitution save only those pitiful crumbs which we fling them from our table in return for their voting in favour of what we dictate, in favour of the men we place in power, the servants of our *agentur*. . . . Republican rights for a poor man are no more than a bitter piece of irony. . . .

Dialogues

. . . you do not know the unfathomable cowardice of humanity . . . servile in the face of force, pitiless in the face of weakness, implacable before blunders, indulgent before crimes, incapable of supporting the contrarieties of a liberal régime, and patient to the point of martyrdom before all the violences of bold despotism, upsetting thrones in its moments of anger, and giving itself rulers whom it pardons for actions the least of which would have caused it to decapitate twenty constitutional kings.

Dialogues

. . . the principle of popular sovereignty is destructive of all stability . . . it indefinitely perpetuates the right to revolution. It puts nations into open war against all human powers and even against God; it is the very incarnation of violence. It makes of the people a ferocious brute which sleeps when it is satiated with blood, and which is enchained. . . .

Dialogues

From the weariness of ideas and the shock of revolutions have come cold and disillusioned societies which have achieved indifference in politics as in religion, which have no other stimulant than material satisfactions, which live only in their own interest, which have no other cult than that of gold. . . . Do you believe that it is for love of liberty in itself that the inferior classes are trying to rise to the assault on power? It is by hatred of those who possess. . . .

Dialogues

What forms of government would you apply to societies in which corruption has stolen everywhere, in which morality has no guarantee

Protocols

It is the bottomless rascality of the *goyim* peoples, who crawl on their bellies to force, but are merciless towards weakness, unsparing to faults and indulgent to crimes, unwilling to bear the contradictions of a free social system but patient unto martyrdom under the violence of a bold despotism—it is those qualities which are aiding us to independence. From the premier-dictators of the present day the *goyim* peoples suffer patiently and bear such abuses as for the least of them they would have beheaded twenty kings.

Protocols

Thanks to this State of things the people are destroying every kind of stability and creating disorders at every step.

The word "freedom" brings out the communities of men to fight against every kind of force, against every kind of authority, even against God and the laws of nature. For this reason we, when we come into our kingdom, shall have to erase this word from the lexicon of life as implying a principle of brute force which turns mobs into bloodthirsty beasts.

These beasts, it is true, fall asleep again every time when they have drunk their fill of blood, and at such times can easily be riveted into their chains.

Protocols

The intensified struggle for superiority and shocks delivered to economic life will create, nay, have already created, cold and heartless communities. Such communities will foster a strong aversion towards the higher political and towards religion. Their only guide is gain, that is Gold, which they will erect into a veritable cult, for the sake of those material delights which it can give. Then will the hour strike when, not for the sake of attaining the good, not even to win wealth, but solely out of hatred towards the privileged, the lower classes of the *goyim* will follow our lead against our rivals for power, the intellectuals of the *goyim*.

Protocols

What form of administrative rule can be given to communities in which corruption has penetrated everywhere, communities where riches save in repressive laws, in which the sentiment of patriotism itself is extinguished by I know not what universal cosmopolitanism?

I see no salvation in these societies . . . except in the institution of an extreme centralization, which puts all public force at the disposition of those who govern; . . . which rules mechanically all the movements of individuals; in a vast system of legislation which takes up in detail all the liberties that have been imprudently bestowed. . . .

Dialogues

MACHIAVELLI: . . . Who makes the sovereigns?

MONTESQUIEU: The people.

MACHIAVELLI: It is written: *Per Me reges regnant.* Which means literally: God makes kings. [Through Me kings reign.]

MONTESQUIEU: That is a translation in the manner of the Prince, O Machiavelli . . . but it is not from the Holy Scripture.

Dialogues

Today it is less a question of doing men violence than of disarming them, less of suppressing their political passions than of wiping them out, less of combating their instincts than of deceiving them, less of prohibiting their ideas than of changing them by appropriating them to oneself. . . . The principal secret of government consists in enfeebling the public spirit to the point of disinteresting it entirely in the ideas and the principles with which revolutions are made nowadays. In all times, people, like individuals, have been paid in words. Appearances nearly always are sufficient for them; they demand no more. One can, then, establish artificial institutions which correspond to a language and to ideas equally artificial; it is necessary to have the talent to strip the parties of that liberal phraseology with which they arm themselves against the government. It is necessary to satiate the people with it until they are weary, until they are disgusted. One speaks often today of the power of public opinion, I shall show you that it is made to express whatever one wants when one knows well the hidden resources of power. But before thinking of directing it, one

are attained only by the clever surprise tactics of semi-swindling tricks;
where looseness reigns: where morality is maintained by penal measures
and harsh laws but not by voluntarily accepted principles: where the
feelings towards faith and country are obliterated by cosmopolitan convictions? What form of rule is to be given to these communities if
not that despotism which I shall describe to you later? We shall create
an intensified centralisation of government in order to grip in our
hands all the forces of the community. We shall regulate mechanically
all the actions of the political life of our subjects by new laws. These
laws will withdraw one by one all the indulgences and liberties which
have been permitted by the *goyim.* . . .

Protocols

Per Me reges regnant. "It is through Me that Kings reign." And
it was said by the prophets that we were chosen by God Himself to
rule over the whole earth.

Protocols

Nowadays it is more important to disarm the peoples than to lead
them into war: more important to use for our advantage the passions
which have burst into flames than to quench their fire: more important
to catch up and interpret the ideas of others to suit ourselves than to
eradicate them. The principal object of our directorate consists in this:
to debilitate the public mind by criticism; to lead it away from serious
reflections calculated to arouse resistance; to distract the forces of the
mind towards a sham fight of empty eloquence.

In all ages the peoples of the world, equally with individuals, have
accepted words for deeds, for they are content with a show and rarely
pause to note, in the public arena, whether promises are followed by
performance. Therefore we shall establish show institutions which will
give eloquent proof of their benefit to progress.

We shall assume to ourselves the liberal physiognomy of all parties,
of all directions, and we shall give that physiognomy a voice in orators
who will speak so much that they will exhaust the patience of their
hearers and produce an abhorrence of oratory.

must benumb it, strike it with uncertainty by astounding contradictions, work on it with incessant diversions, dazzle it with all sorts of different actions, mislead it imperceptibly in its pathways.

Dialogues

I would institute . . . huge financial monopolies, reservoirs of the public wealth, on which depends so closely the fate of all the private fortunes that they would be swallowed up with the credit of the State the day after any political catastrophe. You are an economist, Montesquieu, weigh the value of this combination.

Head of the government, all my edicts, all my ordinances would constantly tend toward the same goal: to annihilate collective and individual forces; to develop excessively the preponderance of the State, to make of it the sovereign protector, promoter and remunerator.

. . . In modern times, the aristocracy, as a political force, has disappeared; but the landed bourgeoisie is still an element of dangerous resistance to governments, because it is independent in itself; it may be necessary to impoverish it or even to ruin it completely. It is enough, for this, to increase the charges which weigh on landed property, to maintain agriculture in a state of relative inferiority, to favor commerce and industry excessively, but speculation principally. . . .

Dialogues

It is useless to add that the perpetual upkeep of a large army continually exercised by foreign wars must be the indispensable complement of this system; it is necessary to arrive at the existence in the state only of proletarians, several millionaires, and soldiers.

. . . Outside, it is necessary to incite, from one end of Europe to the other, the revolutionary fermentation that is curbed at home. Two considerable advantages would result from that; the liberal agitation outside makes passable the repression within. Moreover, in this way one

In order to put public opinion into our hands we must bring it into a state of bewilderment by giving expression from all sides to so many contradictory opinions and for such length of time as will suffice to make the *Goyim* lose their heads in the labyrinth and come to see that the best thing is to have no opinion of any kind in matters political. . . .

Protocols

We shall soon begin to establish huge monopolies, reservoirs of colossal riches, upon which even large fortunes of the *goyim* will depend to such an extent that they will go to the bottom together with the credit of the States on the day after the political smash. . . .

You gentlemen here present who are economists, just strike an estimate of the significance of this combination! . . .

In every possible way we must develop the significance of our Super-Government by representing it as the Protector and Benefactor of all those who voluntarily submit to us.

The aristocracy of the *goyim* as a political force, is dead—we need not take it into account; but as landed proprietors they can still be harmful to us from the fact that they are self-sufficing in the resources upon which they live. It is essential therefore for us at whatever cost to deprive them of their land. This object will be best attained by increasing the burdens upon landed property—in loading lands with debts. These measures will check land-holding and keep it in a state of humble and unconditional submission.

. . . At the same time we must intensively patronise trade and industry, but, first and foremost, speculation, the part played by which is to provide a counterpoise to industry. . . .

Protocols

The intensification of armaments, the increase of police forces— are all essential for the completion of the aforementioned plans. What we have to get at is that there should be in all the States of the world, besides ourselves, only the masses of the proletariat, a few millionaires devoted to our interests, police and soldiers.

Throughout all Europe, and by means of relations with Europe, in other continents also, we must create ferments, discords and hostility. Therein we gain a double advantage. In the first place we keep in controls all the powers, among which one can create order or disorder at will. The important point is to entangle by cabinet intrigues all the threads of European politics in such a way as to play one against the other the powers with whom one treats. . . . Alexander VI practised only deception in his diplomatic negotiations and yet he always succeeded, so well did he know the science of cunning. . . . But for what you call today the official language, a striking contrast is necessary, and there one cannot affect too much the spirit of loyalty and conciliation; the people, who see only the outward appearance of things, will manufacture a reputation of wisdom for the ruler who can conduct his affairs in this way.

To all internal agitation, he must be able to respond with a foreign war; to any imminent revolution, with a general war; but since in politics words must never be in accord with deeds, it is necessary that, in these various crises, the prince be able enough to disguise his real designs under contrary design; he must always give the impression of acceding to public opinion while he does what his hands have secretly prepared.

Dialogues

. . . what is essential is the use against one's enemies of all the arms they could employ against you. Not content with relying on the violent force of democracy, I would borrow of the subtleties of justice their most learned resources. When one takes decisions that could seem unjust or rash, it is essential to know how to express them in fine terms, to give them the highest reasons of morality and justice.

The power of which I dream, far, as you see, from having barbarian customs, must draw to itself all the forces and all the talents of the civilisation in the heart of which it lives. It must surround itself with publicists, lawyers, jurisconsults, practical men and administrators, men who know thoroughly all the secrets, all the strength of social life, who speak all languages, who have studied man in all circles. They must be taken from everywhere, no matter from whence, for these men give surprising service through the ingenious procedures they apply to politics. With that, a whole world of economists is necessary, of bankers, of industrialists, of capitalists, of men of vision, of men with check all countries, for they well know that we have the power whenever we like to create disorders or to restore order. All these countries are accustomed to see in us an indispensable force of coercion. In the second place, by our intrigues we shall tangle up all the threads which we have stretched into the cabinets of all States by means of politics, by economic treaties, or loan obligations. In order to succeed in this we must use great cunning and penetration during negotiations and agreements, but, as regards what is called the "official language," we shall keep to the opposite tactics and assume the mask of . honesty and compliancy. In this way the peoples and governments of the *goyim*, whom we have taught to look only at the outside of whatever we present to their notice, will still continue to accept us as the benefactors and saviours of the human race.

We must be in a position to respond to every act of opposition by war with the neighbors of that country which dares to oppose us: but if these neighbors should also venture to stand collectively together against us, then we must offer resistance by a universal war.

The principal factor of success in the political is the secrecy of its undertakings: the word should not agree with the deeds of the diplomat.

Protocols

We must arm ourselves with all the weapons which our opponents might employ against us. We must search out in the very finest shades of expression and the knotty points of the lexicon of law justification for those cases where we shall have to pronounce judgments that might appear abnormally audacious and unjust, for it is important that these resolutions should be set forth in expressions that shall seem to be the most exalted moral principles cast into legal form. Our directorate must surround itself with all these forces of civilisation among which it will have to work. It will surround itself with publicists, practical jurists, administrators, diplomats and, finally, with persons prepared by a special super-educational training in our special schools. These persons will have cognisance of all the secrets of the social structure, they will know all the languages that can be made up by political alphabets and words; they will be made acquainted with the whole underside of human nature, with all its sensitive chords on which they will have to play. . . .

millions, for all fundamentally resolves itself into a question of figures.

As for the principal dignities, the principal dismemberment of power, one must so arrange as to give them to men whose antecedents and character place a gulf between them and other men, every one of whom has only to expect death or exile in case of a change in government and is in need of defending until his last breath all that exists.

Dialogues

. . . in politics that is a rule the details of which I will follow scrupulously; if you will call to mind the principles to which you hold the most, you will see that I am not as embarrassed by them as you seem to think. . . . You would not fail, no doubt, to speak to me of the principle of the separation of powers, of liberty of speech and of the press, religious liberty, individual liberty, the right to congregate, equality before the law, the inviolability of property and of the home, the right of petition, free consent to taxation, proportionality of punishment, the non-retroactivity of the laws. . . . I have told you that I would proclaim these principles, but I have not said I would inscribe them or even that I would expressly designate them. . . . I will in no way sum up; I will take care to declare to the people that I recognize and confirm the great principles of modern justice. . . . If I expressly enumerated these rights, my freedom of action will be chained to those I have mentioned; that is what I do not want. In not naming them, I seem to accord all and I do not specially accord any; this permits me to set aside later, by means of exception, those that I may judge dangerous.

Look, the nations have I know not what secret love for the vigorous genius of force. Of all violent actions marked by the talent of artifice, you will hear said with an admiration that overcomes all blame: This is not good, so be it, but it is clever, it is well done, it is strong! . . .

MONTESQUIEU: You expect, then, to associate the nation with the new fundamental work that you are preparing?

We shall surround our government with a whole world of economists. That is the reason why economic sciences form the principal subject of the teaching given to the Jews. Around us again will be a whole constellation of bankers, industrialists, capitalists and—the main thing—millionaires, because in substance everything will be settled by the question of figures.

For a time, until there will no longer be any risk in entrusting responsible posts in our States to our brother-Jews, we shall put them in the hands of persons whose past and reputation are such that between them and the people lies an abyss, persons who, in case of disobedience to our instructions, must face criminal charges or disappear—this in order to make them defend our interests to their last gasp.

Protocols

For our policy it is of the greatest importance to take cognisance of this detail; it will be of assistance to us when we come to consider the division of authority, freedom of speech, of the press, of religion (faith), of the law of association, of equality before the law, of the inviolability of property, of the dwelling, of taxation (the idea of concealed taxes), of the reflex force of the laws. All these questions are such as ought not to be touched upon directly and openly before the people. In cases where it is indispensable to touch upon them they must not be categorically named, it must merely be declared without detailed exposition that the principles of contemporary law are acknowledged by us. The reason of keeping silence in this respect is that by not naming a principle we leave ourselves freedom of action, to drop this or that out of it without attracting notice; if they were all categorically named they would all appear to have been already given.

The mob cherishes a special affection and respect for the geniuses of political power and accepts all their deeds of violence with the admiring response: "Rascally, well, yes, it is rascally, but it's clever! . . . a trick, if you like, but how craftily played, how magnificently done, what impudent audacity!" . . .

We count upon attracting all nations to the task of erecting the new fundamental structure, the project for which has been drawn up by us. . . .

When we have accomplished our *coup d'état* we shall say then to

MACHIAVELLI: Yes, no doubt. That surprises you? I will do much better; I will first have ratified by a popular vote the coup that I have carried against the state; I will say to the people, in suitable terms: All was going wrong; I have smashed everything, I have saved you, do you want me? You are free to condemn me or to absolve me by your vote.

Dialogues

. . . in the majority of the parliamentary nations, the press has the faculty of making itself hated, since it is at the service only of violent, selfish, and exclusive passions, since it disparages through prejudice, since it is mercenary, since it it unjust, since it is without generosity and without patriotism; and, last but not least, since you will never be able to make the masses of the people understand of what value it may be.

. . . it isn't only journalism that I intend to repress.

. . . it would hardly be worth while escaping from the attacks of journalism if one had to remain exposed to those of books.

I would decree that in the future no newspaper could be founded except by authorization of the government; right there you have the danger arrested in its development; for, as you can easily understand, the newspapers which would be authorized would be only those organs devoted to the government.

I would reach all newspapers, present or future, by fiscal measures which would check when needed all publicity enterprises; I would subject political journals to what you call nowadays the stamp and security. The business of the press would soon become so unremunerative, thanks to the raising of these taxes, that no one would go into it unknowingly.

MONTESQUIEU: The remedy is insufficient, because political parties spare no expense.

MACHIAVELLI: . . . I have something with which to close their mouths: here come the repressive measures. . . . Two convictions in one year will automatically bring about the suppression of the paper. I would not rely on that alone, I would say to the newspapers, in a decree or a law: "Reduced to the greatest caution in matters that concern you, do not expect to arouse opinion by commentaries on the debates in my chambers. . . ."

the various peoples: "Everything has gone terribly badly, all have been worn out with sufferings. We are destroying the causes of your torment—nationalities, frontiers, differences of coinages. You are at liberty, of course, to pronounce sentence upon us. . . ."

Protocols

What is the part played by the press to-day? It serves to excite and inflame those passions which are needed for our purpose or else it serves selfish ends of parties. It is often vapid, unjust, mendacious, and the majority of the public have not the slightest idea what ends the press really serves. We shall saddle and bridle it with a tight curb: we shall do the same also with all productions of the printing press, for where would be the sense of getting rid of the attacks of the press if we remain targets for pamphlets and books? The produce of publicity, which nowadays is a source of heavy expense owing to the necessity of censoring it, will be turned by us into a very lucrative source of income to our State: we shall lay on it a special stamp tax and require deposits of caution-money before permitting the establishment of any organ of the press or of printing offices; these will then have to guarantee our government against any kind of attack on the part of the press. For any attempt to attack us, if such still be possible, we shall inflict fines without mercy. Such measures as stamp tax, deposit of caution-money and fines secured by these deposits, will bring in a huge income to the government. It is true that party organs might not spare money for the sake of publicity, but these we shall shut up at the second attack upon us. No one shall with impunity lay a finger on the aureole of our government infallibility. The pretext for stopping any publication will be the alleged plea that it is agitating the public mind without occasion for justification. I beg you to note that among those making attacks upon us will also be organs established by us, but they will attack exclusively points that we have pre-determined to alter.

Not a single announcement will reach the public without our control. Even now this is already being attained by us inasmuch as all news items are received by a few agencies, in whose offices they are focused from all parts of the world. These agencies will then be

I do not want my kingdom to be disturbed by noises from abroad. How could foreign news arrive? By a few agencies which centralize the news which is transmitted to them from the four quarters of the globe. Well, I suppose these agencies could be paid, and then they would give out no news except by order of the government.

MONTESQUIEU: . . . now you may go on to the regulation of books.

MACHIAVELLI: . . . In the first place, I shall oblige those who wish to exercise the profession of printer, editor or librarian to secure a seal, that is, an authorization which the government may always withdraw, either directly or by decisions of the court.

MONTESQUIEU: But, in that case . . . the instruments of thought will become the instruments of power!

MACHIAVELLI: . . . I will return to fiscal measures; I will extend to books the stamp which affects the newspapers, or rather I shall impose the burden of a stamp on those books which have not a certain number of pages. A book, for instance, which has not two or three hundred pages will not be a book, it will be only a brochure. I believe that you readily grasp the advantage of this scheme: on one hand I reduce, by this tax, the swarm of little writings which are like the appendages of journalism; on the other hand, I force those who wish to escape the tax to write long and costly compositions which will scarcely sell or which will barely be read in this form. Nowadays there are hardly any but a few poor devils who have the conscience to write books; they will give it up. The economic question will discourage literary vanity and penal law will disarm printing itself, for I shall make the publisher and the printer criminally responsible for the contents of the books. If there are writers daring enough to write books against the government, they must not be able to find anyone to publish them. The effects of this wholesome intimidation will indirectly re-establish a censor that the government itself could not exercise because of the disrepute into which this preventive measure has fallen. Before publishing new works, the printers and the publishers will consult one another, they will be informed; they will produce books which are in demand, and in this manner the government will always be usefully informed of the publications which are being prepared against it; it will bring about a preliminary attachment when it deems necessary and will report the authors to the courts.

. . . Since journalism is such a great force, do you know what my already entirely ours, and will give publicity only to what we dictate to them.

. . . Let us turn again to the future of the printing press. Every one desirous of being a publisher, librarian, or printer, will be obliged to provide himself with the diploma issued therefore, which, in case of any fault, will be immediately impounded. With such measures the instrument of thought will become an educative means in the hands of our government. . . .

We turn to the periodical press. We shall impose on it, as on all printed matter, stamp taxes per sheet and deposits of caution-money, and books of less than 30 sheets will pay double. We shall reckon them as pamphlets in order, on the one hand, to reduce the number of maga-zines, which are the worst form of printed poison, and, on the other, in order that this measure may force writers into such lengthy pro-ductions that they will be little read, especially as they will be costly. At the same time what we shall publish ourselves to influence mental development in the direction laid down for our profit will be cheap and will be read voraciously. The tax will bring vapid literary ambi-tions within bounds and the liability to penalties will make literary men dependent upon us. And if there should be any found who are desirous of writing against us, they will not find any person eager to print their productions. Before accepting any production for publi-cation in print the publisher or printer will have to apply to the authorities for permission to do so. Thus we shall know beforehand of all tricks preparing against us and shall nullify them by getting ahead with explanations of the subject treated of.

Literature and journalism are two of the most important educative forces, and therefore our government will become proprietor of the majority of the journals. This will neutralise the injurious influence upon the public mind. . . . If we give permits for ten journals, we shall ourselves found thirty, and so on in the same proportion. This, however, must in nowise be suspected by the public. For which reason all journals published by us will be of the most opposite, in appear-ance, tendencies and opinions, thereby creating confidence in us and bringing over to us our quite unsuspicious opponents, who will thus fall into our trap and be rendered harmless.

In the front rank will stand organs of an official character. They government would do? It would turn journalist, it would become journalism incarnate. . . . I shall count the number of newspapers which represent what you call the opposition. If there are ten for the opposition, I shall have twenty for the government; if there are twenty, I shall have forty; if there are forty, I shall have eighty. You can readily understand now to what use I will put the faculty which I reserved for myself to authorize the creation of new political papers.

. . . the masses must have no suspicion of these tactics; the scheme would lose its point, public opinion would shy at newspapers which openly defended my policies.

I shall divide into three or four categories the papers devoted to my power. In first rank I shall put a certain number of newspapers whose tone will be frankly official and which, at any encounter, will defend my deeds to the death. I tell you right from the start, these will not be the ones which will have the greatest influence on public opinion. In the second rank I shall place another series of newspapers the character of which will be no more than officious and the purposes of which will be to rally to my power that mass of luke-warm and indifferent persons who accept without scruple what is established but who do not go beyond that in their political faith.

It is in the newspaper categories which follow that will be found the most powerful supporters of my power. Here, the official or officious tone is completely dropped, in appearance, that is, for the newspapers of which I am going to speak will all be attached by the same chain to my government, a chain visible for some, invisible for others. I shall not attempt to tell you how many of them there will be, for I shall count on a devoted organ in each opinion, in each party; I shall have an aristocratic organ in the aristocratic party, a republican organ in the republican party, a revolutionary organ in the revolutionary party, an anarchist organ, if necessary, in the anarchist party. Like the god Vishnu, my press will have a hundred arms, and these arms will stretch out their hands to all the possible shades of opinion over the whole surface of the country. Everyone will be of my party whether he knows it or not. Those who think they are speaking their own language will be speaking mine, those who think they are agitating their own party will be agitating mine, those who think they are marching under their own flag will be marching under mine.

MONTESQUIEU: I am only wondering how you will be able to direct will always stand guard over our interests, and therefore their influence will be comparatively insignificant.

In the second rank will be the semi-official organs, whose part it will be to attract the tepid and indifferent.

In the third rank we shall set up our own, to all appearance, opposition, which in at least one of its organs, will present what looks like the very antipodes to us. Our real opponents at heart will accept this simulated opposition as their own and will show us their cards.

All our newspapers will be of all possible complexions—aristocratic, republican, revolutionary, even anarchical—for so long, of course, as the constitution exists. ... . Like the Indian idol Vishnu they will have a hundred hands and every one of them will have a finger on any one of the public opinions as required. When a pulse quickens these hands will lead opinion in the direction of our aims, for an excited patient loses all power of judgment and easily yields to suggestion. Those fools who will think they are repeating the opinion of a newspaper of their own camp will be repeating our opinion or any opinion that seems desirable for us. In the vain belief that they are following the organ of their party they will in fact follow the flag which we hang out for them.

In order to direct our newspaper militia in this sense we must take especial and minute care in organising this matter. Under the title of central department of the press we shall institute literary gatherings at which our agents will without attracting attention issue the orders and watchwords of the day. By discussing and controverting, but always superficially, without touching the essence of the matter, our organs will carry on a sham fight fusillade with the official newspapers solely for the purpose of giving occasion for us to express ourselves more fully than could well be done from the outset in official announcements, whenever, of course, that is to our advantage.

These attacks upon us will also serve another purpose, namely, that our subjects will be convinced of the existence of full freedom of speech and so give our agents an occasion to affirm that all organs which oppose us are empty babblers, since they are incapable of finding any substantial objections to our orders.

Methods of organisation like these, imperceptible to the public eye but absolutely sure, are the best calculated to succeed in bringing to the attention and the confidence of the public to the side of our and rally all these military forces of publicity secretly hired by your government.

MACHIAVELLI: That is only a question of organization, you must understand; I shall institute, for instance, under the title of division of printing and the press, a center of operation to which one will come for orders. So, for those who will be only half in on the secret of this scheme, it will be a strange spectacle: they will see sheets, devoted to my government, which will attack me, which will shout, which will stir up a turmoil of confusion.

. . . you will notice that the foundation and the principles of my government will never be attacked by the newspapers of which I am speaking; they will never go in for anything more than a polemic skirmish, a dynastic opposition within the narrowest limits.

. . . The result, considerable enough, will be to make the greatest number say: "But you see, one is free, one may speak under this régime, it is unjustly attacked; instead of repressing, as it might do, it tolerates these things!" Another result, not less important, will be to provoke, for instance, such observations as these: "You see to what point the foundations and principles of this government commands the respect of all; here are newspapers which allow themselves the greatest freedom of speech; well, they never attack the established institutions. They must be above the injustices of human passions, since the very enemies of the government cannot help rendering homage to them."

. . . With the aid of the secret loyalty of these public papers, I may say that I can direct at will the general opinion in all questions of internal or external policies. I arouse or lull the minds, I reassure or disturb them, I plead for and against, true and false. I have a fact announced and I have it refuted, according to the circumstances; in this way I plumb public thought, I gather the impression produced. I try combinations, projects, sudden decisions; in other words I send out what you call in France feelers. I fight my enemies as I please without ever compromising my power, since, after having the papers make certain statements, I may, when necessary, deny them most energetically; I solicit opinion on certain resolutions, I urge it on or I hold it back, I always have my finger on its pulse; it reflects, without knowing it, my personal impressions, and it occasionally is astonished at being so constantly in accord with its sovereign.

government. Thanks to such methods we shall be in a position as from time to time may be required, to excite or to tranquillise the public mind on political questions, to persuade or to confuse, printing now truth, now lies, facts or their contradictions as they may be well or ill received, always very cautiously feeling our ground before stepping upon it. We shall have a sure triumph over our opponents since they will not have at their disposition organs of the press in which they can give full and final expression of their views owing to the aforesaid methods of dealing with the press. We shall not even need to refute them except very superficially.

Trial shots like these, fired by us in the third rank of our press, in case of need, will be energetically refuted by us in our semi-official organs.

Even nowadays, already, to take only the French press, there are forms which reveal masonic solidarity in acting on the watchword: all organs of the press are bound together by professional secrecy; like the augurs of old, not one of their numbers will give away the secret of his sources of information unless it be resolved to make announcement of them. Not one journalist will venture to betray this secret, for not one of them is ever admitted to practise literature unless his whole past has some disgraceful sore or other. . . . These sores would be immediately revealed.

... You must know that journalism is a sort of free-masonry; those who live in it are all more or less attached to one another by the bonds of professional discretion; like the ancient soothsayers, they do not readily divulge the secret of their oracles. They would gain nothing by betraying one another, for the majority of them have some more or less shameful secrets.

Dialogues

How are loans made? By the issue of bonds containing an obligation on the part of the government to pay a yearly interest proportionate to the capital which has been deposited. If the loan is at 5 per cent, for instance, the state, at the end of twenty years, has paid a sum equal to the capital borrowed; at the end of forty years, a double amount; at the end of sixty years, a triple amount, and yet it always remains debtor for the total of the same capital.

Protocols

A loan is—an issue of government bills of exchange containing a percentage obligation commensurate to the sum of the loan capital. If the loan bears a charge of 5 per cent, then in twenty years the State vainly pays away in interest a sum equal to the loan borrowed, in forty years it is paying a double sum, in sixty—treble, and all the while the debt remains an unpaid debt.

DIALOGUE AUX ENFERS

ENTRE

MACHIAVEL

ET MONTESQUIEU

OU LA POLITIQUE DE MACHIAVEL

AU XIXe SIECLE,

PAR UN CONTEMPORAIN.

———

« Bientôt on verrait un calme affreux, pendant lequel tout se réunirait contre la puissance violatrice des lois. »

« Quand Sylla voulut rendre la liberté à Rome, elle ne put plus la recevoir. »
(MONTESQUIEU, Esp. des Lois.)

BRUXELLES,
IMPRIMERIE DE A. MERTENS ET FILS,
RUE DE L'ESCALIER, 22.

—

1864

TITLE-PAGE OF MAURICE JOLY'S "DIALOGUES IN HELL," 1864, FROM WHICH THE "PROTOCOLS" WERE PLAGIARIZED.

déchaîneront les factions. Dans peu de temps, ce
sera le désordre partout ; d'intarissables rheteurs
transformeront en joutes oratoires les assemblées
délibérantes ; d'audacieux journalistes, d'effrénés
pamphlétaires attaqueront tous les jours la per-
sonne du souverain, discréditeront le gouvernement, les ministres, les hommes en place...

MONTESQUIEU.

Je connais depuis longtemps ces reproches
adressés aux gouvernements libres. Ils n'ont pas
de valeur à mes yeux : les abus ne condamnent
point les institutions. Je sais de nombreux États
qui vivent en paix, et depuis longtemps sous de
telles lois : je plains ceux qui ne peuvent y vivre.

MACHIAVEL.

Attendez : Dans vos calculs, vous n'avez compté
qu'avec des minorités sociales. Il y a des populations gigantesques rivées au travail par la pau-
vreté, comme elles l'étaient autrefois par l'escla-
vage. Qu'importent, je vous le demande, à leur
bonheur toutes vos fictions parlementaires? Votre
grand mouvement politique n'a abouti, en défini-
tive, qu'au triomphe d'une minorité privilégiée
par le hasard comme l'ancienne noblesse l'était
par la naissance. Qu'importe au prolétaire courbé
sur son labeur, accablé sous le poids de sa des-
tinée, que quelques orateurs aient le droit de par-
ler, que quelques journalistes aient le droit
d'écrire? Vous avez créé des droits qui resteront

A TYPICAL PAGE OF THE JOLY "DIALOGUES IN HELL" PLAGIARIZED BY
THE FABRICATORS OF THE "PROTOCOLS."

vous le verrez. Vous me demandez comment je neutraliserai une rédaction hostile? De la façon la plus simple, en vérité; j'ajouterai que l'autorisation du gouvernement est nécessaire à raison de tous changements opérés dans le personnel des rédacteurs en chef ou gérants du journal.

MONTESQUIEU.

Mais les anciens journaux, restés ennemis de votre gouvernement et dont la rédation n'aura pas changé, parleront.

MACHIAVEL.

Oh! attendez : j'atteins tous les journaux présents ou futurs par des mesures fiscales qui enrayeront comme il convient les entreprises de publicité; je soumettrai les feuilles politiques à ce que vous appelez aujourd'hui le timbre et le cautionnement. L'industrie de la presse sera bientôt si peu lucrative, grâce à l'élévation de ces impôts, que l'on ne s'y livrera qu'à bon escient.

MONTESQUIEU.

Le remède est insuffisant, car les partis politiques ne regardent pas à l'argent.

MACHIAVEL.

Soyez tranquille, j'ai de quoi leur fermer la bouche, car voici venir les mesures répressives. Il y a des États en Europe où l'on a déféré au jury la connaissance des délits de presse. Je ne connais pas de mesure plus deplorable que celle-là, car c'est agiter l'opinion à propos de la moindre

ANOTHER TYPICAL PAGE OF THE JOLY "DIALOGUES IN HELL" PLA-
GIARIZED BY THE FABRICATORS OF THE "PROTOCOLS."

ЕВРЕЙСКОЕ КЛАДБИЩЕ ВЪ ПРАГѢ

и

СОВѢТЪ ПРЕДСТАВИТЕЛЕЙ

ДВѢНАДЦАТИ КОЛѢНЪ ИЗРАИЛЕВЫХЪ.

С.-ПЕТЕРБУРГЪ.
ТИПОГРАФІЯ ТОВАРИЩЕСТВА «ОБЩЕСТВЕННАЯ ПОЛЬЗА»,
ПО МОЙКѢ, У КРУГЛАГО РЫНКА, № 5.
1872.

TITLE-PAGE OF HERMANN GOEDSCHE'S FANTASTIC STORY, PUBLISHED IN RUSSIA IN 1872, CONTAINING THE FIRST DRAFT OF THE "PROTOCOLS" IN THE FORM OF FICTION.

TITLE-PAGE OF THE "PROTOCOLS" IN SERGIUS NILUS' BOOK. THIS
TITLE-PAGE READS: "ANTI-CHRIST AS A NEAR POLITICAL POSSIBILITY
(THE PROTOCOLS OF THE SESSIONS OF THE ZIONIST SAGES). 1902-1903."

Сергѣй Нилусъ.

Великое
въ маломъ
и
АНТИХРИСТЪ,
какъ близкая политическая возможность.

ЗАПИСКИ ПРАВОСЛАВНАГО.

(ИЗДАНІЕ ВТОРОЕ, ИСПРАВЛЕННОЕ И ДОПОЛНЕННОЕ).

ЦАРСКОЕ СЕЛО.
Типографія Царскосельскаго Комитета Краснаго Креста.
1905.

TITLE-PAGE OF SERGIUS NILUS' BOOK CONTAINING THE "PROTOCOLS," PUBLISHED AT TSARSKOYE SIELO, IN 1905.

ція, пререканія, раздоры и вражду. Въ этомъ—двоякая польза: во первыхъ, мы держимъ въ страхѣ всѣ страны, хорошо вѣдающія, что мы властны произвести по желанію безпорядки или водворить порядокъ въ нихъ. Онѣ привыкли видѣть въ насъ необходимое давленіе: мы запутали всѣ нити, протянутыя въ *Государственные Кабинеты всемірною политикой, экономическими договорами или долговыми обязательствами.* Для достиженія этого послѣдняго обстоятельства намъ надо было вооружиться большою хитростью и даже проныриивостью во время переговоровъ и соглашеній: но въ томъ, что называется оффиціальнымъ языкомъ, мы должны были казаться сговорчивыми и правдивыми. Такимъ образомъ гои, *которыхъ мы пріучили смотрѣть только на показную сторону того, что мы имъ представляемъ,* принимаютъ насъ еще за благодѣтелей и спасителей рода человѣческаго.

На каждое противодѣйствіе мы готовы отвѣтить противодѣйствующей Странѣ войною съ сосѣдями, а если многіе задумаютъ коллективно дѣйствовать противъ насъ, то мы завяжемъ узелъ всеобщей войны, ~~и незамѣтно для нихъ подобьемъ ихъ за это.~~

Главный успѣхъ въ политикѣ заключается въ тайнѣ ея предпріятій. слова не должны согласоваться съ дѣйствіями дипломатовъ.

Мы успѣшно вынуждали не разъ къ войнѣ гоевскія правительства, якобы общественнымъ мнѣніемъ, въ тайнѣ подстроеннымъ нами. Одному изъ нихъ мы доказывали свои силы въ покушеніяхъ—въ террорѣ. а всѣмъ, если допустить ихъ возстаніе, мы отвѣтимъ Американскими, Китайскими или Японскими пушками, которыя всегдало въ нашемъ распоряженіи.

№ 5.

(по рукописи протоколъ 2-й).

Намъ необходимо, чтобы войны не давали территоріальныхъ выгодъ Это перенесетъ войну на экономическую почву, на которой нація убѣдятся въ томъ, что преобладаніе зависитъ отъ *нашей помощи,* а такое положеніе вещей отдастъ обѣ стороны въ распоряженіе нашей интернаціональной агентуры, обладающей милліонами глазъ, взоровъ, не преграждонныхъ никакими границами... Тогда наши интернаціональныя права сотрутъ всѣ народныя права и будутъ ими править такъ, какъ гражданское

FACSIMILE OF A NILUS PROTOCOL PUBLISHED IN 1905, WHICH WAS "DOCTORED" BY BUTMI IN A LATER EDITION. THE MARKED PASSAGE SHOWS THAT IN 1905, BEFORE THE FIRST RUSSIAN REVOLUTION, THE NILUS VERSION OF THE "PROTOCOLS" SAID, "WE WILL SHOW ONE OF THEM (THE POWERS) OUR STRENGTH BY MEANS OF VIOLENCE, THAT IS BY TERRORISM."

хитростью и пронырливостью во время переговоров и соглашеній, но въ томъ, что называется „оффиціальнымъ языкомъ", мы будемъ держаться противоположной тактики и
будемъ казаться честными и сговорчивыми. Такимъ образомъ народы и правительства госэ, которыхъ мы пріучили
смотрѣть только на показную сторону того, что мы имъ
представляемъ, примутъ насъ еще за благодѣтелей и спасителей рода человѣческаго.

На каждое противодѣйствіе мы должны быть
въ состояніи отвѣтить войной съ сосѣдями той
странѣ, которая осмѣлится намъ противодѣй-
ствовать, но, если и сосѣди эти задумаютъ стать
коллективно противъ насъ, то мы должны дать
отпоръ всеобщей войной.

Главный успѣхъ въ политикѣ заключается въ тайнѣ ея предпріятій: слово не должно сообразоваться съ дѣйствіями дипломата.

Къ дѣйствіямъ въ пользу широко задуманнаго нами
плана, уже близящагося къ вожделѣнному концу, мы должны
вынуждать гоевскія правительства якобы общественнымъ мнѣніемъ, втайнѣ подстроеннымъ нами
при помощи такъ называемой „великой дер-
жавы"—печати, которая, за немногими исклю-
ченіями, съ которыми считаться не стоитъ,—
вся уже въ рукахъ нашихъ.

Однимъ словомъ, чтобы резюмировать нашу систему обуз-
данія гоевскихъ правительствъ въ Европѣ, мы одному изъ
нихъ покажемъ свою силу покушеніями, т. е. терроромъ,
а всѣмъ, если допустить ихъ возстаніе противъ насъ, мы
отвѣтимъ Американскими или Китайскими, или
Японскими пушками.

Слѣдующій протоколъ.

Мы должны заручиться для себя всѣми оружіями, которыми наши противники могли бы воспользоваться противъ
насъ. Мы должны будемъ выискивать въ самыхъ тонкихъ
выраженіяхъ и загвоздкахъ правового словаря оправданія

FACSIMILE OF THE SAME PROTOCOL IN THE BUTMI EDITION, SHOWING
CHANGES IN THE TEXT AFTER THE 1905 REVOLUTION. AFTER THE
REVOLUTION, BUTMI CHANGED THE "PROTOCOL" TO READ, "WE HAVE
SHOWN ONE OF THESE GOVERNMENTS OUR POWERS BY ASSASSINATION,
BY TERRORISM."

FACSIMILE OF A LETTER BY PHILLIP PETROVITCH STEPANOV, CERTI-
FIED BY PRINCE GALITZINE, STATING THAT BOTH HE AND NILUS
RECEIVED THE RUSSIAN VERSION OF THE "PROTOCOLS" IN 1895, TWO
YEARS BEFORE THE FIRST ZIONIST CONGRESS AT BASLE.

THIS LETTER BY STEPANOV, FORMER PROCURATOR OF THE MOSCOW SYNOD OFFICE, CONFIRMING THAT HIGH TSARIST OFFICIALS WERE INSTRUMENTAL IN PUBLISHING THE "PROTOCOLS" IN RUSSIA IN 1895-1897, EXPLODES THE ANTI-SEMITIC LEGEND THAT THESE "PROTOCOLS" ORIGINATED AT THE FIRST ZIONIST CONGRESS IN 1897.

Congregation Shaare Shamayim - G.N.J.C.
        Verree Road above Welsh Road
        Philadelphia, Penna.   19115

Congregation Shaare Shamayim - G.N.J.C.
        Verree Road above Welsh Road
        Philadelphia, Penna.   19115